Gamers at Work

Stories Behind the Games People Play

_____

Morgan Ramsay

Apress®

Gamers at Work: Stories Behind the Games People Play

ISBN-13 (pbk): 978-1-4302-3351-0

ISBN-13 (electronic): 978-1-4302-3352-7

Printed and bound in the United States of America 9 8 7 6 5 4 3 2 1

President and Publisher: Paul Manning
Acquisitions Editor: Michelle Lowman
Lead Editor: Jeffrey Pepper
Editorial Board: Steve Anglin, Mark Beckner, Ewan Buckingham, Gary Cornell, Morgan Ertel, Jonathan Gennick, Jonathan Hassell, Robert Hutchinson, Michelle Lowman, James Markham, Matthew Moodie, Jeff Olson, Jeffrey Pepper, Douglas Pundick, Ben Renow-Clarke, Dominic Shakeshaft, Gwenan Spearing, Matt Wade, Tom Welsh
Coordinating Editor: Rita Fernando
Copy Editor: Marilyn Smith
Compositor: Mary Sudul
Indexer: BIM Indexing & Proofreading Services
Cover Designer: Anna Ishchenko

Distributed to the book trade worldwide by Springer-Verlag New York, Inc., 233 Spring Street, 6th Floor, New York, NY 10013. Phone 1-800-SPRINGER, fax 201-348-4505, e-mail

orders-ny@springer-sbm.com, or visit http://www.springeronline.com.

For information on translations, please contact us by e-mail at info@apress.com, or visit

http://www.apress.com.

Apress and friends of ED books may be purchased in bulk for academic, corporate, or promotional use. eBook versions and licenses are also available for most titles. For more information, reference our Special Bulk Sales–eBook Licensing web page at

http://www.apress.com/info/bulksales.

For those whose lack of faith
never failed to push me forward.

Contents

Foreword

The worldwide video-game industry is in a state of enormous flux. Vast budget opuses, such as Activision's Call of Duty, sit alongside mobile phone games created by tiny two-man teams. We work in an industry that is more diverse than ever—an industry that is appealing to an ever-broadening and growing mass market. Could we see a day when people interact with computer games as much as they do with television? Could we see a day when the framework of a game helps us cross a cultural divide? These thoughts would have seemed crazy five years ago, but they now appear certain to become realities. Video games are in the most exciting place they have ever been right now.

I have been lucky enough to see this industry go through many, many changes, starting with those early days at Bullfrog Productions, when two of us created a game called Populous on a shoestring, through to setting up Lionhead Studios and selling the company to Microsoft. Along the way, there have been many good times and a few bad ones, too. Therefore, I could really empathize on a personal level with the experiences and stories documented in this book.

As I read this book, I realised that this is the first time that a history of the video-game industry has been told through the personal stories of the entrepreneurs who pushed the business forward. Many of the people featured came from humble beginnings with only passion to drive them. Most experienced highs and lows, while all had their shares of good and bad luck. What incredible journeys we all have had! No mountain is too high to climb. Every challenge can be overcome.

Gamers at Work is a critical resource for new and experienced business leaders—for anyone who feels unprepared for the demanding and seemingly insurmountable trials ahead of them.

—Peter Molyneux
Creative Director
Microsoft Studios Europe

About the Author

Morgan Ramsay is a serial entrepreneur and author whose companies have served the defense and entertainment industries. Currently, he is the founder, president, and chief executive officer at Entertainment Media Council, the first and only association for entrepreneurs, C-level executives, and senior managers in the video-game industry.

For seven years, Ramsay was the founder, president, and chief executive officer at Heretic, where he led initiatives that recognized men and women of the armed forces on behalf of the President of the United States of America, and launched technologies and services for clients ranging from the nonprofit and small business to the Fortune Global 500.

As the author of *Gamers at Work*, Ramsay has interviewed the world's most successful entrepreneurs in the video-game industry, including Atari cofounder Nolan Bushnell, Electronic Arts founder Trip Hawkins, and Sierra On-Line cofounder Ken Williams. *Gamers at Work* was introduced by Lionhead Studios founder Peter Molyneux OBE.

Ramsay serves as a member of the Business Council at the Poway Center for the Performing Arts Foundation, and as a strategy, marketing, and technology advisor to the boards of directors at Coronado Promenade Concerts and San Diego Filmmakers. He has also served as vice chairman at the International Game Developers Association of San Diego.

He holds a bachelor's degree in Communication from University of Phoenix, and also received education in nonprofit management; event planning; advertising, marketing, and merchandising; and retailing from Chapman University, San Diego State University, and Palomar College.

Acknowledgments

I would first like to thank my father, an inveterate and pioneering hardware engineer, for putting up with my enthusiasm for the entertainment software business. Of course, I would like to thank my mother, a former professional athlete and coach, for teaching me the importance of discipline, persistence, and restraint; and my sister for showing me that compassion and idealism are traits one should never lose.

A tip of the hat to the busy entrepreneurs who volunteered their time to this project and shared their wonderful and often humorous stories with me. I was privileged to investigate their ventures, as well as their personal and family lives. I also want to specially thank Peter Molyneux for graciously writing the foreword. In grand tradition, I wish them luck as they boldly continue to break new ground. Without their support and commitment, this anthology would have never been possible.

Thank you, Jeffrey Pepper, for going above and beyond the call of duty; Steve Anglin, for giving a first-timer a chance; Michelle Lowman and Kelly Moritz, and Rita Fernando, for keeping the project on track within its particular constraints; and the entire Apress team for the opportunity to address the challenges of entrepreneurship in this time-honored format.

I would recognize many people for their time, insight, and/or willingness to make introductions: Al Lowe, Alan Wasserman, Andy Schatz, Brenda Brathwaite, Casey Wardynski, Cathy Campos, Cory Ondrejka, David Edery, David Perry, Doug Whatley, Erin Hoffman, Gabe Newell, Genevieve Waldman, Greg Zeschuk, Greta Melinchuk, Guy Kawasaki, Hal Halpin, Ian Bogost, Jane Cavanagh, Jason Della Rocca, Jason Kay, Jeff Braun, Jim Buck, John Romero, Joseph Olin, Justin Berenbaum, Kellee Santiago, Ken Dopher, Kristina Kirk, Mark Friedler, Matt Shores, Megan Tiernan, Mike Capps, Mike Morhaime, Nancy Carlston, Pam Pearlman, Randy Pitchford, Raph Koster, Ray Muzyka, Richard Bartle, Rodolfo Rosini, Sam Ford, Shon Damron, Sue Coldwell, Suzanne Goodman, Tawnya Barrett, and Tim Schafer.

I would also recognize the current and former members of the Board of Directors and Advisory Group at Entertainment Media Council for their support over the years: Adam McClard, Alexander Macris, Alyssa Walles,

Brandon Sheffield, Christian Svensson, Cindy Armstrong, David Cole, Geoffrey Zatkin, Greg Boyd, Matt Esber, Mia Consalvo, Michael Arzt, Robert Stevenson, Steve Crane, Steve Fowler, and Terri Perkins.

Finally, I thank Laureen Minnich of Southern California Transcription Services for the wonderful work she has done for me; photographer Brandon Colbert for bearing through our session; and Jessica Livingston, for writing *Founders at Work*, which was my inspiration.

Preface

Like many projects, *Gamers at Work* began life as something else. Like many startups, as a first-time author, I made many mistakes. And like most people in business, I had no idea what I was doing, but I lucked out.

When I started the project that became this book, I had founded a trade association, Entertainment Media Council, for business leaders in the video-game industry two years before. We had completed the initial recruiting and planning cycles, and I was anxious to execute our plans.

We needed capital to proceed, but prospective investors, from the world's largest studios to leading universities, wanted to see that our little nonprofit organization had actually done something meaningful.

Entertainment Media Council exists to advance the video-game business by leveraging the collective wisdom and influence of business leaders, in order to address the systemic, market-level, and corporate problems that make video games such a volatile industry in which to do business.

I wanted to get people thinking about solutions, and get them involved with us at any level. Most importantly, I wanted to learn more about the struggles with which startups must contend. So, I had an idea: let's profile the challenges of entrepreneurship by blogging interviews with successful founders that explore major video-game companies at every stage.

Feargus Urquhart, cofounder of Obsidian Entertainment, and Chris Ulm, cofounder of Appy Entertainment, were the first two to sign on. While planning their interviews, I realized that posting interviews with such prominent entrepreneurs on a blog that had zero visibility would not do their stories justice. I would be wasting their time and mine.

On my desk, I saw a copy of *Founders at Work*. I thought, "It's a long shot, but I could write a book. Who's the publisher?" I reached out to Apress, and pitched them on a series of *At Work* books, with my book as the second in the series. They were interested, of course, because they were already developing a series. *Coders at Work* had been published not more than a year before. Within a few weeks, we had a deal.

In this book, I have interviewed 18 successful entrepreneurs in depth. Some are on their first company, others are on their umpteenth, and some are enjoying the retired life. I have tried to ask questions whose answers I wish I knew when I started my previous two companies. I have also tried to elicit answers that I thought I would want to know when someday I start a video-game company of my own.

Additionally, I wanted to illustrate the history of the video-game industry through the perspectives of the developers and publishers who played a key role in its shape. In these interviews, I aimed at having each founder tell their story from the time before their startup had taken form on the horizon to the end of their journey and the start of their next.

As a serial entrepreneur and former consultant, I believe that I should know which are the best questions to ask other founders. However, as you will discover when you read these 17 chapters, experience does not make one an expert.

Indeed, experience and expertise should not be conflated. Experience merely provides opportunities to learn and practice. Assuming that we have taken advantage of those opportunities, remembering our lessons and how they can be applied across problem domains can remain difficult, especially when we are immersed in the day-to-day.

Trip Hawkins, who I greatly admire as a business leader, spent years and years planning Electronic Arts, eventually working at Apple alongside the late Steve Jobs to learn the ropes. Despite that rigor and care which undoubtedly contributed to his phenomenal success, Trip excitedly spun off 3DO on a relative whim in 1991, and that company declared bankruptcy 12 years later. Meanwhile, Electronic Arts exists today as one of the world's most powerful publishers of video games.

The excitement of the day-to-day can be impairing. We turn to advisors, consultants, and trusted colleagues because they are third-party observers, sufficiently removed from our labors, who can pierce through the noise and clarify problems. Similarly, we look to magazines, books, and other publications for insight that gives us pause, or perhaps a simple diversion, that allows us to think clearly and critically.

I hope *Gamers at Work* gives you such a reprieve. I expect the stories shared within this tome will impart valuable information that you might have never obtained elsewhere. I hope the storytellers entertain you with their delight-ful anecdotes as they have entertained me. Finally, I encourage you to use this book as a reference, which you can revisit from time to time when you would like to remember how those who have gone before you confronted the myriad obstacles along the road to success.

—Morgan Ramsay
Founder and President/CEO
Entertainment Media Council

Trip Hawkins

Founder, Electronic Arts

 ***Trip Hawkins*** *left his position as director of product marketing at Apple Computer to start Electronic Arts (EA) in 1982, which continues to operate today as one of the largest publishers of video games in the world. EA has since produced many foundational games, such as Pinball Construction Set and M.U.L.E., and best-selling franchises, such as The Sims, Rock Band, and Madden NFL. In addition, many early employees are part of the company's evolving legacy, and they are now recognized as leading figures in the video-game industry.*

In 1991, Hawkins pursued a strategy to provide the company with a direct path to the consumer. The initiative was spun off as The 3DO Company, an independent platform manufacturer and later a third-party developer. Although initially well-received, 3DO was unable to secure a foothold in the highly competitive console market and declared bankruptcy by 2003. Not one to be deterred by past failures, Hawkins founded Digital Chocolate later that same year to develop video games for mobile devices. Today, Digital Chocolate is a leader in the mobile-games category, and controls a wide portfolio of social, PC, and console games, including Millionaire City and MMA Pro Fighter.

Ramsay: Take me back to before you started Electronic Arts.

Hawkins: As a child, I discovered that I was creative and loved to play games. My favorite games were board, paper, card, and dice games that tried to simulate something that I was passionate about: Strat-O-Matic Football and Baseball, Dungeons & Dragons, and Avalon Hill historical war games. I even designed a football simulation of my own using cards, charts, and dice. I noticed that many of my friends thought these games were too much work. In effect, the player had to be the computer. My own game was a minor business failure, but I loved being an entrepreneur. I vowed to do it again, but to be much better prepared the next time.

This was also the golden age of television, so my friends were basically telling me that they'd rather watch television, which was simple and offered high fidelity. In 1971, I heard about computer kits and time sharing, and I decided that the solution was to put the game into the computer, and to have graphics on the screen that looked like a television broadcast. From that moment on, I was very consciously preparing to found EA in 1982.

In 1973, I purposefully spent two years convincing Harvard to let me have my own special field of endeavor called "Strategy and Applied Game Theory," in which I applied computer simulation to relevant social problems, like organizational decision-making and nuclear-war prevention. During the summer of 1975, I got a job at a Santa Monica think tank, Software Development Corporation, that was the computer spin-off of the RAND Corporation. A colleague returned from lunch one day and said he was at a retail store where you could rent KSR-33 teletype terminals for only $10 an hour. I said, "That's great! This is the birth of home computing. I am going to make games that people can play at home on these computers."

My colleague, who had been at Dick Heiser's The Computer Store, which turned out to be the world's first computer retail store, then told me that another company called Intel had introduced the first CPU chip. I spent the next hour trying to plot out how these advances would develop in the home. I concluded that I should let the technology marinate and the hardware base accumulate for a few years, and that in 1982, I should found my game software company. And that is exactly what I did.

Ramsay: What did you do until then?

Hawkins: I finished school and met another objective by working at Apple from 1978 to 1982. My goal was to learn about how to build my own company by working for other entrepreneurs, and to simultaneously help build the supply of computers in homes, since they would be my future customers. When I joined Apple, we had only 50 employees.

Between 1971 and 1982, I refined my ideas about how to make EA successful. I eventually had a pretty good trick bag. I'm a good creative guy, but I also believe that "creativity is the rearranging of the old in a new way." I had seen how valuable it had been at Apple to leverage ideas from the consumer electronics business into our fledgling computer industry.

Ramsay: Can you give me any examples?

Hawkins: One example was the strategic advantage of direct retail sales—not using a distribution middleman. This became a key issue for Apple. I also determined by 1980 that software developers and engineers were like artists, even like divas. My key reference point became Hollywood media, particularly records and books. I studied those industries and found that it had been even more important for them to have direct distribution control and to build strategic value in their sales pipeline.

In addition, I decided to pioneer the idea of bringing the leverage of the recording studio to game development so that developers would have more powerful tools, and so that we could more easily span publication across more computing platforms. I introduced terms like "producer," "director," and "affiliated label" to software engineering for the first time. I even went so far as to mimic the record album in EA's first games, a specific packaging format that was imitated by 22 competitors later in the 1980s. These pillars of strategy were the key founding principles of EA.

Ramsay: When did you start EA? How did you get funding?

Hawkins: I personally founded, funded, and incorporated EA on May 28, 1982. Initially, I worked out of my home and began recruiting artists, channel partners, advisors, and prospective employees. But I began hiring employees in the fall of 1982 and got Don Valentine to let me use an office at his venture firm, which he had offered to me earlier in the year.

I funded the company, including computers, rent, and payroll for the first 12 employees, until December 1982, when I received additional funding from Valentine and other venture capitalists. The first games were published in May 1983, and EA was off and running.

Ramsay: Many entrepreneurs in this business work within founding teams. Did you? Were there any cofounders of EA?

Hawkins: No. A company is either founded by one person, who then hires the early employees, or there is a group of cofounders who work together to found a company on an equal level and who take equal risks. If there is a cofounder, then there cannot be a founder.

Every company must hire employees, but being an early employee does not make you a founder. I have been the founder of three companies, but none of my early employees from 3DO claim to be cofounders. Since I left EA, some individuals have wanted to position themselves as cofounders.

But the facts are that I spent a decade entirely on my own to develop the foundational ideas. I funded the company's first year entirely myself. I was the only one there when I incorporated the company and opened the first office. And I made offers to the early employees and paid their salaries, and in some cases, I even made personal loans so they could buy stock.

Ramsay: How did you know Don Valentine?

Hawkins: I first heard about Valentine in 1978 when his venture capital firm Capital Management—later renamed Sequoia Capital—invested in Apple, around the time I began working there. A year later, I became intrigued when Valentine sold his Apple position prematurely when the company was still private. It gave me the idea that there was something that Valentine didn't like about Apple, which made me curious.

When I was preparing to leave Apple in early 1982, I read an article about Valentine in an airline magazine that claimed he was so intimidating that a visitor making a pitch had passed out in his office from the pressure. At that point, I purposely sought him out because I wanted to have tough mentors on my board. I called his office and arranged to see him in February. He liked my ideas and encouraged me to get on with it. Valentine offered to let me borrow some of his office space for free if I needed it.

Ramsay: Were other venture capitalists just as receptive?

Hawkins: I found plenty of interest from venture capitalists when I began making the rounds in August and September 1982. I received multiple offers, and I don't remember anyone that wasn't interested. There was even competition for the deal that helped me get a better price. This led to an even hotter 1983 for funding companies doing personal and home computer software. After then, the market and funding climate became more difficult.

Ramsay: Can you tell me about the publishing process at the time?

Hawkins: I developed my idea for the "software artist" from working with brilliant developers at Apple, such as Bill Atkinson. These guys were legitimate divas. I decided to study and transfer the principles of artist management from the music industry to software.

I wanted the best game ideas from the most passionate independent artists that were driven enough and good enough to get the job done. I hired a couple of my buddies from Apple, Dave Evans and Pat Marriott, to be my first producers, but I was really the first producer. I sought out the best developers I knew and heard about, and I personally called on them and closed many of the first round of deals.

The typical model was to pay a small upfront advance because nobody else was doing it, and an advance demonstrated that EA had resources, conviction, and faith in the developers. Then there would be milestone payments. The entire deal for Hard Hat Mack was priced at $14,000.

Many of the early developers were teens living at home, developing on their personal Apple II. We would work closely with them to edit, polish, and improve the product until we either thought it was ready to publish or gave up on it. After publication, the artist would earn royalties, initially at 15% of our net revenue, but I made sure we could recoup our advance.

To create the contract, I took a traditional engineering development contract from the lawyer I had worked with at Apple and combined a copy of a music-recording contract, and then I added a bunch of new stuff specific to games. The entire industry copied my contract for the next 15 years.

Ramsay: Were there problems with getting the first titles out the door?

Hawkins: There were always projects that were never completed. Jay Smith, who created some wonderful games for the Vectrex system, was our first big air ball, costing us $35,000. I loved the Vectrex, made that deal, and was very excited because they had a legitimate professional track record.

Ramsay: Can you give me an example how you solved a problem project?

Hawkins: The young developers could be erratic and run late, but they were very passionate and driven, and took reasonable direction, so many things got done. I designed the One on One game, and then hired Eric Hammond to implement it. He was struggling, so we moved him up to our town and had him work in a cubicle near where I was sitting for the last several months.

Ramsay: Which titles were your major early successes?

Hawkins: The best developers from the group that made the six debut EA games were Bill Budge, FreeFall Associates, and Ozark Softscape. Bill made one of the most important games ever: Pinball Construction Set. FreeFall made Archon, which is still one of my favorite games. FreeFall was a married couple, Jon Freeman and Anne Westfall, and another great designer, Paul Reiche. Ozark was put together at my request to make a simple business-simulation game, for which I provided the design of the underlying economic principles, such as the learning-curve theory of production.

I also wrote the manual for the game M.U.L.E., which also remains one of my all-time personal favorites. Ozark, led by the ingenious Dan Bunten, did a stunning array of clever and innovative things in M.U.L.E., and made it quite charming for a business simulation. Pinball, Archon, and M.U.L.E. won a ton of awards, and all three shipped in the first group of games in May 1983.

Ramsay: There are many developers who cite M.U.L.E. as a favorite, too. What's the story behind the game? How did you know Dan Bunten?

Hawkins: I wanted to make a business simulation that would be based on Cartels and Cutthroats by Strategic Simulations, but simpler and better. I called Joel Billings, who founded SSI, but he didn't want to license Cartels to me as a starting point. I then went directly to Dan Bunten, and we became mutually excited about doing a new game. Their loss was our gain.

Dan and I shared a vision for games that was expressed by an old EA slogan: "software worthy of the minds that use it." We wanted games to be good for people in terms of personal growth and social value. Dan got together with his brother and a few other good souls in Little Rock, Arkansas, and formed Ozark Softscape in order to work with me. To play M.U.L.E. properly, you really needed four players and four joysticks. It was ahead of its time, but everyone that played it was completely charmed.

Ramsay: EA began publishing in 1983. Was there competition then?

Hawkins: I tabulated 135 competitors that were already shipping computer and video games when I founded EA. I already understood that I could not succeed with a "me, too" company, but 135 was a surprisingly big number. Also, it was completely intimidating going to the Consumer Electronics Show in January 1983 and seeing competitive game boxes stacked 60 feet high to the ceiling. But by then, I believed passionately in what I was doing differently and was fearless simply out of youthful ignorance.

EA made its conference debut in June 1983 at the Consumer Electronics Show in Chicago. We had a tiny booth compared to many others, but we later learned that we had made the biggest impression, and people respected our approach, which was thick with innovation, artistry, and quality.

Ramsay: Were there any particular competitors that concerned you?

Hawkins: I considered home computers the next wave, and many of the game competitors were small and lacked business experience. Brøderbund was certainly interesting and capable. I loved the Choplifter game they had published, and we competed for good, independent developers. Activision was the largest of the Atari 2600 developers. Activision had done a huge IPO, but I thought they overrated the Atari platform and would eventually burn out. And they did.

Ramsay: Did you consider Atari, which had been operating for at least a decade before EA, a legitimate threat to your business?

Hawkins: I could tell back in 1982 that Atari was going to hit the wall and would take down its game developers with it. The Atari 2600 was over-hyped, but you could literally animate only six sprites, and the entire thing had 128 bytes of RAM. Bytes! It was a glorified Pong machine, so it was only a matter of time before it became a doorstop.

Atari made a famous announcement in December 1982 that was like the Titanic announcing they had hit the iceberg. Their collapse gave video games a bad name, and suddenly nobody wanted to admit that they liked video games. For certain, Atari was a giant sucking sound that hurt the industry from 1983 to 1985.

Ramsay: What about SoftSel?

Hawkins: In June 1982, I visited SoftSel, the dominant game distributor. I went directly into the lion's mouth. I presented myself as a potential customer, but I mainly wanted to size them up as a competitor since I had decided to bypass distributors and go directly to retail.

Distributors are distributors, and I did not care for SoftSel and never did business with them. Again, I came away with a strong conviction that I was doing the right thing, even though it proved to be extremely difficult and required incredible determination over a three-year period. Retailers would never have bought directly from me if they could have cherry-picked our hits from SoftSel. Instead, they had to buy from us because SoftSel did not have our games. As this became a competitive factor, they got very, very mad about it, but I had to worry about what I had to do.

Ramsay: Finding the right people, especially the right leaders, is a difficult task. Was that your experience with hiring managers at EA?

Hawkins: Like Apple, I found that about half of the managers I hired were not very good. In hindsight, when I think about the first 50 managers at Apple and EA, I think perhaps 5% were exceptional and another 40% were solid role contributors. Both companies succeeded despite being held back by the shortcomings of the other 55%. But sometimes managers with dysfunctional personalities were tolerated for far too long.

Over time, as I gained more experience and perspective, I got better at identifying and confronting issues, and either getting them resolved and improved or making management changes. Another positive for both Apple and EA is that I worked hard on creating a strong internal culture and making sure that we were hiring true believers who were passionate. Their tolerance for change, determination to succeed, and willingness to work hard on something they believed in made up for other deficits.

Ramsay: Do you believe that people who work within a strong culture carry its values forward? Many of your first hires now have great careers.

Hawkins: You get out what you put in. I have always invested heavily in defining and building corporate culture. If you don't do it, the alternative forms of organizations are dictatorship and bureaucracy. As the saying goes, things rot from the head. If a company's leadership exemplifies certain values, they will more likely become part of the true culture, which is often different from the officially stated culture.

With a good culture, you have more successful delegation, faster decisions, and better development of people for their own future and that of the enterprise. In my organizations, I put a lot of effort into the learning and teaching environment, and employees are regularly promoted. This was also true at Apple, where, although not a founder, I was asked by the founders to define and maintain the company culture, which I did.

I think Apple lost some things in the 1980s because the founders didn't do enough to drive the culture. Several years ago, I did a rough count and realized over 50 executives who worked closely with me had later become chief executives, many of which were running public companies. I've been a good school for executives. I'm sure the numbers are much higher now.

Ramsay: Why did EA become a public company?

Hawkins: Having been through the Apple IPO in 1980, I founded EA with the intention of being successful enough to go public. I planned to have venture investors and to give stock options to all employees, and I knew the company would need a path to liquidity. I maintained strong relationships with investment banks throughout the 1980s, and it began to look feasible to do an IPO as early as 1986. But I did not think the company was mature enough, and then there was a market hiccup in 1987.

In the 1980s, consoles were underpowered, passé, and EA only made games for more powerful PCs. Computers had mass storage, read-write storage, keyboards, printers, modems, and other features, whereas Atari had made consoles the butt of a joke. But after Nintendo gave rebirth to consoles, it became clear that the low hardware price of a discless machine and the convenience of plug-and-play cartridges would engender a much larger market. The American game industry hoped Nintendo would be another hula hoop like Atari had been, and was ignoring it and hoping it would just go away. I didn't like Nintendo's draconian license agreement, but I felt compelled to enter the cartridge game market.

In 1988, I was looking for an intelligent strategy to enter the console game sector, and the Tengen-Nintendo lawsuit inspired me. I decided that we should focus on the upcoming 16-bit market and enter the market by reverse-engineering the Sega Genesis. I believed that EA would be better off with a cash war chest to deliver on this plan, including deep pockets in the event that we might get sued by Sega. Once I had this strategy figured out, it made sense to go public to establish the war chest. Ironically, we only raised $8 million in the IPO, and EA has never touched or needed to use a penny of that money. I pulled off a great agreement with Sega in 1990, and the cash just kept rolling in, without there ever being a lawsuit.

Ramsay: What impact did the transition from PCs to console game systems have on publishing operations?

Hawkins: It was an enormous change to go from read-write floppy discs to smaller read-only cartridges with high manufacturing costs. We also needed to make different kinds of games with very different user interfaces. For example, the Madden user interface got a complete overhaul, even though it used the same underlying gameplay mechanics, camera angle, playbooks, and player stats. Many of our employees did not like the change and were uncooperative, insisting that we could not make quality games for an underpowered machine like the Genesis.

I knew we had to let go of our attachment to machines that the public did not want to buy, and support the hardware that the public would embrace. I made this argument on the grounds of delivering customer satisfaction and how quality is in the eye of the beholder. If the customer buys a Genesis, we want to give him the best we can for the machine he bought and not resent the consumer for not buying a $1,000 computer.

The majority of employees and developers got on board with our new values and culture, but there were about 30 employees who departed because they thought I was nuts. That was a big number at the time because we probably only had about 200 employees in total. Those that stayed and believed in the plan went on to experience the greatest growth and success period in the 28-year history of the company.

Ramsay: Fast-forward to 1991. Why did you leave EA?

Hawkins: I didn't feel like I was leaving EA, but it turned out that way. From 1988 to 1990, I did my most transformative work at EA, led by a radical strategy to enter the console game business by reverse engineering a new and unproven platform. In 1988, Tengen reverse engineered and sued Nintendo. I watched that situation unfold to Tengen's ultimate detriment.

At the same time, Sega released the 16-bit Sega MegaDrive, which was later branded as the Genesis, in Japan. I really liked this machine and investigated a strategy of reverse engineering it. Doing so would allow EA to have publishing freedom on the platform, which would probably be released in the United States in 1989 and Europe in 1990. EA already had great 16-bit brands and technology that could easily move to the Sega Genesis.

We moved forward, had it figured out in 1989, and had products ready to go in 1990. I then went back to Sega and made a huge strategic deal that made us good partners. The deal would also prove to save EA $35 million in licensing fees and catapult our market cap from $60 million to $2 billion in a two- to three-year period. Once that was all in the bag and well underway, I was still very concerned about future platforms for EA.

I worried that Nintendo and Sega would take steps to make it harder for EA to have freedom in the future. Sony had not yet entered the game business, and the PC was completely dead as a game platform at that time. I concluded that it was time for EA to take a more active role on the platform side—perhaps not to the same degree as Microsoft or Sega, but in some way that we could drive market expansion and publishing freedom. I wanted to see consumers and developers get the chance to have 3D graphics, optical disc storage, and networking.

This effort began with an internal skunk works, but took on a life of its own. I couldn't resist the temptation to spin it out and organize it as a "Dolby sound"-type licensing model called 3DO. From 1990 to 1994, I was chairman and the largest stakeholder of both companies; however, the two companies gradually pulled apart due to conflicting priorities and agendas.

Ramsay: How did you feel about leaving behind something you created?

Hawkins: I was like the father of a rebellious teenager and an infant having open-heart surgery. I felt obligated to care for the infant and knew that the teen was going to make it to adult life. 3DO was in business for 12 years, and twice reached revenues of up to the $100 million level.

For a variety of reasons, 3DO was not sustainable. I made a lot of mistakes, and many of the ideas were too far ahead of their time. I was sad to become estranged from EA because it was my baby. I had always admired Walt Disney as a role model and the fact that he was with his company until the day he died. I regret the misadventure, but I take full responsibility.

Life tests and develops our character, hopefully into something better over time as we learn and understand what is right and true. One thing I do know is that it was somewhat inevitable that I would do something like 3DO because I was trying too hard to push the envelope in those days. I think many of us as younger entrepreneurs are trying to find out exactly who we are and where our edges are, and you don't know where the edges really are until you fall off a few times.

Ramsay: Platform manufacturers not only compete by publishing their own games; they benefit from hardware licensing and third-party properties. Is this business really that lucrative, or are there hidden costs?

Hawkins: Investors like to play monopoly, so they like platforms, but many platforms fail, and many are capital-intensive. In reviewing history, game consoles are now apparently among the riskiest of platform businesses. To be successful, you need custom chips, high manufacturing volume, and tons of marketing. The pace of technology is also very fast, and new models can quickly become obsolete. Nintendo is the only company in that sector that has been consistently successful over a long period.

Ramsay: Why wasn't 3DO sustainable? What were the mistakes?

Hawkins: For starters, 3DO was more than $1 billion short on the capital requirements. Licensed technologies like Dolby sound, Flash, HTML, or MPEG can gradually sneak up on the market, penetrating more devices and platforms over time and becoming de facto standards. This is because the hardware is selling for another reason and the emerging technology is only an additive. I might buy a tape-cassette recorder because I want to record songs or buy music tapes, and I don't even have to know or care that Dolby sound is an option. It is completely different with game consoles, especially in those days where it was winner take all.

A new game console would only succeed on the basis of new games using its new features. Backward compatibility would not drive its success; it had to have new, state-of-the-art games. It turns out that to make a new console good enough to achieve this and to win support from enough good developers, it takes more than $1 billion to build it out and convince others to jump in. Sony committed more than $2 billion, and not only beat 3DO, but pushed aside larger and stronger competitors like Sega and Nintendo.

Sony, Nintendo, and Sega also had strong brand power and great lineups of first-party games. Mario is only on Nintendo, and Sonic was only on Sega. 3DO could lead off with Madden and Road Rash, but as fast as they could, EA put those games on Sega, Nintendo and Sony. Ultimately, the low license fees for 3DO didn't matter. Developers were willing to overpay Sony because they believed in Sony's strength in building the market.

A great deal is made of 3DO's high hardware price, but this mistake is over-rated. First of all, the initial street price was $599, not higher myths that are often reported. Within a few months, I negotiated with Panasonic to bring the price down to $499, which was, by the way, Sony's introductory price the next year in Japan. Sony was very aggressive when they later entered the United States at $299, but by that time, 3DO's price was $349. 3DO would have done better at lower prices, but Sony won, and also beat Nintendo and Sega for a variety of these other reasons.

Ramsay: When did you start Digital Chocolate?

Hawkins: When 3DO was selling its assets in 2003, I began to see the mobile category emerging as the next big change, and challenge, in the media landscape. I love new media. The dot-com bubble had recently burst, and venture-capital investors were more intrigued with mobile after seeing strong growth with the mobile Web in both Japan and Korea.

I finished the business plan in September 2003, received funding almost immediately, and hired the first employees in December. My wife suggested a few names for the company using the word "chocolate." I took that word and put "digital" in front. I like names that are a mash-up of two ideas that aren't yet associated and yet that belong together, defining something new. Digital Chocolate's first mobile apps and games came out in 2004.

Ramsay: Are the games you're now developing very different from what you were publishing at Electronic Arts?

Hawkins: A few years ago I realized, in hindsight, that my big, true ambition ever since childhood had really been about social games. I was always looking for opponents as a kid. With EA, I supported a four-player game like M.U.L.E. in 1982 and Modem Wars a few years later, at least a decade ahead of the Web. I was very passionate about the multiplayer EA Sports games. Even with 3DO, I produced another multiplayer game called Twisted, and we made a daisy chain of joysticks so that a game could have as many as 16 players in the same room. FIFA only supported six players.

However, Digital Chocolate today is making a much more casual games for a larger and more mainstream audience, like Millionaire City. And our games are free to play with virtual goods, which was never the business model at EA.

Finally, these modern games don't want to let players fail, which was "part of the deal" in the old days. Now, you want everyone to feel like a winner. One of the best tools for making that happen is to completely eliminate any need for timing or hand-eye coordination. Too many people find it intimidating or embarrassing to fail on that basis. By contrast, everyone has brain cells and can enjoy basic decisions and tactics, and will even develop pet strategies. In comparison, the traditional arcade games have typically been about hand-eye coordination. While these arcade games were easy enough to play for everyone in the beginning, within a few years, they became too difficult to play, especially in the everlasting pursuit of the next quarter.

Ramsay: Is the "free to play with virtual goods" model sustainable in the long term? There has been much evangelism, but what are the weaknesses?

Hawkins: It is the future. Even in the present, all of the growth at Digital Chocolate is in virtual goods. I am especially excited about the long-term potential for our NanoStar platform that allows a virtual item to be a character with personality, and to then turn that character into a different game asset in a variety of different games. This approach gives the player much more emotional and gameplay value.

Games are going mainstream, so it is only natural that the business model would become less like a theatrical film and converge toward television and the Web. Free broadcast television paved the way for today's hefty cable subscription fees, and the original World Wide Web paved the way for the monetizable Web 2.0. The only major weakness is that virtual goods work well in some game genres but not in others. As television also works better with some genres, the game industry will have to migrate more to what will work better in the future.

Ramsay: Are you concerned that mass-market video games are migrating toward a future where art, entertainment, and fun take a backseat to what you called "the everlasting pursuit of the next quarter"?

Hawkins: The arcade games took a fork in the road, opting to make the games harder to win. The competitive hardcore male player would try harder, and devote more time and quarters. This made games too difficult for the mass market that had been happily playing Pong, Pac-Man, Centipede, and Space Invaders. Also forsaken and misunderstood were the importance and value of social benefit.

Pong was played, socially, in a lot of bars by people looking for social life. The games that followed in the next decade were almost exclusively played solo. We realized that interactive and social media are far better for us than the "boob tube." We now know how to make better user experiences that are simple and convenient and social. And today, we have more and better technology and art. We are also reaching an enormous mainstream audience. It is still a business, so there is nothing wrong with figuring out what people want. It's entertainment, so there's nothing wrong with helping players release hormones like dopamine and feel good about themselves.

Physical exercise and video games are big elements on the short list of healthy ways to use hormone management to improve life and health. We are not Pavlov's dogs, but B.F. Skinner proved long ago that the strongest form of behavioral modification is variable-ratio reinforcement. The slot machine thrives on it, but is a social ill because it is a dehumanizing addiction. In a more interesting, thought-provoking, and truly interactive game design, the principles of reinforcement are very useful. Nobody is going to do anything if, in the end, it doesn't constructively involve your emotions.

Ramsay: In 2006, quality of life became a hot-button issue for EA. Can you provide any insight into the labor environment then? Did you do anything differently with the culture at Digital Chocolate?

Hawkins: I don't know the details, but I've always been interested in organizational culture, and I want to help my employees win and become better people. At every stop in my career, I've defined the personal values for my companies and the business practices to make them a reality. I even did this at Apple at the request of the founders.

As the industry matured, it became a bit more "dog eat dog," and all of the companies were under more pressure. Many companies, including 3DO, failed. Countless people have told me over the years that the culture and quality of life at EA declined after my departure. While this is disappointing, culture is defined by everyone's values, beliefs, and behavior, not just any one person's.

Ramsay: How has Digital Chocolate fostered a culture where employees can thrive and enjoy their success? Have your publishing strategy and offering numerous outlets for creativity played a role?

Hawkins: Digital Chocolate operates throughout the world, and our employees were born in 35 different countries. But we speak English in our offices. As a lazy American, I appreciate this accommodation, and it helps the global organization exchange ideas and feedback, and learn faster. We do our own technologies, design, and brands internally, so there is plenty to be creative about. Projects tend to be pretty short and have small teams.

Over the course of a year, we can crank out dozens of new games, and again, this creates much more opportunity for good ideas to be used. We let everyone participate in generating ideas and discussing plans, and we're committed to the highest level of production values and quality. We also give bonuses and stock options to all employees. For all of these reasons, the results are very good, and our people are highly motivated.

Ramsay: Has recruiting talent for mobile or social games been difficult? I've heard that some developers can be averse to joining teams dominated by business graduates instead of experienced game developers.

Hawkins: We have around 350 employees in five major offices on three continents, and our people come from a variety of backgrounds. I think the most important things are good education, aptitude, and willingness to learn and adapt. In the old days, the ponytails made the games, and the suits got the packaged goods manufactured and put on shelves, and collected the money. There were big operational demands. Today, the ponytails and suits can sometimes be embodied in one person. In any case, the perspectives of art and science need to be blended together. Creative people need to get out of the ivory tower and pay attention to the tests in the Petri dish. And the scientists need to understand that it takes creativity to make something fun.

Ramsay: You've seen this business from every angle, having worked in publishing, development, and even hardware. What would you say are the most serious threats to the growth and long-term viability of startups?

Hawkins: Digital media has collapsed the traditional value chain, so financial and distribution leverage are no longer viable means of controlling shelf space and pipelines. Now, digital platform companies like Apple, Facebook, and Google have the ability to dominate and control entire value chains.

We all have to be concerned that any of them that get too big or become too central could misbehave. In order to favorably influence the platform titans, smaller game publishers and developers will need to find ways to stick together, and have some collective bargaining power and policy viewpoint. Going forward, the business of games will be about how to leverage technology and intellectual property. Startups will have to find ways to contribute in those dimensions, but it is always possible.

Nolan Bushnell

Cofounder, Atari

At the dawn of the 1970s, **Nolan Bushnell** and Ted Dabney set to work on their flagship product with spare parts in hand: Computer Space, which became the first commercial coin-operated game and the first commercial video game. After briefly operating as Syzygy Engineering, the duo formally incorporated the company as Atari in 1972.

Bushnell and Dabney sought to design and license out their games, but upon encountering resistance, Bushnell decided to enter the manufacturing business. During the first year, Atari spent around $500 in capital, hired roughly 200 employees, and brought in more than $3.5 million. Under Bushnell's leadership, Atari spawned many competitors, effectively fathering the video-game industry that we know today.

Warner Communications purchased Atari in 1976. A year later, Atari unveiled the 2600, the video-game console that defined the 1980s and popularized discrete game cartridges. However, as a testament to the company's influence, Atari brought the industry to its knees in 1983, crashing the market. Many dependent companies found themselves out of business or on the verge of failure.

By that time, Bushnell and Dabney had left years earlier, in 1978 and 1973, respectively. Bushnell moved on to expand the Chuck E. Cheese's chain of family-entertainment centers. Since then, he has started numerous companies, including Catalyst Technologies, the first technology incubator; Etak, which created the first car-navigation system; and ByVideo, which created the first online ordering system. Today, Bushnell is widely recognized as one of America's most powerful entrepreneurial icons and one of the nation's greatest innovators.

Ramsay: What were you doing before you decided to start Atari?

Bushnell: I was an associate engineer at Ampex Corporation, working on a video-file system. We were using videotape to create a massive terabit database, back when a terabit was a lot of memory.

Ampex had basically invented the hard drive and became the leader in tape-recording technology. Ampex had a system that they wanted to create, which stored more data online than anybody else. They had a huge contract with the Los Angeles Police Department to store fingerprints. One thing they wanted to do was store a whole bunch of digital information on videotape. It was my job to increase the density of videotape recording.

I was working on a problem called "dropouts," which what you don't realize are found on videotape or any other kind of metal-oxide tape. These are places in the manufacturing process where there's no oxide. It's called a "dropout" because if you write something there, you can't get it back. So, I had to devise a method of doing some significant error correction because it was a nonstatistical thing, and sometimes a dropout would last for 200 or 300 bits. There was an interesting process that we were working on that would cure that. It was basically an RF redundant adding system in that it took advantage of some of the statistical properties of videotape.

Ramsay: Why did you make the jump from videotapes to video games?

Bushnell: I had played games when I was in college and was very smitten with them. I had also been the games manager at an amusement park. I sort of had games in my DNA, and I was waiting for the time when it would be possible to do a video game at a reasonable price. The machine we were playing on at the university cost a million dollars, and that surely couldn't be monetized a quarter at a time. I understood games and the economics of the coin-operated space, and I felt that the minute I could build one that fit those dynamics, I could have a business.

Ramsay: It sounds like your college life prepared you well.

Bushnell: I worked my way through college, and I loved it, and I shifted my major several times. When I was ready to graduate, I could have graduated in mathematics, in philosophy, and in economics, but I chose electrical engineering because I felt that it was the one with the most valuable of those skills.

Ramsay: Who did you convince to start that business with you?

Bushnell: I had a partner, Ted Dabney, who was my office mate at Ampex, actually. He was a brilliant engineer.

Ramsay: When did you talk to him about starting a video-game company?

Bushnell: It was about 18 months later. I really didn't talk that much about the video games that I had played in college for awhile. The catalyst was seeing an ad for a $5,000 computer come across my desk. The ad was for a machine called the Data General Nova 800. I thought that was a strong enough computer at a low enough price. If I could build a unique monitor—a cheap monitor because computers in those days cost about $30,000—then I would have a business.

Ramsay: Did you have any prior experience with starting businesses?

Bushnell: Yeah, I started an advertising company when I was in college. I also started a television-repair company when I was in my teens. I had been pretty much an entrepreneur on and off all of my life.

Ramsay: How about your cofounder?

Bushnell: No, he had always been an engineer. He learned engineering when he was in the Navy, but he was a good cofounder. Dabney was very supportive and very hardworking.

Ramsay: At what point did you decide to give the startup a go with Dabney?

Bushnell: It was probably the summer of 1970. I basically told him that I thought there was an interesting opportunity using the kinds of computers that were becoming available, and that all we had to do was create a very inexpensive computer interface to a regular television set. Dabney had some skills in that direction. We decided that I would do the computer part and he would do the monitor-interface part. That's kind of where we got talking about how we would do the architecture. And before you knew it, we said, "We've got to start a company to do this."

Ramsay: When you talked to him more about starting the company, what were his thoughts?

Bushnell: Well, he thought that the technical challenge was interesting. He didn't understand the marketplace though. I said, "No, there are millions of dollars worth of arcade games sold every year. All we have to do is make sure that it earns money." At least for me, it was totally opportunistic.

Ramsay: Did you two split your roles definitively, specifically with regard to the business? You would work on the computer, and he would work on the monitor interface. But how about your business roles?

Bushnell: Well, I think as we got going, Dabney was more in the analog side of the world—you know, power supplies and things. He was a very, very good analog engineer and knew a lot of digital. Once we started, Dabney ran manufacturing. He was a very handy, capable guy, and he could build anything. I was on the engineering, sales, and marketing sides.

We both took a cut at the accounting and keeping track of things. I think Dabney did it for awhile, and then I did it for awhile. Finally, we just had to get somebody that actually knew what they were doing.

Ramsay: Why was Atari something you had to do?

Bushnell: The whole idea of a video-game business was just too strange in those days. If you mentioned it to somebody, they would sort of look askance at you. I knew that Ampex wasn't going to do it. I had been starting companies all of my life, so it just seemed like the natural thing to do. I really didn't question any alternatives to starting the company and then licensing the hardware.

Ramsay: Was there a lot of focus on hardware then?

Bushnell: It was all hardware. As it turned out, the first video games didn't have Von Neumann architectures at all. They had what we called "digital-state machines." These machines were, essentially, clocked output signal generators that created waveforms that drove the television monitor. If you wanted to change anything, you had to change the hardware. There was no software at all. In fact, the very first game that executed a program was Asteroids in 1979.

Ramsay: Did you put together a business plan?

Bushnell: No, I didn't. In fact, Atari never had a business plan until we went out for venture capital in 1975, when we were doing about $40 million in sales.

Ramsay: But you had engaged in a planning process with Dabney and talked about where you wanted to go and what you wanted to do?

Bushnell: It was more back-of-the-envelope stuff than it is now, because I knew there was no chance of us getting venture capital. You know, the idea was just too strange and new. In fact, we had four years of profit before we could raise a penny of venture capital.

Ramsay: Since there was no formal business plan, do you still have any of the back-of-the-envelope writings when Atari was just an idea?

Bushnell: You know, I don't. I did a lot of that actually in my lab book. I had the mind of an engineer, if you know what I mean, and that was lost somewhere along the way. So, I don't have it.

Ramsay: What was your original plan or vision for the company?

Bushnell: Our original plan was to simply be the technical foundation and to license our games to other coin-op manufacturers. We were able to do that through licensing at Nutting Associates in Mountain View.

Ramsay: Hardware games?

Bushnell: Right, that was 100% of the business until, I think, 1977.

Ramsay: What did you and Dabney risk to start Atari?

Bushnell: Not very much. We both put in $250 each, so our startup capital was $500. The biggest risk probably came a year and a half later when we went to get a bank loan and had to personally guarantee it.

Ramsay: What were your expenses?

Bushnell: The components to build the prototype unit in terms of the computer cost $300. We spent the other $200 on business cards, a couple of power supplies, and an old television set. I mean, Dabney bought the very first television that we converted for $30 from Goodwill.

Ramsay: Wow! It costs more to build a guitar these days.

Bushnell: I know. Well, many of the individual integrated circuits that we were using cost 15, 20, or 25 cents each. I think the most expensive chip on our PC board was 90 cents—and I mean the whole thing. The power supply that cost $20 was one of the biggest costs, not counting the cabinet.

Ramsay: How were you able to get individual components? Today, you can't just order individual components; you have to order them in bulk.

Bushnell: You could in those days, and Ampex had this thing where they didn't mind you taking a few of these components for what they called your own personal inventions. A lot of these things were available to us at Ampex.

Ramsay: I've been told that new manufacturers convince the sales representatives at parts companies to send them samples, which is why in some technologies no two units are the same. Alternatively, they get a parts company to provide all of the necessary components at little or no cost in exchange for a commitment to order future parts from them exclusively. You told me that Atari had money problems from the start, so did you pursue any of these strategies to lighten the burden?

Bushnell: Oh, yeah, that's precisely what we did. I mean, we had to pay for something ultimately, but we would always give the business to the guys that would give us the longest terms.

Ramsay: You were working at Ampex while you were starting Atari?

Bushnell: That's correct.

Ramsay: They didn't see anything wrong with that?

Bushnell: Not at all.

Ramsay: They didn't want to take control of any rights or anything?

Bushnell: No, they actually encouraged us to do "hobby jobs," as they called it.

Ramsay: With a total of $500 startup capital, did you try to get any more money through mortgaging or credit cards?

Bushnell: Nope, we didn't need to really. Once we had the unit going, we were able to license the game, and then the company that licensed it from us paid for the rest of the development and the premanufacturing costs.

Ramsay: How did licensing with Nutting work? What were they thinking?

Bushnell: They were very happy to license with us. They had a dry spell, and they had a single product that their company was built around—a thing called Computer Quiz. It was really a big strip of slides, of 35mm slides. It was a trivia game and had pretty much run its course. Their business devolved into supporting new questions for the trivia machine, but they weren't selling any more than five or six a month of their regular Computer Quiz, so they were really looking for a product. I hit them at the right time.

Ramsay: And what was that product? Pong?

Bushnell: No, this was Computer Space.

Ramsay: Computer Space. I've never seen Computer Space. Was it a live-action game like Pong was?

Bushnell: It was a rocketship flying-saucer game. You've seen the pictures of the cabinet, haven't you?

Ramsay: Yeah.

Bushnell: Yeah, and you'd fly the rocketship around and try to shoot down the saucer.

Ramsay: Was that sort of dynamic on-screen interaction and animation different from what Nutting had been doing before?

Bushnell: Oh, yeah. Remember, they essentially had just an automated slide projector.

Ramsay: Then I'm guessing they were really impressed!

Bushnell: In some ways, I feel like they were actually quite clueless and were kind of jumping at anything that looked like it might rescue them. I think they were in trouble.

Ramsay: So, you didn't face any difficulty with the pitch?

Bushnell: No.

Ramsay: You didn't need a champion?

Bushnell: Actually, I was introduced first to their marketing manager, a guy named Dave Ralston. He was clearly the most excited, and he brought it to the guy who was running the company at the time, a guy named Guymon, and then Bill Nutting himself.

Ramsay: Did you relocate to start the company? Where were you when you started Atari?

Bushnell: Well, the first facility was Dabney's daughter's bedroom and my daughter's bedroom. You know, we worked at home for awhile, and then we went over to Scott Boulevard. It was a 2,000-square-foot garage shop. A garage shop in those days was really where startups happened. You essentially had a couple of offices up front with a nice door, and then in the back, there was a rollup door and sort of a warehouse facility behind.

Ramsay: Location is important for some businesses. How important was it for Atari as a manufacturer?

Bushnell: It was hugely important to get started because we were right in the middle of Silicon Valley, where chips were readily available, and we knew a lot about them. I think that we actually had a manufacturing disadvantage because Chicago was a lot cheaper, particularly for anything to do with things like coin doors and mechanics and stuff like that, because they had been building coin-operated games since the 1920s. In some ways, it was an advantage, too. But our cabinets always cost us more than they did in Chicago, and any mechanical things we needed cost us more.

Ramsay: You mentioned a daughter. You had a family?

Bushnell: That's correct. I have two daughters. I put the two daughters together and turned their bedroom into our lab.

Ramsay: What impact did the startup life have on your family? Many entrepreneurs start out in their early twenties and single.

Bushnell: Well, understand that was very strange in those days. Entrepreneurs generally didn't start being entrepreneurs until they were in their forties—even thirties was strange. In some ways, I was the youngest entrepreneur that the Valley had seen, and I always felt that kind of paved the way for Gates and Jobs and some of the other guys, just because it was so strange at the time.

Ramsay: Was there a publisher-developer industry at this time?

Bushnell: Not really. I mean, most of the companies did internal development because the games were really complex, strange things, which had a lot of DC motors and moving-slide projectors that would put images on the screen. To put that in context, there was a driving game that was very popular and very successful, and it consisted of three separate slide projectors. They would take a piece of film and put it in front of a bright light with lenses, and then they would change where that image was placed on the screen.

There was one, The Chicago Coin Speedway, that was a disk which represented the track. It would move, so that it would look like the car was viewed from a first-person standpoint. You were able to move your car over the track, and there was another disk that put in traffic. It was clever. It was complex. It made a lot of money. And it broke down a lot.

Ramsay: The lack of an industry also meant a lack of proven models. When you started, how confident were you that you would succeed?

Bushnell: Well, remember, we actually started in 1970 and then licensed the products to Nutting. We felt that we had our own company going at the time, even though we were both being paid by Nutting. I don't know how confident I was. You know, I wouldn't have done it if I didn't think we could do it. But when we started, we thought of ourselves as a design and licensing house. We thought we would be guys who would provide a service to other big manufacturers, and we didn't initially intend to go into manufacturing.

Ramsay: Other than Dabney, who was the first person that you brought on?

Bushnell: My babysitter, Cynthia Villanueva. We just brought her in as a receptionist, coffee maker—someone to keep everything working.

Ramsay: And when was this? This was after you had the prototype?

Bushnell: Yeah, this was actually long after. Dabney and I then worked for Nutting, and we were trying to get this into production. It wasn't until both Dabney and I quit Nutting as employees and worked on a project for Bally Manufacturing that we rented our first facility. That was when we hired Cynthia. We had signed another deal to develop things for Bally.

Ramsay: When did you start working at Nutting? Did you leave Ampex?

Bushnell: Yeah, when we got the prototype working, I went around, and Nutting was essentially the only coin-operated game company in the area. I had presented to them. They liked the idea, and they said, "We don't know anything about this technology. We need a new chief engineer if you want to be it." So, in some ways, not only did I not take any real, big risks, but I negotiated a significantly higher salary at Nutting than I had at Ampex and got the company car. So, it was a really good move all the way around.

Ramsay: What year was this?

Bushnell: 1970.

Ramsay: All of this was happening in 1970?

Bushnell: Correct.

Ramsay: A year of change.

Bushnell: It was.

Ramsay: And you were how old?

Bushnell: I was 27.

Ramsay: How many years was Atari just you and Dabney?

Bushnell: One. Just to put it in context, the time frame was that we created the prototype. We got the job at Nutting. We got the unit into production. We then had royalties. I wanted a large stock option from Nutting. They turned me down. I got the contract from Bally, quit Nutting, started the Scott Boulevard location, and hired Cynthia. We started production up, got Pong going that summer, and started to produce it. We then incorporated the company. It was called Syzygy Engineering up until then.

We tried to get Bally to take Pong as fulfillment of our contract. They turned it down. We decided we might as well manufacture a few. We had, I think, just enough money from our royalties and various things to buy the parts for 13 units. We built them, sold them for cash, and we were off to the races. That was all by the spring of 1972.

Ramsay: How much did each of the 13 units cost?

Bushnell: Each unit cost $380, and we sold them for $910.

Ramsay: $910! And people made such a fuss about the 3DO...

Bushnell: Well, remember, these were coin-operated. These were commercial.

Ramsay: What was your first major challenge as a business?

Bushnell: It was always cash—getting enough cash to buy the parts, getting the cash to just buy capital equipment. We were always short of cash.

Ramsay: You were bootstrapping?

Bushnell: You've got it.

Ramsay: How did you try to solve your cash problem?

Bushnell: What we really became experts at was just-in-time manufacturing. We figured out a way that we could trim essentially most of the cost of our product. There were only three to four days between the time it came in the door and the time it left. What that allowed us to do was operate the company with positive cash flow because we had 60 to 90 days to pay for that stuff.

Over and over again, we were able to sell units for cash. Later on, we sold units to finance our receivables, so that we had cash from shipping our product long before we had to pay for the components or the salaries of the people who were working on them.

Ramsay: What would you have preferred to do?

Bushnell: Oh, I would have loved to have gotten an investor.

Ramsay: And you couldn't get an investor?

Bushnell: No, it was a very different world in those days. I think there were two venture capitalists in the Valley: Sequoia and Arthur Rock—and then there was a company called Minrock. It wasn't until probably 1975 that the Mayfield Funds and some of those others came on board. Venture capital was right at its dawning.

Ramsay: $3.5 million a year wasn't impressive to investors?

Bushnell: Oh, it was very impressive, but it was a weird business.

Ramsay: They didn't understand the business?

Bushnell: Yeah. The people at that point had a real problem with the idea that the games that were really popular this year may not be really popular next year. They saw it as the movie business, which it kind of is.

Ramsay: Most businesses don't break even until the fifth year. Atari had a million dollars in profit by the end of the first. Did you ever think that perhaps your financial constraints weren't as serious?

Bushnell: Well, remember, as you're growing, a company is a net consumer of capital, so it was always difficult because we never had enough cash. We couldn't get ahead of the game, and we were using every bit of our capital to fund our growth.

Ramsay: You mentioned that you signed a deal to develop "things" for Bally. What were those things?

Bushnell: You know, that was after Computer Space. We had a contract to do three things. One was to design a multilevel pinball machine. One was a driving game. And the third one was to look at creating a series of games that were very simple. We never really worked on the last one.

We got a multilevel pinball machine that was really, really fun, but they never produced it. Then we ended up not doing the driving game that we were going to do for them and replacing it with Pong. After they turned down Pong the first time, they came back after it was successful and said, "Yeah, let us do that." And so we allowed them to fulfill their contract by producing their version of Pong, which was called Winner.

Ramsay: What's a multilevel pinball machine?

Bushnell: It was a pinball machine that essentially had three playfields, one above the other. You'd start out in the middle level, and by hitting certain holes, the ball would actually drop down to the bottom side, bottom level, or up to the top level. We called it Transition. The top level was kind of a heaven and had a lot of golds, blues, and whites. The bottom level was hell, and that was reds, oranges, and fire. And the middle was Earth. That was greens, browns, and blues.

Ramsay: Were most pinball machines single-level then?

Bushnell: Yeah. Transition was actually the start. I don't know if you noticed, but there are a lot of pathways—you know, steel ramps and tubes and things like that—which lift the ball up off the playfield. We were actually the first ones to do that.

Ramsay: I'd be remiss if we didn't talk about Pong. I know you've talked about this game over the years, but how did Pong get started?

Bushnell: Pong started as an engineering project, but it was really triggered by my seeing the Magnavox Odyssey. Remember, we had been in business for almost two years now working on Computer Space. And somebody said, "Hey, there's another video game that's for consumers, and they're showing it up in Burlingame." And so I had to check that out.

I went up and saw the Odyssey game. I played it a couple of times and signed a log book, so you know, it's no conspiracy or anything. And driving back down, I thought, "Boy, that was kind of disappointing." I saw it as no competition at all.

We had put ping-pong type games on the big computers when I was in college. I thought that was kind of interesting, but I also thought I could make that better. That happened to be, I think, Al Alcorn's second or third day, and I was fishing around for a way to give him a training project. So, I gave him the task of doing a ping-pong game using our digital technology, which was superior. And it was fun. We kept doing extra little things, and it got more fun. Pretty soon, we said, "You know, this is probably a product." That was when I got the idea of seeing if I could get Bally to put Pong into our contract. That was my plan.

I got on an airplane to Chicago, set up an appointment, flew back there, and tried to sell Pong to Bally. They were kind of wishy-washy on it. By the time I had gotten back, we had learned how much it earned in the test location, The Handicap's Tavern, and I thought, "Geez, we can do this. I'm going to go into manufacturing."

The reason why Pong became a controversy is that Ralph Baer, who did the Odyssey, was always really pissed off that Pong was a huge success and that the Odyssey wasn't. And so over the years, he has claimed that I stole Pong from him. And, you know, that's okay. He likes to point out that we settled a patent suit with him. He did have some patents. But although I think we could have beaten it, it was a situation where it was time-constraining.

I settled with him for what we considered a junk royalty. I think we settled the lawsuit for what was then like 0.06% of our sales, but it was a paid-up license. We were in the process of raising money at the time, and it was important for us to get that off the table, because people get concerned about patent lawsuits. So, it was a business decision to settle. It had nothing to do with the merits of the case. In fact, we settled for less cash than it would have cost us to beat the suit that year. The deal was $100,000 a year for five years, and we figured that it was going to cost us $250,000 to $300,000 to defend it for an uncertain outcome. To me, it was a no-brainer. Do it: settle. You should always save today's cash for tomorrow's cash.

Ramsay: How successful was Pong?

Bushnell: We did about 35,000 units. They were each getting about $1,000 a piece, so we made about $35 million on it.

Ramsay: In terms of staff, did you recruit any advisors? Did you know anyone who could provide you insight into the business side?

Bushnell: I had a good relationship with a guy named Bob Noyce, who was one of the founders of Intel. I really looked up to him, and would often give him a call when I had a thorny problem. Jerry Sanders from AMD was another guy that I would tap from time to time. Those were probably the two major mentors who I would say I had in the Valley.

I also tried over and over again to hire a president. And I hired a couple of guys from Hewlett-Packard. I hired my brother-in-law, who was a chief executive officer. None of them worked out because the dynamics of the company were so strange. We had no cash, and we were literally working from hand to mouth, even though our sales were going through the roof.

At the end of our first year, we had done $3.5 million in sales on 3,000 units with roughly 200 employees on $500 paid in capital. Now, I'm really proud of that. Many people have asked me, "What are you the most proud of?" I've said, "It wasn't the design. It was the financial engineering that we had to go through to just keep all the wheels on."

Ramsay: How did you produce 3,000 units in 1972 on $500 in capital?

Bushnell: That was the trick. You basically took the money that you earned and put it back into inventory. If you do the math quickly—let's just do it in tens to make it easy—those ten turned into $9,000, which turned into thirty, which turned into… and so on up.

Ramsay: Who produced these 3,000 units?

Bushnell: We did. We would buy the cabinets. There was a cabinetmaker, and so the cabinets would show up. We would buy the television sets, modify the television sets, install them in the cabinets, and build this one-board computer. We had a bunch of girls stuffing them into the cabinets.

And the only thing that slowed us down was testing, because every one that would come off the line would have minor little problems. Chips in those days weren't nearly as reliable as they are now. So, the testers would find those problems. They would find the faults, and there would be things called "solder bridges" and various other things to get the machine right. And then we would ship them out. We did that over and over and over again.

Ramsay: You didn't partner with another company like Ampex or Nutting to take on some of that manufacturing work?

Bushnell: Nope.

Ramsay: How many employees did you have at the time?

Bushnell: I think by the end of 1972, we probably had over 200 or maybe 300. We were shipping all through 1983, between 150 and 200 games a day.

Ramsay: Which was substantially less than your competitors.

Bushnell: Correct.

Ramsay: How much of that $3.5 million was profit?

Bushnell: We earned that year maybe a million dollars. It was very hard to tell because every penny we earned was put into equipment and desks and chairs and stuff like that—capital expenditures.

Ramsay: Did you have competitors at the time?

Bushnell: Yep. In fact, we sold 35,000 units of Pong. The total market was estimated at about 150,000 units. So, we did a little better than 20% of the market actually, and we didn't have a factory. We were building factories and short of cash against guys who were all set up to turn out 100 to 300 games a day, and they were able to beat us.

Ramsay: Who were those competitors?

Bushnell: Well, we ended up doing a license to Bally after they saw the success of Pong. That was one. Nutting, our old thing, bought a unit and copied it, and they went into the business. There were two or three others from Chicago. A company called Allied Leisure out of Florida. There were actually a bunch of them, probably 20 or 30.

Ramsay: How did Nutting copy Pong?

Bushnell: Well, all these games had a series of components and a circuit board. If you copied the circuit board, you could see the traces on it and plug in those chips, and the game would work.

Ramsay: Was this authorized?

Bushnell: No.

Ramsay: Did you do anything about that?

Bushnell: It was a thing where I didn't copyright the board, and it was one of those times where I just didn't have time to enter into some kind of a big lawsuit. I just figured I could do that later and never got around to it.

Ramsay: Did you care at all that they copied your board?

Bushnell: Yeah, it totally pissed me off.

Ramsay: How did that turn out for them?

Bushnell: I think they made money on it, but copying somebody isn't a good strategy. It's a really good way to put yourself out of business over time. You're being buffeted by the strings of various things. I think they actually copied my second game, too. I think they copied Space Race, but that was not as successful as Pong by a wide margin, and they kind of got in at the tail. I think they actually lost money on Space Race.

Ramsay: Can you tell me about the culture at Atari?

Bushnell: It was a pretty good culture. We had some formalization, but Atari was a little more like the Wild West. The real thing that we were always trying to do was figure out how to keep up with the demand that we were creating and to keep on the edge, ahead of our competition. There were a lot of people who were waking up to the fact that video games were a significant business, so there was a lot of competition. We just had to keep ahead of the pack.

Ramsay: So, competition really defined Atari. How soon after starting up did you have competitors?

Bushnell: A whole bunch of them sprang up within nine months after shipping the first Pong. We had 20 competitors, and as the market moved past Pong, a lot of them started to do a certain amount of their own development. There was a lot of competition.

Ramsay: Did you ever think about buying out your competitors?

Bushnell: We never had enough money. We couldn't support our own growth. If we had more money, we could have grown faster.

Ramsay: How about after the Warner buyout?

Bushnell: At that time, we were growing as fast as we could because the consumer business was just exploding, and we had some good blocks there. The development time of the chips for the consumer marketplace took over two years. So we knew we had at least a two-year window.

Ramsay: What became of your responsibilities?

Bushnell: I was doing a lot of things internationally, opening up markets throughout Europe. After the consumer product, I was really sort of focusing an awful lot of my time on new projects. We had AtariTel, which was going to be our online game business and which was also killed by Warner. I actually think Atari might have been able to be the Internet if the world had been slightly different.

Ramsay: What was this online game business? I'm pretty sure there wasn't broadband then, so what was it?

Bushnell: This was all done by telephones, modems, and what we call "bulletin boards"—local bulletin boards—and then we were going to link the bulletin boards together with T1 lines.

Ramsay: What kind of games would you play on AtariTel?

Bushnell: We really hadn't gotten there yet. We were really focusing on getting the software and modems that could run fast enough.

Ramsay: What was Dabney doing?

Bushnell: Dabney left. I bought Dabney out in late 1973.

Ramsay: How come?

Bushnell: Dabney was a good engineer, but he was really not good at being an executive. I put him in charge of manufacturing, but I think the company was getting scary for him. I wanted to make sure that Ted did well. He was so important in the early days, but I felt that we had to part. I felt that I could scramble financially, so I wasn't worried about Atari. We sold him the route—the coin-operated route, in which there were about 200 games all over the Bay Area, with each game making net $50 to $100 a week—all of the assets, and income. We also gave him $250,000 in cash and notes. His part had more assets than Atari at the time. It was actually a struggle for us to patch the loss of that cash flow, but I knew we would make it. We just had too many powerful and creative people.

Ramsay: What was the post-acquisition atmosphere like?

Bushnell: It was always very busy, a little bit chaotic, but everybody was having a good time. The corporate culture was very, very positive and up-beat.

Ramsay: How much had Atari grown?

Bushnell: I'd say when I left, we were probably at 15,000 to 20,000 employees. But remember, we were doing manufacturing. We had a lot of people who were just screwing screws and stuffing PC boards.

Ramsay: In your opinion, when did Atari peak?

Bushnell: Well, I sold the company to Warner Communications in 1976. I stayed on as chairman until 1978. It was then run by a guy named Ray Kassar, who worked for Warner, and he was able to grow the market with the 2600. Atari peaked in 1982. But he basically stifled all the engineering, so the wheels came off the company around 1983.

Ramsay: What does that mean? How did he "stifle" engineering?

Bushnell: Basically, he treated the engineers like factory workers. Each game in the VCS world was making a huge amount of money, but he wouldn't even let the engineers put their names on them. Because of that, some of the best guys went off and started Activision, Imagic, and about six others. The real heart of the engineering team left.

There were several other guys, like Alcorn and Steve Meyer, who were always trying to push the envelope to do better and better hardware technology. None of the projects they worked on would ever see the light of day. He killed them one after another. He thought that any product they did had to look like it was going to earn back at least $30 million to $40 million because the company was doing almost a billion dollars then. Of course, no product looks like it's going to be that big right out of the shoebox. If you're killing all your babies, you don't ever have any teenagers.

Ramsay: At the same time, Electronic Arts was just starting up. Trip Hawkins mentioned that the market crashed then.

Bushnell: Huge crash.

Ramsay: He said Atari was to blame.

Bushnell: And he's absolutely correct. It was totally Atari's fault. I've always said it wasn't homicide; it was suicide.

Ramsay: What happened? What was the crash about?

Bushnell: It was all about not understanding that they had saturated the market. Atari went into Christmas 1982 thinking they could put another 15 million VCS consoles into the market, but they couldn't. Everybody went off that 15 million number to put in cartridges, so when the hardware didn't sell, the cartridges didn't sell.

When the cartridges didn't sell, a huge rush to discounting went on. People were liquidating inventory at almost any cost, and a huge amount of red ink flew. And many people thought the business was dead at that time. Remember, there was virtually very little game activity for a couple of years. When Nintendo wanted to bring their unit into the United States, they did it very tentatively because many retailers didn't want to hear the words "video game."

Ramsay: How did Atari recover?

Bushnell: It never did.

Ramsay: Let's go back a few years. Why did you sell Atari in 1976?

Bushnell: I needed the capital to use as funding for the 2600. You know, the 2600 was going to be a huge product, and I knew the company just didn't have enough capital. I was going to either take the company public or sell it to an individual with deep pockets. I decided to go with deep pockets.

Ramsay: Were there any internal discussions about selling to Warner?

Bushnell: Oh, yeah, lots.

Ramsay: How did those go down?

Bushnell: We knew we needed to raise money for the 2600 because we just didn't have enough cash to build the inventory. The Christmas season was really about to build up, and we were shipping everything in October and November. That meant inventory and lots of it, but we just didn't have lines of credit or the ability to really pull that off.

Ramsay: So, the discussions were fairly rational yet desperate?

Bushnell: No, it was just that we were looking at selling the company on one hand or taking it public on the other. We had written a whole plan for a public offering.

Ramsay: In negotiating with Warner, was there a long and drawn-out negotiation with them?

Bushnell: Nope, it was pretty much a day.

Ramsay: What did you guys talk about?

Bushnell: Well, we talked about pricing and value, and the form of the agreement. We pretty much agreed that we were willing to sell, and it really came down to what was the best price.

Ramsay: What did you want to gain?

Bushnell: I wanted a very attractive bonus plan going forward. I also wanted to have certain guarantees of autonomy with respect to product lines, but of course, that ended up being all bullshit.

Ramsay: What you wanted to gain, you actually lost?

Bushnell: Right.

Ramsay: After the deal, they had control.

Bushnell: They did.

Ramsay: How did that power shift impact your role?

Bushnell: The first year, not at all. The next year, we started fighting like cats and dogs. And then the wheels came off that fall. Warner claimed they fired me. I say I quit. It was a mutual separation.

Ramsay: What were the reasons behind the separation?

Bushnell: I wouldn't let go of two major issues. One was that the 2600 needed to be replaced with better technology. They were selling software hand over fist, and I said there has to be an orderly transition. I said there just needs to be a new VCS because I was worried about competition, and I knew we had made all kinds of compromises.

The 2600 had only 128 bytes of memory. That's nothing! I knew we could do so much more if we could just add memory into it. Memory had become so cheap since the time we did the original design that there were all kinds of architectures that would make it much better. And they didn't want to do that.

And it sounds crazy, but the other issue was we had a pinball division, and they wanted to build a standard-size pinball machine. I thought that was absolutely foolhardy because we were at a competitive disadvantage on two fronts. First, we were in California. These things were big and cost a lot to ship. Second, we weren't as efficient a manufacturer of these kinds of things as they were in Chicago, because they had been doing pinball machines for 30 years.

Ramsay: You're talking about Midway Manufacturing, right?

Bushnell: Gottlieb, Williams—all of those guys. So, I just said if you try to do that, you're going to end up losing money on every unit. And, sure enough, one year after that fight, they closed the pinball division because they couldn't make any money.

My theory is that Atari was good at innovation. We were able to extract a lot of money from the innovation. When we got into the pinball business, we created these things which were called "wide bodies." We could charge extra for these wide-body pinball machines. I think we charged $400 more, which totally made up for the manufacturing inefficiencies.

Ramsay: Why weren't you able to work out your differences?

Bushnell: I was brash, and I didn't really abide fools gladly. Looking back on it, I think I was a little bit of an obnoxious guy. I would just call these guys stupid, and if you're an executive at Warner and a guy is calling you stupid, it pisses you off. And truth wasn't a defense. I mean, the guys were a little bit thick.

Ramsay: After leaving Atari, what did you think about the various changes that Atari went through over the years?

Bushnell: I pretty much thought they were clueless.

Ramsay: Looking back, what would you have done differently?

Bushnell: I think I would have hired a more experienced manufacturing person. I think that we hired one of the guys off the line and promoted him. While he was a good and hardworking young kid, he really didn't have the gravitas and the understanding. I think that hurt us in a lot of ways.

Ramsay: How so?

Bushnell: We just didn't anticipate problems. You really have to be on top of things when you're running hand to mouth like we were.

Ramsay: What did you do after that?

Bushnell: I had purchased Chuck E. Cheese Pizza Time Theatre a few years before in 1976. So, by that time, I had built up to about six stores. I just went over to the Chuck E. Cheese offices and spent my efforts there, eventually growing the company to 250 stores.

Wild Bill Stealey

Cofounder, MicroProse Software

 *Wild Bill Stealey* and Sid Meier cofounded MicroProse Software in 1982. Their flagship title, Hellcat Ace, was the product of a bet. Although the industry struggled during this time, MicroProse successfully developed and published simulation games, producing a number of hits for Atari, Commodore 64, and other early platforms. The studio initially created well-received, military-themed simulation games, such as Silent Service and F-15 Strike Eagle, but by 1991, the company had released three of the best-selling franchises in video-game history: Sid Meier's Pirates!, Railroad Tycoon, and Sid Meier's Civilization.

In 1989, Sid Meier and MicroProse changed their relationship. Sid began developing games under contract to MicroProse for advances and royalties, instead of being a partner in the company. Wild Bill continued as chief executive officer until the company was acquired by Spectrum Holobyte in 1993. Stealey exited MicroProse after the Spectrum acquisition, and the next year, he started a new simulation game company, Interactive Magic. Meier and two others cofounded Firaxis Games in 1996. Stealey sold Interactive Magic in 1999 and purchased back the company three years later, bestowing the studio with a new name: iEntertainment Network.

Ramsay: Can you tell me about the events in your life that led to the starting up of MicroProse?

Stealey: We better start at the beginning. I went to the Air Force Academy, where I wanted to be a great fighter pilot. I got to be a pilot even with glasses, and flew airplanes for six years on active military duty and then for ten more years in the Air National Guard. Initially, I was an instructor pilot in T-37 aircraft. After that, I was a C-5A pilot and decided C-5A Galaxy aircraft were not the way to make general, so I decided to leave active duty, fly in the Guard, and go to graduate school.

I was on my way to law school when another Air Force Academy graduate asked me, "What kind of lawyer do you want to be?" I did not know what kind of lawyers there were! He suggested that to be a business leader, I needed to go to business school to get an MBA instead. I went to the Wharton School of Business in Philadelphia. I was already a little older than most of the kids coming out of college or in graduate school because I was 30 years old, already a captain in the Air Force, and already had some significant leadership responsibilities. I then went to two consulting firms. I went to Cresap McCormick & Paget in New York City. Later, I joined McKinsey & Company, the world-renowned consulting firm.

I found out that I was a smart guy, but I wasn't a very good consultant. I'm not patient. You have to be patient to be a consultant because you have to listen to people talk for years, and not do anything. You can bill them by the minute. I'm not very good at waiting to get the answer done. Whenever there's a problem, I want to solve it now and go on to the next one. I know there are going to be more problems tomorrow. I spent three years at McKinsey, and then worked for a client in Hunt Valley, Maryland, called General Instrument.

General Instrument was a technology company that built terminals for racetracks and state lotteries. They had a lot of software people, a lot of hardware people, and I was the director of strategic planning for a $250 million division. My job was to make sure we did strategic plans that we could take up to New York and give to corporate. They basically were doing everything by hand.

I'm a smart, lazy person, so at Cresap McCormick, I invented a software planning system that all of our clients could use on dial-up—believe it or not—dial-up time-sharing. I don't know if your readers will know what that means, but you would dial into a remote computer using an acoustical modem. I had programmed financial models on this remote computer, and we could run financial scenarios with income statements and balance sheets even before there were any personal computer spreadsheets. We had made a sophisticated financial-planning model on the time-sharing system.

I decided to bring a similar system over to General Instrument, but they wouldn't buy any computing time. They didn't want to spend the money on remote computers. So, I went looking for a computer because there was a brand-new program called VisiCalc, invented by Dan Bricklin. It was the first spreadsheet application, the same one "borrowed" later by Lotus and later by Microsoft. They saw what Dan had done, and they copied it!

I was looking for a computer that could run VisiCalc, and I found a Trash-80, a TRS-80, with all of 16K of memory. It came in black or amber screens. Your choice... quite a choice! Next to that was a brown computer with a fruit on it and a small bite out of that fruit. I asked, "What's that?" The clerk said, "That's an Apple." I said, "What does it do?" He said, "Well, it's got four colors." I thought, "Wow, we're moving up from amber and black, and we went to four colors." Next, I heard "eh-eh-eh-bam" explosions, and I looked to the right. There was an Atari 400 with a little chiclet keyboard. I asked, "What's that?" He said, "That's a game computer." I said, "What kind of game is that?" He called the game Star Raiders. I went, "Wow. Does it do VisiCalc?" He replied, "Yep." So, I bought an Atari 800, not a 400, because you could put a basic cartridge in it and get up to 48K of memory—pretty exciting, huh?

I used that Atari 800 to do VisiCalc and the planning for General Instrument as the planning director. I was then introduced to a systems engineer named Sid Meier, who was "reviewing" other folks' games they didn't own. Sid didn't feel he was pirating; he was just looking at them for the technology. I said, "As an Air Force Academy graduate, I can't *review* games without paying for them. That's what we called quibbling at the Air Force Academy." I didn't participate, but he had a user group who called themselves Smuggers, as in Sid Meier's User Group. That was March 1982.

In May, Sid and I were invited to Las Vegas to listen to all the sales guys at General Instrument pontificate about how much better they were going to do next year. He was the only technical guy. I was the only finance guy. We sat in those meetings for two days, until Sid leaned over to me and said, "Hey, Bill, I know where there are some games. Let's get out of here. It's really boring, listening to sales guys talk about how cool they are." We went downstairs at Bally's MGM, right there on the famous corner in Las Vegas, and he kicked my butt at every coin-op video game down in the basement.

Well, I'm not feeling very good now because I'm the fighter pilot, he's the engineer, and he's kicking my butt. There was a game called Red Baron. Since I was flying A-37s for the Pennsylvania Air National Guard, I figured I'd kick his butt in the flying game. I sat down and scored 75,000 points. I said, "Okay, Meier, beat that. I'll bet you a quarter." He sat down and scored 150,000 points. I was really torqued now, and he turned to me and said, "This is not a very good game." I said, "What?" He said, "No." I said, "Well, how did you beat me?" He said, "While you were playing, I memorized the algorithms because there's a pattern here. It's not very good. I could write a better game in a week." Fighter pilots don't like to be outbragged, so I said, "If you could, I could sell it." So, now we had a bet.

It took Sid about two months to write a game called Hellcat Ace. He brought it to me in August 1982. I was wearing my three-piece suit with my collar pin, trying to be Joe Junior Executive. He was still the engineer, in his jeans and his tennis shoes. He handed me this 5.25-inch floppy disk and said, "Hey, Bill, you said you could sell this." I'm going, "Oh, my God. What did I do here?" I took the game home and played it in my Atari 800. I wrote him a four-page memo about what was wrong with the flying and combat. I figured that was the end of it. I gave it back to him, and he just kind of walked away and didn't say anything. A week later, he brought the game back and said, "I fixed all of those things you mentioned." Sid really called my bluff with his new version of the game.

In October 1982, I had one copy of Hellcat Ace on a 5.25-inch floppy in a baggie with colored paper as a cover. Sid had another copy. I was on my way to New York for a General Instrument meeting when I stopped in Rahway, New Jersey, got off the train, and found a computer store. I waited until just before they closed at 9:00 in the evening. I walked in and asked the owner, "Can I show you my game?" We sat there for almost two hours, playing Hellcat Ace. He goes, "This is pretty good. I'd like to buy 100." I said, "What? 100?" And he said, "How much are they?" I looked around the store at the typical price and said, "$29.95." He said, "No, no, no, Wild Bill. You don't get it. I'm a retailer, so I get half off, so I can make money, too." If I remember correctly, I made a deal with him for $14.97 per unit. I called Sid and said, "We need 100." Sid was copying Hellcat Ace onto 5.25-inch floppies from one Atari hard drive to another. To make that order, he had a kid, a next-door neighbor, make copies all day for 25 cents a disk. By December, we were selling almost 500 units per month, still in baggies. I continued to visit computer stores and sell a few here and there.

We had published a number for MicroProse, which was really our home phone number. We got a call on that line, and my wife answered. The caller said, "Hi, my name is Jerry Wolosenko. I run a distributorship in Boston. I'd like to buy 500 units of Hellcat Ace." Well, we almost fell on the floor. She replied, "Mr. Stealey, our sales director, is on the road. I'll have him call you." He asked, "You're a small company, aren't you?" She said, "Yes, we're a small company." And he said, "Well, you have Mr. Stealey call me, and I'll teach him about distribution." He actually bought 500 units, and we learned about distribution, pricing, selling on credit, receivables, and retailing from Jerry. In our first year, we did $200,000 in business, and we had $30,000 in expenses for 5.25-inch floppies and baggies from the local Giant supermarket.

Most of the time, I would just get on the phone and call computer stores. I'd ask to buy Hellcat Ace. They wouldn't have it, so I'd yell, scream, and say, "Hey, don't you know anything about games? This is a terrific game. Didn't you see the review in Antic Magazine?" It was the only Atari magazine at the time. I bought one little-bitty ad in there and got one little-bitty review. So, then I'd hang up. I'd repeat this same sales tactic three weeks in a row. During the fourth week, I'd call back and say, "Hello, this is John Stealey. I'm from MicroProse. I'd like to sell you Hellcat Ace." The guy would say, "My God, we've been getting all kinds of phone calls for that game."

I made my own market, and that's how we sold $200,000 worth of Hellcat Ace in the first year. That's how we got started at MicroProse.

Ramsay: How did the name come about?

Stealey: Sid actually named the company. We were talking about the name one day. We couldn't come up with a really cool name because, given that I'm an Air Force Academy graduate, I suggested academy something or even Smugger. He said, "We write prose for microcomputers. Why don't we call the company MicroProse?" He had been thinking about that. As you know, Sid is very brainy. I said, "Sure. It'll be hard to remember, but once they got it, nobody will forget it." From that moment, we were MicroProse, or MPS Software, depending on what you wanted to call us.

Ramsay: Around what time was that?

Stealey: September 1982. Our only objective was to sell enough Hellcat Ace games to be able to charge our cars off to the IRS. That's all we thought we were going to do. From an entrepreneurship angle, when I was in the consulting world, I had met a Naval Academy graduate. We had MBAs from good schools. What really sparked the entrepreneurial urge for us was that we were making very good money with consulting firms; however, we saw that a bunch of guys, who didn't go to a service academy and who didn't get MBAs from good schools, had little companies that were being bought for big bucks by the big companies. We decided that we should find a way to be entrepreneurs, too.

While I was consulting, I gave a $50 million check to a guy who didn't get out of the eleventh grade. What he started was an HVAC company. I talked to him, and we had a couple of beers together. He told me, "Well, Bill, this is really nice. I love when you Ivy League guys bring me big checks." It was the third business that he started, and the third one that he sold to a big company. I said, "Well, Fred, how do you do it?" He said, "I start companies because I know people, and I know how to manage people. I get them going, and then I let the big companies know they're for sale. I always try and do something that I know some big company will buy."

I talked to my Naval Academy partner and told him we needed to do this. We looked for businesses for about two years. We negotiated on a bunch of them. We tried to buy them. We figured that since we're service academy graduates, really smart MBAs, and consultants, we ought to be able to figure out how to run these little businesses. Other guys are doing it very success-fully, and they don't have our backgrounds. We were being a little superior there. It turned out that it's not as easy to just say, "I'm cool. I need a busi-ness." So, we never were able to find one we could afford to buy.

When Sid came along, there was a chance to start a small business and keep my real job. That was an important thing because I had three kids at the time. To be able to keep my real job and run a business on the side seemed like a really good thing to do. I already had it in my head before I met Sid that I wanted to be an entrepreneur because I had seen all of the success of the entrepreneurs who I dealt with in the consulting world.

Ramsay: When you were selling Hellcat Ace, were you thinking about what you were going to do for future products?

Stealey: Sid had two other products: Chopper Rescue and Floyd of the Jungle. Chopper Rescue was the first multi-joystick game ever. In that game, you had one person flying and another person gunning, so you used two joysticks. It was a two-player game that you played on one computer. I sold that to CBS Software for $50,000, which was a big piece of change for Sid and me. It took about a year to negotiate that.

Floyd of the Jungle was the first four-joystick game. I had three kids, so all four of us could sit in front of the computer, try to climb the same maze, get next to each other, and bop the other guy to knock 'em down the maze. When you got knocked down, you fell to the bottom of the maze and had to run to the top again. My kids and I had wonderful times playing that game. It was a classic game. It never sold that well, but I'd take it to a trade show or computer store on a Saturday morning, get a lot of attention, and have fun with a crowd with the game.

I spent a lot of Saturday mornings showing my games at computer stores all over the Northeast. Everybody loved Floyd of the Jungle. I'd sell 50 of them despite the fact that no one else had ever heard of it. We did very well with the game on a small basis. Anytime I went anywhere, they'd buy Hell-cat Ace, Chopper Rescue, and Floyd of the Jungle. I would always sell three games to anybody when I was in the store. We were very successful at one-on-one selling. Every one of the games had something special going for it, and that was the magic of Sid and my ability to stand up and demo. I was the demo king.

As we were finishing our first year, Sid was looking around for new game ideas, and learned how to do line draw on the Atari. He wasn't a trained programmer; he was more of a systems guy. He started Solo Flight, as he thought I could sell another flying game as well as I had sold Hellcat Ace. My request had been to make an F-15 flying game. He next did F-15 Strike Eagle, which became a very successful product for us.

Ramsay: I know you were a consultant for large firms, but did you have any experience with startups or building new organizations?

Stealey: None of that experience, but I was a Wharton MBA with a finance degree, so I understood balance sheets and income statements. I was a consultant for three years. I saw many of the problems that businesses had. As a young Air Force officer, I had the ability to lead flights and small military organizations, so I already had some organizational skills. That's what they teach you at the Air Force Academy: the ability to manage and motivate people. That was key to my being able to get a job done.

Ramsay: Were your expectations realistic?

Stealey: Probably not, but I had low expectations. Remember, all I wanted to do was sell enough to charge off my cars to the IRS—just enough revenue so that my car could be free. And, fortunately, I ended up being a better salesman than that, and Sid made really great games. When we earned $200,000 in sales during the first year and had $30,000 in expenses, I said, "Sid, we got a real company here, let's go for this."

Sid wouldn't quit General Instrument initially. He didn't believe that we had a real company. I quit General Instrument though. I worked for a year with no salary and ended up with three employees by July 1984, a year and a half later. I had three employees plus myself and my wife, and $27 in sales in July. It's hard to pay for employees with $27 in sales, don't you think?

Ramsay: When did you start thinking about the company's future?

Stealey: At every point, even right at the beginning when I told Sid we had a real company. I'm going back to July 1984 through July 1985. I actually went down and took a loan on my Volvo car for $15,000 so that I could go to the Consumer Electronics Show in Chicago and pay our employees for that month. We were doing a new product called Solo Flight, and HessWare offered me $250,000 for the product. Now that's big bucks. I was ready to sell it to them. They found me at E3. They were well-financed, and seemed to have a lot of cash.

I came back to Sid and said, "Sid, we can get this money from HessWare. We can pay for development." He was still working full-time for General Instrument. He hadn't come to the company yet, and was only doing this on weekends and nights, while I was working every day at the company. "I hired this really smart Wharton MBA to make those decisions," he said, referring to me. He didn't want to participate. As I walked out of the office that we had for him, he said, "But you know what? I heard you shouldn't sell the family jewels."

The new Solo Flight game made us competitive with Microsoft, who had the original Flight Simulator. Flight Simulator was owned at the time by Sublogic, a company out of Champaign, Illinois. I said, "You know what? You're right." I told HessWare no, and they went bankrupt the next month. We would have never been paid. I took Solo Flight to the buyers for Sears. I sold 25,000 units to them because Sublogic was giving them a hard time, and wasn't giving them a good discount. We passed a million dollars in revenue that year.

Ramsay: Had you put together a business plan before then?

Stealey: Heck no! Are you kidding me? What I put together is "what can we sell?" What am I good at? Selling. If you look at the first products that did very well... what were they? Do you know?

Ramsay: I'm not familiar. What were they?

Stealey: F-15 Strike Eagle. Why F-15 Strike Eagle? Because Wild Bill was flying for the Pennsylvania Air National Guard. Remember, I had a part-time job flying for the Guard. I was running MicroProse, and on weekends, I made a three-hour drive to Philadelphia to go fly airplanes for the Air Force Air National Guard because that's where I got my extra money to support my kids. I was flying the A-37, which is a great little attack airplane, but it's not the F-15. I told Sid, "I did a really good job with Hellcat Ace. That's what I sold the most of. Give me another flying game. And by the way, I'd like to do the F-15." And he did the F-15 game for me. That was the second game that generated over a million dollars in sales for us.

My approach to business planning is simple. What can I sell? What do people like? How can I keep the expenses way down? Being a finance guy, I did spreadsheets every day. I'd forecast our cash for three months into the future all the time. Always three months. You always want to know three months because products were always going to come out in three months. We were convinced of it. I was always doing cash flow. I knew our cash flow down to the nub every day, every week, and every month. I never wanted us to run out of cash like we did in July 1984.

Ramsay: You were still tracking your financials on your Atari?

Stealey: Yeah, my Atari 800. That was the only computer I had.

Ramsay: What sort of financial burden did you take on at the start?

Stealey: Sid and I put in $1,500 each. After that, he didn't put in any more money. Sid didn't want to take the risk; he said that was my job. I funded the whole thing from there. I'm the one who hocked my car. I took on the financial risks. I hired those people, and I felt a responsibility to pay their salaries.

Ramsay: How many people did you hire?

Stealey: I hired an accountant, a jack-of-all-trades, and one marketing girl to help out. That marketing/admin girl actually became Sid's wife. The lady who was responsible for the finances also worked as our office manager, making sure the office had toilet paper and that sort of thing. She was a jack-of-all-trades, setting up offices at trade shows, and playing our games all day long. Sid's then-future wife's responsibility was to send out press releases, talk to people when they called on the phone about our games, and periodically make some phone calls with me to computer stores.

I was entirely responsible for those people and the business. Sid wasn't interested in the business side. In fact, one of the disagreements that we had years later was that we were too big. He didn't like the company too big. He wanted us to stay small. But I had complete financial responsibility. Whether the company lived or died was my responsibility. Sid was just going to make games at the rate that he wanted to make games.

Ramsay: Why did Sid want the company to stay small?

Stealey: Because Sid doesn't value money too highly. Sid just wanted to do his games and have enough to sell. We used to have to get all his paychecks off the top of the refrigerator. Sid was comfortable. He was just in it to make some games and have a little fun. I was in it to make a big business, and that's a different philosophy. That's all right. He's a programmer, and I'm supposed to be the MBA.

Ramsay: How much time did you spend on the company?

Stealey: In the beginning, every night for four hours, I was calling computer stores and trying to sell our products. And I had two other jobs, right? I worked full-time for General Instrument and traveled for General Instrument. On weekends, I flew for the Pennsylvania Air National Guard. I was managing these jobs while trying to run MicroProse on the side at first.

Ramsay: What impact did the startup life have on your family unit?

Stealey: Luckily, my wife jumped right in and did all the packaging and shipping. That's why I gave her a sizable sum when we divorced.

Ramsay: Did you think about recruiting advisors or management?

Stealey: No. It was better to do everything myself, and get a few worker bees who I could get to do the grunt work. I was in charge of making sure the big things got done, and doing the selling. By 1985, I hired a law firm to do some of our contracts work. That lawyer introduced me to the Young Presidents' Organization. I got invited to join the organization, and some of those members became my informal advisors and best friends.

Ramsay: Did you have office space when you hired the first three?

Stealey: We did have office space.

Ramsay: Where were you located?

Stealey: We were located in Hunt Valley, Maryland, in a little-bitty office space. Our lunch wagon would show up every day at 11:30 AM because we were their first stop. We all would go out and get sandwiches. We would sit around one little conference table, eat, and go back to what we were doing.

Ramsay: Who did you hire after then?

Stealey: The first recruiting that I did after the first three was for two more programmers from General Instrument who wanted part-time jobs. They were Sid's friends. Sid wouldn't do anything but games for the Atari 800. He didn't like any other computers. I hired those two to convert Sid's games because I saw that the market for Atari 800 software was smaller than the market for the Commodore 64. They eventually became pretty famous. One of them became a consultant, and the other started the Jane's series of simulation games at Electronic Arts to compete with MicroProse. Sid refused to go to the Commodore 64 for a number of years. He continued to make Atari games, and we'd have one of these two guys convert it.

In 1985, I also hired my first sales manager, my first executive, Mr. Barbaras. He was a 65-year-old guy, a very Greek guy, who was retired in Baltimore. He had run a 400-man sales organization and taught me things I didn't know about retail and distribution. Barbaras set up an organization of sales representatives. They usually had six to ten lines of product and had specific customers they were really in good with. We were selling to Sears, Target, Wal-Mart, and all of these big department stores. These sales reps were household representatives who normally sold these same retailers plates, dishes, and spoons. We set up that organization between 1985 and 1986.

Ramsay: But you were the sales guy, the demo king. Why did you hire Mr. Barbaras to run your sales organization?

Stealey: Because I was doing product. Again, I'm a product guy as well. I was helping Sid playtest. I was trying to set up an office in Europe, too. I had six or seven employees. I was still flying with the Pennsylvania Guard, and I had quit General Instrument. It was just getting too much for me to manage all of that alone. I turned the sales over to him, and he did a great job.

I was the mufti company guy that the sales guys would bring in when they had a really big conference with a customer. They would deal with all customers for 11 months of the year. One month a year, I'd go around, see all of our big customers, and put on the Wild Bill act. I'd wear my flight suit in there, and we'd talk about fighter pilot stuff. That usually got them buying product.

I had an image in the industry. You can ask Trip Hawkins, the founder of Electronic Arts, about me wearing my flight suit all the time. He used to make fun of me. But how do you remember a small company? It needs something special. All we had was Sid and Wild Bill.

Ramsay: For how long was MicroProse self-publishing?

Stealey: Forever—from the very first day. We never published through anybody else ever. Trip tried to talk me into combining MicroProse and EA in the late 1980s. He said he would do the sports games, and we would do the military games. You know, Electronic Arts was not very successful early on when they were only doing Apple and Amiga products. When EA and Trip decided to reverse engineer the Sega Master System, and started doing sports games for the system, EA really took off. He asked MicroProse to join him in that effort, and I decided it was not the right thing to do. I missed a real opportunity there to combine with EA.

Ramsay: He didn't mention that in his interview.

Stealey: No, he wouldn't. I tell you, the first few games on the Apple by EA were not giant sellers. There were some real classics, but Apple users were notorious for pirating software rather than buying. The Sega deal was their big breakout effort.

Ramsay: You were trying to set up an office for MicroProse in Europe. Weren't you racing against EA to do that?

Stealey: You should have seen us. Trip and I were sitting at a trade show in 1988, trying to convince each other to close down each other's European operations. We beat EA to Europe. We were already in Europe selling products in 1986. We had licensed our MicroProse products to a company called US Gold. They were selling a lot of our products, but MicroProse was not getting a big revenue share or recognition for our own products. I jumped on an airplane, put an ad in a marketing trade magazine, got over 500 resumes, and hired a great marketing guy as the European managing director. We did over $3 million in sales in the first six months of being open in Europe.

Ramsay: Why did you want to set up a European operation?

Stealey: I saw the value of the dollar versus European currencies. I wanted to get some of that European money. I went over to Europe, and the price of most games was £2.95. I decided that was too low a price for our games. We started charging £9.95 retail for our games, and led the way to better prices, and by the early 90s, we were getting £34.95 for our games. My finance degree also came into use there. I knew how to manage the currency side, so we made a lot of money. We probably made $2 million on just currency swaps.

Ramsay: Let's get back to development. What was your product development strategy?

Stealey: "Sid, here's what I want." That's a great product development strategy, don't you think? I'm a military officer. What am I good at? Military stuff. Let's do another flying game. Okay, flying games are hard. Let's do a tank game, and let's call it M1 Tank Platoon. Let's do a helicopter game because helicopters are cool. Sid and I both love military history. One Christmas, I gave him a book detailing the days of the Civil War. Five days later, he gave it back to me. I asked if he did not like the book. He said he loved it, but had already memorized all the key dates and events in it, and thought I might like to read it, too. Sid is brilliant!

Our first really successful products after Hellcat Ace were Solo Flight, F-15 Strike Eagle, M1 Tank Platoon, Gunship, and Silent Service. Sid actually came up with Silent Service because I wasn't a submarine guy, but he knew I liked military things, and Silent Service was a terrific game. That was one of those games that we sold more than 100,000 copies of through Sears all by itself. Sid wanted to do something outside of Wild Bill's military games that we had been doing the first few years. Pirates! came from that thought. Sid started dating one of our early employees. He took her to the Caribbean, and he got lost. She called me and said, "I can't find Sid." It turns out that he was looking at all of the pirate relics in the area and got all excited about pirates. That's how he came up with Sid Meier's Pirates!. Pirates! was one of the first new games from Sid after he did all the military games I had asked for.

Ramsay: Why did his name precede the title of almost every MicroProse game since Sid Meier's Pirates?

Stealey: Because I decided to do that. I decided that the way you make a great company is you make somebody famous. I thought it was better to make the artist more famous than the CEO.

Ramsay: Although you did have your own cutouts?

Stealey: I did have my own cutouts because I was taller than Sid. Sid didn't wear flight suits. I did. We made those cutouts because EA put up cutouts of Chuck Yeager, trying to sell an EA flying game. Those cutouts were only four-feet high. I made my cutout life-size—seven-feet tall! I wonder if there's a picture of any those anywhere on the Web? I bet there is.

Ramsay: You said that the way to make a great company is to make some-body famous. Some developers actually don't like the spotlight. Did you talk with Sid about placing him on the top line? If so, what was that discussion like? How did he feel about it?

Stealey: I think the original idea came about when Sid and I had the chance to sit at a Software Publishers Association meeting. I was on the board of directors at the Software Publishers Association, and he was my famous partner. We got to sit at dinner with the comic Robin Williams. Robin was talking about basketball and basketball stars, and asked why there weren't software stars. I said, "We'll make Sid a famous software star." And that's when we started putting his name on the games.

Ramsay: How did he feel about that kind of attention?

Stealey: He's a shy kind of guy. We had a fun marketing test of his fame when he and I were at an Amiga conference in California when the Amiga was a big deal. I had my wife, he had his girlfriend, and we're sitting at dinner at a little restaurant. I said, "Sid, watch this. I'll show you what marketing can do for you." I went over to the maître d' and I said, "Sir, my client doesn't want to be disturbed." He said, "Your client, who's that?" I said, "It's the famous Sid Meier. He's a famous author. Please don't let anybody bother us at dinner." Before we got out of there, he had given 20 auto-graphs. You know, we were a small company. You do whatever you can do to get a little attention, right?

Ramsay: Many CEOs like the spotlight. Although it was your decision to raise his status, were you ever personally uncomfortable with his shadow?

Stealey: No, because I got to be the CEO, and I got to be the big cheese. He got to be the brilliant programmer. In the end, I probably should have done it a different way. It should have been "Wild Bill's Pirates!" But you know what? Sid is really the programmer. He's really the brilliant game designer. I'm just the business guy, and I was a good marketing guy. And I had some very good marketing people working for me. I was the first marketing guy, but later, we had a lot of marketing muscle.

Ramsay: Who was your marketing muscle?

Stealey: We had Gerry Blair, a great marketing guy. We had Deborah Tillett, one of our really great marketing persons. Deb was a smart, little lady. One of our European managing directors had a little bit of a lisp. We were at the Consumer Electronics Show, and he was talking about the Isthmus of Panama. He had a couple glasses of wine, so he was having a hard time with "isthmus." She said, "Are you having a hard time speaking isthmus?" And he said, "Are you pissing on my isthmus?" The whole table fell on the floor laughing. But that's the kind of marketing person she was. She could take any situation and turn it into fun and enthusiasm. She was really one of the very best, Mrs. Deborah Tillett. The very first marketing guy was Fred Schmidt, who eventually went on to run Origin Systems. Fred is a brilliant marketing guy. Those three people were really marketing geniuses as far as I'm concerned.

Ramsay: Where was Sid's interest concerning game development? What drove him to create: design or technology?

Stealey: Game design only. His first original game after the many military games was the Pirates! game. Later, we were doing the original Railroad Tycoon, and I said, "Boy, this is really a neat game. Where'd you get the idea?" He said, "Oh, from this box." It was an Avalon Hill board game called 1830. Oh, no! Eric Dott, the president of Avalon Hill, called me and said, "Bill, you're doing my board game as a computer game." I said, "I'm sorry." And he said, "Well, don't let it happen again." I said, "Okay, done."

Sid didn't start with a game idea and launch it fully. Sid played with stuff and would do a bunch of startup things, and then lose interest. He started fooling with something, and some of the guys would start playing it. Later, Sid and the guys are in the back, playing another game that he was working on. I heard that all of them—six or seven playtesters now—thought that whatever they were playing was a great idea.

I went to the back and said, "Sid, what is this called?" He answered, "Civilization." I went, "That's a good name. What does it do?" He showed me the game, and I started playing it. I said, "Wow, this is pretty cool!" And I started marketing it.

I put out marketing for Sid Meier's Civilization, got two ads out in the magazines, and then I received a call from Eric again. He said, "Wild Bill, Civilization is my game. You're stealing it." Oh, no again! I went, "Well, let's have lunch." Then I went back to Sid, "Sid, what are you doing? This is a board game, and it's owned by Avalon Hill." He goes, "I know, but I was going to make it better." He didn't care about copyright. This goes back to Smuggers. Copyright? He's just making it better. I said, "We're in trouble now. I've been advertising. I've spent $100,000 telling the market that the game is coming. Now I have to talk to Eric, and we may have to shut this down." He went, "You'll figure it out." Again, he left it to me.

So, I had lunch with Eric. I bought him lunch because I was buttering him up. I said, "Eric, I apologize. I didn't know Sid was doing this, but I think it's going to be a good game. I think we won't sell near as many as you sell as boxed games." You know, this is one of those games you buy in a box and play on a table—tabletop games. "What if I put a card in every one of the games that says 'get $5 off Civilization from Avalon Hill,' and you do the same for me?" After two or three glasses of wine, he agreed—one of his bigger mistakes. He would have made a lot more money if he had said, "Okay, give me 10% of it." All he got was a card in the game box. If he had 10% of Civilization, Avalon Hill would still be around today, right?

So, we then had the "okay" to do Civilization. You may or may not know, but after I left MicroProse, there were all kinds of lawsuits over who owned Civilization. I was gone after all that, but I had a deal. It was a written and signed contract with Avalon Hill. And then at one time, I tried to buy Avalon Hill, but that's another story.

Ramsay: I'd like to hear it.

Stealey: As we became more successful with Civilization, I started looking into buying Avalon Hill, which was in Baltimore, too. The word got out, and a famous baseball pitcher, Curt Schilling, called me and wanted to go in with me to buy Avalon Hill because he had heard the rumors. He was a Squad Leader fan. Squad Leader was one of Avalon Hill's best games. I don't know how that worked out after Hasbro Interactive bought MicroProse. I don't know how all those lawsuits on who owned the name "Civilization" worked out, but I got away with it with just a postcard in our box. That was a good amount of money to spend, don't you think?

Ramsay: Several years into developing the business, what was your first major challenge as CEO—the challenge that really tested you?

Stealey: The summer of 1989. I had a mutiny on my hands by a former Atari president and some of my executives I hired to manage my coin-op game division. In Europe, we had a managing director who couldn't or would not do accounting for funds he had advanced himself from the company. I went over to reprimand him, and we find that he has £200,000 in expenses that he has never cleared from the books. So, I remove him from having anything to do with the finances, and I come back to the US. The following Monday, the same guy calls me and tells me he's in Baltimore. He has flown from the UK on our company credit card! He tells me he's going to quit anyway and start a competing company. It would have been a lot cheaper to hear that news over the phone, but he wanted to spend MicroProse's money to fly to the States to meet with other members of his new company!

So, I return to the MicroProse offices to talk to my financial officer, and he tells me he's quitting to join that new company. I decide to go back to the UK to sort out our operations there. As I'm on the way to the airport, I realize that the managing director and the chief financial officer can't do this by themselves—they had no development! They have a sales guy and the finance guy, and they needed a development guy. I go back in and confront my head of development. He says he's thinking about it, so I fire him on the spot. They were spending MicroProse's money and using our ideas to start their new company, so I fired them all. They were guys who I brought into the company, and I had to replace them. It was very disheartening.

And, you can imagine, now I've lost my financial officer, my managing director, and my key development manager. At the same time, we were raising a bunch of money, trying to get ready to go public. I was negotiating with Sid on his future with the company. He didn't want to have to sign all of the papers or have any financial responsibilities. He didn't want his name on anything that was public. In addition, my ex-wife decided that she didn't want to be Mrs. Wild Bill anymore. You know, there was enough money, and everybody was saying, "I want some of mine, and I don't want to risk it."

Of course, I was still the entrepreneur and still taking the risks. Every year was a risk when I was hiring more and more people. It was a tough summer all around, but entrepreneurs never give up. I found that no one is irreplaceable. I replaced all the executives within one month and kept selling lots of games!

Ramsay: When you had to replace the three executives in Europe, did you personally hire their replacements?

Stealey: I did. The financial officer I hired became one of the founders of MapQuest. I promoted the finance guy in Europe and made him my managing director. He did a great job. And I hired a really good development guy.

Ramsay: Were you more careful about who you hired?

Stealey: Probably not. The ones that left me were incited by an employee, who I will not name, who had gone to jail for six months for tax evasion after he came to work for me. And the whole time he was in jail, he was thinking about this and started writing them notes. He's the one that enticed them all to leave. They figured they could do it better, but of course, they lasted about 18 months and spent about $5 million of somebody else's money. They imploded! I thought that was what they deserved.

Ramsay: You really weren't more circumspect after that experience?

Stealey: No, you know what? As people get to know me, they know that I'm about as circumspect as an old log.

Ramsay: Earlier, you mentioned that you and Sid disagreed about the size of the company. How was that disagreement resolved?

Stealey: In that same summer of 1989, we decided to change our relationship because we were 50/50 partners. Legally, we were 50/50 partners, but I made all the decisions. He could have blocked me if he wanted to, but he never did. So, he wanted to change and not be my partner. He wanted to be just a super contractor. We made a deal. We paid him a lot of money, and we got a contract to do all his games. He got a contract to get paid whether he did a game or not, and was a big part of every game. That's what he was more interested in. He didn't want to take on financial responsibility. He didn't want to be an owner of a public company, so we changed the relationship. So, that summer—between changing the relationship with my partner of now eight or nine years, getting a divorce from my partner who I'd been married to for twenty years, and then three of my guys walking out—I'm surprised I didn't have a heart attack that summer.

Ramsay: That summer was not a good summer.

Stealey: Nope, it was not. In the end, Sid and I worked it out. My ex and I stayed together for another five or six years. Now, we're still friends, but she was very happy that she got all the money I gave her. So, she's very wealthy now, and I'm still working. So there you go.

Ramsay: Tell me about going public. When and how did that come about? Why did you want to take the company public?

Stealey: Because I screwed up. I was offered the chance to be one of the original Nintendo licensees because I had been the keynote speaker in the mid-1980s for the Japanese Software Publishers Association. And I didn't like the idea of it. I did the software, I bought the inventory, and I had to pay

Nintendo $10 for every game I put out? So, I decided to go into the coin-op business. I thought I could take our excellent titles there—I actually still have a copy of the coin-op version of F-15 Strike Eagle in my garage—and I spent about $8 million and sold about $7 million worth. And the $8 million was spent, and the $7 million wasn't enough revenue to pay it off.

I needed to either raise money or go public. Since I owned a ton of stock, I figured going public would be the way to go. You know, today with Sarbanes-Oxley, I don't think it was the right thing. I'm still the CEO of a public company, which really is not easy, but that's the way it is. We decided to go public, basically, to raise the cash so we could grow the company. At the time we decided to go public, I think we were doing about $30 million in annual sales, we owed about $8 million, and we wanted to get rid of that $8 million and have money for development. And that's what we did.

Ramsay: What did you expect to be able to do as a public company that you weren't able to do before?

Stealey: Invest in bigger projects. It probably wasn't the right answer because projects were getting more and more complex. It used to be that we could do a game for a half-million dollars, and then it was costing a million and a half, going toward three.

My programmers were also restless. Our famous products were Sid games and Wild Bill games. Sid's games were Civilization, Pirates!, and Railroad Tycoon. Wild Bill's games were military games like F-15 Strike Eagle, Silent Service, Gunship, and M1 Tank Platoon. My programmers thought they were really, really much better than that, and they could take on Sierra and Origin. Great, that's just what we would do! We built two products, spent over $2 million on each one of them—one each to compete with Sierra and Origin. They ended up being very good products when we got to version K of them, but they never made their money back because we were known for military games. That's all we were known for. I think every successful game company is known for something.

You know, I mean, THQ is around. It's known for what? Nothing—they struggle. Atari, what are they known for? Nothing—they struggle. EA—sports. Activision—Call of Duty. You have to be known for something. We were known for two things, but we tried to do more. I think that was a big mistake. I wasn't enforcing what I thought we could sell. I was trying to say, "Okay, programmers, give me what you want to do, and tell me how much money you want to spend. We'll find a way to sell it." I should have been smarter than that. I should have stuck with what we were good at.

Ramsay: Tell me about the sale to Spectrum Holobyte.

Stealey: When we went public, my board of directors said, "You've been running this company successfully for nine years. Why don't you hire a president in the US, a president in Europe, and let them manage the business? You should take six months off because we think you've been micromanaging the company a little bit. We want to see what other people can do." Now on the board of directors, I've got venture investors, corporate guys, but no one with any experience in a creative business like the game business. Well, at the time, I was just really getting into golf. I thought a six-month sabbatical was a great idea! I made speeches to a bunch of colleges about entrepreneurship. I played golf all over the country. I left the US division in the charge of a West Pointer, a very good friend of mine, and the European division in the charge of a good financial guy.

In the US, we had a bonus plan for the development staff that said the developers could make big bonuses if your team got the game out on time with marketing objectives met, and the game sold well. That made my guys work very little in the beginning of the project, a bit in the middle, and at the end, they worked like madmen because if they didn't make October 1, they didn't get their bonuses.

I left in January and came back in October. I said to the US president, "Where are the 12 games we're supposed to do this year?" He said, "They're a little late." He had changed my bonus plan from a percentage of the revenue based on bonus objectives to overtime. Do you know how long it takes to do software when programmers are on overtime? Forever! In 1992, we shipped one game—500 employees, and we shipped one game. What do you think happened to the cash flow?

Ramsay: It didn't turn out very well?

Stealey: Nope. So, I fired him a week after I got back, and I took over the company. I got some of those games out. Strike Eagle 3 went out like December 13 of that year, and we struggled along with me trying to find ways to get cash. I thought we were going to go out of business by the middle of the next year if I did not find some cash. I was going to have to fire all those good MicroProse people. I had saved Gillman Louie. Do you know him?

Gillman Louie is a venture capitalist. Before that, he was a head of Spectrum Holobyte. He had called me in December 1989. His company was owned by Robert Maxwell, who had just been thrown naked from a boat off the coast of Spain, supposedly by the Mossad. But he was owned by Maxwell, and he was running out of money. He called me while I was getting ready to go on vacation. He said, "Bill, I need $400,000, and I need it tomorrow." I said, "What are you going to get for it?" He said, "Falcon 3.0." I said, "Done." And I sent him $400,000 on a handshake.

So, when I got into trouble in 1993, I was talking to him at the Consumer Electronics Show. He said, "My company wants to get bigger. We'll come buy you." He got Spectrum Holobyte and Kleiner Perkins to buy us. Spectrum Holobyte was $6 million in sales, and we were $50 million. So, really, Kleiner Perkins bought us. They were the big investors in Spectrum Holobyte at the time. In fact, Vinod Khosla, a famous venture capitalist from Kleiner Perkins, was the guy I negotiated with over that.

Ramsay: When did you leave MicroProse? What were the events that led to your departure?

Stealey: At 9:26, June 21, 1993. I signed the paperwork at 9:15.

Ramsay: Why do you know the exact times?

Stealey: I had tee time at 10:00, and I had to get there. I stayed on the board for about six months, but I couldn't take it and left.

Ramsay: Why couldn't you take it?

Stealey: I was used to running the company. Now, I got all these talkers sitting around, nine of them at a table arguing, "Well, maybe this product, but what do you think is good about that product?" They had no clue what they were doing—zero. I'm sitting there going, "Boy, oh, boy. What's happened to my company?" I was now just a board member. I wasn't CEO. I was just the old CEO.

Ramsay: What did do after you left?

Stealey: When I left, I signed a three-year, 250-mile noncompete agreement, but they needed to get something from me during these three years. So, guess what? I get out of my noncompete. I get my airplane back. You know, they still owned my airplane, the Ms. MicroProse T-28. I show up at Spectrum Holobyte in San Francisco, and they owe me money. Gillman Louis has to go get me a $400,000 check. That was great fun.

I started another company in 1995 called Interactive Magic and took that company public in 1998. I sold it in 1999. I took it back in 2002, and that's what I'm running today. So, I've taken two companies public, and I tried to not make the same mistake the third time while I'm running this entertainment network, which is what's left of Interactive Magic today. I'm still an entrepreneur. I'm just on my third game company.

Ramsay: Any regrets?

Stealey: MicroProse was a tiny, little company, and EA came to us and asked how big we were. I told him, "$6 million." He said, "Oh, we thought you were only $3 million." Of course, they were exactly right, but you always pretended to be bigger than you were. That was the game. We always tried to be bigger at trade shows than we really could afford. It really worked well, and that's what helped us grow.

But I think the most important thing is that we all played our products. There were no executives in my company who weren't gamers. If you weren't a gamer, you weren't going to play because we wanted everybody to help make the products better, from our playtest guys to all our executives. I mean, every game that we put out at MicroProse, I must have logged a thousand hours playing. That was our approach. It was a great approach. But we kind of lost that when we went to Interactive Magic. We ended up with executives and not gamers. I'll never let that happen again.

Tony Goodman

Cofounder, Ensemble Studios

 *In 1991, **Tony Goodman** cofounded Ensemble Corporation, an information technology company, with longtime friends John Boog-Scott, John Calhoun, and Thad Chapman. The company later made the Inc. 500 and was recognized as one of America's fastest-growing companies. Ensemble Corporation was acquired by USWeb Corporation in 1997. Two years before, Goodman cofounded Ensemble Studios with John Boog-Scott and his brother Rick Goodman. With the introduction of the Age of Empire series, Ensemble Studios became the leading developer of real-time strategy games. Microsoft acquired the company in 2001. Age of Empires became the bestselling strategy game franchise of all time.*

But as Microsoft's Xbox business was growing, the Windows game business slowed. During the development of Halo Wars, which also became a bestselling title, Microsoft enacted plans to close Ensemble Studios and lay off all of the employees. By January 2009, Ensemble Studios was reduced to the pages of history. Ensemble Studios left behind a tradition of entrepreneurship. Goodman founded Robot Entertainment the next month. Several startups arose from the ashes, spearheaded by former employees, including Bonfire Studios, Newtoy, Windstorm Studios, Pixelocity, Fuzzy Cube, and GRL Games.

Ramsay: When did you become interested in entrepreneurship and technology? Who was your greatest influence?

Goodman: My greatest influence was my father. He taught me how to program computers at an early age. He also instilled in me an ethic about making the world a better place. My dad was a Yale Ph.D. and professor of management science at Southern Methodist University.

When I was in the sixth grade, he brought home a computer terminal and introduced me to computer programming. From that moment, the world of technology became my passion. He would give me the same computer problems that he had given his students to keep me challenged. While this was technically schoolwork, which I hated, my father would say, "Tony, I have a puzzle for you." Immediately, I was sucked in for the rest of the day, solving puzzles and programming. I always looked at the problems as puzzles. I loved puzzles and games, so I just couldn't get enough. Furthermore, programming gave me power and complete autonomy. That's a pretty exciting thing for a 12-year-old.

Using the computer, I discovered a world of limitless possibilities. Programming was the key that unlocked it all. It came to me naturally. I felt like someone turned on the lights. I remember saying, "This is it. This is what I'm going to do with the rest of my life!"

Ramsay: When did you decide to start your first company?

Goodman: I've always had a passion for technology and starting business ventures, even as a child. My entrepreneurial nature was evident by the second grade. While my friends set up 10-cent lemonade stands, I rounded up all the toys I didn't want and sold them to the parents in town in an open market. This was my first taste of business economics, and it was sweet! Business was in my blood. My first venture had worked out really well until my older brother discovered that he was missing some of his favorite toys. But that's another story!

After high school, I attended the University of Texas in Austin, majoring in business for two years. During that time, I had a great time, partying and skipping class. Then a life-changing medical event radically altered my life and the way that I work. I was diagnosed with narcolepsy, a sleeping disorder, which I've had to live with ever since. Keeping up with a rigid college schedule was nearly impossible with narcolepsy. An opportunity arose to assist my father with cutting-edge research. He was developing algorithms that could predict future stock returns using computers and historical data. I dropped out of school and returned home to work with my dad. A year later, he died suddenly, and the research ended.

Soon after, while jogging and pondering my future possibilities, I had a rare moment of clarity. There are two things that I really love to do: play games and program computers. My future was obvious. I should simply follow my passion, start a company, and make the world's greatest games. I sensed that starting a game company would be a large undertaking, and I wanted to do it right. So, I decided to start a business software company first to gain experience and build capital.

My brother, who was working at Lotus at the time, had sent me a present. When I opened it, I found what was then a revolutionary new program called Paradox. My understanding of programming had been without practical application. Paradox advanced my view of how technology was used to solve real-world problems. Paradox provided a powerful programming language, but it also provided simple visual tools for managing data. This intrigued me. Almost all computer tools of the time were clunky and difficult to learn. I immersed myself in mastering Paradox. The ability to develop user-friendly business applications that managed massive amounts of data was intriguing. For fun, I started developing tools for business applications.

I then used my Paradox skills as a consultant for NationsBank. I helped them use Paradox to develop their internal management and reporting systems. At NationsBank, I was shocked to find how much manpower was wasted on re-writing code. Most programs they developed were very similar to other programs that had already been created. Their programmers would always seem to start from scratch every time they began a new project. I thought this was insanity. If you were to build a doghouse, you wouldn't start by chopping down trees to make lumber. You would simply buy the wood precut from a lumberyard. I became obsessive about developing code in a way that it was always reusable. The more programs I wrote, the more efficient I became.

Soon after, I decided that there was an opportunity for a startup that could simply provide efficient programming and project-management services to corporations. We would be more efficient than other software consultants because we would start with a large base of already written components and use these to jumpstart our projects. Since I was already working with NationsBank, they agreed to become our first client. So, I started Ensemble Corporation.

Ramsay: And then you hired your team? Who were your cofounders?

Goodman: The first thing that I did was form an outstanding senior management team. I approached my high-school friend and college roommate, John Boog-Scott, and asked him to join me as COO. I explained to him that I was working on a revolutionary new product called Command Center that would set our company apart. Command Center was an application generator that enabled people to create powerful and flexible business applications without programming. We would sell the product, and then turn these customers into new clients for our programming services business. John had a great job at Andersen Consulting at the time, so I was very surprised when he said, "Great. Let's do it!"

We took on another buddy from high school, John Calhoun, to head up the consulting division. Calhoun was also working for Andersen Consulting and was known to be quite detail-oriented. Soon, the core management team was comprised of four longtime high-school friends when Thad Chapman joined us. Thad became head of sales. He was a natural at networking and developed business connections easily.

The four of us shared a long history, since elementary school. We were like brothers. We worked together, we ate together, we partied together, and we strategized together. We shared the same goals and wanted to build a great company together. Boog-Scott and I formed a great partnership. I had the ability to visualize the future and barge forward. He had the ability to run the company and keep things stable. He was the sanity check on my crazy ideas. I respected John's opinion more than anyone else's. He didn't raise his voice often, but when he did, I knew it was time to listen.

Trust is the most important characteristic of a successful management team. The four of us worked together as one. We were an ensemble—a group producing together a single effect, as in a work of art—thus the name Ensemble Corporation.

Ramsay: Was your flagship product as successful as you expected? What was the main draw of Command Center?

Goodman: We shipped Command Center in September 1991. The product was a complete success and won many awards. We started out selling the product for $339 per unit. It was making news. Everyone that saw it wanted it. We spent many sleepless nights, eating pizza and drinking beer while assembling boxes and manuals to ship. I was insistent that all orders had to be shipped FedEx overnight delivery. On one occasion, we missed the 11 PM FedEx drop-off time, so we sped to the Dallas/Fort Worth International Airport to deliver the products directly. It was a windy Dallas night. When I opened the car door, $5,000 worth of shipping orders blew out of the car and into the night. Self-publishing isn't sexy.

But Command Center was. Command Center was referred to as the "Paradox Appgen Extraordinaire." Data Based Advisor Magazine described the product as having a "sexy, GUI-like interface, and about 18 times the functionality of Paradox alone." I loved the idea that a computer program could be considered sexy. Businesses bought it because it enabled employees to create enterprise-grade applications without programming, and users loved it because the user-friendly graphical environment was elegant and fun to use. This was unheard of in the database world.

Ramsay: Did you have any trouble marketing to enterprise buyers?

Goodman: It wasn't enough that Command Center was powerful and easy to use. We wanted Command Center to actually be a fun experience for users, but fun doesn't advertise well to corporations. It wasn't an attribute that businesses were looking for in enterprise software. We didn't advertise it as "fun." We advertised it as "powerful." We learned that advertising "fun" hurt sales, but once customers tried it, they were sold.

Ramsay: You were developing and publishing software?

Goodman: Yes. Self-publishing was an invaluable experience. We did the design, programming, testing, packaging, documentation, marketing, distribution, sales, and support. We had a good idea about what was required to put out a successful product. This is when it got really crazy.

Before we knew it, we outgrew the garage space with my barking dog, and secured high-rise office space in Dallas. As the business grew, we hired more programmers, and I started laying the groundwork for Visage, our next product that offered an intuitive drag-and-drop environment geared toward reducing development time for forms and reports.

Command Center and Visage fed Ensemble's programming services business. When customers' needs grew, they were already familiar with Ensemble Corporation, so they called us to build custom-designed software systems. As with any great product, Command Center provided us with more opportunities to expand.

Ramsay: And expand you did?

Goodman: As soon as we relocated and the growth wave began, I was unable to continue in a dual capacity as a programmer and the chief executive of the company. I stopped programming, focusing all my energy on the management and strategic vision of the company.

Ensemble Corporation developed custom software applications for small and mid-sized businesses. Six months after Visage, we saw the need for certain areas of database refinement and developed Renaissance, a companion product to Command Center and Visage. Renaissance was the first and only visual data-entry development tool.

The company became known as a leader in corporate information technology. We provided technical expertise to companies with qualified professionals that were experienced in Access, Visual Basic, Paradox, and Power

Builder. We further grew account teams who specialized in client-server relations in Microsoft SQL Server, Oracle, and Sybase. Our clients spanned many industries, from small medical billing firms and restaurants to large commercial banks, major airlines, and Fortune 100 and 500 companies around the globe.

Ramsay: That's quite a portfolio. What about your people and the internal culture at Ensemble? What was your focus in that area?

Goodman: Our focus was on hiring a core of great employees as the business started to grow. My philosophy has always been to build a great place to work and to empower the employees to do their jobs. We continued to listen to those employees, enabled them to make key business decisions, and looked to them to recruit the next generation of employees. We found that if you do your best to cultivate a fun work environment, your employees will want to bring in their friends, who can help make the business even better.

This approach landed us on the Inc. 500. From 1992 to 1996, we had an 843% increase in sales. In 1995, we recognized that the Internet could lead to a new source of revenue for our business, and we began some very early-stage Internet efforts. We were recognized as one of America's "Entrepreneurial Superstars" and one of the fastest-growing private companies by the Inc. 500.

By 1997, Ensemble Corporation was acquired by USWeb Corporation as they were aggregating Internet consulting companies. Some members of the Ensemble team went on to serve on the USWeb executive team, and managed the central United States and Canada operations for that public company. Once the acquisition was finalized, I began dedicating 100% of my time to Ensemble Studios, which I started earlier in 1995.

Ramsay: Did your experience with designing enterprise software influence the design of your games?

Goodman: One of the most valuable things that I learned about developing software was that for users to be productive, the software had to be fun to use. The key is to keep people entertained long enough to be rewarded. This also happens to be the fundamental dynamic of games, and indeed all human experiences.

Ramsay: Well, how is entertainment so fundamental?

Goodman: For example, with programming, I never had to try to do it; it was my passion. It was like solving puzzles, and I enjoyed solving puzzles. I had an abundance of energy when I was programming and never tired from it. This is the core element of succeeding in any business. If a person finds the thing in their life that they love to do most, and they have endless energy to do it, they will eventually succeed.

This became even more poignant because of my narcolepsy. To succeed, despite the effects of narcolepsy, I had to remain super-engaged, doing something that I absolutely loved. Designing software with entertaining user experiences was my savior. When I do something that isn't engaging for me, I fall asleep. If I had to be a tax accountant, I'd be the worst one in the world.

Ramsay: Why is vision important to successful entrepreneurship?

Goodman: Vision is fundamental, but it is different for every entrepreneur. From my point of view, the destination is not always in plain sight. Like wine, it develops into something better, or worse, with time. I believe in exploring new territory and finding opportunities where others have not been. That is what excites me: the challenge to explore and create! This requires a great deal of risk taking, and it's not for everyone. Great leaders must release the status quo. It is exactly this ingredient that creates new and innovative opportunities. Risk and reward are close allies.

Ramsay: You started Ensemble Studios in 1995, two years before the USWeb acquisition. Why video games?

Goodman: I've always loved computer games and had been keeping an interested eye on the game industry. At that time, PC games were about to undergo an important change: from running on DOS to running on Windows. I saw an opportunity in this.

Up until 1995, creating computer games required an onerous investment in writing hardware drivers. There were no standards for DOS peripherals, so game developers had to write their own mouse and sound drivers. To make a game stable, developers would have to write and test special code for every different mouse and sound card available. Since new products were always being released, developers had to continually update and rerelease their game's mouse and sound drivers. It was a technical nightmare, and none of this code had anything to do with making games. Developers had to do all this in addition to creating great games that were better than the competition. This was a significant barrier to entering the video-game market, but Windows-based games were about to change all of that.

The Windows operating system was quite sophisticated when compared to DOS. Windows handled all hardware at the OS level, so game developers would no longer have to develop drivers. That meant that developers could now devote 100% of their efforts toward making great gameplay. It also meant that legacy game developers would lose any advantage that they had gained from their years of investment in hardware drivers. That was going to level the playing field! It was at that moment that I felt the industry was about to explode, and it was time to jump in.

Ramsay: In the midst of all your success, why did you pursue something so vastly different from enterprise software?

Goodman: I loved the business of developing software, but I wanted to create products that everyone would tell their friends about. I wanted to create a pop-culture phenomenon. If you want to create software that people really want, developing video games places you at the center of the universe.

Creating video games seemed like a crazy change of direction to my friends, but to me, it was inevitable. I could have continued to pursue the business that I had been successful in, but I realized that you don't create passion by pursuing success. You create success by pursuing your passion. After years of developing business software, I decided it was time to finally pursue my original passion: video games.

While I maintained my management responsibilities as president and chief executive officer at Ensemble Corporation, I developed a plan for a new venture. Angelo Laudon, one of my key programmers, was also obsessed with games. We would talk about games until the early hours of the morning. In 1995, Angelo and I began to develop a prototype engine that could be used to produce multiple games. Once we began developing the engine, there was no going back. My exhilaration for games could no longer be contained. The floodgates were opened. We were creating something special and could feel it.

Ramsay: How far along was the company at that point?

Goodman: Early in 1995, while still a part of Ensemble Corporation, Angelo and I began experimenting with graphics code in the new WinG library, the technology from Microsoft that would make games possible under Windows. We began formulating our ideas about creating a historical strategy game, inspired by Sid Meier's Civilization.

Our greatest need at that time was to hire our first artist. I looked over dozens of resumes and interviewed 13 candidates. Finally, I decided on an artist who I thought was really talented. I offered him the job, and he happily accepted. The next day, I got a call from a young man, fresh out of art school. Brad Crow seemed very eager to interview. I told him the position was filled, but he came in to speak with me anyway. Within 15 minutes, I thought, "Holy crap, this guy is amazing." I knew that I had hired the wrong guy, so I offered Brad a job on the spot. I called the first artist and made my first ever "job offer retraction." It was an unpleasant thing to do, but you can't afford to make any compromises with early employees in a startup.

By the end of the year, we had a working version of Age of Empires that we were calling "Dawn of Man." The gameplay was in the early stages of development, but it looked remarkably similar to the final product. Units could run around the screen, fight, and chop wood. It was a sophisticated sandbox. We had a fantastic level designer and a first cut of rudimentary gameplay. But we hadn't figured out whether the game was going to be a strategy game like Command & Conquer, a simulation game like Sim City, or a turn-based game like Civilization.

I had remained in contact with a longtime friend, Bruce Shelley, who had previously assisted Sid Meier with the design of Civilization and Railroad Tycoon. My brother Rick and I had met Bruce Shelley at a board-game club at the University of Virginia, where Bruce was attending graduate school. I was young at the time, but had remained friends with Bruce. Bruce had a quiet yet professional presence as a designer in the game industry. Later, he came aboard as the official spokesperson for the Age of Empires franchise.

As our prototype really started taking shape, we decided to incorporate. I incorporated Ensemble Studios in February 1996 with John Boog-Scott and Rick as cofounders. Rick took on the role as lead designer and project manager. I served as CEO and art director. John and I together headed both corporations. We remained within the offices of Ensemble Corporation and shared expenses with them. We hired six people to start: a few programmers and three artists. Angelo Laudon and Tim Dean were Ensemble Studios' first programmers; and Brad Crow, Scott Winsett, and Thonny Namuonglo just graduated from the Art Institute of Dallas. Brian Sullivan came shortly thereafter to help with the design, implementation, and management. That was the beginning.

Ramsay: Many startups bootstrap and reinvest earnings to build their organizations, but you did things very differently with Ensemble Studios. How did that impact the company's ability to move forward?

Goodman: Ensemble Studios began as a pet project of mine while I was running my first company. I originally did this to mitigate risk, but it turned out to be absolutely critical to our early success.

Before the days of digital distribution, the only way to sell your game was through the major retail chains. Those stores only purchased games from the big software publishers, such as Microsoft, Electronic Arts, and Activision. This meant that you had to negotiate a deal with one of the big publishers. However, a common tactic of publishers was to drag out negotiations until developers ran out of money. Sooner or later, a developer would have to sign a deal just to keep the company afloat. A deal signed under those circumstances will result in very unfavorable terms. The big publishers knew they had game developers over a barrel.

The only way to successfully negotiate with a publisher was to have enough money to last as long as the negotiation might last, which could be anywhere from two months to two years. Having the financial backing of my first company afforded us the ability to negotiate with publishers on our own terms. We didn't have to take the first deal that publishers offered. We were determined to beat them at their waiting game. Eventually, Microsoft tired of negotiating and gave us the deal that we wanted. This deal, in turn, laid the groundwork for the next decade of deals we did with them.

Ramsay: What other publishing options did you consider?

Goodman: I briefly considered self-publishing Age of Empires. Self-publishing enterprise software had taught me valuable lessons about the advantages and disadvantages of publishing. In order for our game to be as successful as I wanted it to be, we needed to have world-class software distribution. That is why, in the end, we chose Microsoft. They were the world's largest seller of consumer software with incredible distribution muscle.

Microsoft had distribution channels established in Germany, France, Spain, Asia, South America, and Japan. In the United States, they had strong relationships with American retailers, such as Best Buy, Toys R Us, and Wal-Mart. No one could put together a marketing campaign as strong as Microsoft could when they were motivated to do so.

Self-publishing is a good option for those who want to create a very small yet highly profitable business inside the United States. But I didn't want to create just a successful game. I wanted to create a worldwide phenomenon. I wanted everyone who had Microsoft Windows to buy Age of Empires. For that we needed the global power that only Microsoft could provide.

Ramsay: What else did you need? Did you have a strategy for creating a phenomenon? Is there a formula for a successful franchise?

Goodman: To create a phenomenon, I had to do three things. I needed to convince my employees they would create the most amazing game ever made. I needed to convince Microsoft that Age of Empires would be the most amazing game they've ever sold. And I needed to convince the world Age of Empires would be the most amazing game they've ever played.

So, first, putting together this core team was the most important step in the process. This was my first game, so I got to hire each team member with love and painstaking care. I asked esoteric questions like, "What are your life's dreams and goals?" I sought seekers. I looked for brilliant young programmers and artists who wanted to pursue a grand vision. I hired dreamers who believed they could change the world. Each member had to be both a follower and a leader. I needed followers who were naturally attracted to my grand and crazy leadership style. They were also the future leaders who'd be teaching, by example, new employees to do the same.

As the initial team came together, I settled on the high-level vision for a product that I believed would capture the imagination of gamers. The idea was that you would get to play a game that looked like the epic Greek, Roman, and Egyptian war movies, such as Spartacus and Alexander the Great. From a bird's-eye view, the players would get to build the Great Pyramids or command realistic armies through exotic locations while building their own empire. This vision was the perfect high-level goal for the team I hired. They got it immediately. They didn't require a lot more detail to be inspired into action. At this point, forward progress took on a life of its own. That's not to say the process was easy. It was almost never easy. But even in the hardest times, we were riding a relentless tidal wave of momentum.

Second, at this point in time, Microsoft was having difficulty breaking into the game market. They had a few respectable products, but they had no real hits. I needed to convince Microsoft that Age of Empires would be the game that would make them a major player in the video-game industry. I knew that once they believed this, they would throw all their global resources behind it, creating a self-fulfilling prophecy. Microsoft may not have the most creative marketing, but when they are organized and determined, they are unstoppable.

Bill Gates was instrumental in solidifying Microsoft's support for Age of Empires. Microsoft was already very eager to have their first blockbuster game. Many Microsoft execs were happy to jump aboard with our product, but some, including Bill Gates, had reservations. Eventually though, opinions unified when Gates declared, "This is a product that we will do everything we can to make a classic, like Flight Simulator, so the popularity goes on and on."

The main concern about Age of Empires was the game's depth. Some were worried that Age of Empires was too complex to become a mainstream hit. Gates' commitment paid off. He stated, "Age of Empires is an amazing product. It is so deep that I wondered if the mass market would get into it, but they did in a big way."

And, finally, magazines like to report massive blockbusters or colossal failures. Everything in between is not news. I don't like leaving marketing and public relations to chance, so while Microsoft was doing their public relations campaign, I did mine. The key was to get a "first follower"—a well-known opinion leader who is an early advocate of your product. I built relationships with the most recognized game magazines. Microsoft had dozens of public relations specialists, but the press prefers to speak with the game creators, not software publishers. I invested a lot of time with key editors, seeding the idea that Age of Empires would be "revolutionary" and would become a "phenomenon." They may not have believed me at first, but my goal wasn't to convince them. My goal was to plant wondrous possibilities in their brains and create anticipation, like Christmas for kids.

When the first early previews began appearing, they were using the terms that we seeded: "revolutionary" and "phenomenal." These early opinions were then picked up and echoed by other publications, creating a snowball effect. Eventually, all the publications would get on board with this message just so they didn't look out of touch.

Ramsay: How critical were expansions, bundles, and player-created content? Were these elements part of your vision?

Goodman: To design a successful game, I think about three basic pillars: deliver fantastic gameplay, create a unique graphical look, and fill a void in the marketplace. Age of Empires was the first historical real-time strategy game on the market. Microsoft was convinced, based on a previous experience, that expansion packs never make money, so they weren't interested in doing them. So, that wasn't part of the original plan.

When Age of Empires blew away Microsoft's sales forecasts, we convinced them to publish Rise of Rome, our first expansion pack. That expansion pack was the most profitable game that Microsoft had ever published. Microsoft was then convinced that expansion packs were the best way to make money.

Player-created content was always part of the strategy, although we never attempted to monetize it. We wanted player-created content to be an extra value that our customers got for free.

Ramsay: How did you get in touch with Microsoft in the first place?

Goodman: I first approached Stuart Molder at Microsoft during the 1995 Game Developers Conference. He was giving a talk on publishing games with Microsoft. As he finished his talk, Stuart was mobbed by hopeful game developers who were anxious to show off their game demos. They were hoping for a break that would land them a major publishing deal with Microsoft. The scene reminded me of sports fans jockeying for an autograph from a revered superstar. I could tell it wasn't the best way to rope a bull.

I decided to sit in the back of the room and act disinterested. I never looked up until the mob had dissipated and Stuart was packing up his materials. On my way out, I casually told him that I headed up a game company that included some legends like Bruce Shelley, codesigner of Civilization. This was my ticket to further conversation, as Stuart had appeared on a television show with Bruce. I told him we were working on something big, and I would be happy to let him know when we were ready to demo it. We exchanged business cards, and I departed, hoping that I had made a memorable impression.

Six months later, I called Stuart and left a message that we were ready to show our game. Microsoft had a team down in Dallas within the week. Microsoft was still new to the video game business and was struggling to be taken seriously by gamers. They had not yet made a hit game. They were actively looking for a gem that could plant them firmly in the center of the computer game business. Microsoft was wowed by our demo, and Ensemble Studios was on the dance floor.

It's a validating feeling to be wooed by Microsoft. They are great at giving you attention when they want something. They threw some really crazy parties. On one occasion, they threw a Roman toga party. The entire San Jose basketball arena was commandeered for this soiree. It was the most lavish party that I've been to. Everyone was required to wear a toga supplied by Microsoft. This party featured a table piled high with turkey legs, giant goblets of wine, and female models posing as white statues standing atop columns of marble. There were wild animals, gladiators, slaves, games, fortune tellers, fire jugglers, and more wine. All this was led by the Caesar of ceremonies Alex St. John. The most memorable event was when a fully grown 400-pound lion escaped from its cage and walked the floor freely amid hundreds of drunken, dumbfounded guests carrying turkey legs. Major catastrophe was avoided as the lion was shooed back to his cage without incident. I never saw another giant man-eating cat at a Microsoft party again.

While getting Microsoft to the table was an easy task, negotiations were a long, drawn-out process. We shopped the game to multiple publishers, including Hasbro Interactive, Electronic Arts, and 7th Level. When negotiating with Microsoft, it's important to play the field. Microsoft negotiates hard. They don't respect you unless you do the same. I could write chapters just on negotiating with Microsoft. However, one important rule is "do not get into the ring with Microsoft unless you're prepared to go the distance. If the negotiation takes under six months, you got a bad deal."

Ramsay: Negotiations are often about compromise. Was this your experience with Microsoft? Did you ultimately get a fair deal?

Goodman: Negotiation is often about compromise; however, negotiating with Microsoft is more often about leverage. In my years of negotiating with them, I didn't often see them give in on any points they didn't have to, and I learned not to give in on any. I learned that when negotiating with Microsoft, you will only get what you ratchet away from them. With other companies, I've experienced willingness to compromise. It's just not Microsoft's style though. I felt that we always got a fair deal with Microsoft, but it was always a lot of work.

Ramsay: Can you give me any examples of the sort of things that Ensemble and Microsoft haggled about?

Goodman: Money was the main issue—royalty rates versus the development advance. The greater the cost that the developer is willing to pay for on the front end of the project, the higher the royalty rate the developer deserves on the back end. We would have liked to have retained the intellectual property rights to Age of Empires, but since this was our first game and we had no track record, I didn't think we had the leverage to swing it. I also wanted control over marketing, but we never saw eye-to-eye on that point.

Ramsay: Was a sequel or trilogy part of the deal?

Goodman: No, we were a little naïve at this point. Our first sequel proposal included eight games over four years. This was crazy, but Microsoft was drinking the same Kool-Aid that we were, and they thought it was a great proposal. I'm sure glad that we didn't sign the deal, because we would go on to average two years per game. We would have been locked up for 16 years.

I did know that the next Age of Empires game would be a medieval game, but that game wasn't negotiated until long after the first Age of Empires shipped. Six months into the development of Age of Empires II, we still had not finalized the deal terms with Microsoft. To compel Microsoft to compromise on terms, we made a difficult decision to stop work on the project, which jeopardized the holiday ship date. When Microsoft sent their production team down to Dallas to see the latest progress, they found the entire company playing ping pong, billiards, video games, and board games. We were doing anything but working on Age of Empires. That caused something to happen up at Microsoft, because within a week, we had finalized the deal terms that we had been negotiating for six months.

The third Age of Empires topic was the most controversial. Some of us wanted to do the colonial time frame, and some of us wanted to move straight into World War I and II. It was the subject of heated debate within

Ensemble. Microsoft was very happy to keep their distance from this topic, so they left the issue to us.

Ramsay: How was working with Stuart Molder?

Goodman: Stuart was great to work with. He was a true believer in our game and our development team. He stuck behind us, and ultimately convinced Microsoft to bet the farm on Age of Empires. This turned out to be a game changer for Microsoft. Age of Empires was first of the two monumentally successful franchises that gave rise to Microsoft as a worldwide videogame powerhouse. For several years, Age of Empires was responsible for as much as 50% of Microsoft's game revenue. In 2003, Bungie's Halo would launch Microsoft to even greater heights, leading to their dominance in console games.

Although we relinquished the Age of Empires intellectual property to Microsoft in our first deal, we were still able to maintain significant negotiating leverage for future versions of the game. This was due to the technical complexity of our game. It would be extremely difficult for another developer to faithfully reproduce our gameplay experience. This ultimately led Microsoft to acquire us in 2001.

Ramsay: What do you mean by "technical complexity"? What would make reproducing the gameplay experience difficult?

Goodman: We built our own proprietary engine, and there were many components that were very difficult to reproduce. One extremely complex part was our pathing algorithms. When you click on a unit and it needs to move somewhere, it must find the most efficient path from point A to point B. When scores of units are moving at once, each unit's moves can block or unblock potential pathways for any other unit. We literally had hundreds of units moving all at once, and all of them were potentially affecting every other unit. As a result, the routine became extremely complex.

Another very difficult problem was computer synchronization. You can have up to eight players in a game, and each player might have 50 or more units move around at once, yet all eight computers needed to stay perfectly synchronized. This needed to happen 30 times a second. That was an exceedingly difficult network programming challenge. Age of Empires I was even more difficult because we supported this over dial-up connections.

Ramsay: Tell me about the Microsoft acquisition in 2001. Did you approach them about selling?

Goodman: Shortly after the release of Age of Empires I in 1997, Microsoft approached me on numerous occasions and expressed interest in Ensemble

Studios joining the Microsoft family. They made a few lowball offers, but we didn't enter serious discussions until we released Age of Empires II in 2000.

When I founded Ensemble Studios, I resolved to not sell for under $100 million. That resolution may have been more of an aspiration than a calculation, but it became an invaluable metric around which I managed Ensemble Studios.

Ramsay: How did you determine that figure?

Goodman: Your company is worth only what you can convince someone to pay. To do this favorably, you must address three factors: revenue, which determines a minimum value; potential, which determines a maximum value; and time. To close the sale, you need to create a vanishing window of opportunity.

Revenue is determined by financial data. A company is minimally worth some multiple of its profitability. Age of Empires II was on its way to becoming the bestselling PC game of all time, so our financial health was outstanding.

Potential is determined by strategic synergy. A company's maximum worth is the benefit it brings to the acquirer. Prior to Age of Empires I, Microsoft had not built a reputation as a top-tier game company. To obtain a premium value for Ensemble, I had to convince Microsoft that purchasing Ensemble Studios would redefine their image in the world of video games.

And to control the sale, you need to control the timing. Cash-rich companies can afford to take their time. They will always hold out for a better price if nothing motivates them to close. To create a deadline, I had decided to work with a new publisher for our next game. This gave Microsoft two options: buy our company or compete with us.

Ramsay: Why did you sell? Was Ensemble not doing well?

Goodman: Ensemble was doing fantastic. The best way to leverage success is with a powerful strategic partner, like Microsoft, who benefited from the deal. We were the perfect match at that time.

There are typically two types of sale: fire sales and strategic acquisitions. The first type, a fire sale, occurs when a financially troubled company is willing to sell for cheap in order to avoid bankruptcy. The second type, a strategic acquisition, is a premium-priced sale that occurs when the acquirer needs something that the acquired has in order to complete some larger strategy. Our purchase was strategic for Microsoft at the time, as they needed us to take them to the next level as a game publisher.

We determined that there was an excellent fit between us and that we both benefited from the acquisition. Then we engaged in a lot of negotiation regarding long-term commitments, strategic plans, franchise direction, control, and key people. In the end, it all came down to the sale price. I had to draw a line in the sand. Finally, many months after negotiations had started, Ed Fries and I agreed upon a final acquisition price during dinner at the Third Floor Fish Café in Redmond, overlooking Lake Washington.

That said, I've always had a passion for games, but even more so was my desire to build something great and enduring. It was a tough call to sell Ensemble. The company was my prized possession, and I had a deep attachment to the family I had built. I nurtured the employees, giving them opportunities that they wouldn't have had otherwise. I wanted to enrich my own life by enriching the lives of my employees.

My philosophy at that time was to give out stock options to align the goals of employees and management. Too many times have I seen companies whose owners make a lot of money and the employees get nothing. In those cases, selling is only good for the owners. So, I had created a stock option plan where all of the employees benefited from a successful acquisition. That aligned everyone's long-term goals. I knew that it was time, and I felt that I had achieved that success.

Ramsay: How did you feel about losing ownership of an organization in which you invested a great amount of time and resources?

Goodman: No one likes losing ownership of something like that. Parents don't like seeing their children go off to college, but it is a necessary part of the life cycle. Microsoft underwent some bad experiences with acquiring companies and trying to control them, so they were in a good mindset to acquire us and allow us to maintain the formula that made us successful in the first place. They were ready for hands-off management.

Ramsay: So, you weren't at all fearful that Microsoft would take over and run your firm into the ground?

Goodman: I wasn't worried about that. I never got the impression that they would try to take over. Ironically, any difficulty between Microsoft and us working together came from a lack of involvement, rather than too much.

Microsoft underwent a difficult time in the first decade of the 2000s, trying to find a good strategic plan for PC games. They had a tenuous time with trying to define their PC game strategy. They ended up with a vague PC plan, while relying more and more on PC games to generate revenue for their budding Xbox business.

One sign that things were a little off-balance at Microsoft was their meeting process. I never knew who would show up to a Microsoft meeting. We had a monthly studio manager meeting. There were seven studios, so one would conclude that seven studio managers would attend the meeting. I would walk into a room with over 20 attendees. I never knew who all of the attendees were or why they were there. I rarely even knew the agenda. It's difficult to accomplish anything with a room crammed full of random people and no agenda.

Ramsay: But you personally stayed with Microsoft?

Goodman: I had a contract for only two years, but I stayed for eight years until Ensemble closed. I was proud of staying longer than my minimum two years. I valued loyalty as an employer, and I believed that I should value it as an employee as well. Over the years, Ensemble had a very low rate of employee turnover. However, Microsoft Game Studios saw increasing turnover in high-level management. With each management change came a new and disruptive strategic direction.

Ramsay: You had various projects in the pipeline before the closure. What were these projects? Why were they canceled?

Goodman: Some of the games we canceled ourselves. Other games were canceled by Microsoft. Some projects were discontinued after Microsoft management changes. The projects were determined to be too expensive and risky or not "in our area of expertise." Thus, we would start over on something new.

It was frustrating for employees to invest so much time on projects that never shipped. The end result was that we ended up doing a lot of Age of Empires sequels. This was fantastic, but we wasted half of our efforts on starting and stopping other new projects which were never brought to fruition.

One great game we had in the works, and in which we had invested two years, was a massively multiplayer online game set in the Halo universe. After multiple prototypes and demos, we finally achieved buy-in from Shane Kim, the general manager at Microsoft Game Studios. The game was bold and beautiful, and I was sure that this product would be a massive blockbuster for Microsoft. It was a very exciting time at Ensemble.

Ramsay: Did that excitement last?

Goodman: After another change in management, Microsoft shifted their direction, killing the Halo project in the process. Soon after that, I flew from Dallas to Redmond for a private meeting with Shane to assess the situation. It was during that meeting that he told me that Microsoft decided to "internalize" the development of Age of Empires and close down our company. While this was difficult news to process, Shane asked me if I was interested in buying Ensemble back from Microsoft. He indicated that they would come to terms on a price with some type of deal to develop the next Age of Empires.

While Microsoft may have been in the position of power to close the studio, I told him that I wasn't interested in reacquiring my company, but that I would entertain starting up an independent studio. I suggested to him the possibility of a new studio that would develop the next game in the Age of Empires series. Shane expressed interest in that, so we began working on a deal to do the next Age game as new independent studio, now known as Robot Entertainment.

Ramsay: What was your vision for this new company?

Goodman: The short-term vision was to capitalize Robot Entertainment by reinventing Age of Empires for an online, free-to-play social-game world. Our long-term vision was to develop original properties that would take Robot into a new era of games. Our intent was to shape Robot into a creative, employee-owned company.

Robot was a company born from extraordinary circumstances. When Microsoft informed me that they were going to close Ensemble, I set my mind to turning this devastating event into a great opportunity. We formulated a plan that would allow us to create a new, progressive game company with the remarkable talent of Ensemble.

The objective was to strike a deal with Microsoft to develop the next version of Age of Empires as an independent company. Our plan was bold. We had to create a design that was so compelling they would be willing to hire back a team whose studio they had just shut down. This strategy relied upon our greatest strength: our reputation as world-class designers of real-time strategy games. By leveraging what Ensemble did best, we funded and launched Robot.

Ramsay: Are you still oriented toward creating phenomena? Or has your experience tempered your more youthful aspirations?

Goodman: My experience has reinforced my youthful aspirations! I believe that creating a phenomenon is more important than ever before. With the rise of mobile and social games, there are more games than at any time in our history. The question is: why do some great games become blockbusters while others remain unnoticed?

Making superior gameplay is only part of the equation. To create a phenomenon that is a runaway success, one must create a powerful group perception. People move in groups. They want to be part of something greater, and this is what a phenomenon is all about. For example, the social phenomenon of The Beatles was just as important as the music itself. Alone, one might listen to an album, but a phenomenon can turn a group of listeners into screaming fans. Creating a phenomenon is an art form.

Ramsay: What do you want to do going forward?

Goodman: My tenure at Robot was shorter than I planned. Despite my love for Robot and its employees, it was soon evident to me that my talents and Robot's needs were not a perfect match. In the early years at Ensemble, I hired each new individual according to my own personal criteria. Robot employees are close friends who I had worked with for up to 15 years. In that time period, our relationships had evolved. I was no longer their mentor and father figure. Time had inevitably changed that. It also became clear that my aspirations were not the same as Robot's aspirations. It was difficult to accept at first, but Robot and I are on separate paths.

My contributions as CEO at Robot were completed after we successfully transitioned from a vision to a flourishing game studio. I've handed the reins over to extremely capable individuals who had been waiting for their opportunities to run a great studio. I remain the largest owner of the company and a member of the board. I stay close at hand to advise on important matters. After spending a decade and a half creating, building, and guiding the team that shaped the Age of Empires phenomenon, it's again time to follow my passion and produce a new phenomenon.

Feargus Urquhart

Cofounder, Obsidian Entertainment

*In 1996, **Feargus Urquhart** began serving as president of Interplay's role-playing games division. Two years later, the division was launched as Black Isle Studios, which became one of the most celebrated role-playing game developers in recent history.*

Through 2003, Urquhart managed the development and marketing of the Fallout series, the Icewind Dale series, Planescape: Torment, and the externally developed Baldur's Gate series. Prior to the studio's closure, resulting from serious financial difficulties at Interplay, Urquhart left with a core team from Black Isle to start anew.

Urquhart and Chris Avellone, Darren Monahan, Chris Parker, and Chris Jones cofounded Obsidian Entertainment in 2003. The studio has since been responsible for original and licensed properties, such as Star Wars: Knights of the Old Republic II, Neverwinter Nights 2, Alpha Protocol, and Fallout: New Vegas. A successor to Black Isle's former glory, the studio continues to develop next-generation, cross-platform role-playing games.

Ramsay: Tell me about the closure of Black Isle Studios.

Urquhart: That was a pretty tumultuous time. I had almost left Black Isle a year before in 2002. I ended up staying because I hoped that we would be able to turn things around and help Interplay get out of debt. My desire to leave was based on the frustration that Interplay was losing money year after year, despite the fact that every game we shipped—both internal and external—made money, and in many cases, a lot of money.

At some point, that really grates on you. It's that feeling that no matter how well you do, the company you work for will just slip another five feet back each year. I held out another year, hoping that things would turn around. But Interplay lost the Dungeons & Dragons license in late 2002 or early 2003 after we had been working on Baldur's Gate 3 for about two years, which was a big morale hit to me and everyone working on the game. Following that, it seemed like it was the right time to move on.

Ramsay: When did you begin talking about Obsidian Entertainment?

Urquhart: I really didn't talk to anyone about starting a new company until after I had left and was then approached by other people. Things then grew pretty quickly over the next few months, and by the end of that time, there were about seven of us, five of which were the owners of the company. A couple of months later, we were able to get Star Wars: Knights of the Old Republic II signed, which made it possible to bring on another ten people in about a month. By the end of 2003, we had around 20 people.

Ramsay: Who were the five owners? How did you know them?

Urquhart: The five owners were, and still are, Chris Parker, Darren Monahan, Chris Avellone, Chris Jones, and myself. As for how we met, it all started at Interplay in the early 90s.

The first of the owners that I knew was Chris Jones because we were in quality assurance (QA) together back in 1992. Chris was a huge Wolfenstein 3D player. I was shocked at the time he spent trying to find all the secrets by sliding along the walls, pressing the spacebar. Chris eventually moved out of QA, became a programmer, and then an engine programmer on Fallout, Arcanum, and a new engine that, unfortunately, died with Black Isle.

I met Chris Parker when he was working as my lead tester on Blizzard's Lost Vikings 2. After he got his chemistry degree, he moved out of QA as well and became a producer in Interplay's Sports division. In 1996, he came over to Black Isle as a producer on both BioWare's Baldur's Gate series and the Icewind Dale series, which we developed internally.

Chris Avellone created adventures and source books for a number of pen-and-paper role-playing games before coming to Interplay as a designer in the then-named TSR Division. I met him in the first few days of taking over the division, and he quickly went from working as just one of the designers to the lead designer on Planescape: Torment.

Last, but not least, is Darren Monahan, who I met, much like Chris Parker, because he was working in QA on one of my titles. He then moved out of QA to become a programmer in Interplay's Tech Group. Darren later transferred to Black Isle when we needed another producer on Icewind Dale.

So, we have all known each other for a long time, and thankfully, we liked each other enough to start a company together.

Ramsay: How did you fund your company at first?

Urquhart: Chris Parker, Darren Monahan, and I put most of the startup costs on our credit cards. I think the total investment came to somewhere between $100,000 to $125,000. This investment allowed us to run payroll; obtain medical insurance; incorporate; buy equipment such as desktops, servers, and networking; and pay the security deposit for our office space. We paid ourselves salaries, but only minimum wage. We had to be able to run a legitimate payroll because no medical insurance company would insure us until we had run and paid either one or two payrolls.

We were able to stop paying out of our pockets after we got our signing amount from the Star Wars: Knights of the Old Republic II agreement. That got us through the first couple of months, and then we were able to start getting paid on milestones. After about six months, the company was able to pay all of us back the money that we had put in.

I'm happy that we bought the software and hardware we needed in the beginning. We purchased legitimate copies of 3ds Max as soon as we needed to use them, and we purchased licenses for Windows and Office with every workstation that we put together. We switched to Dell after the first couple of months. Other than being able to say that we were running our company legally, ensuring we had licenses meant that we could move forward at full steam. We spent quite a bit of our cash reserves to do this initially, so we had to be very careful with other things. When we had more cash available, we were able to hire the people we needed to hire, instead of dealing with a debt of illegitimate software or a network infrastructure that was not made to push 5 GB builds of our game around.

Ramsay: Is the rate at which the company expanded typical for startups?

Urquhart: Yes and no. For a new studio that is starting off to be a multi-project studio working on large games, I think our growth was typical. We started with a core staff of 7 and grew to 20 pretty quickly. We then grew between 20 or 30 each year for the next four years.

However, what might not be typical is that one of our goals as a startup was to become a multiproject studio. This meant we pushed to get multiple projects so that we could grow the company to around 80 to 100 fairly quickly. With our reputation in the industry for making role-playing games, we were able to get these projects, and that fueled our growth. That was a double-edged sword though. It was great to be able to grow quickly, rent new office space, buy new computers, and all of that. But that sort of growth also meant that we had to learn how to manage increasingly large teams working on increasingly complex projects.

I sometimes wonder how things would have been different if we had stuck to one large project and one small project. Doing that, it's very possible we could have grown our methods and our processes along with our staff, which would have probably led to a smoother last few years.

Having said all of that, one piece of advice that I received early on was, "If you are getting deals, sign them." But not to the extent that you have five deals and two teams. Contracts come in waves, and when the waves are hitting, you need to take them.

Ramsay: Excellent advice. I've never heard that before, but I can certainly see the wisdom. Who told you that?

Urquhart: Lars Brubaker, who was president at Reflexive Entertainment then. We started in the industry at about the same time at Interplay. Lars left Interplay earlier than I did and started up his own company in the late 1990s, but we have kept in touch ever since. We still have lunch pretty much every month.

Ramsay: What other challenges did you face in the beginning?

Urquhart: Looking back, the beginning seems easier than the last few years. If I had to pick some challenges from back then, I would say figuring out the ownership of the company, finding a fair way to do medical insurance, and making sure that we were continually thinking about the future and not just trying to get our first game done.

The ownership issue was a little tricky because it was valuing who should get what at the very beginning, which can make some people feel undervalued and others feel greedy for asking what they think is fair for them to have. It seems we did pretty well. Unless I'm mistaken, everyone is still fine with the decisions we made those seven years ago.

Medical insurance is a distinctly American issue, but we wanted to ensure that we were fair to single and married people. We decided to cover single people 100%, spouses 50%, and children 25%. That felt fair because we were giving married people a good benefit, but not so much that single employees would feel married people were getting compensated so much more than them. After a few years, we found that nobody really even thought about medical insurance as something one person was getting more than another, so we changed spouses to 75% and children to 50%. While I'm on the subject, medical insurance costs about $1,300 per month, and we cover about $1,000 of that, with the employees covering the other $300. That's before tax though, so probably only about $200 in actual cash.

Lastly, keeping focused on getting new projects while successfully making our first game was something I think we did pretty well. While I contributed to the development of our first title, Star Wars: Knights of the Old Republic II, it was work that didn't require my attention every day. I wouldn't hold anyone up if I needed to focus on new projects for a day or three. Ultimately, this made certain that I could be looking for new projects, but that I was not so removed that I was out of touch with what we actually do each day. I think that if we had not focused on these things, transitioning from our first project to our next would have been far more of a challenge.

Ramsay: How important to you is being a hands-on leader? Do you think other entrepreneurs should be directly involved with development?

Urquhart: The quick answer is that being a hands-on leader is very important to me. We are in the business of making games. If I completely lose touch with that, I don't think it would be possible for me to be an effective leader. I am also supposed to the most objective person at Obsidian, so if I'm not familiar with the how and why of developing our games, then I can't be effective in that role.

The other thing we talk a lot about at Obsidian is that as the "old guys," we shouldn't abdicate our experience. What I mean by that is that we actually do know things from our 15 to 20 years of experience, and we shouldn't stay silent when there are pieces of advice or methods that we know will work, or for that matter, won't work.

There is a very big caveat about being a hands-on leader, and that is being hands-on does not mean being in the way. I've had to learn that I can be involved in the design of the products or even implementation, but I need to make sure that I'm not stopping anyone else from doing their job because of my "actual" job of being CEO. In my position, I may have to suddenly leave for a couple of days to show off another product or visit one of the console companies. While I'm doing that, it is really frustrating for the team to be waiting for me to finish my development work.

I absolutely think that entrepreneurs should be involved in the actual creation of the games they make. I try not to be a weight on others with the development work that I do. I also try to keep myself focused on my role as the main business development guy at Obsidian. I have to make sure that I'm doing that job as well. If I become too involved with our games, then that job suffers. In the end, it's a big balancing act that I constantly reevaluate.

Ramsay: Star Wars is a major property. How did you get that opportunity?

Urquhart: It was great being able to work on a Star Wars game. I've actually been able to hit the nerd trifecta by working on Star Wars, Star Trek, and Dungeons & Dragons games in my career. When it came to actually signing a deal with LucasArts, it was a collection of relationships and our reputation from Black Isle Studios that brought us the opportunity.

I had met Simon Jeffrey, president at LucasArts, through Lisa Jensen, who had worked with Simon at Virgin. Lisa was in charge of public relations for Black Isle. We were also doing a lot of work with BioWare, and I had known the cofounders, Ray Muzyka and Greg Zeschuk, since working as producer on Shattered Steel, their first commercial product.

When we left Interplay, I contacted Simon to see if he was looking for another Star Wars role-playing game. I was actually thinking the game would be an action role-playing game for the Xbox and PlayStation 2 using the engine that Snowblind Studios had created for Baldur's Gate: Dark Alliance.

However, he said that BioWare was moving onto other products, and LucasArts was looking to have a sequel to Star Wars: Knights of the Old Republic done fairly quickly. I thought about the offer for all of about five minutes, and then called Simon back and told him we would do it.

Ramsay: Is being established critical to winning the big contracts?

Urquhart: In my experience, your reputation, combined with your relationships, really helps you get contracts as a third-party developer. In fact, unless you have an incredible demo already running on one of the consoles or a great track record, getting the larger contracts is extremely difficult.

Ramsay: Lucasfilm has been said to be particularly restrictive with the Star Wars license when third parties are involved. Was that your experience?

Urquhart: Actually, our experience with Lucasfilm was not that at all. In the end, they really only asked us to change three or four things about the game. For example, they did not want us mucking around with Alderaan, and we had the horns on one of the races turned the wrong way.

Now, the reason I think we were allowed more freedom is because of how we have always treated licenses. We look at a license as a privilege to play and develop in their worlds. We respect that privilege.

We immerse ourselves in them and make sure we are doing everything right. In the case of Star Wars, our chief creative officer, Chris Avellone, spent every waking moment for three or four months reading everything he could get his hands on, even this pretty poor series called Teen Jedi or something like that. After such a great investment of time, he became our resident Star Wars scholar and was able to make sure everything we were doing would stay within the bounds of the license. That's how we have always treated the Dungeons & Dragons license as well.

Ultimately, the worlds and rules belong to the licensors. We may not agree with everything they've done, and we may even ask if we can change certain things. But their fans love it for what it is, not for how we can change it. So, by trying to change it too much, we really are doing a disservice to the fans who are going to buy the game.

Ramsay: You've worked closely with BioWare for a long time. When did that relationship come about?

Urquhart: As it seems to happen a lot in my career, it was happenstance. BioWare had pitched, and Interplay had signed, a mecha game called Metal Hive, which was later renamed Shattered Steel. The game's original producer, Rusty Buchert, needed to focus on other things, so I was put on the project. I ended up doing some design for the game, and I wrote the voice-over lines for almost all of the movies.

While working on the project, I had a chance to get to know Ray and Greg really well, so they shared with me another game they were working on. They were calling the game Battleground Infinity, which was a role-playing game with some real-time strategy elements that they were developing for the PC, using pretty much the very first version of DirectDraw for Windows. To be honest, the first demo wasn't that far along, so they started pitching the game to a lot of other publishers.

They showed me another demo a few months later, and a light bulb turned on in my head about how we could make the game into a Dungeons & Dragons game. There was initially some resistance at Interplay, but I have to give credit to Trish Wright, the vice president of marketing, for listening to me and getting Brian Fargo, the chief executive at Interplay, to come see the demo. Right after seeing the game, he said that we needed to sign it up and make a Dungeons & Dragons game.

That one moment was the start of the Baldur's Gate series, BioWare's Neverwinter Nights, and Black Isle's use of BioWare's Infinity Engine to make both Planescape: Torment and the Icewind Dale series. It's interesting to think, "What if that five-minute meeting had never happened?"

Ramsay: What were the difficulties of using BioWare's tools to develop Planescape: Torment and the Icewind Dale series?

Urquhart: With Planescape: Torment, the challenges of using BioWare's Infinity Engine all come from trying to use the engine before Baldur's Gate was finished. That meant we had less than a year before we shipped to work with the final version of the engine.

But because of how we approached the game, we weren't really in that bad of shape. We did what I think everyone should do when using a piece of technology: use it for its intended purpose. In games, that means using it to make a game that's similar to the type of game that it was originally developed to make. Since Planescape: Torment and Icewind Dale were designed to have very similar structures to Baldur's Gate, we were able to use much of what the engine did without implementing too many new capabilities.

Ramsay: You were using the Infinity Engine before BioWare had shipped Baldur's Gate. Are scenarios like that common?

Urquhart: I think that sort of technology sharing was something that occurred more then than it does now, but it probably still happens at publishers, across development teams at larger developers, and during console transitions. Typically, when work begins on a second game to use a particular engine, developers will either work with the unfinished technology while planning to transition to the final version and dealing with the assortment of problems that result or start development when the first game to use the engine is supposed to done. Unfortunately, things don't always happen as planned.

During console transitions, technology sharing happens more often because teams are waiting on the upgraded versions of the engines they are developing on, such as the Unreal Engine, but they don't want to wait until that first game comes out on the new platform. If they waited, they would start development two or more years after the new platform launched.

Ramsay: At Obsidian, have you faced similar challenges?

Urquhart: The largest challenges we have had with technology at Obsidian have come about from not taking my own advice about using third-party tools. With Neverwinter Nights 2, we felt we needed to swap out the renderer and create an entirely new world editor, while keeping the back end of BioWare's engine for the rules, scripting, and core systems. But, as we started changing things, it was necessary to change even more.

What we didn't plan for was how those changes would impact our schedule. We quickly fell behind, and we weren't where we wanted to be after six months of development. What we should have done at that point was to just stop and restructure how we were developing the game. That would have meant moving off a majority of the designers and artists until we really had the systems and tools ready for them to use.

On Alpha Protocol, we ended up in a similar place, but for different reasons. We underestimated all of the RPG systems that we would have needed to create to layer atop Unreal Engine 3. Now, Unreal Engine 3 is much more than just a renderer, but when it comes to all of the things that make RPGs tick, it has never needed to have them. We ended up doing something very similar. We had people trying to create levels, gameplay, and content before the systems were really there for them to use. They could create levels that functioned, but they functioned for a game like Gears of War and not what we were ultimately trying to create. It wasn't the engine's fault though. We didn't adequately take the systems work into account.

Ramsay: When Neverwinter Nights 2 fell behind schedule, what was the publisher's view?

Urquhart: Ultimately, I think Atari was okay with the delay after the game was released. Nobody is ever happy in the midst of a delay though. We should have readdressed where we were, and made a new plan to use our remaining budget and resources to make the best game we could. But it's always hard to stop midway through a project and really evaluate how to best move forward. Actually, it's really scary, too. The reason is that you are trying to keep to your milestone schedule, so that you can continue to get paid. Having to call your publisher and say we have to stop and come up with a new plan could mean that you could get your project canceled and lose any of your own money that you have put into it.

Ramsay: Which is more advantageous: using third-party proprietary tools, licensing middleware, or building your own?

Urquhart: Whether you build your own engine or use a third-party one absolutely depends on the project; although, I think it is beneficial for any developer to either have their own technology or focus on one specific engine. Jumping back and forth between different engines doesn't help with a developer's ability to efficiently make games.

However, there will always be projects, particularly sequels, where it's just better to use a certain technology, even if you're unfamiliar with it. An example would be that we used Bethesda's internal technology to create Fallout: New Vegas. We were able to start where the Fallout 3 team left off and not only use all the tech they created, but all the assets as well.

I should probably add one last thing about using technology. We have been the most successful when we have used an engine that has been used to make the type of game that we are making. Anytime we have deviated from that, we have hit roadblocks. As you deviate more and more, I've found that there isn't a linear relation between the quantity of changes and the challenges we've hit; it's more of an exponential one. The first deviation is not big deal, the third one could create any number of problems, and the tenth one could add three or five times the amount of problems.

Ramsay: Generally speaking, are the savings from reusing technology and game assets so substantial that they outweigh the drawbacks? Would you say that such reuse is a competitive advantage?

Urquhart: In my mind, there are two ways to look at the reuse of assets and technology. First, from a production standpoint, if you can reuse a lot from a prior game, then the time between starting the project and creating that first finished level is much faster. That's a benefit because levels are what players actually play, and the more time you can focus on making and iterating on levels, the better chance there is that the levels will be good and polished. There is also the benefit that the team will be working with finished technology and tools.

Many of the games that I have worked on that have been a challenge have been that way because the tools and asset pipelines were very late in coming online. In particular, designers and artists would fight the technology to make the game, or they would have to continuously go back to levels that were "done" to add in features or fix things because aspects of the engine or assets were changed.

Second, from a creative standpoint, we have to be careful about how similar the game feels to the last game. If nothing new is added, then the game could feel too much like the last game. What we have tried to do is make sure that we add a story with a different twist, add new gameplay options that change how the game is played, add new art that makes at least some elements of the game feel very different, and change as much of the user interface as possible. The user interface of the game is what the player sees from the first second of gameplay to the last second. When we change the user interface, the game will look and feel different.

Ramsay: Can reuse ever stifle creativity or tank a project?

Urquhart: Reuse can stifle creativity, if the team lets that happen. A car is made of an engine, tires, chassis, doors, and a few other things. However, there are car designers that can make that look new and fresh. The team has to figure out how to take what's given to them and put the parts together in ways that are interesting and fresh to the player. Like cars, they do need some new gadgets, paint, and paneling, or it can be a harder job.

In my experience, we've always done a good job of reusing things in ways that haven't led to a project tanking. I think the reason for that is we remember that while we're using the same blocks, it's really our job to arrange them and present them to the player in fresh ways. When you have the opportunity to make more story-focused games, a new narrative with interesting characters can really engage a player, even if a lot of what they are seeing and doing is similar to what they did and saw in another game.

Ramsay: The Fallout series began at Black Isle. Bethesda Softworks now holds the license. What is the feeling at Obsidian about returning to the franchise that you created with less control?

Urquhart: Bethesda was great about giving us a lot of freedom in making Fallout: New Vegas. They gave us some very high-level suggestions about what they wanted, and we then came back with a pitch. They were happy with about 95% of the pitch, and for the other 5%, they had very specific reasons as to why we could or should not do what we had suggested. As we began development, we submitted a lot of our new ideas to them. Todd Howard at Bethesda was very open to our ideas. Throughout development, there were only a very few things they wanted us to not change or not use.

Getting to work on Fallout was a great experience. Personally, one of the things that made me the saddest when I left Black Isle was probably the notion of not ever being able to make Fallout. Luckily, that didn't turn out to be true, and so we now have Fallout: New Vegas.

Ramsay: How do you deal with criticism of your games? What impact do reviews have on the company?

Urquhart: I think I go through the different phases of grief; although, I usually skip denial and go straight to self-loathing!

On a more serious note, I find reading criticism of our games very hard, but I can't avoid the task. As CEO, hiding from reviews is not going to benefit our company or our games. So, I read them, and they remind me about what we need to think about, how we need to focus our efforts, and how to look at the press and the industry as a whole. We are not an island, and we need to take critical perspectives into account. The job becomes harder when you think about the impact of bad reviews on your future as a developer. Bad reviews increase the difficulty of getting deals, and they may close doors to contracts that may have once been available.

Ramsay: What are some of the lessons that you have learned?

Urquhart: We developed Alpha Protocol, and the game has not received great reviews. For a game that we worked on for more than three years, the reviews were tough to see. It's easy to blame outside forces, such as the technology you've licensed or how your publisher made it hard for you to make the game, but it's essential for us to be introspective and ask, "What could we have done to facilitate production? How could we have improved our relationship with the publisher?"

We need to absolutely understand the expectations of our publishers and ensure that there are no gray areas at all. I can point to many rocky areas in our publisher relationships where we did not understand what our publishers were expecting from the game or from our next milestone, what shows they wanted us to attend, marketing materials they planned to use, and a myriad of other things. Understanding and then agreeing on those expectations have been difficult sometimes with our more recent publishers, but doing so has led to things going more smoothly.

We also need to recognize that we are a contractor working for our customer—the publisher. It's our job to represent our opinion and let them know what we think, but it's their money, and it's their decision regarding what should ultimately be done. Acting like children, putting our foot down and telling them they are dumb, isn't helpful, even if we do it behind their back. That doesn't mean we have to do everything they say though.

Ramsay: When is walking away from a project right and justified?

Urquhart: If the publisher is directing a project toward a very different direction than what we had initially agreed upon, then we have to remember our right to walk away. That can be very difficult contractually, but it has to be done if we are ultimately being asked to do something that is impossible, unethical, or harmful to our reputation. Walking away would be what any normal contractor would do under those circumstances.

Ramsay: Where do you see Obsidian going in the future?

Urquhart: More role-playing games. It's what we—and especially I—love to do. I think developing role-playing games is a great challenge, and they are something I've learned a lot about since I started working on them in 1995.

We are looking at new ways to fund our games and how we could develop our own games with our own money. Steam, Xbox Live, and the PlayStation Network have really made distributing our own games possible.

Our reputation for making a certain kind of games actually makes getting the word out about our games easier, but it's a resource that we haven't tapped for our original properties yet.

Ramsay: What advice would you give to anyone looking to found a studio?

Urquhart: That's difficult to answer. I think we were able to form Obsidian as a result of our time in the industry, our relationships, and our focus on developing role-playing games. Having all of those resources makes starting a studio easier when you don't have access to a lot of capital. All of that let us start Obsidian on our credit cards.

Thinking about our early days, the studio leadership needs to think about how they can reduce the risk that a publisher might perceive when determining whether to sign the studio. All of the things that we had going for us were things that reduced the publisher's risk in going with us.

I think there are several ways to reduce this risk. You can have a demo that shows what the studio can do. You can have people with experience in the genre working on the projects you are pitching. You can offer to do products like sequels and expansion packs. Basically, you can encourage the publisher to believe that you are running a smart business. Of all of those, I strongly recommend the sequel and expansion pack route. These products generally use the engine from the previous or core game and reuse a lot of assets. This makes developing those games less risky, which is something a publisher will absolutely understand.

Now, in starting our studio, we always ran Obsidian as though success was predetermined. That means we ramped up people when they were available, offered 401(k) plans as soon as we could, and we got serious about running the company as a business pretty much right away. We argued about medical coverage to make sure we offered the best we could, and we spent a lot of our initial money on a great network infrastructure and good computers. We were also very upfront with everyone that came to work with us about how performance reviews were going to work, what they would get when the company was successful, and where we were trying to take the company. That is probably the best piece of advice I can ever give anyone who is looking to run or is running a development studio.

Be upfront and honest with your employees and treat them like adults. Tell them the good and the bad about what is going on with the company. Doing that will build trust between you and them, and it will make sure they believe in you, not just in the good times, but also in the bad.

We do this at Obsidian by having meetings every two weeks where we talk in-depth about the projects and the company. And I make it a point to personally take at least one person in the company out to lunch every week. By updating everyone as a group and then letting them ask questions one-on-one, we head off paranoia and build trust.

Tim Cain
Cofounder, Troika Games

After producing Fallout at Interplay, Tim Cain left the company with Leonard Boyarsky and Jason Anderson, frustrated with the decision-making processes there. In 1998, the trio cofounded Troika Games, and secured a deal with Sierra Entertainment to publish the award-winning Arcanum: Of Steamworks and Magick Obscura in 2001. When the studio closed four years later, the company had developed only two more titles: The Temple of Elemental Evil and Vampire: The Masquerade— Bloodlines. Financially, none were hits, but all are cult classics.

Cain and his cofounders were designers, artists, and programmers. They were not interested in business planning or the long-term viability of the company. Success meant making the games that they wanted to make. They surmounted many obstacles through dogged persistence and sheer luck, but they eventually found themselves ill-equipped for the myriad challenges of their final project.

Ramsay: Tell me about the day you left Interplay. Why did you leave? What were you thinking?

Cain: While Fallout was in production, I was unhappy at how development worked at Interplay. People who didn't play games, or didn't even seem to like games, were making decisions about how to market the game, what features it should have, and when it should ship.

Worse, decisions were being made that changed the game and required us to do substantial changes, and these decisions could and should have been made months earlier. For example, the UK office said no children could be harmed in the game, but children had been in the design for years. Another example: Interplay spent a lot of money for an external marketing agency to develop treatments for the box and ad, and they were terrible.

My artists produced better work on their own time, but marketing did not want to use them. However, when Interplay's president, Brian Fargo, saw their work, he liked what he saw, so the art was used. My role as producer appeared to consist of arguing with people and trying to defend the game from devolving into a lesser product.

In July 1997—Fallout would ship three months later in October—I had decided that I did not want to work on Fallout 2. I submitted to my boss, Feargus Urquhart, a review for my line producer Fred Hatch that recommended he should be promoted to associate producer and assigned Fallout 2. Although the review was not processed, Feargus gave Fred the game to see how he would perform. When the first designs were submitted, I really didn't like them. Neither did Feargus, nor did Brian Fargo.

Leonard Boyarsky and Jason Anderson, who were the two artists and designers on Fallout with whom I would later start Troika, didn't feel any different either. So, Leonard and Jason wrote a different storyline for the game, which Brian liked more, but he told me he'd like to see what I could do. When I asked Feargus about Fred's promotion—his review was now long overdue—he told me that while he wouldn't make me do Fallout 2, the promotion wasn't going to happen, and Fred wouldn't get the sequel.

Feargus planned to give Fallout 2 to the producer of Descent to Undermountain if I didn't take it. While I personally liked that producer, I hated Descent. I thought the sequel would suffer under similar direction. I told Feargus that I would do the sequel and began working on a design.

Before leaving for Thanksgiving, I informed Feargus that I was thinking of quitting. I wanted him to know how I was feeling about development and how deeply I had been affected. I was worried that the same problems I had experienced during the development of Fallout would persist during the making of Fallout 2. Feargus said he understood.

When I returned, he asked if I had made a decision. I had not, and so I began work on Fallout 2. I worked out a new design and made an aggressive schedule to get the game out by the end of October 1998. I then started working on the game as lead designer and producer.

But the same problems resurfaced. For example, to save time and money, I had decided to have the same internal artists make the box for Fallout 2.

Feargus was upset that I had made such a decision without consulting him, but when I talked to Marketing, they were fine with the idea. But then Sales decided to change the box size and style, which would create problems for making the second box look similar to the first. In a meeting with Sales where Feargus was present, I was told that the decision was made and "there will be no further discussion on it."

I decided I had enough. Leonard and Jason, who could tell I was unhappy, had told me weeks earlier that they were unwilling to work on the sequel without me. Rather than simply quit, I remembered that Brian had told me years ago, after a programmer had quit under bad circumstances, that he wished people would come and talk to him rather than quit.

I went to Brian in December and told him that I was unhappy and wanted to quit. I decided to be frank and honest, and told him that other people also weren't happy and might resign with me. He wanted names. I told him about Leonard and Jason. Other people declined to be mentioned.

Throughout December and January, the three of us met with Brian to discuss the problems and see what solutions might be found. We wanted to meet with Brian as a group to prevent any misunderstandings that might arise from separate meetings. In fact, I wanted Feargus there, too, but Brian only included him once toward the end. Brian seemed surprised that I was getting resistance to doing Fallout 2 my way. His attitude was, "You did well on the first game, so just do it again on the second."

Unfortunately, this meant running to Brian whenever anyone tried to force their own ideas into the game, which didn't seem like a good working environment. We discussed this problem and raised other issues at these meetings, such as converting our bonus plan to a royalty-based plan. Brian did not like the idea of royalties. As for how to handle creative control, Brian said I could divide the responsibilities with Feargus, so I could handle Marketing and other departments directly, and they would have to effectively treat me as a division director. This seemed unsatisfactory to me, but Feargus seemed very unhappy that his own authority and responsibilities concerning Fallout 2 would be greatly reduced in this plan.

It was unclear how some issues would get resolved, such as budgeting for equipment and maintenance, since I didn't have a division director's budget. Brian handwaved these issues, saying that we'd work them out.

At that point, I regretted not abiding my original instinct to walk out and trying to work things out with Brian. In mid-January, I decided to leave the company. I told Feargus, who accepted my resignation and asked me to work until the end of the month. We went to talk to Trish Wright, the executive producer, who was unhappy to see me leave but accepted it. She warned me that Brian might be very upset, but I wanted to tell him that day. I returned to my office and told Leonard and Jason that I had quit, effective at the end of the month. Then I went and told Brian.

As expected, he was not happy. We talked for an hour, but the meeting was cut short because I had a dental appointment. While I was at the dentist, Leonard and Jason also decided to tender their resignations. I didn't speak to Brian after that day, and I finished out the month with my team.

My team was surprised and unhappy, having heard nothing of my months of meetings with Brian. I met with them to make sure the design for Fallout 2 was up-to-date. And I met with Feargus; my replacement, Eric Demilt, who would produce Fallout 2; and other designers, such as Chris Avellone and Zeb Cook, who would assume my design responsibilities.

I made sure that everyone understood the new design and where all of my documents were located on the local network. Phil Adam, the head of human resources, met with me once, to get my view on why I was leaving, but I otherwise did not interact with Brian or the administration.

On my last day, I packed my personal effects and went to Human Resources to process out. I was redirected to Legal, where I was asked to sign a letter that reminded me of my confidentiality agreement. I learned later that Leonard and Jason were not asked to sign such a letter. And then I went home, wondering what to do, now that I had a good title under my belt but had effectively cut ties with my last company.

Ramsay: When did you approach Leonard and Jason about Troika?

Cain: I talked to Leonard and Jason the day after we quit about their plans. None of us had approached any companies before we quit Interplay. Personally, I was too busy trying to document my plans for Fallout 2 to even think about what to do next. So, we sat down and talked about what we liked about Fallout and what we didn't like, and one theme became clear: we really wanted to make a fantasy computer role-playing game.

We had avoided the fantasy genre when we made Fallout, and that was a conscious decision to distance ourselves from the large number of competitors already on the shelves, such as the Ultima series, the Might & Magic series, and all of the games based on Dungeons & Dragons (D&D). But we felt that we had earned the right to work in that genre, and we had a number of ideas that would make our game stand out.

The desire to mix magic and technology was present from the outset of our talks, so really, you could say that the basis for Arcanum formed very quickly.

We wrote down our ideas for technology levels, for the effects of technology on classic fantasy races like elves and orcs, and for the role of magic in such a world. Everything seemed to come together very quickly, and we were pleased with our outline for the game.

Originally, we never planned to make our own company. None of us were businessmen, but we did enjoy working together. We went to several local companies, such as Blizzard and Virgin, but they were more interested in hiring us to work on one of their existing games under development than to work on an original game. After a few weeks, we figured that our game would only be made if we formed our own development company and found a publisher, so we switched tactics and began approaching companies for a contract and not for employment. That's when we created Troika.

The name came from something that Feargus would call us back when we worked on Fallout. As producer, I would be responsible for signing off on various game assets, such as the manual, the box cover, and any advertisements. However, I am not very artistic, and I am color-blind as well, so I would usually bring Leonard and Jason along with me to check that the art was appropriate on these assets. Feargus started calling us "the Troika," and after we had left Interplay and thought about making our own company, we liked that phrase enough to use it for our company name.

We incorporated on a suitable date: April 1, 1998. We didn't get a publishing deal until summer. We worked out of our homes until we moved into offices in October. And that's when Troika really began.

Ramsay: None of you had experience on the business side of running a studio. Did you find someone to play that role?

Cain: We never did get a business person. In hindsight, that was probably our biggest mistake. We would work on a game until it was finished, then we would scramble to find our next contract. We should have had someone whose full-time job was to secure funding for us, so we could concentrate on making games. Instead, we were always overworked and stressed. We did find a great lawyer who specialized in legal contracts in the game industry, but that only helped after we found a deal.

Ramsay: How did you chart out the future of the company? Did you at least go through the business-planning process?

Cain: We didn't chart out anything. We tried to get our first contract, and we did. As soon as we had it, we concentrated on nothing else. We focused on that game—designing it, programming it, and producing its art assets.

We were developers first and foremost. Running the business was an afterthought—an extra chore that we did between developing games.

Ramsay: What happened next? What was your first challenge?

Cain: Our first big challenge after incorporating was finding a publishing deal. None of us had any contacts in the industry, so we just cold-called places. We went to Activision, Sony, and a few other big publishers, but everyone seemed more interested in hiring us than funding us. Finally, six months after we quit Interplay and four months after forming Troika, when we were feeling the most despondent, we got a call from Sierra that changed everything.

Scott Lynch was a newly promoted vice president of development at Sierra, and he had loved Fallout. Scott was very excited about our ideas for Arcanum, and more importantly, he wanted to get us signed quickly so we could get started on it. He was even willing to make unheard-of—at least to us—concessions in the contract, so that we could get funded quickly. I think the whole negotiation period took less than a month. And we had a great contract! The big challenge now? They wanted a working prototype of the game in 90 days.

Ramsay: Then you began hiring the first employees?

Cain: Ninety days was insane, but we didn't know it. We were excited to get the contract. We had come off Fallout and Fallout 2 at Black Isle, where we had worked crazy hours. I worked up to 14 hours a day, seven days a week, for the last three months of Fallout. I figured I could do that again.

The working prototype that Sierra wanted was a sample level from the game. They wanted the player to be able to walk around, cast some spells, and engage in combat. They wanted one or two creatures to fight, a structure of some kind to enter, and some interesting effects. And we decided to do particle effects and real-time shadows. Of course, they also wanted a user interface on top of everything.

Unfortunately, the programming challenge proved to be beyond my abilities in that time frame. Since Sierra was paying us for the prototype, we used some of that money to hire another programmer, and the two of us worked crazy hours along with Leonard and Jason to get that prototype done. We started from nothing—no code base, no art, nothing. And we managed to make a really good prototype.

Ramsay: What was the size of your team during prototype development? How large did the Arcanum team eventually grow?

Cain: There were just the four of us: we three founders and one additional programmer. When we finished the prototype and Sierra accepted it, we rented office space in Irvine and were joined by three more people. Over the next few months, we hired five more, for a total of twelve people. I am still amazed to this day that we developed Arcanum with only twelve people. For three years, we worked long days—between ten to fourteen hours per day—and most weekends, usually Saturday and sometimes Sunday, too. This is what you can do when you are young, idealistic, and optimistic.

Ramsay: There were no concerns about crunch, quality of life, and the impact on productivity? How did you reward employees for performance?

Cain: When we hired everyone, we told them we wanted to keep the company small and lean. While we knew there would be long hours, everyone would have opportunities to work in many different areas of the game and have ownership of those areas. That's why the credits for Arcanum simply state our names and not any titles. All of us made Arcanum. We blurred the lines between programmers, artists, and designers—hence the name of our company. One person would create animations and write dialogue, while another would implement combat and design quests. We were kind of like communists, which made our company name even more appropriate.

In that communist vein, we also decided to pay everyone the same salary, so we hired only senior, experienced people. If the game brought in any money, we would split the amount 50/50. Half would go to the company and funding our next game. The other half would be split evenly among us. At the end of the project, that's exactly what we did.

Ramsay: You were working long hours, with undifferentiated roles, hiring only experienced people, and paying employees without concern for merit. That doesn't sound like a sustainable model.

Cain: We couldn't keep working at this pace or with this flat hierarchy. It was difficult to plan a schedule when everyone had an equal say in all matters, and we felt that we needed to structure our team better.

After Arcanum shipped, we rearranged ourselves into a hierarchy with leads, seniors, and staff members. We planned our design work carefully, trying to avoid the crushingly long hours we had endured for the last three years. We started working on a Lord of the Rings game using the Arcanum engine but with a completely different art style. We worked with Sierra and the Tolkien estate, and we created a really fascinating storyline for the player, which paralleled the original fellowship storyline. But Sierra pulled the development into one of their internal teams, which was extremely disappointing. Then out of the blue, we ended up being courted by two different publishers, and both of them had offers to work on licensed games.

We accepted both offers and split into two groups. One group worked on a D&D game for Atari, while another began work on a White Wolf Vampire game for Activision. I was in charge of the first group, while Leonard and Jason headed up the second.

Ramsay: These games were The Temple of Elemental Evil and Vampire: The Masquerade—Bloodlines, right? Were you able to reuse the Arcanum engine?

Cain: Yes, we used a heavily modified Arcanum engine for Temple. We were lucky that we had reserved the rights to the engine in our contract with Sierra, because they retained the rights to the property. The new engine used 3D models for the characters instead of 2D sprites, and the background art contained masks to let the 3D characters pass behind the 2D background images.

Of course, we converted all of the system mechanics to D&D version 3, and then 16 months into the project, we converted the mechanics to 3.5. I am very proud of the game for being completed in 20 months. It may not be my finest work, but it was done quickly and is incredibly feature-rich for such a fast project.

On the other hand, Vampire was done using Valve's Source engine. That's the same engine used for Half-Life 2, Left 4 Dead, and many other games. In fact, we were the first external developer to make a game with Source. We actually finished Vampire before Half-Life 2, but we could not release our game before Valve released their game.

Ramsay: When you were negotiating with Sierra, did you try to obtain the rights to Arcanum? Why did you keep the rights to the technology instead? Would you recommend asking for technology rights to other developers?

Cain: We tried to keep the rights to Arcanum, but Sierra was investing 100% of the capital. They really wouldn't budge on this issue. So, we asked for the rights to keep all technology involved in its development, including all tools and the engine itself. Sierra agreed, which was a delightful surprise.

I advise startups to ask for whatever they want. The worst a publisher can do is say no, and they probably will, if they are providing the majority of the funding. But sometimes they will give you what you want. We were able to make Temple so quickly because we already had an engine ready to use.

Ramsay: Temple had a very short development cycle, and the mechanics were revised during the last stretch. What went right? What suffered? If you had more time, how would the game have been different?

Cain: The original schedule for Temple was 18 months, which was and is un-thinkable for a full-featured role-playing game. I tried to convince Atari that we needed more time. When I failed, I reduced the scope of the project and cut several classes from the design, including the druid and the bard, both of which had many specialized rules for their abilities. Atari asked for those classes to be restored, implying that the game contract depended on it, so I added them back. But very little manpower was available for design. I hoped that by picking a classic module for the base design that I would save many hours of design time, but we could have probably made a better product in that time frame by developing our own game world.

What suffered? Well, we had very little time to write dialogue, or develop quest lines, or balance treasure amounts. Our tight schedule left only two people, Tom Decker and myself, any time to do these tasks. I was also the producer, and Tom was in charge of localization. We had too many chores and not enough time to do them. It certainly didn't help that, in the middle of development, Wizards of the Coast published the D&D 3.5 core rules revi-sions. We had a difficult choice: launch the game with out-of-date mechanics or change those mechanics in the face of an already tight deadline. I asked Atari for more time, specifically for three months. I told them that this was an issue they should have foreseen. Did they not know about the revisions? But they didn't want to budge. Finally, they gave us an extra two months, bringing us up to twenty months.

In that time frame, we did a great job on the combat system, which was a masterful interpretation of the D&D rules married with an intuitive inter-face. Even people who did not play D&D could quickly grasp basic combat, and many of the more advanced combat feats were supported as well. I think it helped us immensely that many of our programming staff were D&D fans, and they already knew the rules very well.

In hindsight, given a longer schedule, we would have made our own IP in-stead of using The Temple of Elemental Evil, and I believe that world would have had the rich characters and storylines that people had come to expect from Troika. And, of course, the game would have shipped with fewer bugs and design issues than it did. But that is starting to sound like the moral of the Troika story: if we only had more time.

Ramsay: Troika also had some trouble with release timing. How did Valve's embargo on Vampire impact the company?

Cain: Well, the embargo caused several problems. First, while the game was held until Half-Life 2 shipped, we were also not allowed to keep the title in development. Activision had us work on the game until a certain point, and then they froze the project. We'd have continued to improve the game, especially by fixing bugs and finishing incomplete areas, but they didn't let that happen. They picked a version as the gold master for duplication, and then they held that version close until the ship date. We fixed some bugs, but they didn't want to pass new builds to quality assurance.

Second, while our game was being held, Valve continued to make improvements to the Source engine—improvements we couldn't add to our game. It was frustrating to play Half-Life 2 and see advancements in physics, modeling, facial animation, and other features that our game did not have.

Finally, the embargo really demoralized the team. They had finished a game that couldn't be shipped, or changed, or talked about. And when Vampire was shipped, the game was compared unfavorably to the only other Source game on the market. Needless to say, we lost some good people during that time. They quit in frustration and went elsewhere.

Ramsay: Even if there was a need for the title to be published before Half-Life 2, Valve made that impossible. Why did Activision freeze the project?

Cain: Just to be clear, I came over to the Vampire team after the first two years of development, and my role was to provide programming leadership and work on areas of the game code that needed immediate help, such as creature artificial intelligence and file-packing issues. So, I never interacted with Activision during development.

With that said, the Vampire game had been under development for three years. While that's not a long time for a role-playing game—Fallout had taken three and half years to develop, and that was a simpler game made almost a decade earlier—Activision had become impatient and wanted the game shipped as soon as possible. They wanted to cut areas of complexity, we wanted to maintain quality, and the game was caught in a lopsided tug-of-war. In the end, Activision "won," and the game was shipped with many bugs, cinematic cutscene issues, and incomplete areas.

Ramsay: Can you give me some examples of these problems?

Cain: Some of the most egregious examples included the game crashing when a Nosferatu player character finished a particular map. This was caused by a bad map value in a script that teleported a Nosferatu to a different map than other player characters because Nosferatu were not allowed to appear in public places. The crash was discovered after the embargo, along with the disheartening fact that no one in quality assurance at Activision had ever tested the Nosferatu character.

We were also working on smoothing out the walking animations of characters during in-game cinematic sequences. The embargo occurred during the middle of this process, which left a great many characters skating or stuttering during those sequences. And the warrens near the end of the game were barely populated with creatures when development was frozen. No balancing or dialogue was added at all.

I don't have to restate how demoralizing these issues were to the team. All of these problems were easily solvable with more time, but that time was not available.

Ramsay: Was there any ill will toward Valve?

Cain: No, we weren't really angry with Valve. They made their deal with Activision, and part of that deal was that any Source-based game had to be shipped after their Half-Life 2. Valve had the luxury of pushing out their ship date repeatedly—and they did—to ensure that their game was great. We were hoping for the same luxury, but Activision didn't grant it.

Now Activision, on the other hand, did get a bit of our ire. When we discovered that we could not ship before Valve, we never imagined that Activision would ship Vampire on the same day as Half-Life 2. For several reasons, a much better idea would have been to ship Vampire a couple of months later. It would have given us time to polish our game with a stable engine. It would have given the consumer something else to buy that used the Source engine after Half-Life 2. And a later release would also not have put us in direct competition for consumer dollars during our important first few weeks on store shelves, because we all knew that consumers were going to choose Half-Life 2 over Vampire. And, really, was the cost of a few more months of development really that much more than the years we had already spent on the game? No, I may not be a businessman, but that seemed like a bad choice on Activision's part.

Ramsay: Sounds like a reasonable solution to me. Did Leonard or Jason make these arguments to Activision?

Cain: Leonard did a lot of the interacting with Activision, and he did suggest this course of action many times. As far as I knew, Activision either ignored the suggestion or complained about how much time Vampire had already taken. They really did not want to put any more money into the game than they absolutely had to, but at the same time, they demanded triple-A quality. It was quite schizophrenic.

Ramsay: In the end, this ordeal brought about the collapse of Troika? What happened after Vampire shipped?

Cain: Leonard, Jason, and I went looking for a new contract even before Vampire shipped, since we were done a few months before. Leonard pursued Fallout 3, which ultimately went to Bethesda, who outbid us. I landed us a contract with the Department of Defense to modify Temple to make it a training ground for military artificial intelligence. The idea of military AI learning in a Dungeons & Dragons world amused me to no end. But that contract only covered three people for about six months. After a few months of searching, we ended up laying off half of the employees, with severance pay, so we could keep the office open.

We actually had the opportunity to get contracts for several different games, but none of them were role-playing games, and none of them were games that I had any interest in playing. Leonard wanted to take them to tide us over, but I didn't want to do that. I figured, why should we have a company if we were not making the games we wanted to make?

I didn't particularly enjoy running a business, and Leonard and Jason didn't either, so we decided to shut down Troika while we were still in the black. We could pay our remaining employees severance and insurance, so they could find other employment, and we kept the office open for a month to make their transitions easier. In fact, we kept Troika going as a business for six months, with me running it from my house, so employees could file for insurance under COBRA, which is easy and fairly automatic. If we had closed, they would have had to apply for HIPPA, which is much more complicated. It was the best we could do.

In the end, Vampire shipped in November 2004. We closed the office in February. And Troika officially ceased to be a company in September 2005.

Ramsay: Looking back, do you think you should have pursued contracts for the games you didn't want to do? In several months to a year, there might have been more attractive opportunities.

Cain: Oh, I think I will always wonder about that, but honestly, I have no regrets. Troika was a wonderful experience while it lasted, but I am not a businessman. I did not want to live a life of pursuing one contract after another, of negotiating with publishers, or of dealing with employees and landlords. I got into this business to make games, and I am getting to do that more as someone else's employee than as a company owner.

Ramsay: Would you say that Troika was your first and last venture?

Cain: I will never say never, but yes, it's very likely that I will never start my own company again. Owning your own company is something that many people dream about, but I've been there and done that. It's just not for me. Now with that said, I wouldn't rule out the possibility of making a game on my own, smaller in scope than my previous games and something designed for a particular platform, like an iPad game. I still have ideas that I'm not sure how to express in a big game, but those would likely be ideas I could pursue in a small one. You never know what the future holds.

Ramsay: What are you doing now? Are you happy?

Cain: I left Carbine Studios in July 2011, and I decided to take some time off. While I did interview at some game companies—mostly at places that approached me when word of my Carbine departure got out—I was not actively looking for work. Instead, I was thinking about all of the different kinds of development work I had done before, and I was trying to decide which work I liked the most and which I didn't like. Given that August 2011 marked the thirtieth anniversary of my first game industry job, I thought it was a good time to stop and take stock of my career.

During lunch with Chris Jones, an old friend and colleague from Interplay and Troika and an owner of Obsidian, he mentioned that I seemed happiest when I was not at a big company in a management role. He said I had seemed the most happy when I was programming Fallout 1, and he thought I should consider that kind of job—one where I could take an active hands-on role in the development of a game, but at a small company.

So, I approached a startup in Seattle and offered my services. After the interview, they offered me a job, but there was one catch: the position would not begin until April 2012. When I mentioned this to Chris, he suggested that I spend the balance of my time doing programming work at Obsidian. I came by the Obsidian offices and liked the people I met and the projects I saw, and I started working there on October 11, 2011.

And who knows what may happen next? If I like Obsidian and they like me, I may stay. Or I may join the startup in Seattle. But one thing is clear to me. Going forward, I am going to pick jobs based on how happy they will make me, and not on how much they pay, how much responsibility I receive, or how much they may advance my career. I have done those things, and I wasn't happier for it. I suppose these are the kind of life lessons that everyone has to learn for themselves at some point. This was my point.

Warren Spector

Founder, Junction Point Studios

*In nearly three decades, **Warren Spector** has created or cocreated several of the greatest franchises ever conceived, including the System Shock, Deus Ex, and Thief series. He has earned himself a well-deserved reputation as one of the video-game industry's most highly regarded game designers.*

Spector founded Junction Point Studios in 2005 and spent the next two years pursuing an opening to develop his own ideas. However, through Spector's relationship with the Creative Artists Agency, he was presented with a chance opportunity to work with Disney's most established icons, including Mickey Mouse, Yen Sid, and Oswald the Lucky Rabbit. As a show of commitment, Spector's company was subsequently sold to Disney.

In 2010, Junction Point released Disney Epic Mickey, a more complex and ink-stained take on the world of Mickey Mouse than seen before. Although polarizing, Disney Epic Mickey was the fastest-selling game in the history of Disney Interactive Studios. Presently, Spector helms the studio under Disney as vice president and creative director.

Ramsay: At Ion Storm, you produced two hit series, Thief and Deus Ex, and I think "hit" is an understatement. Why did you leave?

Spector: Leaving Ion Storm was one of the toughest things I've had to do in my career, but also one of the most necessary. I left for a whole host of reasons. First and foremost, I was feeling out of step with Eidos' mission.

And, remember, Eidos owned Ion Storm at the time. The company was greenlighting concepts I wasn't wild about—stuff like Backyard Wrestling, 25 to Life, Crash and Burn, even to an extent the Hitman games, which I thought, and think, were swell games. They were just challenging for me in terms of their content. I wanted to do stuff like Deus Ex and Thief, which I saw as different... more, I don't know, thoughtful. I guess they were almost art projects in a way. I remember being at E3 in 2003, the year before I left, and looking around the Eidos booth thinking, "One of these things is not like the others." I realized I was the piece of the puzzle that didn't fit.

So, yes, I thought about leaving for awhile before I actually left. I was also itching to do a startup—something I had never really done. I found myself thinking, "I make enough mistakes of my own. I don't need to be dealing with other people's mistakes, too!" And, on top of all that, I had an idea for digitally distributed episodic games that didn't fit into any publisher's plans back then. Ironically, I still haven't been able to try the episodic thing! Anyway, all of that added up to me leaving the studio that I started in 1997. Rationally, I knew it was time, but emotionally, it was hard. I loved the team, the people, man. We had been through hell together and created some great stuff. Leaving them was hard. I can't even put it into words.

Ramsay: How soon after leaving did you set up a new operation? Was there a period where you were thinking about what to do next?

Spector: I had a noncompete to deal with when I left Ion Storm and Eidos, so I couldn't start anything right away. Frankly, I needed a little downtime anyway, so it worked out just fine. I left Eidos in the spring of 2004, but it wasn't until the beginning of 2005 that I could start anything real. Having said that though, I knew exactly what I wanted to do when I left. I spent a ton of my downtime thinking, plotting, and planning.

Honestly, the fact is that I wanted to do something that didn't fit in with what Eidos wanted to do. And that was a big reason for leaving in the first place. I loved my team and hated to leave, but there was something I wanted to do—had to do—that overrode all of that. I can't imagine doing a startup unless you have a high level of clarity about what you hope to accomplish.

Ramsay: You started Ion Storm Austin before. Had you created organizations from scratch previously? Or were you under the impression that the process would be exactly the same?

Spector: I have to admit that I was hopelessly naïve and really did think that having started remote studios for external partners had prepared me for doing a real startup. Man, was I wrong! I had built studios from one person— me—to full development operations. I had been responsible for profit and loss and all. But I never appreciated how much support I had received from existing finance departments and human resource departments and so on. I got an education in a hurry, I can tell you!

The biggest thing that separated my startup experience from my start-a-studio-for-someone-else experience was the knowledge that there was no safety net. There was no bank account out there to draw from, other than my personal one! On top of that, there's a world of difference between wanting to convince someone to let you make a game you want to make and the knowledge that if you don't convince someone to let you do something, then the money spigot's going to dry up, and all the folks counting on you are going to be out of work.

I was stunned at how quickly I went from "we're going to change the world" to "how do we make the next payroll?" I was determined to do a startup without taking money from investors. I wanted to build on development advances alone. Everything became about keeping the doors open and the lights on long enough to do the cool stuff I knew Junction Point was capable of doing. I'm as proud of the fact that Junction Point never missed a payroll as I am of anything I've done. I only had to foot the bills a couple of times!

Ramsay: Before you were worrying about payroll, what was the first thing that you thought you should do to get started?

Spector: In retrospect, I was astonishingly arrogant when I started Junction Point. I had an unshakeable belief that I could get meetings with publishers to convince them to fund my projects and fully fund my startup effort. A track record of something like 20 shipped games opened a fair number of doors, and 20-plus years in the business gave me a pretty solid contacts list!

Ramsay: Were you concerned about funding? How did you intend to raise capital to get the company up and running?

Spector: As far as funding went, I knew I didn't want to go the venture capital route or the angel investment route. I'd seen too many friends and colleagues fail as a result of having to meet the needs of external investors. I hedged my bets by signing with the Creative Artists Agency (CAA). They were into alternate financing schemes, which I found really attractive back in 2005. Even if that didn't pan out—which it didn't—I was committed to doing a startup backed by publisher advances. I figured I could only deal with one boss and I'd need a publisher anyway, so why not get them to be that boss and the studio's sole funding source?

Ramsay: Did you write a business plan, or did you jump directly into pitching to publishers?

Spector: I never did a business plan per se. I just wrote several project pro-posals and went on the road pitching publishers. Surprisingly, things mostly worked out. Junction Point never missed a payroll, never needed external funding other than publisher-paid milestone payments, and I only had to cover the studio's expenses a couple of times.

Ramsay: Why exactly did you avoid venture capital? Some studios have made that work to great effect.

Spector: Plenty of startups and software developers have been venture-funded, certainly. But I've also seen venture-funded developers fail because their funding partners demanded results on too short of a timeline that didn't match development realities or that forced growth at such a rapid pace that company culture and product quality went out the window.

I wanted Junction Point to be about the games, not the money. Also, I was just at a place in my career where I didn't want anyone telling me what to do—arrogant, I know, but there it is. I didn't want a board of directors or money guys or anyone, really, telling me how to run my game-development studio. I figured I could always walk away from a publisher that didn't want what I wanted to deliver, but you can't walk away from the bank!

Ramsay: What were the alternate financing schemes that CAA was advo-cating? Why didn't they work out?

Spector: I don't think I should be the one to talk in any detail about what CAA or anyone else was or is thinking about with regard to game funding. Suffice it to say, it was a more movie-like funding scheme than the game business had seen to that point. I was intrigued by that.

Ramsay: Some entrepreneurs I've talked to had families when they started their first companies. Did you?

Spector: I've been married to the lovely and talented Caroline Spector since 1987. No kids—just us and the pets. I was lucky in that I didn't have to worry about missing my children growing up! And I'm even luckier to have a wife who's the most understanding person on the planet, as well as being a gamer herself. It didn't hurt that she used to work in marketing at a game company! She knew what she was getting into when we got married.

Doing the startup was just more of the same for her and for us. However, to be clear, I did invest some of my own money in Junction Point. There were critical moments when I had to tide us over, but my partners and I always found a way to get back on solid ground, and I was reimbursed for most of what I paid out. That got a little dicey at home, but as I said, my wife's in-credibly understanding and supportive.

Ramsay: Who did you convince to tackle this new venture with you?

Spector: I had a partner, Art Min, when I started Junction Point. He was an ex-Looking Glass guy. We'd worked together on several projects. I was the creative guy, and he was the tech guy. We focused on business, but in very different ways. I tend to want to fail gloriously, while my partner was more cautious. We made a pretty good team. We started by building our senior development staff, people who could do "real" work and manage teams.

Most of the crew came from Ion Storm when their Austin office shut down. There was some convincing to do, but both Art and I had personal and professional connections of long standing with the people we wanted. It didn't hurt that most folks could see the writing on the wall at Ion Storm!

There were no guarantees; that's for sure. In fact, any time I hear anyone in the game business talk about staying at a company, or leaving to go to another one, because of stability or safety, I tell them there's no security to be had in the game business. If that's what you're after, find another line of work. It'll be less interesting, I guarantee that, but you might feel better. You have to be willing to embrace chaos. You have to thrive on it!

Ramsay: Did you have any external advisors who could help you troubleshoot business issues?

Spector: Art and I had a team of agents at CAA working with us, and I've always valued input from Mike Grajeda, my ex-boss at Origin. We consulted with them pretty frequently. And at the end of the day, CAA set up our meetings with Disney and engineered that deal.

But honestly, it's not like I had a mentor or anything. When I started in games, I certainly looked to Richard Garriott and others for guidance and advice. But by the time I started Junction Point, I really wanted to see what I could do on my own or with a congenial partner, so I didn't look for external advisors, really.

Ramsay: Did you find out what you could do on your own? Did you find out what you couldn't?

Spector: I certainly learned a lot in the year between leaving Ion Storm and Eidos in 2004 and starting Junction Point in 2005. I learned even more in the two years when Junction Point was independent. As I said before, I was surprised at how quickly you have to shift from "how do we change the world?" to "how do we make rent and payroll next month?" That took me a bit by surprise. I learned just how much support even non-congenial partners provide, in terms of the administrative and bookkeeping tasks associated with running a business.

I also learned how much I enjoyed living and dying by my own mistakes. I used to joke that I make enough mistakes on my own and don't need any help from outside parties! That turned out to be truer than I expected. Finally, I learned—or more accurately, was reminded—how much I enjoyed being in a pit with a small group of people, passionate about a project. Running a studio as part of a larger organization takes you away from that. It's inevitable. And it was great being back in the pit.

Ramsay: Junction Point was independent for two years until its sale to Disney. What were you doing during in that time?

Spector: Like most independent studios trying to compete in the triple-A space, much of the time was spent conceptualizing ideas and trying to find funding partners for them. We generated several original concepts—some of which we did find deals for and were able to take to prototype, and some of which just died. We worked with a couple of Hollywood directors on concepts, including John Woo. We had a development deal with one publisher to make "Ninja Gold," a game concept we developed in collaboration with John. We did some work for Valve on some Half Life stuff. We developed and got a deal for a huge fantasy game called "Sleeping Giants." And we got a contract with Disney to do the Disney Epic Mickey game, which eventually led to the acquisition and to us walking away from all those other projects and opportunities.

Ramsay: When did Disney Epic Mickey come into the picture?

Spector: In the fall of 2005, I was out looking for a deal. As an independent, you're always out looking for a deal! I had two concepts that I was pitching: the "Sleeping Giants" fantasy game and a science fiction idea that was basically Deus Ex with the serial numbers filed off and fiction more in keeping with the postmillennial era than with the pre-millennial conspiracy-obsessed world.

Back then, I was represented by CAA. My agent at the time, Seamus Blackley, suggested we include Disney in our publisher pitch tour. I told him, "I love Disney, but they're not gonna be interested in M-rated sci-fi and fantasy games." He said, "They're changing and doing some interesting stuff. Talk to them." So, we visited Disney.

I remember vividly walking into a conference room in Glendale and pitching my totally non-Disney-like ideas. I watched as all the senior execs in the room started fiddling with their BlackBerries. I was thinking, "I'm gonna strangle Seamus when we get out of here. What a waste of time." But it turned out that they were texting each other, asking if they should pitch me on their Mickey Mouse game concept! When I got done, they asked if I was interested in any licensed games, to which I replied that I'd kill to make a Scrooge McDuck game. And, at the time, I had a concept kicking around the back of my mind for a monster-of-the-week game based on the ABC show Night Stalker. They said, "What about Mickey Mouse?" I said, "No."

I didn't make games for kids. Disney was pretty solid about Mickey as a character aimed squarely at youngsters. But they went to great pains to assure me they were looking to broaden Mickey's appeal, and asked if they could show me a PowerPoint presentation, prepared by a group of interns in Disney Interactive's Think Tank. What did I have to lose? I said, "Sure." The lights went out, and they showed me their pitch. I was hooked. The idea of Mickey using paint was there. The Blot as a villain was there. The return of Oswald was there. And the idea of a world of forgotten characters was there. The lights came on, and I said, "I'm in." Then came years of turning ideas—great ideas—into a shipping game.

Ramsay: How involved were you with the getting the deal with Disney?

Spector: I'm a bit of a control freak, so I was pretty involved. I tried to be clear with CAA about what I wanted and needed. I let them run with the day-to-day discussions, but when it came time to dot the final i's and cross the final t's, I was in the room with the agents, lawyers, and executives.

Ramsay: In that moment when you signed and Junction Point was officially a Disney studio, what were you thinking?

Spector: I was a kid in a candy shop, mostly. It was kind of an incredible story, actually. We all had decided that we'd announce the deal at E3 in 2007, but in the morning, before the Disney press conference, there were still a couple of deal points unresolved. I remember standing outside the room where the conference was being held, listening to the throng of reporters filling the room. I was looking at Graham Hopper, who ran Disney Interactive, as he held out the contract and a pen. I had one phone held up to one ear talking to CAA, and another phone held up to the other ear talking to my attorney. It was crazy. We had to start the press conference late because we couldn't start until I signed! But sign I did, and like I said, I was a kid in a candy shop.

I will say that I had to wipe some tears out of my eyes as I entered the press conference room because I was walking away from the characters and world of "Ninja Gold." When you put your heart and soul into something, there's always some pain when you walk away from it. And I felt like I was letting John Woo down, which hurt. But I told myself, "How often do you get a chance to work with a character like Mickey Mouse?" I had to let modern-day ninja Kat Sato go. But mostly, I was thrilled. I mean, my mom's only response when I told her I'd signed with Disney was, "It's about time!" What does that tell you?

Ramsay: What did becoming a Disney studio provide you?

Spector: Becoming part of Disney, aside from allowing me check off another box on my to-do list of life, provided a level of stability it would have taken years to achieve had Junction Point remained an independent developer; that is, assuming Junction Point survived long enough to become stable at all! To say the least, having a big company behind you is comforting.

In addition, the number and quality of resumes you get goes way up when your job listings include the word "Disney," especially on the art front! Being part of Disney allowed us access to talent—animators, writers, audio people, and so on—that's second to none. The creative folks at Disney are amazing, and more than willing to share their experience and expertise.

And, finally, there's access to 80 years of creative history. Disney has created some of the most memorable intellectual property on the planet. Being able to tap into that was, and is, incredible. I could walk out into the middle of the street right now and scream, "I created JC Denton!" And no one would have a clue what I was talking about. Tell people you worked on a Mickey Mouse game, and you're going to get a reaction. That's incredibly cool, and it's something only Disney can offer.

Ramsay: Earlier, you said that you "got an education in a hurry" when you started Junction Point. Now that you can depend on the resources that a large enterprise can provide, was that education all for naught?

Spector: I wouldn't say that education was for naught. Learning is learning. And even if I weren't using all that hard-won experience, I suspect it would come in handy someday, probably in a context I can't even imagine. But the fact is that I do use that education all the time. Running a Disney studio involves interactions with strategic planning and finance people all the time, and there's frequent interaction with other lines of business. Slate planning and budget planning are big at Disney, so it all comes in handy.

Ramsay: How successful was Disney Epic Mickey?

Spector: I'd describe Disney Epic Mickey as wildly successful, in most ways that matter. For starters, even though it was released on just one platform, the Nintendo Wii, it's by far the bestselling game I've ever worked on. It generated more revenue than anything I've ever worked on, and it certainly made money for the company. From that perspective, it's all good.

Of greater importance to me, if not to Disney overall, it accomplished most of its creative goals. We wanted to remind the world that Mickey Mouse could be a hero, one who appealed to kids and adults. Look at the demographics of who bought the game, and we clearly got Mickey in front of people who might not have thought of him as being aimed at them before. And when you talk to players, you hear them saying they thought of Mickey differently than they did before. He was edgier, more mischievous, funnier, more surprising, and best of all, a real hero. So, put a tick in that box, too. Awareness of, and affection for, Oswald the Lucky Rabbit was way higher after the game than before it. So, there's a tick mark there.

And, best of all, we really touched people in a way none of my games, at least, had before. I've never received more heartfelt fan mail. Response from fans has been overwhelming.

The one area where I might have wished for more was in the review scores. Our Metacritic score was good, not great, but two things about that. First, we clearly polarized critics, garnering as many perfect scores as we did, well, let's just say "terrible" scores. No one was middle of the road. You either loved us or hated us. That's way better than creating something mediocre! And, second, if you gave me a choice of review scores and awards or true and genuine love from fans—kids and adults, and men and women—I'll take the fans every time.

I look at Disney Epic Mickey and feel nothing but pride. The Junction Point team created something special. That's good enough for me.

Ramsay: With that success, are your early struggles more distant?

Spector: I think I had the arrogance required of anyone doing a startup at a time when their business is, to be kind, going through a transition. In 2005, who knew what the game business was going to look like five or ten years later? We still don't know. To think you could find success in chaos requires a certain amount of arrogance, I'd say. I was also pretty committed to making the games I wanted to make, publishers and players be damned.

I've always said that my only obligation is to make a game that sells one more copy than necessary to get someone to fund my next one. That's pretty arrogant, if you ask me! Am I more cautious now? Hell, no! If anything, I've gotten worse! I'm too old to mince words, to settle for mediocrity, or to make games that aren't personally meaningful to me. If that's arrogance, so be it. What I do know is that caution never led to greatness. And while I might fail—heck, you could argue that I've always failed—I've never started a project I didn't think could be great and never tried for anything less than greatness. Caution be damned!

Ramsay: Have you reached the point where you've thought about succession? Or do you plan to stay with Junction Point forever?

Spector: Who knows what tomorrow will bring? I thought I was going to retire from Origin—get the gold watch, the pension plan [laughs], the whole nine yards. That didn't quite pan out! I certainly have no plans beyond Junction Point. Having said that, I'm at a point in my life—I'm 56 years old—where I spend more time than I used to with the word "legacy" sort of hanging in midair in front of me, like a movie subtitle. What am I leaving behind? I want to do everything I can to make sure my work means something, to make sure that I've made a difference.

And I'm much more mindful of, as you say, "succession." I'm making very conscious efforts to get out of the way of the folks coming up behind me at Junction Point. I can see my studio director, Paul Weaver, taking over from me on the studio side of things. I can see my design director, Chase Jones, taking the creative lead on projects. I'm pushing them to do just that right now, and they're doing great. I'm doing that partly because it's the right thing to do, but also because I long ago made a list of the things I wanted to accomplish in my life, and there are still some things I haven't done. Luckily, I can do most all of them with Disney, so my hope is to finish out my career here. We'll see how it goes.

Ramsay: Do you have a formal system in place to cultivate new leaders?

Spector: As anyone who has worked with me will tell you, I'm not the most process-oriented guy in the world, so anything I do tends to be pretty informal!

Here's how it tends to go: I work with a lot of people. I figure out who's on the same page with me, creatively and in terms of studio culture and so on. I talk to those folks constantly, guide them where I can, give them more and more responsibility, and give them the benefit of my insight while letting them make their own mistakes. It isn't rocket science, and it isn't terribly structured. I've always tried to make room for the next generation of people who want to make the kinds of games I love, and I think I've had some success seeding the medium with like-minded people, as folks like Richard Garriott and Steve Jackson did for me.

What I will say is that I'm much more conscious now—more so in the last year or two than ever before—of the need to plan for the future; to make it a formal thing, and to push people to take my job away from me. I'm still working out the details, but that's critically important. I want Junction Point, and games like Deus Ex and the Ultima games and Disney Epic Mickey, to go on after I'm retired. Heck, someone better make some games I want to play!

Ramsay: What's the studio culture like?

Spector: If you want to know what the culture's like at a studio, don't ask the guy who founded and runs the place; ask the people who work there! But if you want to know what I hope the culture is, or becomes, probably the best thing to do is consult the studio mission statement (Figure 7-1).

The Junction Point Studios Mission Statement

To create great games, we must create a great work environment. For us, a quality workplace is one which is positive, warm, friendly, respectful, healthy, and smart. Specifically, our culture embodies the following ideals:

- We value collaboration among members of the same discipline but also across disciplines.
- We encourage everyone to speak his or her mind without fear of judgment or ridicule.
- We talk openly about any problems we see and work to ensure that problems are addressed quickly and don't linger.
- We recognize that everyone can contribute to the creative process and actively encourage everyone to do so, regardless of title or position on the org chart.
- We hire the most talented, dedicated practitioners of the art of game development, but, as important, we look for people with the potential to grow during their tenure with us and/or who can contribute to our own growth and the enhancement of our development culture.
- We encourage personal and professional growth, helping one another to grow, both personally and professionally. We are all teachers and students.

Figure 7-1. The Junction Point Studios Mission Statement

From a practical standpoint, the utility of the studio's values is in each employee asking, "Am I thinking of team and project first, and putting personal goals second?" It's in hiring the people who seem likely to fit into or enhance our culture, and who buy into our primary and secondary values. It's in finding ways to involve more people, not fewer, in all aspects of development, asking, "If roles were reversed, would I feel a sense of ownership in this situation?" It's in asking, "Now that I've finished my work, is there anything I can do to help that other guy?" It's in asking whether you can help someone do or be better, regardless of the circumstances.

The most important part of studio culture for me is what I describe as "respectful argumentation." Lots of folks I've worked with find the idea of argumentation inherently stressful, even destructive. I don't feel that way at all. I want to get into it with people, to argue with 'em, to test their ideas, and have my own tested. But that might just be me...

Ramsay: How has your role changed? What are your responsibilities?

Spector: Since I got into this business, I've described my job as "doing whatever a team needed me to do to ensure their success." If that meant ordering pizzas, I ordered pizzas. If that meant designing game systems, I designed game systems. If that meant acting as a barrier between team and publisher, I did that. If that meant directing the game, I directed.

My role has varied on all 20-odd games I've worked on, often changing during the course of development. At this point, my primary role is to get concepts started: "Here are the kinds of games we should make," or "Here's a high-level look at a game we're going to make." I do a bit of blank-screen conceptualizing, but more often these days, I'm focusing on the bigger picture—overall slate management; culture issues; and outward-facing communication to Disney, to press, and to the public.

I have a tendency to turn into a critic, with veto power, at some point in preproduction, after I'm confident that the leadership team on a given project "gets" what game we're making. I stay in that role throughout production. Honestly, I've always found the production phase of projects pretty dull, and over the years and right up to today, at Junction Point, I've been lucky enough to be able to surround myself with great implementers—people who live for the thousand and one details that have to be worked out every day.

Then, at the end of a project, I get more actively involved. That end phase, where you're making critical tradeoffs and turning an unpolished but playable game into something really fun, is really interesting to me. I think, as part of Disney, I spend more of my time in outward-communication mode than I used to. It's a big, big company, with lots of stakeholders and lots of moving parts, but the difference in my role today is one of degree, not of kind. I mostly like it, really.

Given my age and where I am in my career, I think it's more important to help bring up the generation of developers coming up behind me than it is to be "The Man" on an individual game. I want to leave behind a cadre of people who make the kinds of games I like to make and play, so I have something to do in my dotage! Do I want to do more than I'm able to do these days? Of course! But I still get to do plenty of fun, creative stuff. It's all good.

Ramsay: Speaking of responsibilities, how much time do you have for yourself when you go home each day?

Spector: The last year of Disney Epic Mickey's development was rough, in terms of my personal life. I mean, game development has always involved long hours and commitment at a level which lots of people find onerous, but I've always loved being immersed in my work. I have a wife—25 years of marriage and counting!—who understands and indulges me when it comes to my hours! But the last year of Mickey was brutal—necessary, but brutal—with long hours at work, and lots and lots of travel. In the last three months of 2010, I was home for ten days. Ten days!

Honestly, as a 56-year-old game developer, the hours started taking a toll on me physically, in a way that I never experienced when I was younger. Luckily, I'm surrounded by people who noticed and who care. Go figure! I have an assistant now who's an absolute lifesaver, and Disney got me an executive coach. One sounds indulgent, and the other sounds crazy and New Age-y, doesn't it? Well, don't knock it till you've tried it.

Having an assistant has been great, and I kick myself for playing the "I'm not important enough to need an assistant" game as long as I did! And coaching started making a difference from the very first session. I'm trying hard to achieve a better balance of work and personal life. I'm delegating more, mentoring more, and focusing on the things only I can do, instead of all the things people want me to do. It's helped. I feel a little guilty though, truth be told! Still, while I'm far from living a balanced life, I can at least see one out there on the horizon, and that's pretty comforting.

Doug and Gary Carlston

Cofounders, Brøderbund Software

Doug Carlston was the cofounder of Brøderbund Software where he was chairman and chief executive officer. Brøderbund published a number of notable products including The Print Shop, the Carmen Sandiego line, and other great game and educational products. Before Brøderbund, Doug earned a law degree at Harvard University, practiced law and built houses in Maine. During Doug's tenure at Brøderbund, it became one of the most influential software development companies and went public in November 1991. Doug left Brøderbund after the 1998 sale to the Learning Company. After Brøderbund, he was chairman of ICplanet for two years, and thereafter was a director or chairman at Public Radio International, and A. H. Belo Corporation and still today, at MoveOn.org Political Action, and Tawala Systems, Inc.

Gary Carlston, also cofounder of Broderbund Software, was raised in Iowa where he left one physical education credit short of a high-school degree to study German in Bavaria. He eventually graduated from Harvard University with a degree in Scandinavian Studies. Gary coached women's basketball in Sweden for four years. He and his brother Doug started Brøderbund Software in the proverbial garage in 1980. Gary, whose initial role was marketing the programs his brother produced, initiated a distribution agreement with the Japanese Starcraft Group that *rapidly drove Brøderbund's success and reputation. Among later responsibilities, he managed the entertainment and education division. He left in 1989 moving to New Zealand with his wife, Nancy. In 1991, he moved to Colorado, restored a ranch, built an ice rink, and adopted four children. Gary moved back to New Zealand in 2007 and started a vineyard. Now he lives in Mill Valley, California and tries to play as much guitar as possible.*

Ramsay: What were you two doing before you started Brøderbund?

Doug: I had been practicing law and building houses in Maine. I learned programming in high school, and programming helped pay for college and law school. When the first personal computers came out, I bought a TRS-80 from RadioShack, and started programming the most boring parts of the legal business and job estimating. Neither set of programs used the full capabilities of even the early personal computers.

I wrote some games to develop my programming skills and for fun. I sold those games through a Florida company called Adventure International, and it wasn't long before the revenue matched my other sources of income. The oil shocks of the 70s had dried up the housing market, and I was bored with practicing law, so I was looking for an alternative.

Gary: I had spent the previous three years trying to get a couple of other businesses started, one with a friend and one with my brother Doug. My brother had moved out to Oregon from Maine to share an apartment with me and had brought his TRS-80 computer with him.

Most of my work experience prior to Brøderbund was as a women's basketball coach in Sweden. My degree was in Scandinavian Languages and Literature. I couldn't imagine why Doug wanted a computer. I had played Pong in college and could not conceive of a more riveting technology.

Ramsay: When did you decide to start a software company?

Doug: When I visited Gary in Oregon, where he was running March of Dimes for the Eugene area. I broached the idea of starting a company.

Gary: I was completely broke when we started Brøderbund. Doug had written a couple of simulations that were being published by a Florida outfit. Doug decided that it might be fun to try to sell his own software and asked me to join him, but I responded that I was in enough debt from two earlier stillborn entrepreneurial efforts. "Well, you can pay your share of the rent," he pointed out, so I agreed to take a stab at it.

Doug: Gary made the first sales call, which was unusually successful.

Gary: I got on the phone while he was out and sold $300 worth of software on my first call to Ray Daly at the Program Store in Washington, D.C. Doug was very pleasantly surprised when he got home. In the next six months, I think we only sold about another $500 worth of product.

Doug: Ray Daly already knew my name from Adventure International and was happy to buy from us. Weeks after we started, we drove down to San Francisco for Jim Warren's old outfit, the West Coast Computer Faire. We didn't sell much, but we found a source of terrific games from a Japanese trading company called Starcraft.

These games were a major factor in our first year's success. In the summer of 1980, Gary came down to San Francisco on a one-way ticket and sold enough software to keep us fed and to even buy a ticket home!

Ramsay: Founding duos typically split responsibilities. Who worked on the technology side? Who worked on the business side?

Doug: I mostly programmed, and Gary mostly did everything else, but he coded one project himself. We shared some jobs like disk duplication and answering the phone. We tried to sell all kinds of things, including tax programs I had written and some early educational products, such as Dueling Digits, and a line of accounting software. But it was the games that sold.

Gary: Doug flatters me when he said I coded one project myself. I "ported" one of his Galactic Saga series games over to the Apple II. The game was written in BASIC, and Applesoft BASIC was pretty similar, so I just asked Doug whenever I didn't understand something. I mostly tried to sell software, get packaging and printing done, and those kinds of jobs.

Ramsay: Doug mentioned that you found a source of games in Japan?

Gary: The story of how we got the rights to the games from Starcraft that first year is a funny one. At the West Coast Computer Faire, we saw how much more technically advanced their game programs were than anything in America. Doug and I decided to write a letter to a Japanese computer magazine, fishing for any games that might have been written over there to try to acquire the rights.

We didn't think too much more about it until one day, while Doug was out east, I received a call from a Japanese man, Minoru Nakazawa. He was at the airport, had seen our letter in the Japanese magazine, and wanted to come see me to talk about US distribution rights. I figured I had about 15 minutes to make our apartment look like a legitimate business before he showed up. We had two computers and nothing else businesslike.

As it happened though, I had read an article while at my dentist's office the day before about doing business in the Middle East. Not the Far East, mind you, but it was the only advice I could think up in the 15 minutes I had before Mr. Nakazawa rang the doorbell. The article had said that Middle Easterners like to do business with people of their own social class, but that in dealing with Americans, because they've discovered that anyone can make money in America, they look to educational status as the primary indicator of class. Well, Lord knows Doug and I had no money anyway, but we did both go to Harvard, and I happened to have a recent issue of Harvard Magazine handy, which I promptly put on the coffee table.

The doorbell rang. Mr. Nakazawa introduced himself and walked in, and then suddenly blurted out, "Ah, Hahvahd!" We talked about world events, literature, and whatnot for more than two days. Then, Mr. Nakazawa told me that he had only visited us as a negotiation tactic to drive up the price when he went to visit a "legitimate company" down in Los Angeles.

However, he had enjoyed talking with us so much that he wasn't going to Los Angeles at all, and we could have the rights to produce as many copies of his games as we could physically copy in the amount of time that he would visit us when he returned. We worked around the clock with the masters of the games he brought over, and they caused a sensation in the computer world around Christmas 1980.

What's amazing about this little trick with Harvard Magazine having worked is that Mr. Nakazawa is probably the only person in all of Japan it would have worked on. He came from a merchant-class family, but his only friend growing up was Emperor Hirohito's second son. He showed us photo albums of his growing up in the 1930s, and there he was in his Little League uniform with Emperor Hirohito and his son by his side. The result of this upbringing is that Mr. Nakazawa seemed to be in a social class all by himself: a commoner, but a friend of the Emperor. Somehow, our Harvard educations gave us enough cachet that he could deign to do business with us. It's the only substantial benefit that I ever got from my Harvard education, so it seems to have been well worth it.

The "everything else" I did became a much bigger job at that point. One of the stunning impacts of our publishing these Japanese games is that every top-notch programmer in America wanted to know how they did it, and most of these programmers then went to work for us.

Ramsay: So, Brøderbund was initially a two-man operation. When did you expand the company and start filling the ranks?

Gary: Once we had the Japanese games, we were really busy. We had our first employee around December 1980, I think. His name was Brian Eheler. Doug may recall the story better than I do, but I think we picked him for the $19 tax credit we got for hiring the chronically unemployed.

We're still friends with Brian. He and another couple came and helped us stuff the plastic bags with the little printed sheets and the 5¼-inch disks or cassettes. There wasn't any professional packaging in the games end of the software business yet. Somewhere in there—maybe a little after Christmas 1980—we tried hiring a bookkeeper, but she didn't know what she was doing, so that lasted about two days.

Doug and I induced our sister, Cathy, to leave her job in Manhattan as the Christmas buyer for the Lord & Taylor stores, and to come out and work with us. I think we had about six people in spring 1981. At some point during this time, the Eugene airport was socked in by fog for two weeks, and we couldn't ship any products, and therefore did not receive any income. We decided that wouldn't work. Besides, the Oregon rain was not popular among the three of us. We packed up our bags and formed a convoy, and headed south with Brian Eheler and Chris Jochumson, who was one of those good American programmers who had joined us earlier.

We got down to San Rafael, plopped ourselves down, and continued working in a house as we had in Oregon. The UPS trucks drew the ire of the neighbors, and we very quickly had to find legitimate office space. We also found a legitimate bookkeeper, just about first thing.

We moved down into San Rafael on what had been the site of a Computer-Land store and just kept growing. After about a year in San Rafael, I think we had about 30 employees, and we were looking to become more professional—not too professional, mind you. About this time, in August 1982, I severely injured my leg playing soccer and missed three months of work. When I returned, it was to put together a product development team. I was done with sales forever! Yeah!

One very funny story came out of this period. We felt that we needed to go beyond a bookkeeper and hire a chief financial officer. So Doug and I went through the process and narrowed it down to two candidates. We went to dinner, decided on one, and gave him a call to hire him that night. The next day, the guy we thought we had not picked showed up. We had mixed up the two! His name is Bill McDonagh, and he eventually became president of Brøderbund. Bill is now a respected venture capitalist today. He loves this story. He's the kind of guy you could tell this sort of thing to.

Ramsay: Were you competing with Atari and Electronic Arts for talent?

Doug: Atari was viewed as a platform, not a competitor. We used a publishing model, offering royalties to authors, and until 1983 or so, our primary competitors were the other Apple II-focused companies: Sierra On-Line and Sirius Software. Some of our programmers published through multiple channels, depending upon who responded first with the best offer.

EA came along in 1983 or so and started out with a similar model. They tried to tie people up with multiple product deals and definitely took some game developers away. However, our interests were much broader than those of EA at the time. We published accounting software, productivity tools, and educational software. Games were only the majority of our sales in 1980, which was our first year.

Initially, we had no programmers on staff. We tried an experiment in 1983 with staff programmers working on original work, with poor results, and people wanted both salaries and royalties. In 1984 or so, we offered them a choice: go out-of-house with a nice royalty deal and advances on projects in which we were interested but no salary, or stay in-house, focus on what we needed done—mostly ports of products from one platform to another or educational projects designed by in-house designers—and get a salary but no royalties. Part of the problem was that projects were getting much larger and the day of the individual developer was rapidly coming to an end. A successful project needs musicians, graphic artists, animators, writers, and managers, as well as engineers. To pay the engineer a royalty and the others only salaries seemed unfair.

Half of the engineers went outside as a group and negotiated royalty deals with us and others. The rest became normal employees, just like everyone else. We spread credit for products widely—some of the credit screens on early computer applications rival the credit screens of major motion pictures!—and peace was restored to the kingdom.

I do think most people feel that Brøderbund was a great place to work. I still get dozens of letters and e-mails every year from former employees, telling me that it was the best work environment they ever experienced. And I think that was mostly due to a very straight, honest culture that took into account normal human needs. People called it family-oriented, and it became that as we all grew up and started to raise our own families. Once when we were considering a merger with EA, a writer quipped that the negotiations were a case of "the Walton family meeting the Mason family"—not quite fair to either company, but there were big cultural differences.

Ramsay: You developed and published other types of software in addition to games. Do you think this capability was a competitive advantage?

Doug: What we were trying to do was emulate a book publisher and fill different niches. We also discovered early on that evergreen products were far more profitable than consumables. The early thinking was that all games were consumables; they could sell well for a short period of time, but would then disappear. It wasn't until years later that EA came up with the concept of evergreen games—sports games that updated data and code on a regular basis but kept their fan bases.

Our most profitable products were mostly nongames, if you include Carmen Sandiego as an educational product rather than as a game. By far, the most profitable was Print Shop. Carmen was probably second, followed by Family Tree Maker, 3D Home Architect, Bank Street Writer, Living Books, and Kid Pix, which all made the top ten and all had well over $10 million in revenues. So, it wasn't just knowledge that we gained from publishing nongame products. Of course, Myst was up there, and other games, too.

Ramsay: In 1984, you had a good number of employees, and then staff and contract programmers. What was the next step?

Gary: My recollection is that we were operating in a hybrid mode with internal programmers and an acquisitions program looking for "raw" products developed by individuals or groups outside the company. We also allowed our staff programmers to develop products on their own time, outside the company, and earn royalties. Print Shop was one such product.

I left the company for nearly two years in this time frame. I was kind of pushed out by the venture capitalists because I wanted to be in a creative position rather than a managerial role. I was brought back after this hiatus because the company was stalled on finding new products. And Carmen Sandiego, which had been my idea, had become a big hit.

There was strategic tension within the company on whether our model should be to create proprietary product lines and extend them or whether to accept the notion that these products would die out and would need to be replaced. I was a proponent of the proprietary products approach.

Doug: Our model was still primarily focused on public products submitted by outside authors, but we had started to build some internal capability, too. It was hard to get what we wanted to be able to publish just by waiting for good submissions, although that is where the bulk of our products came from. The first big products that didn't fit the book-publishing model— products that had big internal components that didn't just involve converting a product to another machine or adding music or graphics—were Carmen Sandiego and, to some extent, Print Shop. Both were published in 1985. We had given ideas to outsiders before, such as Dueling Digits, but they were still straight royalty arrangements.

Carmen was designed internally, largely from an idea Gary came up with, although Gene Portwood and Lauren Elliot, both on staff, augmented the idea. It was then coded by a staff programmer, Dane Bigham, who received royalties, as was our tradition. As it became increasingly apparent that products involved a lot more than just programming, this caused a big fuss.

In this case, the programmer had not been responsible for the idea, data, music, or graphics. This eventually led us to decide to not offer royalties to staff, but instead to include them in other company-wide benefits, like stock options. About half of the staff programmers left when we made that decision, but most of them contracted with us, as well as with others, as outside programmers on royalties.

Print Shop was different. It was the brainchild of two guys: David Balsam and Marty Kahn. Marty had come aboard as an employee, but specifically exempted Print Shop, then called Perfect Occasion, as a prior project that he had been working on before he came to Brøderbund. We accepted it as a royalty deal, and changed it from a screen-output product to a printed-output product. That was no mean feat at that time, as every printer had a totally separate printer driver that had to be written for it before it could handle any graphics. We eventually wrote over 100 different drivers.

We then OEM'd it all over the place with printer companies, trying to get people to buy personal printers, which was just beginning to be the case. Marty eventually went off payroll and worked full time outside with David on new versions until around 1989, when they went in different directions. We took over the coding of new products under the Print Shop name.

Internal design and publication remained relatively rare, however. What became common was the internal design and extension of product families. So, in addition to many extensions for Print Shop—such as Print Shop Companion, Graphics Libraries, Photo Organizer, and Page Layout—and then Carmen—such as Where in the USA, Where in Time, and Where in North Dakota—we also took published products that were sourced externally like Kid Pix and did the same thing—such as Kid Pix Companion.

So, the internal staff mostly converted products for use on new computers and did extensions. The first wholly internal line was Living Books, which was the brainchild of a graphic artist at Brøderbund named Mark Schlichting. He came to us in 1989 or so with a one-page proposal to make interactive, animated versions of popular children's books, and that eventually became a $30 million business all in itself.

However, virtually every other major hit we produced came from external sources and was published under a royalty agreement. The only exception I can think of is Family Tree Maker, which we bought along with the company that produced it in the early 90s. Three D Home Architect, Myst, Dazzle-Draw, Lode Runner, Treehouse, Ancient Art of War, Bank Street Writer, On Balance, BannerMania, and Zoombinis were all externally created products that were published under royalty agreements. The model stayed the same throughout the 18 years of the company's existence.

Ramsay: Brøderbund seems to have hemorrhaged employees at several points along the way as a result of salary-royalty decisions. How much trouble did these periods of contraction cause you?

Doug: I think only 4 or 5 programmers out of a total staff of 180 left in 1986 over the decision to not pay royalties. They formed an outside group called Presage, set up offices in San Rafael, and secured several contracts from us. They also got work from others.

To the best of my recollection, the only programmers who moved out were Dane Bigham, Scott Schram, Steve Ohmert, Mike Wise, and I think one other. Not much of a hemorrhage. Two of our designers left a year later, Portwood and Elliott, over similar issues. They wanted to be compensated directly for the success of the products they worked on.

I should note that virtually everyone in the industry eventually abandoned the royalty system of payment for internally produced products. The products just involved too many people in too many different areas, and it was a crazy way to try to pay people. Instead, we gave everyone in the company options in company shares, which eventually proved far more valuable than the royalty shares would have been.

The only other time we lost people in any number prior to the layoffs of the late 90s was in 1989, when our salaries began to be perceived as well-below market. We hired a human-resources consultant, Mel Croner, to compare our salaries to the marketplace, fixed a few categories, and changed the perception inside the company. Even then, I don't think it was more than a half-dozen people over a period of months. I do remember being upset about it because we lost a couple of good, young product managers that I really wanted to hold onto.

Ramsay: When Gary was pushed out by the investors, what were you two thinking as cofounders and brothers?

Gary: I don't think you should make too much of the conflict between myself and outside investors or Doug. The conflict between laid-back company founders and corporate financial types is pretty universal. As far as brotherly disputes go, any two partners would have clashed frequently in such a fast-changing industry. I recall some competitors in 1982 saying that we wouldn't survive as a company because of the brotherly disputes between Doug and me, but in reality, they had it exactly backward. It was because we were family and wanted to not disappoint our parents and the rest of the family that we were able to get through it as long as we did.

The investors had their own interests at heart, and moving me along in 1984 increased their share of the company. I had also expressed to Doug that it wasn't much fun anymore, so it probably didn't look to him like there would be any reason to intervene. As the character of the industry changed from "family"-run companies to professionally run ones, a lot of founders were probably considering when would be the best time to bail out.

It was nice to be able to come back a year or two later and feel appreciated, but it's not an event on the same level as the return of Steve Jobs. When I eventually left for good in 1989, the same year as our sister Cathy, I imagine that Doug may have even felt envious. As a result of my experience, I would never take venture capital again. But I don't think that's a unique point of view. Besides, I'm through starting companies.

As far as the debate about what the assets of the company were—proprietary products, developers, distribution channels? Have these issues really changed for anybody? Nobody knows how to weigh that stuff properly. Look at how Apple has turned conventional thinking on its head by controlling markets without owning the content. "Content is king" was a given a few years ago, so a lot of people had it wrong.

Ramsay: Also in 1984, you bought Synapse Software and tried to sell electronic novels?

Gary: We were friends with the owners of Synapse, Ihor Wolosenko and Ken Grant. It was an effort on our part to get into the adventure game and Atari markets. It didn't work out especially well, as Synapse adventure games had become dated in the marketplace, and no new innovations were forthcoming. The Atari market, obviously, didn't have legs.

Doug: We bought a number of companies over the years, usually for their product lines. In the case of Synapse, it was to give us products in the Commodore and Atari worlds, where we had no representation. All the companies tended to know one another, and we all frequently talked about joining forces. In the end, we took over Synapse but paid nothing for it, as it had a negative book value. I don't think their products did very well. Some acquisitions, like the one that brought us Family Tree Maker, did very well. Others, like PC Globe and TMaker, were more modest successes.

Ramsay: What were the events that led to the company's going public in 1991?

Gary: I had already left Brøderbund by that time, so I was not involved in this decision. The company had venture capital. There had to be some mechanism for them to achieve liquidity.

Doug: We went public in order to allow our VCs to sell their shares. Most venture capital funds have ten-year duration, and we had taken money in 1983. It was time. The company was flush with cash, so we raised no money for the company, but instead we permitted any shareholders who wished to sell their shares. Our VCs—Burr, Egan, Deleage & Co. and Arthur Trueger and his company—both sold, as did Jostens, Inc., which had bought a small portion of the company in 1987 when they were trying to get into the software business.

Ramsay: The company was eventually sold to The Learning Company for a staggering $420 million in stock. Doug, you left the company in 1998. Was selling the company a good move?

Doug: The company sold in 1998 due to a variety of factors. A number of senior managers had retired. The Internet was causing a collapse in sales in the packaged software consumer business—except for video games, an area we were not in—and our stock value had declined in two years from $2 billion to about $400 million. This was dangerous because we had over $200 million in the bank, and there was a danger that someone could buy the company with its own money! In the end, most of the shareholders were convinced that the offer from SoftKey, which was also known as The Learning Company, was as good as we were going to be able to get, and that the shares might continue to lose value if we held on. My departure was forced by the new owners.

Ramsay: What happened to the company after you had three of your shareholders exit?

Doug: The company kept growing through the 1990s, which is why the market cap kept going up, until suddenly it didn't. We had two years of losses in 1996 and 1997, although we still had over $200 million in the bank, so we weren't in any danger. Rather, we were facing competition that pulled stunts like selling their Print Shop competitor, Print Master, for $29.95 with a $30 rebate, mostly just to drive our stock price down. It was part of SoftKey's rollup strategy. It was so successful that the stock dived until our market value was only about twice our cash on hand. In other words, you could buy half the company with its own cash if you took it over. This was a very dangerous situation, and one that ultimately led to the successful take-over and destruction of the company.

Ramsay: Did you have any idea why the new owners wanted you out? What was leaving Brøderbund like for you?

Doug: Sure. They intended to lay most of the people off to make their company look very profitable, then flip it to an ignorant purchaser who didn't do their homework. They found such a purchaser in Mattel, and the strategy worked. Mattel paid $3.4 billion for the whole mess. Mattel bled money for a year, and then sold the whole operation—Brøderbund and all the other companies that made up SoftKey, which was later renamed The Learning Company—for a dollar. I was sorry to be pushed out of the company, but I was happy to be gone during its final dismantlement and destruction. These guys destroyed 1,500 jobs.

Ramsay: Doug and Gary, what did you do after your respective departures from Brøderbund? What are you doing now?

Gary: I went to live in New Zealand to write a novel. I then moved to Colorado, restored a ranch, and adopted four children. Then I moved back to New Zealand and started a vineyard. I now live in California and play guitar. On into the sunset ...

Doug: I started a few Internet companies. I now run one called SportsDashboards. I also sit on 11 nonprofit boards: Ploughshares Fund, MoveOn.org, Dominican University, Internews, Albanian American Enterprise Fund, The Long Now Foundation, Sweetwater Spectrum, Salzburg Seminar, NOVA, Carlston Family Foundation, and the Albanian American Development Foundation.

Don Daglow

Founder, Stormfront Studios

*Although **Don Daglow** founded Stormfront Studios, as Beyond Software, in 1988, he had already established himself as a pioneer.*

Daglow has a number of firsts to his credit, including the first computer baseball game, the first computer role-playing game, the first commercial sim game, the first game to use multiple camera angles, and the first graphical massively multiplayer online game. In addition, he is the only executive who has led development teams on every console generation.

Stormfront Studios was created in pursuit of an opportunity. There were few, if any, developers at the time who understood the black art of publishing. Having worked as an executive publisher at Brøderbund Software under Gary Carlston and as a producer in the early days of Electronic Arts, Daglow was perfectly suited to build a company with such expertise.

The company operated for 20 years, selling more than 14 million units and producing more than $500 million in revenue, until its closure in 2008, when a lucrative contract was lost to the volatility of the video-game industry.

Ramsay: What were you doing before starting up Stormfront?

Daglow: I was working at Brøderbund Software as executive publisher for the entertainment and education division. Brøderbund was a family business. It was started by Doug and Gary Carlston and their sister, Cathy. Doug ran the productivity side of the operation and was the chief executive for the company overall. Print Shop would probably be the best-known title that came off of that side. Gary ran the entertainment and education division as a senior executive.

Executive publishers ran the day-to-day operations, working for each of the Carlston brothers. I was running the group that published entertainment products and education products, such as the Carmen Sandiego line. We were doing the distribution for SimCity, which was published by Maxis. I was in charge of acquisitions, project management, and both external and internal development for the products.

Ramsay: So, why did you decide to go from there to starting up Stormfront?

Daglow: I felt like there was an opportunity. One of the things that we used to talk about with others was those who end up entrepreneuring eventually get itchy and want to do something on their own. How do you describe that emotion? It's difficult to describe, but if you feel it, you recognize it. At that time, I felt there was a vacuum.

When those of us who were doing acquisitions for the major publishers compared notes, we'd always talk about what we really needed. We needed more developers who understood what it's like to publish games. We talked about that a lot, and at some point, I thought, "You know what? To have a developer like that, it would have to be founded by somebody who had publishing experience." Now, of course, what you don't think about at that moment is the fact that there's a lot of development experience you need to have, too. When you're an indie developer, it's a very different experience from being a publisher, but that's the perspective you gain later. I thought I could found such a group, and I could fill that gap.

Ramsay: Why is having that understanding important?

Daglow: Well, I wanted to create a development studio that understood what it was like for publishers—the realities of publishing games. Publishing games is a much tougher business than a lot of people realize, and although it has changed dramatically in 25 years, the fact is that it's still a very tough business. That understanding wasn't just a matter of recognizing where the developer and the publisher had shared interests, but rather, it was about being able to reflect that understanding in day-to-day interactions with publishers.

Ramsay: Specifically, what should developers have understood about publishing video games?

Daglow: I'm thinking back over 25 years now. If you have worked at a certain job, you have a deep understanding of where money gets wasted in that kind of business, where opportunities are to save time, and where opportunities are to save money. You have that unique perspective because you've done the work. If you and I worked in automobile repair and race-car tuning, you and I could talk at a level about car racing that others simply could not. Someone who was the best repairman at the local Toyota understands a great deal about car repair, but he might not get what we talked about. He wouldn't necessarily be able to take part in our conversation the same way.

I think when people share that specialized knowledge and experience, they can finish each other's sentences. I think it's that sense of affinity that people react and warm to. With 20/20 hindsight, I think that's what I was in search of providing when I founded Stormfront. For the first ten years of the organization, I think there were real benefits to just understanding how stuff works.

Ramsay: Can you give me a few examples?

Daglow: On the practical level, it was a matter of knowing how the sales process worked inside a publisher. Every publisher does it a little differently, but every publisher has a process by which a producer takes a game through the firing line to get it approved for funding and published. At every publisher, what those things then and now had in common is a financial calculation: "Can we make money off this thing?" And there is an "Is this fun to play?" evaluation. It has to pass both tests. You could argue that in some ways there's a third test, which is "Can we market this to people? Do we have a way to get them interested? Do we know how to sell it?"

Once in a while, you'll see a game that's really fun, and you think you can make money off it, but you have no idea how to sell it because it's impossible to explain. You can give it an hour. It's a fabulously fun game. But, of course, standing in a store, you don't have a chance to have potential customers play for an hour. In theory, reviews and editorial and the press should solve that problem, but it doesn't always work that way. If you break it down, certainly, there's a financial evaluation, there's a fun evaluation, and to some degree, there's a separate "can we communicate this and market it" evaluation. Everybody does it a little differently, but at the end of the day, the publishers who succeeded were remarkably similar in that they did those kinds of evals, and then they simply added their instincts.

A great example is Brøderbund. The guys at Cyan had done a game called The Manhole on the Macintosh back when Mac games were a very small business. Doug Carlston liked The Manhole and thought that product showed talent. He said, "We should go talk to those guys and see about doing another game from them because those guys show talent." Of course, that turned out to be Myst, one of the biggest hits of the 1980s and 1990s.

There were only four or five people in the room when Doug said that. I remember thinking at the time, "The Macintosh is such a small market, and it's hard to make much money there." So, it stuck in my head. When it turned out to be such a spectacular success later, I was kind of like tip-of-the-cap to Doug. He recognized that talent.

So, thought number one is that publishing is a combination of a formal evaluation of money and play value, and marketing combined with just pure human intuition. Doug's intuition about Cyan is a great example of that intuition, and it's a great story because they were in such a small pond, were such a small player, and it turned out to be so big. In any era at any publisher, for a developer to have been part of those sales pitches in-house, and to understand the arguments and the debates that happen, where a producer is likely to be shut down, and what a producer needs to be able to present to the management of a company in order to get a yes are extremely important.

Well, when the producer does that presentation, they're already sold. They're selling for you as a developer. If you're a developer and you understand what the producer's going to have to do, you may not know exactly what the debate is going to be, but you know the kinds of questions and challenges marketing can put forward and the other kinds of challenges and questions that finance tends to put forward—even operations. You know what makes the sales force tick. There are certain things the sales force looks for in a game in order to give it a good projection—a good estimate for sales. Understanding all those things is invaluable to a developer because you become your publisher's partner, your producer's partner. Your producer is pitching on your behalf, but you're the one providing him or her with most of what they pitch. If you're doing that, understanding the process they're going to go through really helps.

Ramsay: Did you have any prior experience with startups?

Daglow: I worked for Electronic Arts very early in their history. I had been involved with starting up a division at Mattel, developing the Intellivision. On day one of that organization, there were five of us at the start, so that was kind of a guarded in-house introduction to startups. EA was very much still a startup when I got there in 1983. There were three producers doing product, and I was one of their three. Brøderbund was a little more mature, but nonetheless, they still had the startup mentality. I had been in the startup culture in Silicon Valley for several years, and I had a chance to adjust to that.

Ramsay: What were your expectations? Did you think that starting up a new company would be similar to starting a division?

Daglow: No, I knew we had had layers of safety nets and layers of bureaucracy. Safety nets and bureaucracy tend to mirror each other. The more safety nets you want, the more bureaucracy and oversight you're going to get. The less safety nets you're willing to go with, you give yourself the potential, although not the guarantee, for less bureaucracy and oversight. So, I understood that part very well.

I had pictured, however, starting a team that would stay under ten people, because independent developers of that era were not very big. I was used to teams like Interplay, where they had three to five people early in their history. Likewise, I worked with Maxis at the very start of the company with just a handful of people. So, I was picturing a much smaller scale than we ended up having.

Ramsay: You've referred to "startup culture." In your view, what is startup culture?

Daglow: Oh, boy. Let me try to take a shot at a less than one-hour answer. You can do an entire presentation on just that.

First, the startup is more likely to use project management techniques like agile. They usually have tighter deadlines, shorter development cycles, and fewer sign-offs. In a startup, there's a sense that everything is moving faster. When people move to startup environments—at least ones which are prospering—they normally say, "God, everything around here is double speed; everything is moving so fast." Sometimes it's very disorienting, but decisions tend to be made fast.

In a large corporation, you could need 25 signatures to get a game package approved. I've seen startups where you might need only two formal sign-offs, and it would be smart to also get two informal approvals to maintain relationships and make everybody feel like they're in the loop. So, here's the difference between getting 2 sign-offs and getting 25 sign-offs: There's a sheet put in a big envelope, and the envelope makes the rounds at 25 different stops. On average, it might stop for two or three days at every stop. That's two months to get a sign-off. In a startup, you might get one in a day or two. In a startup, fewer and smaller meetings are more likely to involve discussions and brainstorming instead of status and review.

Another aspect of startup culture is the dress. In a traditional, larger company back then, you were required to wear a coat and tie; it was not a choice. If you were not a manager, you could dress more casually, but once you became a manager, you had to wear a tie. When I was at Brøderbund, the traditional dress was still a coat and tie. At a startup, business casual was a t-shirt or open collar. That's changed in the intervening years, but it was a dramatic difference back then.

Tom Peters, who wrote the In Search of Excellence books that were big in the 1980s, had a great way of putting it. I'm paraphrasing. Traditional companies would go "ready, aim, aim, refine aim, refine aim, refine aim, and fire." Startups would go "ready, fire, refine aim, fire, refine aim, fire, fire, refine aim, fire, fire, fire, fire, fire, refine aim." I thought that was exactly what it felt like. Instead of spending a long time letting the executives jockey for position and figure out who could control this, how they were going to control it, whose turf it was on, and how everybody's butt was going to be covered, the idea was to get something to market. That has now become a science in the new business culture—that whole idea of how you get sent out in a hurry, sell fast, and then learn from your failures. There are books on that now. There are classes just on that one concept. In the early days in Silicon Valley, that was definitely part of the culture. You didn't have long; you had to get going with whatever you had to do. You couldn't take time to make decisions and worry about turf because, if you took any time at all, you'd be dead without ever even getting a shot off.

Ramsay: Do you think the agility of a startup is the result of having not only one layer of management, but also a lot of risk?

Daglow: I think flat organizations definitely come out of that startup culture. Flat organizational design definitely grew in the 1980s Silicon Valley, where so many of these things seem to have been pioneered. Flat organizational design was very, very much part of that culture. People were consciously trying to avoid creating big departments that could control things and slow everything down.

If you were in a venture-backed company, and you didn't have a lot of money coming in, the clock was ticking. It's like one of those movies where the hero has been poisoned in the first five minutes, and they have to find the antidote before the end of the movie. There's a sense of urgency. Well, a lot of venture-backed companies have that same sense of urgency, especially when you add in competition. Anybody who is doing business in a traditional way gets outmaneuvered.

Ramsay: What did you want to accomplish with Stormfront?

Daglow: This will sound naïvely simple, but what I wanted to do was build great games, make money, potentially create a big hit, and make quite a bit of money.

Ramsay: Did you put together a plan to pursue those goals?

Daglow: I was in the process of doing that when I did the first pitch for our baseball game. I actually succeeded in selling it right at the start, so the business plan changed from being a sales-oriented business plan to more of a project management sort of business plan—who's going to do what, when, how, and how that all will work.

Ramsay: What risks did you take?

Daglow: I knew that what I was basically trying to do, like all developers, was to get paid on advances against royalties. Make sure you live off those advances. Don't overspend. Don't get out in front of what those advances cover because you can't get in too deep of a hole. The worst thing that happens is if it doesn't work out, you have to go get a job. I expected that we needed to stay within our means, build the game, ship it, and see if it could do well enough that we could get to build another game. That's one of the oversimplified paths I've talked about with other developers: building a game gets you the chance to build the next one. You hope that by doing a good job with building up an organization, you'll have some reserves and a real company.

Ramsay: How much did you invest into starting Stormfront?

Daglow: I started out with $14,000.

Ramsay: Was all that your money?

Daglow: Yeah.

Ramsay: Where was your first office?

Daglow: We changed buildings and neighborhoods, but we were always in San Rafael, California.

Ramsay: Why were you there?

Daglow: It's my hometown. It's an area that's a hotbed of game development, so when your hometown is a hotbed of game development, it's very convenient.

Ramsay: Did you have a family?

Daglow: Yeah, when I started Stormfront, our sons were five and just turning nine. My wife and I had been married at that point for 12 years.

Ramsay: How old were you?

Daglow: Let's see. Let me do the math. It was 1988. I was 36.

Ramsay: There have been a few founders in that age bracket.

Daglow: Maybe there's something about those mid-30s.

Ramsay: Most entrepreneurs I've talked to were in their mid-20s.

Daglow: Yeah, my problem was, when I was in my mid-20s, the game business hadn't been invented yet.

Ramsay: Was $14,000 a significant amount for you to invest?

Daglow: Oh, yeah, that was a lot of money for us. We were not in the position where we were independently wealthy, so $14,000 was "OK, let's hope we don't lose this, but we're going to take the chance. We'll bet on ourselves."

Ramsay: You had a lot of support at home?

Daglow: Absolutely. Throughout my entire career, I've been fortunate to have a wife who has always been extremely supportive of my trying things, and going out and doing new games. I've had exceptional support at home. It would be very, very difficult to do something like this if your partner did not support you emotionally, let alone financially. The financial approval and support are very important parts, but I think the emotional support, the cheerleading, and your partner believing in you are ten times as important as the money.

Ramsay: Did taking these risks economically impact your family?

Daglow: Oh, yeah, during the first three years of Stormfront, we battened down the hatches. We had been spending money right and left to start with, but we reduced our spending pretty dramatically. It was a time when we saved every penny and we watched every penny.

Ramsay: You didn't have to take on a second mortgage, relocate, or anything like that? You were just very conservative?

Daglow: We didn't, but your credit-card debt builds up during those times. I can't give you a detailed analysis, but it's my memory that we were carrying a lot more credit-card debt afterward.

Ramsay: Were you the sole founder?

Daglow: On day one, I was the one who organized the company and held founder's stock. There were a handful of other guys, who also had options, who came in very, very early. So, there are different definitions of "founder." In terms of them being there right at the start, they should be considered founders.

Ramsay: Who were they? Who were those few?

Daglow: The guys who were there at the start were David Bunnett, our art director; Mark Buchignani, who was a programmer; and then he came a little later, but Hudson Piehl, who was another programmer. And Katie Jack came on very early and was all things administrative.

Ramsay: Did you have to convince anyone else to join you on this venture?

Daglow: I think for anybody who comes and works for a startup, there's an amount of faith that's involved. There were a handful of team members who started out early on at the company, and although I was the one who had put up the money, and they were employed and getting paid, there's still an act of faith there.

So, we sat and talked about it. I remember those discussions were more like, "Are we crazy if we do this?" I didn't feel like we were in sales mode. I was talking out loud about whether it was worth doing or a good idea to do, and the conversation ran along those same lines. In a venture setting, you're like, "Hey, we just got funded. Here are all the reasons we're going to be great. Come work for me." Instead, you're setting out on your own with next to no money. You know, allowing for inflation, we invested over $30,000 today. If you're just a regular family, that's a lot of money. But if somebody gives up other sources of employment or potential jobs to do this, and it peters out, that could be damaging to their careers, too. So, everybody had a stake in this.

Ramsay: Were you ever quietly worried that you wouldn't succeed?

Daglow: Oh, hell yeah. Unless somebody is a trust-fund baby or has been handed something in their lap, I don't see how you can't have that thought in the back of your mind. If you don't have the thought, you're not living in the real world. Denial might be an effective management technique, but I prefer to recognize the risk. In fact, I like the idea of listing risks, ameliorating them, and directly addressing them, rather than sticking your head in the sand.

Ramsay: Were those risks explicitly identified in those discussions?

Daglow: No, in fact, I became aware of that style of management when it became more formalized in the 1990s. In 1988, we certainly had that approach, but it wasn't a formal management style. It was simply an awareness of, and being focused on how to overcome, your risks. If you're a caveman and there are sabre-toothed tigers in the neighborhood, you're going to spend some time thinking about how to avoid the sabre-toothed tigers.

Ramsay: How important was mentoring?

Daglow: We worked very actively to try to encourage that, and to try to have a lot of different kinds of cross-training. We tried to encourage mentorships. When I look back, I think we did a lot of it, but I think we could have done even more.

Ramsay: When did you start cultivating new leadership?

Daglow: I started trying to do that right from the beginning of the company.

Ramsay: When some founders get started, they either go out and immediately get people to manage operations for them or they find people to advise them and help them along. What did you do?

Daglow: I had a board of directors at the start because we were set up as a corporation. I had experienced people with financial backgrounds because I've obviously done a lot of product development. I'm not formally trained in marketing, but I had worked with really good marketers. So, I had the chance to have wisdom rub off from some very smart people. I worked inside the industry, so I understood the game business. But I didn't have a background in finance. I tried to load up on advisors with financial expertise.

For day-to-day administration, I mentioned Katie Jack. She's just really highly intelligent. She ran the day-to-day business side, and that allowed me to focus on the product pieces. She was running the operations of the company. In terms of actual finance, we had outside accountants, but Katie did a fabulous job with the day-to-day operations of the company and just keeping the trains running.

Ramsay: What was your role in the beginning?

Daglow: I was, in effect, what we now call creative director. I was also the chief executive officer, and in that role, I led the company overall. And this wasn't a large company in that first year. I think we peaked at eight people. But I was running the company. The biggest thing I was doing was acting as design director on the game that turned out to be Tony La Russa's Ultimate Baseball.

Ramsay: How did that project come about?

Daglow: I had done baseball games before, so that was an area of expertise and passion for me. I designed World Series Baseball for the Intellivision, and hired Eddie Dombrower in 1982 to work on it. I was also lead designer on Earl Weaver Baseball at Electronic Arts, and there, too, I worked with Eddie.

I don't know if you've ever met Eddie, but he has also had a very long and successful career in the game industry. Eddie has a really unique background in the very early days of computers. He was an innovator in how you displayed animated figures. World Series Baseball was the first game that used camera angles to display the action. I always try to make sure I mention Eddie because that partnership was one of those one-plus-one-equals-five relationships. We were able to take ideas and the design, and make them a reality. We were especially able to make the graphic presentation work so well.

When I went to do Tony La Russa Baseball, Eddie was already committed on other projects, so we built it ourselves. I did the simulation, staff design, and the overall look of the game, in the same way that Eddie and I did for World Series Baseball.

Ramsay: How much thought did you put into whether that title would be your best bet for moving the company forward?

Daglow: There had not been a major new baseball game for a couple of years, so it felt like there was an opening in the market. It was also the thing I was the most passionate about doing. I probably would have done it anyway, even if there wasn't such a good market opportunity.

Ramsay: How important is it for a founding chief executive to be passionate about each of the company's products?

Daglow: I've seen a variety of very successful chief executives. I think the answer depends on which one you're dealing with. If you're a chief executive in the game business and you were trained as an engineer, you've got to be passionate about the technology that enables great new games. If you were a game designer, you better be passionate about the kind of game you're creating.

The other kind of chief executive, I think, is the professional manager. I have seen outstanding managers who are passionate about building really effective organizations, and who are passionate about building teams and businesses where people want to come to work in the morning instead of going, "Ah, I have to get to work."

I think either of those ways works if you have a professional manager as the chief executive who is passionate about building teams and companies, and generating revenue in a sustainable way with a team that's highly motivated. You just need other people on the team who are really passionate about the product or service.

Ramsay: Which way worked for you?

Daglow: I think it has been the product passion, but for lack of a better term, I'm a social person. I like team building. I like being around teams. I like being part of teams, so I have that passion, too. I would like to think that the people I work with know I enjoy working with them. A combination of the two has been very effective for me, but I go back to thinking about the passion with the product first.

Ramsay: There are a lot of small developers who, when they start out, think they're focusing on putting out that one game. They're not thinking about several titles later. They're not thinking about the company. Were you thinking about building just one game or an entire catalog?

Daglow: We actually ended up working on several titles because, at that time, I think if you were a developer and you were only working on one thing, it was very hard to cover the cost of the infrastructure. So, a little later, we got assignments from publishers on other titles.

With Strategic Simulations, which had the gold-boxed Dungeons & Dragons games that were tremendous hits, they had to stop development on the Gold Box games when they needed to implement a new engine. They had to take all the programmers in-house and start them working on a new engine, which became the Dark Sun Engine. They gave us the Gold Box Engine and the Forgotten Realms location, and said, "Well, we're going to miss a year on a new Gold Box game, and we don't know that we'll actually continue the series. Let's have you start a new series of Gold Box games. Let's have you do another Gold Box game to fill that gap while our programmers are working on Dark Sun." So, that's how we got our second major title. That's also when I chose Neverwinter as the location for that game.

Right after I founded the company, I had been working with Quantum Computer Services, which later became AOL. I had been working with Steve Case back when they were a tiny company with about 40 employees. I had signed a deal with them when I was at Brøderbund. And right after I founded Stormfront, they contacted me and said, "Let's work together." So, right from the beginning, that gave us two projects. I had that deal, and we had the baseball game very early on.

We did a couple of small games for them at the start, and then I had chosen Neverwinter as the location for the Gold Box game we did for SSI. In doing that, I realized that I was doing online games with AOL, and I was doing Dungeons & Dragons games with SSI. Nobody had done a graphical massively multiplayer online game yet. Several teams had tried, but nobody had succeeded in shipping one. I looked at that, and said, "Wait, I know how to do this because I understand how the Dungeons & Dragons system works on one hand, and I understand how online works on the other." I called up Steve Case, and Joel Billings and Chuck Kroegel at SSI, and said, "If you guys want to give it a shot, I can give you a graphical MMO, and we can be the first to have it." And that's when Neverwinter Nights was born. We needed to get TSR, which controlled Dungeons & Dragons. All of those guys bought into the project. That started about one year after Stormfront started. We did two smaller games before we got to the point of doing Neverwinter Nights.

Ramsay: You used the term "MMO." Was that term in use in 1989?

Daglow: That's a good question. I think you're right. I think that terminology came later. That terminology came about during the 1990s. I'd have to go back and look at the old game magazines to really find what terminology was being used at the time, because it was not MMO. Online role-playing game? Persistent world? I forget exactly when "persistent world" came in as a term.

But the idea of adding graphics to role-playing games, which until then had always been text only, was new. The idea of being able to add graphics to them and have multiple players playing online simultaneously, well, that was the holy grail. We were fortunate to be that nexus. The right team members at the right time helped to figure it out.

Ramsay: You had Neverwinter Nights in development. Where was Tony La Russa's Ultimate Baseball? What did you ship first?

Daglow: The first titles we actually shipped were the small online games we did with AOL, which is funny now because of the growth of the online game business.

The baseball game took us a year and a half to build, so that came out in 1991. So, after we had done a prototype, we went to Tony La Russa, who was then managing the Oakland Athletics. We went to the Oakland Coliseum, showed Tony the prototype of the game, which was basically pretty pictures for its era, but it didn't have any artificial intelligence yet. We asked Tony if we could call the game "Tony La Russa Baseball" and if he could design the artificial intelligence. I had worked with Earl Weaver doing the same thing on Earl Weaver Baseball. So, I said to him, "What we'd like you to do is provide the brains." And he said that he would like to do that, and signed up. He ended up coming onto our board of directors, serving for almost 20 years.

Ramsay: What do you mean you had him "design the artificial intelligence"?

Daglow: There is an art to that because, basically, we had to ask him questions, and we had to take the answers and get the machine to use them in our artificial intelligence tool.

With Earl Weaver Baseball, we had an aggregate amount of time of initially a couple of days and thereafter when we could meet with Earl. We had long lists of questions which we asked him, and out of that process, we were able to build the artificial intelligence. Now, Earl had written a book about baseball strategies, so reading that book obviously saved a lot of time because we could start with everything he wrote in the book, and then we could go on from there and ask questions. And, frankly, there was less we could do because the game was initially designed for the Amiga, and computers of the day couldn't do much. We had the chance to ask him a ton of questions, and he answered them. What people would say about Earl Weaver was, "God bless the three-run homer." Are you a baseball fan?

Ramsay: I'm not a sports guy.

Daglow: OK, well, in baseball, there are all sorts of strategies. I'm going to oversimplify here.

One strategy is you get a team that gets on base, is very fast, has good defense, and has good pitching. The other team won't score very many runs. You will make something out of nothing with stolen bases, with walks. You'll get a few runners on, and you'll get a few runs. If you don't allow the other team to score very many runs, and you can manufacture a few, you could win a lot of games. There are teams that have won the World Series with that strategy.

Another strategy is "God bless the three-run homer." You have some guys get on base. You have a bunch of big, muscle power hitters. The power hitters hit a lot of home runs. You've got some guys on base when they get the home runs. And you have a decent pitching staff, so your pitching staff won't give up too many runs. You'll get a bunch of runs, and you'll win the World Series. That's another strategy that teams have won with. Earl Weaver is the poster manager for that strategy. In fact, that's his quote. He's the one who gave the name to that strategy.

So, Earl was an old-school baseball guy. When I told him he thought very mathematically, he looked at me like I was nuts. On the other hand, who is the manager who was the first in history to start keeping statistics on how each batter did against each hitter or against each pitcher? That was never done before. Earl got a series of index cards. He had a college kid help him do it. He had index cards on how each pitcher did against each hitter. Earl had more detailed statistical knowledge than other managers did, and he used that to influence his decisions. That's thinking mathematically.

There was one time sitting in his office, which was one of the great experiences in my life. Imagine you're sitting with one of the most famous thinkers in the world on a topic that you're interested in, and he reaches into his desk and pulls out a stack of index cards. If it were economics, that stack of index cards might be what won him the Nobel Prize. Earl Weaver is in the Hall of Fame. One of the reasons he's in the Hall of Fame is because of his stacks of index cards. He reached into his desk, pulled out his index cards, and showed them to me, which he normally wouldn't do. That was a fabulous, fabulous moment. Eddie and I had access to that level of feedback from Weaver, so that was fabulous.

La Russa is a very different sort of a manager. People would say that you couldn't have two managers who were successful but who were more different. Their careers only overlapped for a few years in baseball, but what they have in common is that they both think very mathematically. Tony, likewise, went far deeper in terms of research and analysis than other managers of his era, and he just naturally thinks in mathematical terms. Both of them, each in their own way and each for their own era, thought more mathematically than did their competitors. And that's why we picked them.

Ironically, later in his career, a lot of people said that La Russa was the computer manager who was utterly dependent on computers. They actually went from underestimating his analysis to thinking that he was completely ruled by computer charts, when, in reality, he was not. We worked on La Russa Baseball with him over a period of eight years with fairly regular contact, going back and forth with refinements. You can imagine how much we learned from his mathematical approach. I would read some of these articles about La Russa and Dave Duncan, his pitching coach, being guided by computers, and I thought it was completely nutty what the press would say about them. On the other hand, the analysis they did on other things was so deep that I think the press didn't really realize how deeply they understood what was going on through their charting.

Back to your question about how we did the baseball games with both Earl and with Tony, we got to the point where we could watch a game that they were managing, and we would have a good idea what they were going to do. The trouble is that the other teams are scouting these managers, also looking for tendencies. If a manager always tries to have a runner steal a base in a certain situation, they lose the element of surprise. If the other teams figure it out, pretty soon they're throwing out all those base runners because they know that's what's going to happen. Managers have to be deliberately unpredictable. Allowing for that, we got to where we just studied the managers enough that the only thing that would surprise us, typically, was when they were being deliberately unpredictable. That gave us the ability to then build the artificial intelligence where it really did reflect their thinking. In Earl Weaver Baseball, the computer manager thought like Earl, and then we made adjustments to it. In Tony La Russa Baseball, there were a lot of settings you could change to make it think differently, but the default setting was it thought like Tony, and it really did think like Tony.

Ramsay: So, you worked with them directly? You didn't just let them have at it and say, "We'll be back in a few weeks"?

Daglow: Yes, we did not ask them to write stuff up. We did not ask them to create charts. It actually was much more time-consuming this way because they would sit with us for hours, talking and asking questions. We would come in with these long lists of questions, and we'd just keep running through them. We'd ask one question, and we'd be talking about stuff for an hour. Sometimes, we'd ask a question, and we'd get a one-second answer; then we'd ask our next question. But the key was absolutely being prepared. We would spend days and days of specific preparation, and then we had a questions list we were building continually over time, looking toward the next meeting.

And I'll tell you a funny Tony La Russa story. When we first showed Tony the prototype and said that we'd like to negotiate a deal with him to be the artificial intelligence, he said he was interested. We were talking to his agent about the deal. Even before we signed the contract, my phone rings one day. I pick it up, and it's Tony La Russa. I was thinking, "Oh, this deal is going to blow up. Something is going wrong because we haven't signed the deal yet." We were in contract negotiations with his agent, and I thought that was the "I've decided to not do this" or whatever else call. Instead, what Tony told me—and this is quintessential La Russa—was, "Look, when the deal is finished, we're going to have a contract that calls for a certain amount of my time to help you build this game. Forget what's in the contract. Tell me what I need to do for this to be a great game, and I'll do what you need. It has to be within reason—obviously, common sense—but with anything that makes any sense at all, tell me what you need, and I will do it for you." I was sitting there with my jaw dropping.

That's what makes La Russa tick. He does nothing halfway. He either does it totally or he doesn't do it at all. There is no halfway with him. I think there's a correlation between that total commitment La Russa shows, when you talk about managerial styles, and the success he has had. What's funny is that I've now been associated with Tony for 22 years. He has kept his word for 22 years since that conversation, which is pretty striking.

Ramsay: Did Tony ever tell you why he okayed the baseball game?

Daglow: Back at the start, he said it looked good. That conversation was over 20 years ago, so I only vaguely remember it, but the thing I remember him saying is that we seemed committed to doing something that was really good—that we were not just trying to build something that was pretty, and take some money and run. But the idea was that we were really committed and fanatical about building something that was great. Earl Weaver Baseball had been Game of the Year, so we had success with that, and I think he certainly had done research. He had checked us out and recognized that had happened in the past.

It meant a lot to me when La Russa won Sports Game of the Year from Computer Gaming World. I wanted to do at least as well for Tony as I had for Earl Weaver because Tony was so committed. Earl had been great. It's just with Tony, we had the advantage of being nearby, and we had this continual access for years and years and years. When we won Sports Game of the Year, I felt like I had honored what I owed him, in terms of giving him everything we had the same way that he does. He sets that incredibly high example for everybody.

Ramsay: Was that game published by a third party?

Daglow: Yeah, the game was published by SSI.

Ramsay: Why did you choose Strategic Simulations? When did you start pitching the game to publishers?

Daglow: I started pitching it right in late 1988. We initially were with another publisher who went bankrupt, so then we had a chance to go back and start again. When that happened, we already had a relationship with SSI because we were doing the Dungeons & Dragons game with them. When our baseball game became available, they signed it, and we ended up publishing with them as well.

Ramsay: In terms of product development, were you more driven by technological innovation like id Software or game design like John Romero? What was your focus?

Daglow: John Carmack is only an acquaintance of mine, so I can't comment beyond the fact that I think we perceived them as being technology-driven. John Romero is actually a good friend, who I like and respect a lot.

I like being able to have both design innovation and technical innovation on any game. I always start with the goal to push the envelope at both ends. At the end of the day, though, games have to be fun, and any strategy that is not built on the idea of games being fun is a doomed strategy—no pun intended. All the technology in the world and all of the design theory in the world would not have mattered if Doom were not fun. If you scratched John Romero from the equation, you'd lose a lot of technical expertise and design savvy there. And I think there's no question that if you have real strength in both those areas, it's helpful. I think if you look at Brenda Brathwaite, who John is teamed up with now, she did not start out as a programmer, but over the years, she has acquired a tremendous amount of technical savvy. You can just see it in her work—the combination of understanding the tech along with the design.

Ramsay: Did you want to focus on a specific genre?

Daglow: I actually started the company with what we called the three-legged stool strategy. And I understood, having been through the video-game crash of 1983, that the industry was not the world's most stable business. So, I felt like I didn't want to be in just one genre.

I love RPGs, and I love baseball. It was no coincidence that we were doing very different categories in creating RPGs and baseball. So if baseball or RPGs developed a problem, we'd still have the other category. It was also no coincidence we were doing both online games and not online games. We had the AOL relationship and the SSI relationship, and then later an EA relationship.

The idea was simple: don't become dependent on any one platform, on any one genre, or on any one client because, despite the absolute best efforts of people, stuff happens. To have diversity in our client base and our products was a goal from day one.

Ramsay: You said to have diversity for your client base and products for goals from day one. I worked in branding for many years, and a common refrain was that successful companies need to be known for something. They need a niche—something they can own. How did being all over the place with clients and products affect the Stormfront brand?

Daglow: The fact is that we were known for both baseball games and later sports games and role-playing games. Role-playing game fans saw us as a role-playing game company. Sports game fans saw us as a baseball game company, and later as a sports game company. But we were accepted in both genres, and I think that helped a lot. Periodically, we had done educational software off and on, and I think that helped pay some bills. The fact that I had a master's degree in education gave us credibility when we did those titles. We didn't try to do just any old game, and I think it's good that we didn't do that.

Sports is a big category. We did a lot of different kinds of sports teams over the years. And role-playing is a big category. We ended up doing a lot of different kinds of role-playing games, and the online expertise obviously also helps. So, I think you're absolutely right that you need to be known for something.

Ramsay: Was reputation a factor in your business dealings, getting publishing deals, teaming agreements, and things like that?

Daglow: The game industry is small, and reputation still travels very quickly. The industry was even smaller and tighter-knit then.

Ramsay: Between 1988 and 1989, you were in the middle of development of the Tony La Russa Baseball game, Neverwinter Nights, and a few smaller games. What was your first major business challenge, either as a company or as a new founder?

Daglow: I think the challenge will sound very familiar to many people, and that was simply the combination of having so much work to get done and the timing of cash flow, because when you're paid by the milestone, you do the work before you get paid. In essence, you do the work on spec every month. If it's accepted, you get paid. If you're asked to make a few changes, and they delay the payment until the changes are made, you get paid a little late. Of course, your bills and your payroll come due right on time, no matter what. So, managing that cash flow to keep everything running was certainly the hardest part, especially when we were working 80- to 100-hour weeks just to get all the work done.

Ramsay: How often did that happen?

Daglow: It happened. There were a lot of bursts like that, especially for me, as I was both CEO and lead designer, between 1988 and probably 1992. On the weekend, I believe I saw every soccer game and every baseball game my sons ever played. For afternoon games, I saw the second half of an awful lot of them, but I didn't get to every one. Those were things that were, for our family, not negotiable. And then I would simply work a lot of long hours.

Ramsay: At what point during the company's life cycle would you say that you were on sure footing?

Daglow: In the game business, that's always relative. There was a point in 1991 when I thought we were. That was the summer when the first Dungeons & Dragons game, Gateway to the Savage Frontier, became a hit. Tony La Russa Ultimate Baseball became a hit in 1991, and Neverwinter Nights on AOL launched. By today's standards, Neverwinter Nights would not have been considered a huge game, but it started bringing in money. And that got us to the point where the company had paid off the credit cards and had a little money in the bank. We weren't getting rich by any means, but the paranoia about cash flow and the sense of every payroll being an adventure had subsided a little bit. It became a little more straightforward to manage, so I could sleep a little better. But solid footing is always relative.

One of the things about being a game developer is if you have a one-year-long project, you can do a great job and make a little money, but it'll take you an extra month to find your next game. That month will burn all the money you made in the prior year and maybe more. That's the peril of being a game developer. Once you have costs and salaries and overhead, when you're not working on a game, all that eats you alive very, very quickly.

Ramsay: Every payroll was an "adventure." What did you mean?

Daglow: When you're developing games, especially if you're a young company, you get paid by the milestone. So, you complete one month of work, and you send that in. If the publisher accepts and approves it, they pay you. If for some reason they don't accept it, and they want to make changes, they don't pay you until after you've made those changes. You don't have guaranteed revenue, but your payroll is guaranteed in the sense that every two weeks, you have to pay salaries.

The tough part of running a business is you have both unpredictable revenue and predictable expenses. Now, if something goes wrong with your unpredictable revenue, and your predictable expenses continue, that's not a fun pattern. When those moments come where you've got payroll due at a given moment, that's why it's an adventure—because you're trying to make sure you get cash in fast enough. If a publisher takes an extra week to sign off, it can create a real disturbance for a developer. The system has run that way for decades.

Ramsay: Can you tell me about one such specific adventure at Stormfront?

Daglow: I don't remember specifics anymore, but there were cases where we had a publisher, and a new manager came in and wanted to put their own stamp on the product. They wouldn't accept milestones until we made changes. It was kind of a proof of loyalty. They wanted a developer to prove to the new manager that the new manager was the new boss in town. Well, you go in and you make the changes, but it might take an extra week or two, and now you're a week or two late with a significant, large check. You can have cases where publishers get in financial trouble, start to stall on payments, and be late on payments. That can chain-react for developers. All those kinds of problems are things that developers routinely deal with.

Ramsay: Paranoia about cash flow seems to be a recurring theme throughout this conversation. Was there anything you did or thought about doing to alleviate some of that pressure?

Daglow: Early on, you could do everything perfectly on a 12-month project and finish the project. Then if it took you one month after that to find your next project, which is easy to do, that month would eat up all your reserves. You would have had a perfect year in which you had done a fantastic job, produced a successful game. But in just one month without a project, all your expenses could destroy it all. What we found ourselves doing was searching for new projects earlier and earlier.

Ramsay: Were you in the black?

Daglow: We were in the black in 1991.

Ramsay: With multiple launches and hits. Were you feeling more secure about your cash flow—more certain about the future of the company? Or were your cash-flow worries lingering?

Daglow: No, at that point, we felt more confident, which is why we started moving toward publishing ourselves, rather than going through a publisher. In the early 1990s, we published the first two Tony La Russa Baseball games with SSI. We published Tony La Russa Baseball 3 ourselves, and so that meant more risk. It also meant that we would get a bigger share of the rewards ourselves.

Ramsay: How confident were you?

Daglow: I think we were less paranoid, but I don't know how you'd put a number on it. If you decide you're going to try publishing yourself, there are a bunch of extra expenses. If you feel confident enough to undertake those expenses, you've got to be feeling pretty good.

Ramsay: Did either your cautiousness or your confidence ever cause you to miss any good opportunities or take on any bad ones?

Daglow: Not that I recall. Nothing comes to mind in terms of a big opportunity where a lack of confidence caused us to pass it up. I think there were a lot of opportunities we could have chased that would have been dumb to chase, and I think we were smart not to chase them. There are lots of things which look wonderful, but they're not. The number of interesting ideas that will actually make you money is not that great, but it's really easy to talk yourself into an idea being fantastic. We did a lot of original products, but we tried to be very selective.

Ramsay: 1991 was also the year that the name of the company changed from Beyond Software to Stormfront Studios. Why did that happen?

Daglow: We found that there were several companies using the name Beyond Software. There was a computer store in Arizona or Oregon, and then there was another small developer. The name was generic enough that we felt like we never really owned the trademark clearly. We determined that we needed to get a new name—a name that we could actually own.

We went through a lot of names, thinking about the right name. We must have gone through 35 names, of which none cleared trademark searches. It was a frustrating process of going through name after name to find that they were all already taken. Only after that did we finally get to the point where we came up with Stormfront Studios. We trademarked that, and we had our unique name.

Ramsay: What were some of the other names that you considered?

Daglow: I still remember "Light Source" because it was trademarked six months before we searched it, and it turned out to have been trademarked by a good friend of mine, Ty Roberts. I thought it was ironic that here was a name we wanted, and we had missed it by only six months, and a friend of mine had been the one to register. I don't remember any of the others anymore.

Ramsay: What was attractive about the name "Stormfront"?

Daglow: The person who came up with the idea for the name was Sara Stocker, who was a producer on our team and remains in the industry. When a storm front blows through, the weather changes. It's dramatic. There's all this imagery of rain and rebirth, refreshing and cleansing—something new and fresh. And, in a way, nature starts over after the storm front blows through. So, all those ideas of something new, something dramatic, something that changes everything when it blows through—I liked all those parts of the imagery.

Ramsay: After the name was changed, did you encounter any problems with name recognition? Did the name matter?

Daglow: It mattered, but we changed the name at the point at which we were about to ship two major products. Our Gold Box games for SSI and Tony La Russa Baseball 2, if I remember correctly, were both about to ship. It might have been Neverwinter Nights; I forget which one. But we had two big product introductions. We changed the name to take advantage of product introductions because if we introduced those products with the old name, then it would've been much, much harder to change the company's name. And it would've been much harder to have the public and the game industry follow along with the change.

We sold the old name of the company, and it ended up becoming part of Beyond.com. In owning it, we would have had to constantly enforce it. By selling it, we didn't get a lot of money, but it was enough to pay for a press release, new stationery, sending out cards to all our contacts, and all the new things you have to do when you change your name. When we sold the name, we got enough money to pay for all those things.

Ramsay: Did the name ever become part of the studio's identity?

Daglow: I think that the people had a strong identification with the company, and the company name was part of that. Frankly, I think David Bennette did a fabulous design on the original logo, which stayed largely the same over time. It was a lightning bolt. I think people identified strongly with that. This is my interpretation. I saw that the logo was used widely in things that the team created, so if we had a team-designed t-shirt or something like that, people actively included the logo. We had different kinds of jackets and things with the logo on it, and people liked that. I get off on the symbolism, but I think, in retrospect, that the team was especially fond of the logo.

Ramsay: So, the logo became a flag around which the team rallied?

Daglow: I think in many ways it did. But it's always easy for managers to say how the team was passionate about this or passionate about that, and very often, managers are the worst gauges of the team's passion. Managers have a tendency to project their own feelings onto their team, so what they really report are their own feelings. That's why I always hesitate to report how the team felt because I like the idea of the team being able to speak for themselves, rather than having the manager presume to say how they feel. So, given that, it certainly seemed to me like there was an attachment, but I'll let them be the ones who say that.

Ramsay: What about you? How did you feel?

Daglow: Oh, I liked the name, and I got very attached to it over time. We had a lot of people who stayed for 5 years, 10 years, and in some cases, close to 15 years. For the long-term people, it just kind of gets ingrained. Again, I'm speaking for others here, but when you work for a company for over ten years, there's a pretty deep bond that gets built there. For the people who worked at Stormfront for a very long time, I feel a very deep bond.

Ramsay: OK, it's 1991. You've had multiple launches and hits, and you've changed the company's name. What was your next step? What was the next challenge for the company?

Daglow: We started laying the groundwork to be able to publish ourselves. I think we started to bring it into fruition by 1993. The problem was—and this is an interesting tale about evaluating risk—once we had laid the groundwork, hired the team, and set ourselves up as independent publishers working on baseball games, our idea was to publish baseball games and continue to be a developer of other kinds of titles. So, we continued to work on the role-playing games and the online titles as a third-party developer. That meant that all the revenue we got from those sources would continue.

In baseball, we planned to become a publisher because we thought we really knew that segment. We had the most successful title in the segment. And I knew that in 1994, the contract between the baseball union and Major

League Baseball was going to come up, and there was the possibility of the baseball strike. But I remember thinking the union and MLB have learned enough from prior problems with strikes and stuff that they aren't going to take it too far. We won't have something crazy. So, we brought out Tony La Russa Baseball 3, and it turned out that baseball and the players union had the most destructive strike—the longest strike—in the history of baseball.

That was a disaster for us because people were angry at baseball. People were frustrated with baseball. We had only about 60% to 65% of the sales that we had projected. And, of course, you have almost all of the same expenses, and you lose a third of our sales—that's going to take you someplace bad. We had another game called Old Time Baseball, which was a nostalgic baseball game built on the same engine. So, out of all that, we lost well over a million dollars in the process. If there had not been a strike, I think it all would have been successful at some level.

I don't think we would have had a mega hit like a Tetris or a SimCity, but I think we would have had a solid hit. We would have made quite a bit of money, and it would have gone well. But with the strike, we'll never know, because we didn't have a control group. In the face of the strike, we got very strong positive feedback on the game. We got very strong reviews and won some awards, but the sales did not cover all the extra expenses. We had picked the absolutely worst time to become publishers. In the end, we had to say, "This was a bad idea. The baseball market itself is severely damaged. What we have to do is lick our wounds, become third-party developers again, and take it from there."

Ramsay: Was a million dollars a lot of money at the time?

Daglow: That was a gigantic amount of money for the company.

Ramsay: How much was the company operating on then?

Daglow: Our revenues per year back at that time were probably in the order of between $6 and $8 million a year. Now, adjusted for inflation 20 years later, that's more money in today's dollars. A company that's averaging $7 million dollars in revenue a year loses a million bucks—that's a pretty big hit. That came close to taking us out, but we were able to regroup, sign new contracts, and go on.

Ramsay: How do you handle a situation where you have no control over those external market forces?

Daglow: In my case, in that particular situation, I recognized that I had underestimated the risks. I knew that there was a possibility for a strike, and by proceeding anyway, I had really exposed the company to that risk. So, step one was for me to look at myself in the mirror and say, "You have to learn from this. This was a bad mistake." It was a mistake of overoptimism and overenthusiasm, and that's a lesson I have to carry forth in my career as a manager and try to not do again.

What we now know from history is that both sides believed, at that moment, they were in the ultimate showdown, where their economic success rested on not compromising. And that's why the 1994 baseball strike wiped out part of the 1994 and the beginning of the 1995 season, the postseason, and damaged baseball so terribly. Now, in retrospect, both sides recognized that they both had collaborated on almost killing the goose that laid the golden egg. But, unfortunately, just like my mistakes which I learned about in hindsight, the two sides in the 1994 baseball strike also realized their mistakes only in hindsight.

Ramsay: So, you went from being in the black in 1991 to being in trouble by 1994?

Daglow: Yes, 1994 and 1995. Given that we didn't have a lot of reserves, I think that we were back in the black by 1996 because we had no choice.

Ramsay: How did you recover?

Daglow: We simply said we're going to focus on being third-party developers. We're going to stop trying to be publishers and go back to executing on that plan.

Ramsay: And that worked?

Daglow: Yeah, it did. Plenty of fingernail-chewing, I'm sure. After 15 years, you don't remember the details. You just remember that was a pressure-filled, tight, and nervous time. I remember the feelings and that we got through it.

Ramsay: When would you say was the height of Stormfront's success?

Daglow: I think we had peaks on different products. In the online world, we had a peak between 1991 and 1993 with Neverwinter Nights on AOL. It wasn't gigantic financially, but it was nice and a lot of prestige for us being the first ones to do a graphical massively multiplayer online role-playing game.

The game Air Warrior, which was a plane combat game, preceded us. That was the first. The numbers were much smaller in those days, but it was what you'd now call a persistent world. And that product, in part, inspired me to believe we could, in fact, get away with Neverwinter Nights.

The early Tony La Russa Baseball games, which were published at about the same time, were a peak for us with a very different audience. Those sold well. We won some Sports Game of the Year awards. And at about that time, the regular Gold Box Dungeons & Dragons games were also hits. Certainly, we did the first PC version of Madden Football in its modern form for EA Sports. We created the NASCAR racing franchise for EA Sports, which was huge. We had another peak in the early 2000s when we did Lord of the Rings: The Two Towers, which was a massive, worldwide hit.

So, often in the game business, one of the things that we were taught long ago was all hits are flukes except sequels, which is why you see so many sequels. But when you hit one as a developer, it produces those peaks. Because we lasted 20 years, we had multiple peaks, and then there would be smaller peaks within those bigger peak periods, and so on.

Ramsay: There were many peaks and valleys?

Daglow: Yeah, and if you hadn't had a hit for a couple years, sometimes you'd start looking in the mirror and you'd go, "Gosh, why haven't I had a hit for a couple of years?" You have to be able to continue without that worry disabling you.

Ramsay: How many employees did you have during the 1996 recovery?

Daglow: You know, I don't remember specific numbers. There were times we got bigger and times we got smaller in the ensuing years, but from the early to mid-1990s until we closed the company, we stayed not too far from having 60 to 65 people on the team. I didn't want the company to grow much bigger, but there was a critical mass we needed. I wasn't trying to build a huge head-count company. What I was trying to do was build a company that would really produce high-quality titles within the size that we would allow ourselves to be.

Ramsay: Obviously, the talent you hired was really important.

Daglow: I believed at the time that we had a fabulous team. In hindsight, I believe even more that we had a fabulous team.

Ramsay: How large did Stormfront grow?

Daglow: We ended up having an average of 65 people for probably our last 15 years. We would have had times where if we were working on smaller projects, we'd let things shrink down to a smaller team, and we peaked somewhere in the low 80s. I don't remember exactly when that was. But I felt that if you got too much bigger than about 65 or 70, when you finished one project and started another—even if you were working on three projects at a time—the cost was just incredibly tough to take during that transition time. So, we declined the opportunity to grow. We felt like we weren't going to deliver consistent quality, and all we'd do is get in over our heads.

Ramsay: When was the next peak after the baseball strike?

Daglow: Actually, the next peak after that was not that much later. It was when NASCAR exploded, which was probably two years after we went back to just being developers. It's when NASCAR really took off.

Ramsay: What were you doing? What were your responsibilities?

Daglow: At that point, we had four teams inside Stormfront, so I was running the company overall as chief executive. Each of the producers or senior producers, who ran the four teams, reported to me.

Ramsay: How did your role change between the start and then?

Daglow: In the earlier days when we were smaller, I was lead designer on our titles. Once we got to where we were running multiple teams, I delegated the design responsibilities, so each team included people who were working on design. And then I had a supervisory role, but I stopped being lead designer on our titles in the 1990s.

Ramsay: Why?

Daglow: I realized there's a point when an organization gets big enough that I think you have to make a choice. Not everybody has looked at this the same way, but if you try to be lead designer on three different games at once, it's very hard to do. Some would say if your focus is divided that much, maybe it's impossible to do. If you're designing a wide variety of genres, you're probably designing in some genres where you have more skill than in others. Once you get to where you have a big enough organization, if you're the only person who is in a lead design role, you have to develop more people in the organization.

In a small team, you can empower the entire team, and it's not an issue. But in a larger organization, you have to develop more people who are playing a design role, and they have to feel like their careers are developing. So, you can't take all the fun jobs for yourself and leave whatever is left for other people.

There was a point when I thought that I had to either keep Stormfront smaller, and keep doing things the same way, or let the company grow by delegating and developing other team members. I chose the latter.

Ramsay: Did you enjoy your new role?

Daglow: You know, it's interesting. I really liked the people who I worked with. I really enjoyed working with them. I enjoyed that coordinating part. The fact is that we had multiple teams working successfully that had stepped up and opened more opportunities for us as a company, but I absolutely missed design. There was no doubt that I missed it. I missed that part of the job.

Ramsay: Did you have any creative influence as a manager?

Daglow: I did, but there's a difference between influence and control. If you hold the reins really tight, then other people are going to feel like they're nominally the designer and not really the lead. Responsibility and accountability have to go together. If you're going to loosen the reins enough to say that somebody else is, in fact, the lead designer, you can be a foil. You can provide feedback. You can be a counterpoint. You can be a conscience. You can be a backup. You can be all those things. But if you're holding those reins really tightly and pulling in the horse constantly, that's not delegating. Delegating is a very hard thing to do.

Ramsay: Did you ever try to be hands-on and participate in the creative process of some games?

Daglow: I kept my hand in all through that, but I believe in supervising creative work in a way that holds the bar high without demotivating the people on the team by making them feel too controlled or like they don't have freedom to take the initiative. I think that's a balancing act that you can work at for an entire career and still be learning.

Ramsay: I think the NASCAR game was released in 1997.

Daglow: First, we did Andretti Racing for PlayStation 1, and that came out right at the beginning of PlayStation. That had three different kinds of racing. It had open wheel, or what we now call "indy." It had a dirt track, where you were sliding around. And it had stock cars. That game was successful enough that EA went back and got the NASCAR license the next year.

A game that ships in 1995 will be NASCAR '96 just because you need to have a fresh year on it. Once the thing has stayed on the shelf, if the year on the box is the last year on the calendar, that product is dead. When you look at the names on the box, typically they ship in the year prior to the number on the box.

Ramsay: So, you probably spent a year or two working on that first NASCAR game?

Daglow: Once we got into the late 1990s on the EA Sports titles, we were on a one-year cycle. You had one year to do each game, and you'd update it. You tried to update it as much as you could each year, and create something that was worth buying the game new again.

Ramsay: Did the one-year cycle apply to your role-playing games?

Daglow: I don't actually remember anymore how long we took on those. Those were a case of looking at the game you were trying to build, and you built the schedule off that in terms of what was sensible for the game.

The one-year cycle for EA Sports titles grew out of the way the products were marketed, and the fact that they discovered that a lot of consumers dearly loved the games. If you could get a lot of new features in year to year, they would come back, and they would buy it each year. They'd get the updated rosters, the updated stats, and the updated players or drivers or whatever. Then what you were really killing yourself to do was get additional features in there so that people would not be complaining that they had to buy an entire new product just to get the updated stats and players or whatever. Instead, they'd go, "Hey, look at these great new features. Yeah, I bought it two years in a row, but you know they added a whole bunch of features this year." That was kind of the standard we were striving for: to make people feel like they got something of value.

Ramsay: Was the one-year cycle an EA Sports strategy?

Daglow: I think it evolved that way, and then a lot of other people then picked it up. There are a lot of instances where EA pioneered aspects of game marketing that other people saw was really smart. They then emulated or tried to leverage it. I think it's a strategy that evolved because they simply discovered that the audience was there—that the audience was ready to buy those games.

Ramsay: How challenging was it to develop NASCAR '98 and then NASCAR '99 on that one-year cycle?

Daglow: I think with all those titles, each successive year becomes harder. When the hardware generations change, suddenly you have a much more powerful machine, and now you can introduce a bunch of new features. When you're in the first or second iteration of a console, you can add features because you've got a great new idea. You can add features simply because you learn that box better. You learn how to better code for the machine. With each generation, you have some more abilities.

Once you get to the third or fourth iteration on the same machine, then you tend to have used up a lot of the ideas you had. You've used up a lot of the little technical tricks that you discovered on your second or third outing. And the last one or two years on a given console can be especially challenging because you're going, "God, what am I going to do to give the user extra value this year?"

Ramsay: Were there any production difficulties? Did EA Sports address any production issues related to one-year cycles by providing extra resources or anything like that?

Daglow: There's nothing that particularly sticks in my mind about the NASCAR games. To tell you the truth, we were working very closely with them on a lot of products during those years, and I'm sure there were lots of favors back and forth every day.

Ramsay: What was the atmosphere like during that time? Was the attitude around the workplace very positive, or did production cause a lot of chaos and consternation?

Daglow: I think there was a bit of both because when you have that many deadlines on that many games, inevitably, that produces schedule pressure. In having a lot of games where you have only 12 months to get things out, I think it increased that sense of time pressure compared to the era before that. If you look at the early 1990s, being on time to market was always a huge advantage, and being late with games was always asking for disaster.

But dealing with 12-month cycles just means you have less margin for error. If you have an 18-month project, and you take something and you divide it into 18 pieces, now you've got a little more than 5% of the project in each piece. If something goes wrong, you've got the other 95% to try to cover for whatever problem you discovered. If you've got something broken into 12 pieces—well, really, it's more like 11—now you're getting to the point where you have almost 10% of a game in each piece. Some years and SKUs were harder than others, but being on an annual cycle, it just turned up the stress.

Ramsay: Were there any stressful events that stand out?

Daglow: Like every studio in the industry, we had a lot of discussions about how to best balance work, in terms of how do you deal with crunch. We would have annual off-site planning meetings, where we just talked about how we could get better at whatever it was we were going to be doing the next year. And I think those off-site meetings were very helpful because that was one time each year we just went off for an entire day and said, "OK, we're just going to talk about trying to do our jobs better." I know it's probably not realistic to have thought we were going to get crunch out of the system. Banishing it completely didn't feel realistic, but getting it more under control each year felt like not only a possibility, but a worthy goal.

Ramsay: Can you tell me about the duration of the typical crunch period at Stormfront?

Daglow: We had some projects that were just a few weeks at the end that were tight, or where you had a handful of one- or two-week periods going into milestones that were tough. And we had a couple where there were several months of really tough long hours before we shipped. The feeling was that this was punishing for everybody involved, and we had to be able to do better than this.

Ramsay: Did you figure out the cause?

Daglow: You know, I think that with 20/20 hindsight, there's a variety of things that caused it. At the risk of oversimplifying the issue, I think some of it was just due to the eternal optimism of human beings. We tend to think we can do things faster than we really can, so when you go back and you estimate, you start from individuals in small teams and assemble that up to a big project. If everybody in the project is a little overoptimistic about how much they can get done, that aggregates to a pretty significant delta. You can say, "OK, well, Irving told me this will take one week." Instead of thinking it was five days, I'll think seven days. And then you start tweaking the estimate, but once you start tweaking it, then you're just guessing. Putting in some kind of contingency time is important.

I think another factor is that if a publisher saw that you were reasonably on track, some of the publishers were trained to then go back and ask for additional features: "Hey, it looks like the project is looking pretty good, but for this game to sell, we need to have this, this, and this." Some publishers would do that very aggressively and withhold payment if you didn't have those features, and they were effectively getting those features for free. They came out of the developer's skin. Some publishers did that more than others. Reputations would get around, and developers would be more hesitant to work with some publishers who they knew did that. At Stormfront, we were able to say either no or that we just would not work with that publisher again.

What can happen is that you can have one component of a game that you thought was going to be straightforward, and then it's not. Or you have one component of a game where you said, "Oh, we know how to do this ambitious new thing. We're going to do a big upgrade of the artificial intelligence." And then you get in the middle of the code, and the team is struggling. Whatever was the galvanizing idea about that update, that component of the game isn't happening, and instead of being smarter, the artificial intelligence is dumber.

Everything else can be right on schedule, but that one component could drag everything else down. Now, do we bring in more programmers? Do we abandon the feature? Depending on the circumstances, there are different ways to look at it. Any and all of those things produce crunch, and part of what makes it hard to get rid of is the fact it can be a variety of things that feed it, including the idea of people coming back and asking for more features.

Ramsay: What were some of the things you tried to solve crunch?

Daglow: At the start of every project, we would do a postmortem. We would run through the lessons learned from the prior project, which tended to be at a point when everybody was kind of worn out and tired at the end. And we'd say, "OK, let's try to learn from those things on the next one." If the prior project had been especially crunchy, then we had a pretty long list of things we wanted to make sure we didn't do again. Here's a planning mistake that contributed to crunch. Here's a communication problem. Here's a case where the publisher came to us and said that we absolutely, positively have to add this feature. We don't want to be in a position where we get stuck. So, I think it was an ongoing process.

It isn't the kind of thing where you wake up in the middle of the night and you go, "Aha! I can make this much better if I just do this one thing." There's this continual drive for a better result, and a continual evolution of what you're doing and trying different things. And, frankly, a lot of it, too, is based on the skills of the people. As our team got more experienced, that was a positive factor in trying to make projects run better.

In years when we had less money, it was tougher when a publisher came back, trying to push us for extra features. In years when we had more money, it was easier to say no because they couldn't blackmail us because we didn't need money. And years when we really did need money, they had more leverage on us, and we could be treated more unfairly in those years.

Ramsay: How effective were your solutions?

Daglow: I think that we had periods of crunch throughout our history. We continually got better at planning. I think we learned a lot, and having a lot of veteran people helped a lot. In all of our different eras over 20 years, we did have crunches, which is one of the things that would just eat at me. It's not something you set out to do.

Crunch is destructive to teams. Short periods of it, I think, are probably inevitable, but something that's long and sustained is really destructive. If the short periods are so constant that they almost run together, they're not short anymore. When those things happened, I always felt like, "Crap, I've got to be able to do better than this." I think we continually got better and we continually learned, but we also had times when it happened. And, frankly, some of those were tied to publisher leverage, where publishers simply were upping the content by leveraging us because they knew we needed money. And at other times, there basically had been mistakes that we made where we were overly ambitious or misestimated.

Ramsay: What were the events that led to the closure of Stormfront? Did those events start long before 2008?

Daglow: The short answer is yes. Taking a well-established company and changing its strategy and business model is like turning a battleship. We could see the changes coming. We actually did a pretty good job of anticipating what the changes were. What I didn't do is turn the battleship as fast as I needed. You don't want to upset people. You're trying to have the team feel like they have a voice in things. You're trying to give them some autonomy. You have a lot of rationalizations, but the fact is I did not turn the battleship fast enough to recognize the changes that were happening. We had become specialized, and we did not unspecialize fast enough from being large, console game developers. From about the advent of the PlayStation 2 to the current generation, the requirements for large console games rapidly increased.

As the budgets for those games got bigger, more and more publishers said, "We're not spending this kind of money outside. If we're going to spend that much money to develop a game, we don't want to pay anybody else royalties, and we want the team under our control, so we can manage the process if they get off-track." I'm oversimplifying, but that was the general line of thinking for publishers.

When the budgets were smaller, they thought, "We're not going to think of every good idea ourselves. There's a lot of talent out there. We'll do some games in-house, and we'll do some games externally. We're more likely to get certain kinds of hits from external groups, and we're more likely to have certain kinds of titles do better in-house. We'll have a mix of both, and it will reduce our risk." Once the budgets went up, that strategy no longer made sense to publishers. The strategy that made sense to them was, "Hey, have control. You've got so much money at risk here, and the bigger a project gets, the more lawyers and the more accountants are involved because the more nervous everybody is about something going wrong." So, how do you protect yourself? You have more accountants, you have more lawyers, and that pushes the prices up still further.

That change meant that every year, there were fewer projects that external studios could do in the console space. That supply of potential work kept declining and declining and declining. And the number of studios kept declining and declining and declining. So, we were in a position where we were one of the lucky ones still working, but we recognized the number of studios was declining and the number of projects was declining. We needed to think about how we were going to focus on emerging markets like mobile and handheld games, which had not been a focus for us ever. We needed to think about going back to online. And we started working in all those spaces.

But we started working on it seriously two years later than we should have because we had a team of people who loved console games. That's what they were there to do. And that was simply too late.

The specific event that precipitated the end for us was we had a very large original game we were doing with one of the major publishers. It was a dream project in a lot of ways. It was going to show off the capability of the team wonderfully. We had a schedule that was long enough to be able to really focus on quality. We had a really strong team—all the things you look for—and then our client was acquired. And when our client was acquired, the titles that they had that were in the early stages of development were terminated, our project included. We had $20 million in business evaporate off our books in ten days. When that happened, there wasn't any way to turn the battleship. At that point, we didn't have the resources to go forward, and we shut down operations.

Ramsay: When you shut down, was Stormfront solvent?

Daglow: I guess it all depends on what you mean by "solvent." We shut down at a point where we could pay the last salaries for people. We still had bills we could not pay after that, so we went out of business.

Ramsay: Was the closure a graceful exit, or did employees arrive the next day to locked doors?

Daglow: You know, every circumstance is different, and the degree of control that you have is different in each case. In our situation, we called everybody into the conference room and explained what had happened. We said the company wasn't going to be able to go on.

Ramsay: What was that like?

Daglow: Well, obviously, it was very tough for me after 20 years. That was a long way from my favorite moment in my life. There were people in that room who had worked with me continually for 15 years. We had gone through a lot of ups and down, but to have it not work out really felt bad. These things happen though, so you just have to move on.

Ramsay: You started your new company, Daglow Entertainment, three years later. What were you doing during that time? What did you do after Stormfront closed?

Daglow: For awhile, we had a project that we thought we were going to sign. That project looked like it would bring the company back to life, so we spent three months chasing that project. But it turned out that the people who were organizing it never got their funding. After that, I started doing freelance creative work and business consulting, and that's how I made a living between the time Stormfront closed and the time when I started Daglow Entertainment.

Ramsay: Stormfront lasted 20 years. That's between 15 and 19 years longer than most developers. When you look back, are you happy with what you accomplished? How do you remember Stormfront?

Daglow: You know, I think this may sound corny, but if you work in a company that long, it cuts a part out of you that leaves a big empty hole, and you're left feeling both very sad and very empty. But you still need to get up and go on.

Ramsay: What are you doing now?

Daglow: You know, games are what I do. I was originally trained to be a playwright. Before the game industry existed, I worked as a teacher and as a professional writer. But pretty much from the beginning of the industry, this is what I've done for a living, and I still love building games. I still love designing games. I love working on them and leading teams. For better or worse, this is what I'm committed to in my life's work. I am focusing now on wherever I can when I have a choice, working on the design component of games instead of delegating that, which means that the new company is going to stay smaller than Stormfront. I want to continue to play a critical design role.

Ramsay: Are you picking up where you left off in terms of looking at opportunities in emerging markets?

Daglow: That's a great example of where there is continuity. The way we build games now is so different from the way we did it a few years ago because you have online, and you have shared work groups across continents. You have Skype. We have all these tools and new methodologies. With the explosion of online and social games, all sorts of massively multiplayer online games, and the indie community, there are so many different ways to build and distribute games.

In those respects, everything I'm doing is actually quite different because it's a different era and the methods are different. But within Stormfront's era, I had seen tremendous changes in how we did things over those 20 years, too. That's just a normal evolution.

The thing that I find myself continually drawn to is the idea of doing things where there's something new about them—where we're trying to be the first to do something or trying to do something no one has ever done before. That increases both risk and reward. Sometimes the reason it was never done before is it wasn't fun. In the end, it's all about fun. There's the danger of doing things that have never been done before just to show off this technology, but it's not fun. I've had plenty of ideas that never panned out and where what I was trying to do for the first time didn't work, but I've been right a number of times, and it's what I love doing.

John Smedley

Cofounder, Verant Interactive

 With the impending launch of PlayStation 2, the leadership at 989 Studios, the first-party software house of Sony Computer Entertainment America (SCEA), refocused the studio on PlayStation products in 1999. The PC games group that was headed by director of development **John Smedley** was then excised. Along with 56 other refugees, Smedley cofounded Verant Interactive to operate EverQuest, on which development had started three years earlier in 1996.

SCEA continued to support EverQuest through Verant, whose passion for and commitment to creating the seminal massively multiplayer online game paid off. In 2000, the successful launch of the title inspired Sony Online Entertainment (SOE) to acquire Verant. Strengthened by the resources that only a large enterprise could provide, the Verant team, as SOE, set to work on EverQuest II and a number of hit titles, including PlanetSide and Star Wars Galaxies.

EverQuest evolved into a successful franchise with seven games on multiple platforms, more than two dozen content expansions, iconic characters, and a series of novels, among other extensions. The franchise has also played a central role in the video-game addiction controversy, and has been the subject of academic research. Today, SOE is a leader in the massively multiplayer online game category, helmed by Smedley, who serves as president.

Ramsay: What were you doing before you decided to start Verant?

Smedley: My time in the industry started around 23 years ago. When I was 19, I started a company called Knight Technologies, which did contract work on the Apple IIc, Apple IIe, and Atari Links. Knight was a very small business, but I created some games there. I then worked at Park Place Productions until the company went under.

In 1993, Russell Shanks, Andy Zaffron, and I started up a studio in San Diego for Sony Imagesoft, which became Sony Computer Entertainment America (SCEA) and then 989 Studios in 1995. We started developing what later became EverQuest in 1996. A guy named Steve Clover came up with the name. In 1999, we were working on PlayStation 1 products, and the PlayStation 2 was just about to come out, but I was also doing PC games.

Ramsay: How did you get involved with setting up the San Diego studio for Sony Imagesoft?

Smedley: Park Place Productions was doing a project for Sony, and then went out of business. Park Place was in bad financial trouble at the time. We contacted Sony, and they let us start up the studio in San Diego. We did sports games for many years.

Let me tell you, I hate sports games. I despise them. I produced the MLB Pennant Race and NHL FaceOff games. I was director for half of the studio. The other half was managed by a guy named Chris Whaley, who did football. I'm not a sports guy at all.

Ramsay: You were the director?

Smedley: I was a director of development. Chris Whaley was a director as well. We tried to split this studio down the middle. He was responsible for football, basketball, and some extreme sports. I was responsible for baseball and hockey. It was a fun time. Although I don't like sports, I enjoyed making games a lot, so it was an interesting experience. I worked with some very talented people and had a good time doing it. My real passion though was making PC games, especially online games.

Ramsay: When did you start up Verant Interactive?

Smedley: Kelly Flock, who was president of 989 Studios, felt that as the studio was going into development of PlayStation 2 games, it wasn't a good idea to also be working on PC games. 989 Studios was the first-party software house of SCEA. So, although Kelly had initially okayed us to work on PC games, he felt like he needed to be making only PlayStation 2 games. Kelly effectively told us that our jobs were going to end, but that we could spin off a new company to operate EverQuest and continue developing the game post-launch.

Sony invested $4.5 million over three years into the game, and owned a very small minority share of the company. We were lucky enough to have a real hit on our hands with EverQuest. Sony maintained ownership of the game. All we did was operate it, but we also got the rights to Tanarus, PlanetSide, a sci-fi game that ended up becoming Star Wars Galaxies, and a bunch of technology that we were working on.

Ramsay: Was your previous experience with Knight Technologies sufficient experience to prepare you for starting Verant?

Smedley: Running a company just takes discipline and focus. It's not that the nuts and bolts of the physical part of a corporation are not hard. We had 56 people, including the office manager and network people. Russell and I have a lot of experience with managing people, so it wasn't particularly hard. You just need to watch every game every single day, ensure that customer service is doing its job, and know that everybody in the company is focused on making games the best they could be. That sort of discipline requires meeting with teams every single day, playing our games, and talking to customers.

I personally took a lot of calls from customers. I felt that I had to stay in touch with the user base, stay up-to-date with the day-to-day, and make sure that I was not sitting in an ivory tower. That was something that I was able to do with a company that size, and it was a lot of fun.

Ramsay: Why was EverQuest such a big deal to you at the time? How come that's what you wanted to do?

Smedley: EverQuest was the first commercially successful 3D massively multiplayer online game. We had a passionate group of people that made a game that they wanted to play, and it worked out really well.

Ramsay: But you were set up specifically to develop EverQuest. How confident were you that EverQuest would do well?

Smedley: I wasn't when we started. At the time, Kelly didn't think EverQuest would last very long either. Who knew back then that it would last? I was confident in the idea. I was confident that we would make money. I just didn't know how much, and I didn't know how long the game would last because there were no previous games of this type that lasted. I mean, we're in the thirteenth year now, so who knew?

Ramsay: How high were your expectations?

Smedley: My expectations were high. I was thinking we'd get maybe 100,000 users, but EverQuest exceeded that number on a massive scale. It is hard to plan for that kind of success until you've had the experience. Now, we've come to expect that kind of success.

Ramsay: Did you envision Verant doing more than operating EverQuest?

Smedley: I did. It's the same vision that we maintain today at Sony Online Entertainment. We want to bring massively multiplayer online games to many different genres. We love making online games here. We were working on a strategy game called Sovereign, and someday we're still going to make it. Sovereign was a massively multiplayer real-time strategy game. It was amazing. Going into different genres has been a really big focus for us. We had PlanetSide, which we made into the first massively multiplayer first-person shooter. So, these were big things that we were trying to do.

Ramsay: Did you put together a business plan?

Smedley: It wasn't necessary because our business plan was already fully in effect. We had games in development, and we had expected revenues, so we had a full profit-and-loss picture ready to go right from day one.

Ramsay: What did you have to give up in order to start Verant?

Smedley: Well, our jobs and our safety within Sony. It was a lot of risk because nobody knew what the market was going to be like. The only successful example was Ultima Online, and even that had only 100,000 subscribers. We couldn't live off that. Maybe doing sports games would have been less risky, but the idea of doing them was not appealing. I intensely love online games, and I really can't stand sports games, so for me, it was a no-brainer. I already had two kids at the time, which made the risk a little scary. It was for everybody, but it worked out well.

There was also a big financial burden because we didn't have the certainty of knowing that our salary was going to be there for long. We didn't have the bonuses and all of the really strong financial incentives that you have within Sony. Walking away from all that was terrifying.

Ramsay: What impact did the startup life have on your family?

Smedley: I don't remember much of my first two kids' early lives. I really greatly regret that. It's a mental toll that is hard to explain to people that haven't done it. You're constantly thinking about work. You're never home from work because it's your company and the well-being of every single person in that company is your responsibility. That's the toughest thing. When you're within Sony, you have this nice and safe framework.

When you're just out on your own, payroll only gets made if you make enough money, so you have to make sure that happens. And it's not just about making enough money; it's about making sure that the money you do make is in the right place, that it's the right account, that all of your health-care expenses and taxes are paid up, and all of the little details with the payroll service are handled. It's a hell of a lot of work, but it was also so much fun. It was just an immensely fun time.

Ramsay: Since you already had an organization set up when you left 989 to start Verant, who came along with you?

Smedley: Basically, the entire studio that I ran—the 56 people who were working on PC games—came with us. Almost everybody was a developer or a producer. It was awesome. The exceptions were my assistant, Marsha Gygax, who became our office manager, and the IT guy, Jeff Bolaris. I miss those days. Now, when you build an organization, you have 500 people, and you've got all kinds of middle management and all that stuff. It's a lot different today than it was then.

Ramsay: Were you the sole founder? Or did you have cofounders?

Smedley: Every one of those people cofounded that company with me. So, all 56 are equal cofounders. Just because I happened to be running it doesn't mean they weren't just as important. And I don't mean that in a "hey, we're one team" way. I mean, literally, everybody was a cofounder. Every one of them had stock options, and it was a risk for them. Almost every one of those people could have chosen to stay at 989 to do sports games or to work at another local company. They could have gone somewhere else, but they chose to believe in the dream, and they got rewarded for it.

Ramsay: If Russ had decided to stay at 989, do you think you could have achieved the same success on your own?

Smedley: I don't know. Russ has been a big part of this success, too. I wouldn't have had as much fun doing it. You've heard the cliché that it's a lonely job? It absolutely is. It's hard to explain how lonely this job is sometimes because you have to make very tough decisions every day. The tough parts have more to do with the fact that the buck always stops with me, and knowing whether I'm making the right decisions. Sometimes I need to bounce ideas off someone, and that someone is Russ.

Ramsay: Did you have any external advisors who you could lean on for assistance with business issues?

Smedley: No, we were on our own. Luckily, I had been making games for quite awhile at that point. We had a lot of experience with running the group, so on the management side, we knew what we were doing. For payroll, we got a payroll service. For health care, we used a benefits company that worked with us on all that stuff. I mean, it was just a lot of logistics work.

The network side was probably the area where we were the most challenged because we had to maintain a very strong network. On that front, we learned as we were going. I was personally logging in to the Cisco routers. I could actually mess with the Versatile Interface Processor cards almost as well as any of our network engineers at that time. They've long since passed my skill in that regard. Russ was right there doing work with our database. We didn't have database engineers then. There was a guy who was assigned to do the database, and somebody who taught himself Oracle. When the company's that small and you're learning this stuff, it's just a very different animal. It's an everybody-does-everything kind of a business then.

Ramsay: Who else was focused on the business side?

Smedley: Russ, who is our chief operating officer now. At 989, he was one of the producers, and we went to Mt. Carmel High School together. Our CFO at the time, John Needham, also attended Mt. Carmel. Although we graduated together, we didn't know each other then. So, that was kind of a very big coincidence.

Ramsay: The timeline for Verant and Sony Online is very confusing.

Smedley: Okay, so it's very simple. Verant began January 1, 1999, and it went through to about May 2000. Then, Sony Online Entertainment acquired the rest of the stock that they did not own. I can't disclose the amount, but they owned a significant minority. We sold the remainder to them, and Sony Online Entertainment then owned Verant. Within a few months, they shut down the rest of Sony Online Entertainment, and we effectively became Sony Online Entertainment, so that's why it's confusing to people.

Sony Online Entertainment was actually headquartered in New York at the time. They had Station.com, which offered a bunch of free-to-play casual games. It wasn't lighting the world on fire, but it was there. So, what happened is they shut down New York and Los Angeles, and we became Sony Online Entertainment. Kelly Flock, after he saw that EverQuest did well, came in to run it for awhile, and then, after about a year, I began running it.

Ramsay: Sony had invested a lot of money into EverQuest. How much pressure did they put on the company?

Smedley: Almost none. Because it was such a new thing, they saw us as the people that made this amazing thing, and they just let us do our thing.

And so there was pressure, but just to keep it going is basically the way I would put it. They weren't in our faces. It wasn't like that.

Ramsay: Was the relationship between Verant and Sony smooth and uneventful? Or was there tension?

Smedley: It was very smooth. I mean, really, there were no problems at all.

Ramsay: They had no questions about performance?

Smedley: Well, sure—always. But they were just standard management questions. They left us alone to do our jobs and supported us. That's the best way I can put it. I don't mean that as a "hey, they just left us alone, and we did everything ourselves." When we needed new equipment, they took care of it. When we needed help with network issues, they took care of it. It was a terrific relationship.

Ramsay: Did you have to provide some measure of certainty that their investment was going to good use?

Smedley: The answer is yes. They got to see the monthly numbers, so they knew for themselves what the game was looking like.

Ramsay: What were your next games after EverQuest?

Smedley: We had EverQuest 2 in development; Sovereign, a 3D real-time strategy game that we were working on; and PlanetSide. Subsequent to that, we got Star Wars Galaxies going as well.

Ramsay: How did you decide what products to develop?

Smedley: We just decided on the games we wanted to make. The best way to do it is when you get people that say, "Hey, we have a great idea," and everybody says, "Yeah, that is a great idea. Let's do that." And that's how we decided what to make.

You can't make a game that people aren't passionate about playing, and that's kind of what makes us who we are. We are passionate gamers to begin with. I personally go home and game for four hours a night. That's how I get my enjoyment. I'd prefer to do that than watch television any night, and people here feel the same way. We always make sure to put people on teams where they're passionate about what they're doing.

We were also strategically looking at genres we felt were going to have big potential down the line, particularly real-time strategy games and shooters. Looking percentage-wise at the PC game market, these were genres that were over 15%. The shooter genre was over 25%, and the role-playing game genre was over 25%, so you knew those were good markets to be in.

Ramsay: That sounds somewhat informal. What was the culture like?

Smedley: "Agile" is probably the best way that I could put it. We were sort of the underdogs. While we were at 989 Studios, the rest of the studio really didn't like us. They called us the "goblins-and-ghouls guys." They used to openly laugh at us.

EverQuest was the subject of a great deal of ridicule within that studio. It was frustrating at times because I understand it. They were making sports games, and we wanted to make this Dungeons & Dragons-like online game. They didn't get it. They thought it was stupid—a waste of time and money. They understood after the launch, but it was a frustrating experience. That transformed us into this underdog company that had a point to make. We wanted to go out there, kick ass, and make our game the best. That is a very strong motivational tool. It's like a bunch of geeks in high school who got their asses kicked for playing Dungeons & Dragons at lunch. That's who we were, and it was awesome.

Ramsay: Were there any problems caused by that conflict?

Smedley: All the time—every day. The real reason Kelly spun us out was because he wasn't sure what would happen and believed it was smarter to focus on the PlayStation business.

Ramsay: How much thought went into research and marketing?

Smedley: Market research, absolutely none—no market research whatsoever. Marketing is a different story. We did start putting really heavy focus on marketing because we knew that we needed good marketing to take it to the next level. So, we started almost immediately with a marketing campaign.

At 989, we had this horrible relationship with the marketing guy there. He was just not very good to us, and he hated EverQuest, so we got basically no marketing whatsoever from him. In fact, during the first year we were at E3, he actually told his people to not tell others where our booth was. I'm not kidding. The people who were there are now here, and they even remember the story. It's very funny. He just outright hated EverQuest and wanted to work on only PlayStation stuff.

Ramsay: What tools were used for the marketing campaign?

Smedley: Back then, it was all print ads. There was no online. It was weird. I mean you're talking early days here. It was all print. And what's funny is how slow that was to change. Even to this day, even in our offices, there are still a lot of people who love seeing their games advertised in a magazine, even though nobody reads magazines anymore for online games. It's kind of stupid, but...

So back then, it was all print, and we would go at it hard. In fact, I remember Rob Smith, who was then the executive editor at PC Games, was the first one to give us coverage. I still see him, and every time I see him, I shake his hand. He's still an industry journalist. We also made the cover of TV Guide, which was kind of the highlight of, in my opinion, the EverQuest franchise. You know that you have hit mainstream when you're on the cover of TV Guide.

Ramsay: As a result of that mainstream attention, EverQuest caught a lot of flack, didn't it?

Smedley: Yeah, it did. There was a whole bunch of people saying, "Hey, are people addicted to this game?" They called it EverCrack. We had a kid who killed himself while he was playing our game. That was very, very depressing.

Ramsay: How do you respond to something like that?

Smedley: I talked to the mother for a long time on the phone. It was incredibly uncomfortable because she was convinced that our game was at fault. The simple reality is that any form of entertainment can be taken to an extreme. The incidence of men beating their wives when football season is over is huge. At some point, people get too into something, and just like any other form of entertainment, it's best with moderation. But not everybody games that way, you know.

Ramsay: Did you ever make a proactive public relations effort to head off these allegations?

Smedley: We did. I wouldn't say it was proactive. It was reactive because this is one of those kind of stories that you don't even think about until something like that happens, and then you're like, "Oh, wow. Okay."

Actually the boy's mother, Elizabeth Woolley, convinced me to put an alarm clock into the game. To this day, there's an alarm clock in EverQuest. The alarm clock was like a reminder to "hey, get back into the real world." And it's very interesting to see World of Warcraft and many other games have that feature. Warcraft even has a "remember to leave Azeroth" notice sometimes.

I think there's a recognition in our industry that people can get addicted, but I just think it's like any other form of entertainment. We just need to gently remind people that there's other stuff out there. Other countries actually take this to a higher level. In China, they have what's called the anti-indulgence system, and we are forced to put mechanisms in the game where if you play past a certain point, it starts giving you big negatives for playing. They call it the "rest system." If you play more than five hours or eight hours or whatever it is, your character gains a lot less experience—pretty interesting.

Ramsay: How did the sale of the remaining stock to Sony Online Entertainment come about?

Smedley: I got to know Yair Landau, who was on the Sony Online Entertainment board at the time. We talked, and he asked, "Hey, what do you think about us buying you?" We said, "Sure."

Ramsay: Were you having any money problems?

Smedley: No, things were going along nicely. They were funding the other games, even though they owned a minority share. By that point in time, EverQuest was a success, and we knew we were in good shape.

Ramsay: How quick were you to say "sure"?

Smedley: Very quick. He had been kind of kicking the tires for awhile, and we'd been talking. It was an ongoing discussion, and I knew that we wanted us back as part of the Sony family. I really like Sony. It's a great company, and I liked the management at Sony Online.

Ramsay: When founders hit the sell button, it's usually because there's either a great payout or a quick exit. But you stayed on with Sony...

Smedley: Well, the payout was nice. I felt like I had put a lot of work into it, and a bird in the hand is worth two in the bush, so that was fun getting that kind of payout. It was also because I wanted to have the deep resources to be able to act on much bigger visions. So, it was nice.

Ramsay: You didn't think you could stick it out as an independent firm?

Smedley: Oh, sure, we could have, but it would have taken a long time. I saw the opportunity in the online game market, and there was an opening for us to become the leader. But to stay the leader, it was going to take money; it was going to take deeper pockets than we had.

Ramsay: After you sold Verant to Sony Online Entertainment, what was your first major challenge?

Smedley: It was getting used to the corporate mindset again. It was that we weren't this little ragtag company anymore—that we were part of Sony once again. We had to get our heads around the bureaucracy that comes with big companies. What I miss the most about the Verant days is that there was no bureaucracy. We just moved.

Sony's actually really good about that. There's not a ton of bureaucracy in the way, but there are always some layers no matter what company it is. There are going to be some layers there. When you have 56 people, you're a lot more nimble than when you have 500. So, the major challenge was getting used to being less nimble. In a small company, having meetings to discuss business models or long-term strategy would involve 4 or 5 people, but in a larger company, those meetings became 30-person affairs.

Ramsay: You said that owning the rights to some of the games you brought over from 989 was very important. Why was that important since you ended up selling the entire company to Sony anyway?

Smedley: Well, you have to look back in time. It was all about our decision making then. It was important then that we owned our own code and that we could develop other games. That was very important to us.

Ramsay: Although costs have risen in most areas of the game business, the requirements for massively multiplayer online games were already high. How do you determine what's feasible now? Has your process for selecting new projects evolved since Verant?

Smedley: Before, it was literally a bunch of people in a room. Well, it's not that there wasn't much of a process. When a company that's making games has to make a decision on what to make next, it has to be based first on the passion of the people making them. We are in this business because we like games, so we make decisions about our next games based on what we want to make. We might choose three or four different ideas which we like, and then we whittle them down to one, based on market research and whether the whole team is behind the one that we want to do.

Now, it's largely the same process, but with a lot more market research behind it. There's a greenlight meeting. We have a budget each year, we have what are called "to-be-determined" projects, and we're allowed to basically make the kind of games we want to make. Now, that means as a company, we have to be responsible and have a good expectation of return on our investment, but we're able to make those decisions ourselves. It hasn't changed much since Verant, with the exception that we have a lot more experience now. There's a lot of history to guide our decisions, and that helps a great deal. But what we don't do is work backwards and ask, "What game is the market missing?" We don't do that.

Ramsay: In which areas does it help?

Smedley: We can now look at historical data. If we want to make a western game, we could go look and see what games have been successful and what games haven't. Prior to Red Dead Redemption, I couldn't tell you whether it would have been stupid to make a massively multiplayer online game out of a western. I still wouldn't make one though. So, you can look at historical trends in the market and see what genres are popular. When you're going to spend $60 million to $150 million on a game, you've got to make darn sure that you're in a genre that sells.

Ramsay: How has your role changed since Verant?

Smedley: I could have a more direct impact on everything we did at Verant. As we've grown, that is no longer true. I have to delegate a lot more, and I'm not able to be involved in every decision.

Ramsay: And you're no longer doing any programming?

Smedley: Oh, no. God, no. I wasn't coding at Verant either, other than some tools that we used to manage the games.

Ramsay: We talked about the culture at Verant. How would you describe the culture at Sony Online?

Smedley: I would call it very family-oriented. We've had people here that started when they were 18 as testers. They've literally grown up inside the company. They've married and had families. It's not uncommon at all to see dogs around here, and people bringing their kids into work because they didn't have a babysitter that day. It's just sort of expected. It's kind of the way we are.

We also have a very flat organization. Most of the people in the company know me. They know that they can talk to me. There's not some big, inflated hierarchy here. I think that's bred a very open atmosphere. I'm very open with numbers. I share information with our employees, and, so far, that has never bitten me. I'm a very open person, so the company knows for better or worse when we've had good times and when we've had bad times. The company's aware of everything that's going on.

Ramsay: How do you deal with criticism? I know that the critics can sometimes get very personal.

Smedley: I can handle criticism when it's about our games and not about the people who made them. There have been times when people attack the teams here. I get very freaked out by that, but I'm not bothered at all by criticism. That just comes with the territory. You need thick skin if you're going to do anything creative that the public is ever going to see.

Ramsay: Do you ever change how you do things based on that feedback?

Smedley: Sometimes, but it just depends on the criticism. Like, if somebody criticizes our art, and we agree, then we make the art better. Sometimes it's criticism of our game, and what they're criticizing is by design. We listen, but we decide that's who we are and leave it at that.

Ramsay: We've talked a bit about public relations and crisis management. How do you deal with situations where you've had to effectively take your online business offline?

Smedley: Well, we've had many of those. For example, we went through the New Game Enhancements (NGE) with Star Wars Galaxies in 2005. They can be tough. They can be very trying. Every one is new and different.

One thing I really like about this company is that it's made up of a lot of very supportive people, so people know when I'm in full concentrating mode. People just stay out of my way and don't talk to me much about unrelated issues, which is exactly what I want at those times. I need to focus on what we were doing, try to keep the company informed, and try to keep morale up. Sometimes morale is difficult to keep up in those situations, but you just have to get through it. You deal with it. That's the best way you can do it. It's just part of the job.

Ramsay: Can you walk me through what you were doing during the NGE?

Smedley: In the case of the NGE, we realized very early on that we had made a mistake, but it was the kind of mistake that couldn't be reversed because of our partners at LucasArts. So, we got active with our community, and we let the community know why we had made the decisions that we had. I answered a lot of e-mails. I probably got 10,000 e-mails on that, and that's a conservative estimate. While I didn't answer every one, I'll bet I answered 8,000 or 9,000 of them. I responded to some of those e-mails simply by saying "sorry." We went into heavy communications mode, but the problem is people didn't like the message. Sometimes the best thing you can do is to simply be consistent, apologize, and work through it. And that's exactly what we did.

Ramsay: The NGE completely revamped Star Wars Galaxies. There were many unhappy customers, and even major news outlets covered the story. What did you do to "win back" Star Wars fans?

Smedley: In that particular case, there was really nothing we could do. I would say that was probably our darkest hour as a company. Because the decision was made with LucasArts to move forward with the NGE, we basically made substantial changes to the code base and radical changes to the game itself. And where we ended up was nowhere I wanted us to be. It was a mistake, and at some point, you just have to acknowledge a mistake. It wasn't one we could recover from.

Ramsay: What was the decision-making process that led to the mutual decision to move forward with the NGE?

Smedley: The NGE came about while we were working with our partners at LucasArts. A guy by the name of Jim Ward was running it at the time. He insisted on a major change to the game, so that he could put a lot of marketing money behind it. We were working with him, talking about what were the major changes and what things people were complaining about the most. His research showed that combat was the biggest thing, so we made the decision to change that.

Ramsay: So, we've talked about how you confront social crises and operational crises. Our industry frequently faces the possibility of political crises as well. Where do you stand in the video-game violence debate?

Smedley: I strongly support the Entertainment Software Ratings Board (ESRB). I believe parents need to do their jobs. I was standing in line at midnight for the Call of Duty release. I'm standing in line, and there are mothers there with 10-year-olds. First of all, the next day was a school day. Second of all, they were standing in line with a 10-year-old to buy an M-rated video game. Come on, do your job as a parent.

There are a lot of people who feel very strongly that every parent can make a decision for their kid, and I believe that. That's what the rating system is for, but people will bring their 10-year-olds to R-rated movies. I went to see The Hangover 2, and I looked over and there was a row of 10- to 12-year-old boys and some adult males. What are you thinking? Seriously, you're going to bring them to see this movie? Okay. What can you say?

It's a tough thing because I'm such a strong believer in the rating system, but on the flip side, I also think the rating system is there so that adults can have games like Grand Theft Auto and Modern Warfare. I definitely think that GTA is a piece of art. I think it's a great game, and the fact that you can do all kinds of bad stuff, well, so what? It's a video game. Just don't let your kids play it.

Ramsay: Fantasy violence is a core feature of massively multiplayer online games. How much attention do you give to the efforts to defeat the anti-violent video-game bills?

Smedley: A fair amount, but that's because I personally believe the ratings are enough. They're just like they are with movies. It's enough to tell parents how they should act through ratings guidance. It's also enough that the big GameStops and their competitors don't sell M-rated games to minors. And the enforcement rate is amazingly good. They always do those secret-shopper studies, and the results are always in the 80th to 90th percentiles. Sure, there's always some idiot who will sell the wrong game to a minor, but for the most part, it's effective. That's all we need. We don't need Congress legislating or Senator Yee telling us how to enforce it. I don't think that's the government's job.

Ramsay: Do these macroenvironmental factors ever affect decisions and the workings of your business?

Smedley: No. We support the ESRB very strongly and, therefore, that's enough. Every chance we get, we'll support any of the ESRB's efforts, or the Entertainment Software Association's (ESA) efforts to stop these suits. I'm glad that our ESA membership dues go toward helping stop that stuff.

Ramsay: Let's talk about SOE today. You're running a larger company. You have many more offerings. What are your core businesses?

Smedley: Our core business is running our massively multiplayer online games. That's still where a lot of the revenue comes from. The subscription model is still there, but we've also changed over to "free to play" for some of our newer games. Our microtransaction business is probably our fastest growing business. That has been growing 150% to 180% year over year, and continues to grow like crazy. And our console business is growing. We're trying to get our overall revenue to be roughly half from PC and roughly half from console. To date right now, our overall revenue is more like 20% console and the rest is PC.

Ramsay: Microtransactions are when you sell virtual goods and services in the game, right? Can you tell me more about that business?

Smedley: It's a very unique business because there are categories that we're just now defining. I'll give you some ideas. Services, for example, is a big microtransaction area, but we're learning that it has a lot more to do with retail. We have to constantly change up how we present things to people, and we're learning that if we have "deals of the day," they do three times what other SKUs sell. So, it's a merchandising thing, and we need to make sure that the pipeline is constantly filled. It's a very new business for us, so I can't say that we've figured it out yet.

Ramsay: What are the difficulties of doing microtransactions?

Smedley: That's another interesting piece for us. You need a pipeline for microtransactions. It's almost like a consciously thought-out pipeline of artists, designers, and programmers. You need to constantly come up with new stuff. You need people who specialize in that, and we have a couple of people whose entire jobs revolve around strategizing on pricing, merchandising, how we show stuff to our customers, and doing sales. It's a very, very interesting and exciting part of the business now.

Ramsay: How is that content priced?

Smedley: A lot of the pricing now is based on what's worked before, but sometimes we come up with completely new things, and we need to figure out what the market will bear. We tend to go higher at first to see what the market will take. We're learning where the grooves are and what people will accept.

Ramsay: So, you don't use the markup method?

Smedley: Oh, no, not at all. If we did that, we would have never entered this business because it wouldn't always make sense. We'll make something that took us three weeks to make, and it'll sell one unit, while something that took an hour to make will sell a million units. We're getting better at this, but there's no formula yet.

Ramsay: Do you still have the Platform Publishing label?

Smedley: We got rid of it. It was a bad idea—something that we tried. We wanted to use our ability to publish and market games, and distribute them to take third-party titles to market. But we never found the right title to do that with. I shouldn't say it was a bad idea; it just didn't work.

Ramsay: Was the label created post-Verant?

Smedley: Oh, yeah, most definitely. No, it was something we just decided to do internally in maybe 2004 or 2005.

Ramsay: You've done a number of games, including PlanetSide and Free Realms, but you've built EverQuest into an established franchise. Why? Given your past success, have you looked into creating similar franchises?

Smedley: Absolutely. In fact, PlanetSide is actually a case in point. I can tell you that we're about to announce PlanetSide 2. We're very focused on that.

Ramsay: What goes into the thinking behind developing a franchise?

Smedley: A good example is Free Realms. One of the things we decided early on was the age range that we wanted. We wanted roughly 10- to 13-year-olds to play the game. We decided that we needed a mascot that would cross all the games, so we made one called Chatty. We purposefully designed a look to the game that would be friendly to the age range that we were looking for, and we knew that we wanted the game to be kind of a whimsical, almost like Shrek, online game. It really resonated with people here, so we put a lot of thought into how you grow that franchise. It has worked out quite well for us because of that.

Others kind of evolve into being franchises. With EverQuest, we actually did not set out to make it a franchise. It became one. We were at a different point in our life cycle as a company then. Now, we do that purposefully. But it doesn't always work out right, and sometimes you can make something that you think is going to be a franchise, but doesn't turn out to be one. So far though, we've had a good track record. We're just going to have to wait and see.

Ramsay: What are the unique challenges of building massively multiplayer online games based on licenses?

Smedley: Well, the number one challenge is that you're restricted on the content that you can put in, and this happens all the time. The two biggest licensed games that we've dealt with are the Star Wars franchise and the DC Comics franchise. In both cases, we can't just do what we want creatively. We actually have to get approval, and many times there are creative people on the other end who want to be involved and lend their own creative energies. Surprisingly, that actually works out pretty well most of the time, but it places a lot of restrictions on what we can do. For example, you're not going to see blood in the Star Wars universe. We made a Clone Wars game, and we couldn't have Darth Vader in the Clone Wars game for a very obvious reason that you don't normally think about.

There are points in time when you get the license, and things change that affect what you want to do. Dealing with licenses is a tough challenge sometimes.

Ramsay: In your experience, have you found that licensors exert much control over their licenses?

Smedley: Absolutely, but, in fact, it really depends. For example, the regime at LucasArts now is really nice and good to work with. Back then, it was different because Jim Ward was a different personality. People and relationships matter immensely, and we are super happy with the LucasArts relationship.

Ramsay: How much more freedom do you have now?

Smedley: We have a lot of freedom, but what we do with it still has to be within the boundaries of the license. Although we have that freedom, there's always that knowing we have to treat the license with respect.

Ramsay: How does using third-party intellectual property differ from building original intellectual property?

Smedley: The difference is mostly that with licenses, you've got lines that you can color within, and that's something that you need to give a lot of thought to. When you're working with your own intellectual property, you can make it up as you go. If you need a new piece of lore, you can just make it. We can do that a lot of times with licenses, but not always. And you can come up with a unique look. With Star Wars Galaxies and DC Universe Online, the look had to be fully approved by their respective licensing parties. I still like licenses, but we're going to do a lot less in the future.

Ramsay: Why?

Smedley: At some point, we, as a company, want to build more original intellectual property. We think that's a big part of our job. Being profitable by making great games is number one, but right behind that, I would say making new intellectual property that Sony can use is an important part of what we do.

Ramsay: SOE has a history of developing and publishing titles which are exclusive to consoles, handhelds, or PC, but you've recently brought MMO games to the PlayStation. Why is that?

Smedley: Well, nobody with PlayStation is telling us to do it. We made that decision because we think there's a market there, so we've made the conscious choice to move our products in that direction.

Ramsay: Does being part of Sony limit the platforms you can work with? For example, you can't develop Xbox games, right?

Smedley: Well, yes and no. It does, but we're a part of Sony, so we wouldn't want to develop Xbox games. We're fighting for the home team here, and Xbox is our competitor. That's how we view it. The guys at Sony Electronics can't launch their stuff on Samsung televisions either. It's just who we are. We're Sony. Everybody else is a competitor.

Ramsay: Have cross-platform online games proven more challenging, creatively and technically, than PC exclusives?

Smedley: Insanely more challenging. There are moments when you just want to tear your hair out, but luckily, mine's all gone.

Yeah, it's tough because there are things that you don't think about ahead of time. For example, many times our updates for games are ready on the PC long before they're ready for the PlayStation 3 because we had to get them approved through Sony Computer Entertainment. SCE has to make sure that they run properly on the system. That could mean as much as a month of lag time. We would love to put out the PC version early, but we can't do it because the audiences will scream at us. We probably didn't realize how strongly they felt about that ahead of time. It's interesting.

Ramsay: What are the technical challenges?

Smedley: The limited memory of the PlayStation 3 or any console, really. Although the PlayStation 3 is the most powerful platform, the console is still not a PC, so there are so many more limitations which we have to abide. On the flip side, you get hardware that's the same in each unit, and that helps us because we know that our game will run the same on every system. That makes it nicer, but it's still challenging. We found the PlayStation 3 to be a great machine to build for. It's just... it's work.

Ramsay: How do the markets for the PC and PlayStation differ?

Smedley: There's a lot of noise whenever you release something on the console. It's a much bigger spike of noise. If you release something on the PlayStation Network, they know that every week there's going to be something new on there, so people go to look. They're trained.

Also, the console doesn't have the legs that the PC does. A good game can gain word of mouth on the PC a little easier than a good game on the console. On the console, a game that was released five months ago tends to be forgotten, but on the PC, the tail is longer. The numbers on the console can be much larger though because the noise around releases is so much louder.

Ramsay: Do you try to find a middle ground to appeal to both? Do the characteristics of an online game for the PC and an online game for PlayStation appeal to different markets?

Smedley: They do, and we're just learning that. We're not good at it yet. It's something that we need to work on.

Ramsay: What's the competition like in the massively multiplayer online console game market?

Smedley: Well, I'll let you know when it comes. I'm not even being glib about it. The truth is I don't know. There are only two companies that have ever launched a massively multiplayer online console game: Square and us.

On the PlayStation 2, we were not very successful with our first massively multiplayer online console game, EverQuest Online Adventures. It did okay, but we launched it around the same time they launched the network adapter for the PlayStation 2. I think what we learned from that is "wait until the installed base is there." We thought we should wait until there's a machine with built-in networking, like the PlayStation 3. It was a great experience though, and it was a really good game, but it wasn't a big success financially because we were selling to a small base. Square blew us out of the water. This time around, it's a totally different story. They're not on the PlayStation 3, so it's a totally different story now.

Ramsay: Within the last few years, Sony Online has been digitally distributing games through third parties. How is that working out?

Smedley: Steam is huge. We certainly can't discount the reach that they have. I use Steam all of the time myself. At the same time, we have to be careful because, just like with iTunes, we can get to the point where one company has too much power. In this case, Steam has handled that very well. There are plenty of competitors, but they don't demand exclusivity.

Valve is really good about conducting themselves well and maintaining a balance, but you're starting to see other companies like EA with their Origin download service. EA is pulling the plug on providing Steam content because they're worried about that iTunes kind of effect.

I still like having third-party distribution. In the future, will it always be that way? Maybe not. At some point, we could decide to keep our products on our site, but we'll see.

Ramsay: You've been doing digital distribution through Station.com for awhile. Was there a point at which online games were distributed exclusively at retail? When did that change?

Smedley: Very early on. In 1999, they were distributed that way, but that's now changed. I would say right around 2002 or 2003.

Ramsay: What was the consequence of that shift?

Smedley: We got to keep a higher percentage of the profit that way, but the single biggest thing was that it enabled us to take a little longer. The lead time—to put code on the disc—for retail was a little longer then, at roughly four to six weeks.

Ramsay: I want to talk more about alternative business models and how their emergence is impacting your business today. Why was free to play attractive?

Smedley: One of the biggest barriers to getting people into the massively multiplayer online game market is simply getting them to spend the money—the upfront money to try the game. The free-to-play model removes that barrier. It gets them interested, and then they can decide whether they want to pay a monthly subscription or do microtransactions.

Ramsay: Was Free Realms your first free-to-play game?

Smedley: Yes, it was our first free-to-play game.

Ramsay: How did Free Realms come about?

Smedley: It basically came about when we started looking at the free-to-play market and saw amazing games like RuneScape, which were doing phenomenally well. We just decided that we'll give this a try. We wanted to make a kids game. Many of us have families, so we wanted to make a game that families could play together. We decided that would be a good idea.

Ramsay: Is there a strong relationship between the free-to-play model and virtual goods?

Smedley: Certainly, but they're optional in both. Our style of free to play is what I call "freemium," which is where we still have a subscription and we give more features to subscribers. We still like recurring revenue. We think that's still a very powerful model, but it's true free to play. We just encourage people to get a subscription by putting features behind a pay wall.

Ramsay: Do you use virtual goods as a gate for content in free to play?

Smedley: No, that's not our policy. We think that they should be separate. The gate for content is typically just membership. Now, that may not be true in the future. We may try something else, but at this point, we haven't done anything like that.

Ramsay: Social games have exploded in a very short time. Have you pursued that opportunity yet?

Smedley: Well, we've launched four different social games, and we just decided that it was not a market we liked. They are exploding, but you had to be one of the first movers, in our opinion, to really make money. We were not a first mover. At this point, the only big social games company that's making real money is Zynga. All the other ones are money losers.

Ramsay: There won't be any more social features in your games?

Smedley: I'm sure there will be, but social features are a different story. Certainly, we believe strongly in that, but we're not going to be making Facebook games anymore.

Ramsay: Do you think social games have to be developed from the ground up as social games? Do you think that "social" isn't just a tactic, but rather a completely new product category?

Smedley: I think it's both. A great example is Battlefield 3's social service Battlelog. It is a tactic, but it's also a completely new category.

Ramsay: So, you'd design a game to be social from the start?

Smedley: I think it helps if you have that in mind when you make it, but I think Call of Duty Elite is probably the best example of how to bolt it on afterward.

Ramsay: Many companies are betting on mobile games. Have you done anything in the mobile area?

Smedley: Not as Sony Online per se. But we helped with some early on. It's not going to be a core thing we do. It's not for us.

Ramsay: How come?

Smedley: It's just not what we do. We don't have to make all games for all people. We also don't make Xbox games. It's just not something we do.

Ramsay: Are you interested in cloud distribution, like what Gaikai is doing?

Smedley: We are, and that is an emerging category. I don't know that we need anything special. It's not very hard to do technically, so I don't know that we need a third party to do that, but we are very interested.

Ramsay: You could play EverQuest on Facebook.

Smedley: Yeah, it sounds nice, but there are some practical limitations to it that are very real. That's why you're not seeing this huge explosion of services being used. I think it's real. I think it's a real opportunity, and I think I would use it more to get people interested.

Ramsay: With the rise of social games and free to play, there's a tendency to let games design themselves through metrics. Are you concerned about this trend?

Smedley: I am. In fact, I think a lot of the games I'm seeing out there are doing that. I don't enjoy most of the games on Facebook because I feel like the whole point of these games is to click on the next thing. I don't feel like there's enough game there. Now, the games are improving. A good example is CityVille, which is certainly much better than Mafia Wars. They are increasing in quality, but there's still, I feel, too much focus on the payment, and not enough focus on the game.

Ramsay: You believe games should be fun before they're monetized.

Smedley: Yeah.

Ramsay: You had several collectible card game studios...

Smedley: We still do. We just moved them to San Diego.

Ramsay: What was the thinking behind those acquisitions?

Smedley: I believe very strongly in the microtransactions built around games like Magic: The Gathering. I'm a big Magic: The Gathering fan. We've been very successful with the same model—with microtransactions added on top. Digital goods of all kinds are of great interest to us.

Ramsay: What characteristics do you look for in a potential acquisition?

Smedley: Well, the culture has to be a good fit. First and foremost, we are looking for great people, and, second, we want great tech. If the culture is a good fit, then we like to make the acquisition. If it's not, then we pass.

Ramsay: Verant was an independent game company for about a year before it rejoined Sony, and you've been heading Sony Online since then. Do you see yourself trying your hand at another startup in the future?

Smedley: Yes. I've still got an entrepreneurial streak, and I think it's my dream to someday do that again.

Ramsay: Based on your experience, what advice would you offer to someone looking to start an online game company?

Smedley: I would say, "Be passionate, and don't be afraid to do it." Just give it a try. There are some brilliant companies formed by people who have never made a game before, but they were smart and super passionate about what they wanted to do. If you have that combination, you can achieve some great stuff, but you've got to be passionate about it.

Ken Williams

Cofounder, Sierra On-Line

*Sierra On-Line was initially On-Line Systems, started by **Ken Williams** in 1975 as a computer network consulting practice. Enthused by a text game the two had discovered, his wife Roberta convinced him to develop a game she had designed. Mystery House was released in 1980, becoming the first graphical adventure game.*

After Mystery House, six more titles were released. Having relocated from Los Angeles to Oakhurst, a short distance south of Yosemite National Park, the company was renamed Sierra On-Line in 1982. While barely surviving the crash of 1983, Sierra was then rescued by King's Quest: Quest for the Crown in 1984. The success of that game altered the company's direction forever.

Over the next decade, Sierra produced 27 critically acclaimed games in the King's Quest, Space Quest, Leisure Suit Larry, Gabriel Knight, and Phantasmagoria series. However, in 1996, Sierra was acquired by CUC International, and Ken and Roberta departed the following year.

Currently, Ken and Roberta are happily retired. While the couple spends their time circumnavigating the globe in their Nordhavn yacht, Ken continues to develop software. He has also written three books about their travels and misadventures.

Ramsay: Take me back to before you started Sierra On-Line.

Williams: I have childhood memories of wanting to start a company and be successful. I remember telling people in high school that my plan was to start a company and retire by the time I was 30.

I was able to skip a year of school and start college a year early at 15. Roberta and I met when I was 16. At first I studied physics, but one day on a class outing at UCLA, I saw my first computer. This was a long time ago, approximately 1972, and the computer industry was just beginning. The computer was a big, clunky beast, but I remember being fascinated by it and immediately enrolling in computer classes. Soon after, Roberta became pregnant, and it was time to think about a real job.

After two years, I dropped out of school to attend a nine-month computer trade school, in computer programming, called Control Data Institute (CDI). The school wasn't particularly great, but it gave me what I wanted most: access to a computer. I have a natural talent for programming and graduated at the top of my class.

From 1972 to 1979, I worked in a wide variety of software jobs in Los Angeles, including Children's Hospital, Bekins Moving and Storage, Financial Decision Systems, Aratek Services, Informatics, McDonnell Douglas, and more. I had a few full-time jobs, but most of my work was as an independent contractor specializing in online networks. My consulting practice was called On-Line Systems. This was at a time when the idea of terminals connected to a mainframe computer was just getting started.

Just as my life changed when I saw my first mainframe, I knew the second I saw a microcomputer that my life would change forever. I saw a TRS-80 and knew there was a huge opportunity to write software for it. But rather than a TRS-80, there was another new computer coming onto the market that had a lot of buzz: the Apple II. In addition to my networking background, I had done a lot of work with databases and compilers. My plan was to put a Fortran compiler onto the Apple II. The only other company doing language development was a tiny outfit called Microsoft.

However, one night I was working late on one of my contract programming projects, doing some development work on a terminal hooked to a mainframe at MIT, when I noticed a computer game. I played it a bit and thought Roberta might like it. The game, called Colossal Cave Adventure, was all text and began just by saying, "You are at the end of a long road, standing in front of a well. What would you like to do?" You then could type in anything you like, such as "look in the well," and the game would respond. Roberta was captivated and wound up staying up all night to finish the game.

A week later, she took me to dinner at a nice restaurant to pitch me on the idea of dumping my compiler project and starting a game that she was already at work designing called Mystery House. Within a few months, I had quit my various jobs, sold our home, and moved to Yosemite to focus on developing games. It was because of the move to Yosemite that we renamed the company from On-Line Systems to Sierra On-Line.

Ramsay: Why did you relocate to Yosemite? That sounds like a fairly nontraditional location for a video-game company.

Williams: We always had idealistic fantasies about moving to a little log cabin in the middle of the woods, and getting out of the city. We thought it would be a much better environment in which to raise our children, and I was sick of all of the traffic in Los Angeles.

In the early days, our location worked for us. The idea of living at Yosemite, with the hiking and wilderness, helped us recruit young programmers. It was a cool place to live. It also seemed to work for the kids. We lived on a lake, and waterskiing became a family ritual.

I also had a belief that it was part of why Sierra succeeded. I was under the impression that companies in the Bay Area swapped employees regularly. I refused to hire anyone who had worked at a competitor. I wanted our employees to do things "the Sierra way." I wanted to give our customers the kind of product that couldn't be bought anywhere else. I didn't want our employees looking at competitors' products and copying. I wanted our products to break new ground and go places our competitors weren't.

Unfortunately, as the company grew, there started being problems. It really came to a head when I phoned the executive search firm in San Francisco that was supposed to be finding us a vice president of Marketing. "Why do you keep sending us C players?" I asked. "Because A players won't move to Yosemite," came the response. They were right. Yosemite isn't on the fast track for most professionals, and even if they wanted to live in Yosemite, their spouses or families might not. Our location was crippling our ability to hire senior management.

It was also a problem for our family. There were no private schools, and the public school in Oakhurst, where we were based, was rated among the lowest in California. None of our children's peer group seemed interested in college. We had moved to Yosemite in 1980, but by 2003, it was clearly time to leave if we wanted the company to succeed—as well as our family!

Ramsay: With a family of your own, do you think you were more cognizant of the more human needs of your employees? Did this influence how you thought about "the Sierra way"?

Williams: The sad truth is that I was not much influenced by family. Both Roberta and I are workaholics. If I'm awake, I am generally at my computer. I have been retired for 13 years, but I still try to write some code every day.

My philosophy of business has always been that business is war. You need to decide if you want to win or lose, but there isn't an option to just show up. To beat the other guy, you need to get there sooner, hire better people, work harder, start earlier, focus on every detail, and have all of the luck you can get. I can't remember ever taking my sons to a baseball game. I never coached any team for the kids or went to a PTA meeting. I prided myself on trying to go weeks without small talk with my secretary.

We were young, and wild parties did occur, but these were exceptions. At Sierra, my "business is war" attitude generally prevailed, and anyone who needed family time didn't understand the problem.

Ramsay: So, you had just moved to Yosemite with your family and decided to start developing games. Did you have enough money to get started?

Williams: Prior to starting Sierra, we had already been thinking about moving to Yosemite. We had two small children and discussed often "raising them in the woods." We thought that by getting out of Los Angeles, our children would be sheltered from all of the drugs, crime, and other big-city problems. We had been saving money, and I had been trying various entrepreneurial ventures, thinking that something might work.

When we first started Sierra, it exploded immediately. The first game, Mystery House, was programmed by me with art and design by Roberta. Music in those days was just "BEEP!" We couldn't afford any packaging or advertising. The "box" was just a Xeroxed piece of thick paper, along with a disk, in a Ziploc bag. We didn't have a printer, so we cut words from magazines for the text on the box. We did run a black-and-white ad that cost about $200 and which was also hand-assembled with magazines, scissors, tape, and a copy machine.

There was never any doubt that we were onto something. I sold the first games by driving around to the few computer stores that existed. Because I was knocking on doors at computer stores—there were very few on the West Coast—I contacted other young companies to ask if I could sell their software. I forgot whose games we sold. I think Adventure International and perhaps some others. We couldn't make games fast enough! I wound up selling the distribution side of the business to a friend, which became Softsel, a large software distributor, and focusing on games.

My recollection is that we moved to the mountains in Coarsegold within a couple of months after selling our first game. If it hadn't worked out, we always could have moved back to Los Angeles. But I don't remember ever worrying that it might not work.

We were funded for the first year from my checking account until an East Coast venture capitalist, Jacqui Morby, from TA Associates showed up on our doorstep. She explained what venture capital was. We didn't need the money, but she talked me into it. We were very naïve at the time.

Ramsay: Did taking venture capital turn out to be a good decision?

Williams: When Sierra started in 1980, I was 26 years old. My interest in venture capital had more to do with the connections and guidance we would receive than the cash. I liked the idea of having a board of directors who had "been there before" and who could help me with some of the business decisions and opportunities ahead.

As it turned out, venture capital almost sunk Sierra. At the time of investment, we were completely focused on software for the Apple II. The venture capitalists saw a huge opportunity in the larger video-game market and encouraged Sierra to shift development resources to games. Roberta and I were skeptical about entering the video-game market, and even if it was the right decision, we were not completely committed. Almost certainly, our lack of commitment contributed to the disaster that ensued.

It is a miracle that Sierra survived our flirtation with video-game development. I have forgotten how much money we raised, but I believe it was around $10 million. This money was plowed into development for the Atari, Commodore, Nintendo, and Coleco game machines. A huge chunk of the money was spent on inventory. In 1982, while Sierra was coding and starting production for our games, the video-game market was in its gold-rush phase. As we were ready to go to market in 1983, the entire video-game industry imploded. We were caught with a warehouse of worthless inventory. Atari, who had built millions of E.T. cartridges, was forced to truck their inventory out to the desert and bury it. We knew how they felt.

Our venture capitalists, who invested in Sierra to ride the video-game wave, lost faith in Sierra. The focus at board meetings shifted to selling the company. Activision offered $1 million for Sierra. We came within inches of taking the deal. We also met with another company, Spinnaker, which had received investment from the same investors. Their goal was to merge Sierra into Spinnaker. This would have occurred had Roberta not dug in her heels and decided firmly that we were going to continue Sierra with or without the venture capitalists. We mortgaged our home, borrowed on credit cards to the limit, laid off most of the staff, and just dug in.

Ramsay: Entrepreneurship isn't for the faint of heart. Were both you and Roberta completely invested at this point? How far were you willing to go?

Williams: When Sierra hit tough times, I was too quick to write the company off. I actively participated in discussions with the prospective buyers. Roberta and I wouldn't have received any money out of a sale. We would have been left penniless, unemployed, and living in the boondocks. That said, I was young and believed myself incapable of failure.

I remember thinking that the VCs had invested the money, we had played the game their way, and were shot down due to market conditions. There was some anger at the situation because I had worried from the beginning that our segueing into video games would be a disaster. However, we did take the money, we did build the games, and I was the captain when the ship sunk. Finger-pointing would accomplish nothing.

Most of the money lost belonged to the VCs, and it seemed fair to me that they should have a voice in the disposition of the company. Their hope was to combine their dog investments and try to assemble a company that could survive. One way or the other, I was confident I'd be fine, and that if Sierra didn't work out, I'd just start a new company or be a leader within a consolidated company. Be it right or wrong, I had no lack of self-confidence. I was certainly disappointed, but I didn't really see it as the end of my world.

On the other hand, Roberta believed in Sierra. She had no interest in merging the company with anyone. She was confident that we could turn the company around, and that we should bet the ranch on keeping the company going. I hated the idea of irritating our investors, and I didn't like the idea of pledging the few assets we owned.

Our difference of opinion came to a head when our board invited Spinnaker's management team to present at a Sierra board meeting in San Francisco. Spinnaker was a heavily financed educational software company out of Boston. Although it wasn't specifically said, all of us knew that the goal for the meeting was to talk about Spinnaker and Sierra joining forces, which was the polite way of saying "sell Sierra to Spinnaker."

For the meeting, I wore a jacket and tie. But Roberta, who was also on Sierra's board, well, she refused to fancy up. She appeared for the board meeting at least one hour late in jeans and a t-shirt. She diddled around for her first few minutes in the meeting room, making coffee, and then asked, "What are we discussing?" After one of our investors explained that we were discussing how an industry-leading company could be built by combining Sierra's leadership in games with Spinnaker's leadership in education, Roberta responded, "No, thanks. We have no interest." She followed with some candid and derogatory comments toward Spinnaker, throwing the meeting into turmoil and ending discussions.

Roberta was right, of course, and quite a lady. We went through some tough times, and had to lay off most of the company. The company shrank overnight, from over 100 employees to about 12. The board fired me as chairman of the board and assigned one of the investors, David Hodgson, to the role of chairman. We maxed out our credit cards, mortgaged our home, and Roberta went to work for the company full time as our accounts payable person while also continuing to work on her games.

Our turnaround came amazingly fast. Roberta had a game in development called King's Quest. I presented it to IBM, who was working on bringing out a new home computer, the PC Junior. I also presented my idea for a word processor that would be based around pictures, or icons, rather than text links. IBM signed an agreement with Sierra that gave us the funding we needed to build these products. In return, we gave them some very cool games to showcase their new machine. Once the products hit the market, they were a huge success. Sierra was back on top of the world. Within a year, I was restored as chairman. All talk of selling was long forgotten.

With 20/20 hindsight, it is hard to imagine how I ever agreed to consider selling Sierra. I was in my 20s, had never seen tough times, and was probably a bit overwhelmed. I also remember laying off 80% of the staff as one of the worst days of my life. Oh, well. As they say, that which doesn't kill us tends to make us better people.

Ramsay: After King's Quest, did you immediately start hiring back everyone you had to let go? What happened?

Williams: IBM gave Sierra funding to do a few products for the PC Junior, including King's Quest, a graphic word processor called Homeword, and I also think there were some action games. Luckily, IBM didn't ask for exclusivity.

In fact, my recollection is that IBM was sensitive about allegations of industry dominance. There were concerns that IBM could be busted up by the government. This worked in our favor, in that IBM paid for the code, but then we had to be very careful in contract negotiations to ensure we had the rights to sell to their competitors. So, we were able to take our games and have them immediately ready for competing computers, in particular, the Tandy 1000.

Although the PC Junior bombed, RadioShack became a huge customer for us, and revenue started flowing rapidly. I don't remember if we rehired most of the people who were laid off or not. I'm sure we rehired some.

Our flirtation with bankruptcy changed me forever. Whereas prior to our video-game disaster, I thought money was easy and plentiful, I became extremely conservative. I swore never again to put the company at risk of failure, and I was very careful to not hire more people than we needed, and to flush people immediately who weren't pulling their weight.

As part of this conservative attitude, I made the decision to focus on brand extension, rather than trying to launch new products. By doing King's Quest II or Space Quest II, the revenue projections were much more accurate, and less money had to be spent on creating brand awareness. The troops, Sierra's staff, hated the idea that new ideas were shut down so quickly, but it was part of my strategy of trying to build a company that could survive any attack. The tough times were a real wake-up call, and I was in no hurry to repeat them.

Ramsay: What kind of success did you have with this new strategy? Was the hit to morale worth it?

Williams: With the success of King's Quest, Sierra discovered the formula that brought us tremendous success. I began to think of the business as being about building franchise properties, and then extending the franchises and creating new franchises. I also began to speak of our customers using terms like "cost of acquisition," "retention rates," and "lifetime revenue."

Internally, we started to market as though we were serving product to a giant fan club. We tried to think of our relationship with the customer as much bigger than a single product. We knew that if we treated customers with respect, and gave them far more than they bargained for with each purchase, they would be back for many more. More importantly, they would be willing to try an unknown product just because it had the Sierra name, and this would allow us to launch new franchises. Our strong customer relationships also allowed us to survive a few highly visible turkeys along the way, which might have destroyed other companies. Our customers felt they had a personal relationship with the company, and the fact is that they did. The relationship for them and for us was much bigger than any one product.

Ramsay: What "turkeys" were those? How destructive were they?

Williams: Sierra's best-known turkey was a game called Outpost. The reviews were so bad that one publication reviewed it under the name "Compost." The name stuck. Outpost wasn't actually a bad game. It looked beautiful, and Sierra invested a fortune in making it. I don't remember how much—probably a pittance by modern standards—but I recall the game shipped very late and heavily over budget.

The problem was that the game just wasn't fun. It had many beautifully rendered 3D sequences, but these slowed the gameplay and became boring after awhile. We knew fairly early in development that we had a problem. Early showings of the product generated high consumer demand, but I wanted to keep the game in development until I felt it was ready for release. No one at the company was playing the product. I was constantly leaning on the product's designer to fix the problems, but rumors around the company were that he was exhausted and out of ideas for what to do.

After months of costly delays with no forward progress, I made the decision to ship the product. Many people said that I should have held the product for further tweaking. Had I believed it would make a difference, I would have. Who knows? Perhaps I was wrong and we should have kept working on the product. We'll never know. Outpost sold well, but it also had a lot of returns. Overall, we lost money and reputation over the fiasco.

On a more personal level, I was very frustrated with the last released sequels to two of Roberta's series, King's Quest VIII and Phantasmagoria II. Phantasmagoria had tremendous advance buzz, and the game was awesome. The only major complaint was that people didn't want to see it end. Gameplay was fairly short but intense. Everything about the game was pioneering, and Phantasmagoria became Sierra's first game to sell a million copies. I wanted Roberta to launch into Phantasmagoria II immediately, but she had started on King's Quest VIII, which would also be a money factory.

Rather than wait on Roberta to become available, I made the decision to have Lorelei Shannon, who had understudied with Roberta on King's Quest VII, to design Phantasmagoria II. Lorelei did a fine job, but you can't fool the public. In the creative world, fans are buying the person behind the product, not just the product. They knew Roberta's style and wanted a Roberta game. It's as if a bestselling author had a book ghostwritten. Within a few pages, the fans would know they had been duped and feel disappointed, regardless of the quality of the work.

Phantasmagoria II was also slammed by a completely unanticipated problem: Sierra's acquisition. As part of the acquisition, Sierra's distribution was handed off to a competitor, Davidson Software. When Davidson's management team realized that Phantasmagoria II had content that was typical for horror movies but arguably offensive, there were voices that said "kill it." I doubt Davidson would agree, but there is no doubt in my mind that Sierra's sales force would have sold materially more units of Phantasmagoria II than Davidson's. Probably one of the greatest series ever created was killed by inattention.

Meanwhile, Roberta was having even less fun with King's Quest VIII. As part of the company's acquisition, I was sidelined. Roberta had been accustomed to coming to me when there were creative differences with the team. Artists, programmers, and musicians working on a game often liked to insert things which allow them to show off their own creativity. Sierra was able to attract top talent, and these were people who wanted to showcase what they were capable of. One of my biggest challenges was to keep the entire team pushing in the same direction. If left to their own devices, a 20-person team might create something that feels disjointed with no central vision. I constantly fought the battle of trying to harness and focus creativity. This usually meant supporting my designer and helping the team understand why it was in everyone's best interest that they execute the designer's universe, rather than try to slip in ideas of their own.

Without me around to support her, Roberta lost control of the project. Characters and character interaction started showing up in the game that Roberta didn't put there. The game started transitioning from an adventure to more of a fantasy role-playing game, with battles taking on much more importance. Roberta was frustrated and complained to me constantly, but I was powerless to help. Finally, she said, "I want my name off the game. I am walking on the project." This did not go over well. Her vocal nonsupport of the game would kill revenues. A negotiation occurred, during which some game changes were agreed to and money changed hands. It was a sad situation with lots of finger-pointing, and the game suffered. Roberta was not surprised that the game sold poorly.

Ramsay: What did you think about being acquired?

Williams: I had convinced myself that Sierra was so strong that we could never fail. I also believed that any company that acquired Sierra would try to get inside of what made Sierra special, instead of destroying what they had bought. A structure was put in place that I believed would ensure that Sierra was a success post acquisition. Unfortunately, the rules that we established were ignored, and Sierra's acquisition was a disaster for the acquiring company, Sierra's employees, and Sierra's fans. It hurts me to think about it.

Ramsay: How did the acquisition by Davidson come about?

Williams: Walter Forbes, the CEO at CUC International, had a vision to consolidate the key players in the consumer software industry and create a dominant company. His idea was to "roll up" all of the leading players into a mega company that would dominate the industry. As part of that strategy, he met with LucasArts, Brøderbund, and Davidson. My recollection is that Sierra actually wasn't part of the original game plan, but was added later in the process. I had no idea these discussions were going on and was blindsided when Walter asked me about acquiring Sierra. I don't remember if this occurred before or after the Sierra acquisition was consummated, but I remember participating in a very strong effort by CUC to acquire Brøderbund.

To this day, I vacillate on whether Walter Forbes was a genius or a crook. The Walter I knew was ahead of his time and a true visionary. Ultimately, a jury convicted him. CUC was found to have been conducting massive fraud. He and his president, Kirk Shelton, were said to have fabricated nearly a half billion in profit and jailed. But I never heard the evidence against him, and I will never completely believe in his guilt. That said, he was definitely not honest about how Sierra would be managed post acquisition.

Ramsay: How did Davidson kill the Phantasmagoria series through inattention? Why couldn't the series recover?

Williams: Sierra and Davidson were successfully acquired simultaneously by CUC. As part of the acquisition, all distribution responsibilities were consolidated under Davidson. Davidson's background was in selling educational software. Their retail sales force couldn't make the adjustment of going from selling kids' learning games to explaining to Wal-Mart why they should keep an R-rated product on their shelves.

We also heard that Jan Davidson, Bob Davidson's wife, was personally offended by Phantasmagoria and wanted it shut down. I appealed to Walter Forbes to intercede, but Davidson's heart was not in selling R-rated products, and the product died. With Davidson running the sales force, there was no reason to make a third Phantasmagoria, as it would have met the same sales challenge.

Ramsay: When Roberta would come to you with her grievances about creative differences, were you ever concerned that your interference would be viewed in a negative light?

Williams: Pre-acquisition, when Sierra was Sierra, there were certainly allegations of favoritism when I would take Roberta's side in creative discussions. My response was always, "Go write a game that sells 500,000 copies, and I guarantee I will favor you."

Generally, how Sierra worked was that each project had a designer. I picked the projects and assigned the budget. The budgets were based on a combination of the designer's past success and sales of similar products in the niche. For instance, if the game was a race-car game, and industry sales stats indicated that racecar games averaged 100,000 copies, then I would give the team a budget based on 100,000 copies. In those days, I did all budgeting based on a 20% R&D budget. In other words, if I thought I would sell 100,000 copies at $22 wholesale, then I was forecasting $2.2 million in revenue; 20% of that number is $440,000. If the designer felt they could build the game for $440,000, then we could proceed. If not, then the project wouldn't get built.

Once the project started, I held the designer responsible for all creative decisions on the project, including the look and feel of the advertising and packaging. If the designer exceeded their sales forecast, and delivered the project approximately on budget, they would be given a bigger forecast and budget for their next project. If they delivered a bomb, unless it was an anomaly within a long career, their career was over as a designer. The rules were very simple and firm. Winners moved up the ladder, and losers lost.

Ramsay: Can you tell me more about how Sierra would be structured after the acquisition?

Williams: It was agreed, in writing, that after the acquisition, I would retain complete control over Sierra's product development and marketing organizations. I would be named vice chairman of the acquiring company. An Office of the President would be formed at the acquiring company, and I would be one of three persons in it, along with the existing president and the chief operating officer. A software board would be formed, too, and Sierra would have two seats on the four-person board. None of this was ever done. Immediately after the acquisition, it was made clear that these things had only been said so that I would agree to the acquisition. I would never have agreed to the acquisition had I not believed that a structure was in place that would allow Sierra to succeed.

Ramsay: Few games have creators with Roberta's name recognition. Did you believe in cultivating creative leaders on other products?

Williams: Absolutely. Sierra always featured our designers and had a large number of great designers. Over the years, we cultivated about 30 individuals who I trusted to design and build products. These people were known to our customers. Their games had instant demand on release.

Sierra was a publishing company. Our primary assets were the stable of authors we had spent years cultivating and the processes we had in place to build games. Post acquisition, all of this fell apart, and the two gentlemen who engineered our acquisition, Walter Forbes and Kirk Shelton, are still in jail today.

Ramsay: What did you do after you left Sierra in 1998?

Williams: There's an old saying: "If you ever sell your company, get as far away as you can, as fast as you can." I should have kept that saying in mind. However, instead, I tried to stay and make sure that the company was in good hands. I remember that one of my mission statements at Sierra was that I wanted to create a company that would survive longer than I would. I thought I had done it.

It was amazing how little time it took them to destroy the company. I had thought that there was some risk that the "corporate types" wouldn't understand how to build fun games, but I always assumed that I would be able to give them gentle nudges in the right direction. I thought that they would be happy to have the help. I knew that I was dealing with a bunch of Harvard types who would need some time to learn the business, but I didn't know I was dealing with crooks.

After the sale, I felt virtually every emotion at one time or another. Sierra had been 17 years of intense pressure. The sale left me wealthy, able to relax, and it was a great feeling of not having to jump on an airplane every few days. On the other hand, I went from the fast lane, where everyone returned my calls, to being an outsider. There was a time when I could call virtually anyone and get through. Suddenly, I was a has-been. And then there was the trauma associated with watching them destroy the company and the damage it caused the employees. People were being wiped out financially—people who had worked for me for many years and had done nothing wrong. It was insane and incomprehensible.

On one hand, I felt responsible, in that I should have known these guys were incompetent. Except, how could I have? If the auditors couldn't figure it out, how could a software entrepreneur, thousands of miles from corporate? I remember telling Roberta that I couldn't believe the board meetings at the company that acquired us. They had very little to do with the company's operations. There were lots of golf stories, kidding around, and very little substance. Sierra's board meetings were always tense and very serious. I felt like a fish out of water.

There are other emotions that I'm not particularly proud of. One line I used to say a lot was, "There is no one working at Sierra who isn't confident they can do my job better than I can." I always had a sense that everyone around me thought I was an idiot and could easily do my job better than me. It bugged me on some level, but not very much. I knew that my job was trickier than people thought and that the hardest thing to say in business is no. I had to turn down projects regularly and always be the bad guy. In some cases, I shut down projects where the team was absolutely convinced they had a mega hit, but it just didn't feel right to me. In some cases, I was right, and in others, I was wrong. I explained to people that my goal was to grow the company and please the customers, not to win a popularity contest.

When the new owners spoke to the teams, they all assured the new owners that they could survive quite happily without me. The developers always had things they wanted to do that I wouldn't permit. I had fairly rigid rules for what I'd approve, how I wanted the system to work, and what staffing should be. With me gone, everyone got what they wanted, which in a creative enterprise can quickly create problems. It shocked me that the new owners didn't call me to review many of the decisions, and ultimately, they discovered that they should have. I feel somewhat vindicated by all that occurred after me and that perhaps people now realize that they should have listened to me.

Overall, I just feel sad about the whole thing. I feel happy that we created such a great company, but sad that I sold to crooks who destroyed it all. I was personally tired of running Sierra and a little burnt out. I felt it was time for me to move on, and thought I had the company sold to someone who would take over all the bureaucracy, but allow me to continue building great product. It didn't work out that way and was a total disaster.

Ramsay: When you look back on Sierra and what you accomplished, what are your thoughts?

Williams: One benefit of selling the company was that I was finally able to do some things I've always wanted to do. Probably like every person who has ever managed a team of creative people, I was jealous of my people. I always felt trapped as a corporate bureaucrat while everyone around me was having fun doing cool things. I wanted to be creative, too! I loved writing code, but there was just no time. I had to live my life vicariously through my engineers and designers.

Finally, after the sale of the company, I could do some writing. I enjoy writing and have written three books. My books are not that good, and I'm not a great writer, but that's fine with me. The writing is somewhat its own reward, and within the small niche that reads my books, they are very popular. The books chronicle Roberta's and my adventures as we cruise around the world on our boat. I'm a computer geek, not a ship captain, and the books work because people are able to watch me struggle with a whole class of puzzles that are completely new to me.

On the coding side, I'm also having fun. I now write code probably 20 to 60 hours a week. I'm building a dot-com type of company, which I believe can someday revolutionize its category. I've always been interested in networks and empowering people to communicate in new ways. My product, a website maker, seems boring on the surface, but some of that is because I have a small team and we can't move very fast. I have a clear vision for where I want to take the product and a schedule for getting there, but I'm not in a hurry. I miss the days of having hundreds of programmers and being able to move quickly, but not so much that I want to go back to managing a large team. If I do something radically new and different five years from now instead of one year from now, that's fine with me. I'm having fun, and I'm in no hurry for the fun to end.

When I look back on my career, there were some things I did very well and some things I wish I could go back and do over. In many ways, particularly at the beginning, I was very immature. I was just a dumb kid in the right place at the right time. Had the industry not been growing so fast, I'd have been wiped out quickly. However, I did have some core values which were with us from the beginning, and which, when I look back, impress me that I was so wise for such a young kid. Specifically, I was very focused on the relationship with the customers and with building a long-term relationship. We ran the business like a large fan club. We knew that if we took good care of customers, they'd take good care of us. It was more than a saying; it was how we did business. Every decision revolved around the long-term relationship.

I was also very firm about the ownership of intellectual property rights. I understood that we needed to own everything. We were also compulsive about wanting to forge our own path. We never got into doing "me, too" products. We always saw ourselves as leaders and felt that we had a responsibility to do cool new things. Overall, I'm very proud of what we did, and I'm sorry that it ended.

Once in awhile, I think about "dropping back in" and building another game company. But it will never happen. Those days are behind me. Other than wishing it had ended differently, I don't regret a thing.

Lorne Lanning

Cofounder, Oddworld Inhabitants

*After leaving the Hollywood visual-effects business, **Lorne Lanning** and Sherry McKenna cofounded Oddworld Inhabitants. Lanning had created a fictional universe called Oddworld, and believing in the power of video games as a storytelling medium, he set out to realize his creative vision. Immediately, he persuaded McKenna, a leading computer-graphics producer who had worked with talents such as The Doors, Michael Jackson, and Mick Jagger, to join him.*

Although financed by a venture-capital group, the investors sold its stake to GT Interactive, which became the studio's publisher of record. Oddworld Inhabitants went on to sell more than 6 million critically acclaimed games in the Oddworld universe, generating more than $200 million in revenue. However, Oddworld Inhabitants suddenly ceased its studio operations after the release of its last title in 2005, as part of a conscious yet controversial decision to reevaluate the business.

Lanning and McKenna have worked together for more than two decades. While they maintain the Oddworld franchise, especially with the rise of digital distribution, the duo, alongside Pogo founder Daniel Goldman, have started a new company, Xmobb, to pursue opportunities in social media.

Ramsay: What were you doing before Oddworld Inhabitants? Why did you make the decision to start a video-game company?

Lanning: Before Oddworld Inhabitants, Sherry and I were in the film business, and we were doing visual effects. At the time, I was a visual-effects supervisor at Rhythm and Hues, which is today one of the largest visual-effects firms in the world. I quickly saw, from being in Hollywood for awhile, that owning your intellectual property was not going to happen in that town, regardless of whether the medium was television, movies, or whatever. I started looking at how computer-graphics animation could be used in a place where I could create and control the destiny of our own properties, and our own stories and characters. That was a massive driving ambition. I wanted to tell these stories because I didn't want to be a miserable guy—another frustrated director in Hollywood and just complaining. I wanted to actually materialize my dreams.

So, I started looking heavily at what was happening in the game industry. Around 1992, being close to technology, chips, and how computer graphics worked, I thought the writing was on the wall. Right about that time, I convinced Sherry McKenna, who was at the time a superstar computer-graphics producer in Hollywood, that we needed to start a game company. A game company was the only place where we would eventually be able to use computer graphics to tell stories that we care about and not just stories that make money—stories that actually have some substance and relevance in the world. Twenty-one years ago, it was obvious to me that we were going to end up where we are now as a civilization, and I wanted to start telling stories that retooled the old myths and gave us some semblance of sanity. And that led to games.

I also convinced Sherry that the time was now. If we didn't hit that window, we probably never would. The people in film wouldn't be able to cross over in the years to come. As I put it then, there's a lot of dumb money being thrown around, and they don't understand necessarily who's going to win and who's going to lose, so we have to get in now before they figure it out. It took me two years to really convince Sherry. And then she had enough of me trying to convince her and said, "If you can raise the money, I'll start the company with you." She was never expecting that we actually would raise the money because we wanted $3.5 million. That was ridiculous for a game budget, according to conventional wisdom.

To me, it was obvious that games were going to have $50 million budgets. If you said that in 1994, you were insane. No one would listen to you. The more you understood how the entertainment business worked, how mass media worked, the more you could predict where games were going to end up. So we took that path, and there was no looking back. It has been a wild ride ever since.

Ramsay: You didn't want to wind up miserable in Hollywood? How was Rhythm and Hues? Were you miserable there?

Lanning: Well, not with the company. I think the company was as good as it gets. John Hughes, Charlie Gibson, Pauline Ts'o, and Frank Wuts were the founders, and they ran a top-notch organization. They all have an incredible amount of integrity. I was really lucky to land there. Well, actually, I begged my way into the door. I took a 50% pay cut to move from TRW Aerospace to Rhythm and Hues because I wanted it that bad. They were really honorable people and prudent about how they were running their business. But I wanted something different. I wanted to tell stories.

I think I had the John Lasseter dream. I wanted to make those stories happen. I felt like that was part of what my life was about. The industry of Hollywood, not the company, was such that those dreams are very elusive. The more you studied what was happening on the ground, the more those dreams felt like they would never be. It's like our impression of Iraq or Afghanistan. We have one view from being on the outside, and then there's this whole other view when you're on the ground. Being on the ground, I just saw what a stale town Hollywood was.

There are shelves full of books written about the dysfunctions of Hollywood, but really, it's like a California town that had already been mined back in the 19th century. It was like most of what was really good was already gone. Now we have these industries—television, film, and music—that were very obviously going to die. As much as we want to view them as we do today, when you look at the music industry, it's dead. Oh, we can say people are still making money on concerts and stuff, but just look at the revenue; just look at the charts of the financials from a Wall Street perspective. The music industry is dead. It had its heyday. Napster changed everything, and iTunes changed it more. The old ways had to change, and the people who held on to those old ways did not change. As a result, we saw the music industry just collapse.

The movie industry isn't far behind. The budgets are just so enormous, and that's a hit-driven business. You're into a single project for hundreds of millions of dollars. It's like, "Are you kidding me? This is a movie. This is entertainment. You've got more money here than multiple third-world nations combined, and you're dumping all of that money into a single movie?" Bigger budgets mean you've got another level of bureaucracy. We're seeing this inflation happen in the game business today, too. That inflation has changed and is continuing to change the dynamics of how people work. We're seeing more checks and balances, more paranoia, more people in the loop, more studio notes, and everything else that ultimately adds up to less fun and creativity. Hollywood very quickly lost its appeal to me.

Ramsay: How quickly did you go from wanting to work at Rhythm and Hues to wanting to get out?

Lanning: That was after five years. There's this old Japanese story. I don't know if you've heard this. Did you ever hear about the samurai who goes up to the top of the mountain and talks to the old wise man in the cave? How do I know when my time has come? How do I know when my moment for greatness is here?

So, there's this samurai. I'll tell you the story, if you don't mind. There's this samurai and he's feeling like, you know, "What do I do now. I'm at the top of my game, but I feel like I'm destined for greatness. I'm going to go talk to the old sage in the mountains." So, he goes across the valley, across the plains, over the hills, up the mountain, and climbs all the way to the top. He gets into the cave, and he's like, "Old wise man, how do I know when it's my time to be great?" And the wise man says, "Well, here's what you need to do. You need to go back down the mountain, go back over the hills, go back across the plains and across the valley, and get to the ocean. When you get to the ocean, start walking in. When you get your knees deep in water, keep on going until it's up to your waist. When the water gets to your chest, keep on going. Eventually, the water is going to be up to your face. Keep on going. Do that." And the guy's like, "Are you serious?" And the wise man's like, "Yeah, do that, and you'll get your answers."

The samurai just thinks this sounds crazy, but the guy is the old wise man in the cave, so he goes back down the mountain, over the hills, across the plains, across the valley, and finally gets to the beach. He walks into the ocean, and the water gets to his knees. He keeps on walking, and the water gets to his waist. He keeps on walking, and the water gets to his chest. He keeps on walking, and the water gets up to his face. You know what? He's going to go for it, so he just keeps on walking.

A minute later, he can't walk any farther because he's completely underwater and about to drown. He comes up for air, and he's like, "What the fuck?" He's totally pissed off. He storms back across the valley, across the plains, over the hills, and climbs up the mountain. He charges into the cave, and he's like, "Dude, you know what, wise man, why did you make me do that? I almost drowned." The wise man says, "Yeah, but how did you feel?" The samurai replies, "I needed air." And the wise man says, "Well, that's when you know it's time for you to make your move for greatness."

The point of that story is that you know it's time to make your move when you can no longer take what you're currently doing. That's the essence of that story. How did I feel when I was underwater? Like I was going to die, like I had no options. That's how I felt. Like I was going to die, like I had no options, like I was trapped in a career. It had nothing to do with the people or the company. It had everything to do with my own dreams and ambitions. I wasn't really making them happen. I was developing my skill sets. I was making a lot of decent money. I was on the cutting edge of imagery and computer-graphics technology. I was working with awesome people, but I wasn't telling stories. Telling stories is what I wanted to do. At the same time though, I wanted to make a lot of money.

I've always believed that people wind up slaves to the economy. What would we be like if we didn't have to work every day? What would we be like if we didn't have to go have a job? What are all of the things that we'd want to do? What do we actually do because we have to make money? Because I grew up poor, that was always something that made me think, "I want to do what I want to do, and I want to make money doing it because I spent a lot of my life being poor, and I don't like being poor." So, that's sort of the moral to my analogy. I needed more air and felt as though I had no choice but to make a change. When you feel that way, you do something. So, what I did was I convinced Sherry to start Oddworld.

Now, in the meantime, I had been writing stories. I was really learning a lot about what was happening in, let's say, the red-pill reality. You know, like in The Matrix, the reality outside what people perceive in the media—what's really going on. The more I learned about what's really going on, the more I felt a strong desire to tell stories because, quite frankly, the blue-pill reality was really starting to piss me off. I just couldn't believe the bullshit that people were being hoodwinked into on a daily basis.

I believe that stories have the power of change. Stories can help people who recognize certain difficult-to-perceive and even harder-to-believe landscapes of our world. Regardless of whether the subject is international banking, the war machine, or whatever, the more truth that's revealed to us, as opposed to the bullshit we're told, the more I felt underwater. And I had to tell stories because I felt like we were living in a dreamworld.

I really wanted to tell those stories. And I wanted to tell those stories through the most popular media, which had drawn me to film in the first place. I eventually realized, "Oh, film is not ready to make CG movies yet." This is before Toy Story had come out. The film studios were not ready to take the chance. At the time, it cost at least $100 million to make a decent movie, and somewhere between $60 million and $100 million in CG, and that hadn't been proven yet. Who was I to fool myself thinking that I'd be the one to get that money to do the first CG movie?

Combine all of these factors and the fact that I really need air. I was looking around, asking myself, "Where can I breathe? Where can I breathe what I'm about?" I settled on... video games? I looked at that, and I said, "I got it." I mean, I got games.

I had a paper route as a kid. In New England, I'd get into a little diner on my route to have some hot chocolate and play some pinball or whatever as often as I could. Anyone who had a paper route where they'd deliver papers at 5:00 in the morning while it's 10°F below outside would understand. It was just so damn cold out. That got me really playing games—loving games—and then my dad started working at ColecoVision.

I understood why games were fun, but I wasn't really a hardcore player. I was more interested in going out, riding motorcycles, and trying to get laid instead of sitting at home, playing any games that were out. I wasn't quite a member of the game-playing youth culture, but I was always somewhat close to it, and I did enjoy games when I played. When the technology evolved to where I felt that what I had come to love—3D computer graphics—was able to become the medium for games, then I decided that was the time to take that chance and really go for it.

Ramsay: At Rhythm and Hues, did the company ever look at applying CG to other media, such as games?

Lanning: Yeah, they actually tried making one of their own games. It was after Sherry and I left. It was called *Eggs of Steel*, and, if I remember correctly, it didn't do so well. At the time, we were trying to convince the company to do games. Games weren't something they had envisioned, but they were listening, and they were curious. They were interested in exploring games as a revenue channel—an area to supplement the movies that they ultimately wanted to make. But games aren't like that. You can't look at games lightly. You can't say, "Well, let's do some games and make some money on the side." It's not going to happen.

I had the good fortune of knowing that then because I had made friends with people in the industry early. I remember the first guy who really opened the door for me to come in and look at his studio was Tommy Tallarico, who was at Virgin at the time. I visited the studio, and I saw how they were doing what they were doing. I was doing a lot of homework on the industry, and I realized this is magic that these guys are doing.

The Hollywood guys were telling me, "Ah, they look like crap. Why are you interested in games? The graphics suck. There are no stories. They're just toys." I was like, "Don't you see the alchemy here? These guys are squeezing out 60 hours of entertainment with 56K of RAM on a budget of $500,000.

You're spending $100 million on a two-hour movie that someone might watch twice. Think about that. You have to start paying attention."

Adaptation is one of our greatest skills. The world is changing underneath our feet at a more accelerated rate than ever before in known human history, and that means you have to be agile. You have to adapt. You can't stick to beliefs that don't really have foundations in repeatable sciences today. You'll get run over too quickly. You could come out with a game back when Myst did, and you didn't have to worry about being ripped off for a few years. Today, if you come out with something clever, Zynga is going to have you cloned overnight, right? It's a different landscape today.

Hollywood, the visual effects supervisors, the art directors, and the good artists weren't interested in games. There were a few, but most weren't. They just didn't get it, in my opinion. They didn't see why games were going to be huge—unbelievably huge. They weren't looking at games as the entertainment medium of the future.

Now, while games have had a lot of successes since then, they're not the medium of the future yet. There are a lot of different moving parts that kind of fucked that up—one called the PlayStation 2—which was when we stopped paying attention to the development environment. We really screwed the pooch on the audience and the development community. Because hardware engineers in the game business didn't understand the art of actually making games and they dictated the designs—in this case, I'm speaking specifically about Ken Kutaragi—they caused games to suddenly start costing a lot more. The culture was such that developers would tolerate rather than resist. If you came out with a movie camera like the PlayStation 2 in Hollywood, you would have been out of business in two minutes. No one would have used it. They would have told you where to stick it. But that's not how the game industry operated.

The game industry was subservient to hardware manufacturing, whereas content-driven industries are not. In my mind, games weren't really a content-driven industry. They were a challenge-product-driven industry. If you had a great challenge that made people have fun playing the game and it was a solid product, then you could win, you could sell, and you could stay in business and make more. In Hollywood, if you didn't have a story that really engaged people, you didn't have a movie. The game audience was really tolerant of certain shortcomings and not of others, so the audience didn't care about graphics if they could get good gameplay. The reviewers thought they were graphics authorities though. It was a joke, right? We'd look at reviews, and we'd be like, "These guys think this is good graphics? They're clueless."

So, there were different human-consumption patterns and desires that made one film or game succeed over the other.

Times have changed. Now, it's hard to tell the difference between what we're seeing. If we're in a bar and we see a game on television, we ask ourselves, "Is that a game, or is that footage of a game?" The line is blurred. In the 90s, the differences between film and games were pretty obvious. But I guess I'm tripping on all of that to just say that games were so obviously the future to me. They were the future because of the ratio of how much content you could create versus how long an experience that created for the audience.

When I started, when we were doing animation, we were charging a million dollars per minute. That was the going rate for quality CG in Hollywood. At Rhythm and Hues, that was the rate. When you looked at the game Myst, most people were spending 20 or more hours in that game, and it had a total budget of $500,000. If you looked at a product where you spent a million dollars per minute to tell a story, that minute would forever be the same throughout history. But with a game, different people play different ways for different amounts of time. Some will spend more, and some will play twice. The economics of games is simply completely different. If you're paying attention to that, you see it's just a matter of time.

As computing power increases, image quality increases; therefore, our ability to tell stories with games will improve. The reason we had confidence in that was because we weren't really looking at the industry as much as we were looking at human behavior. And you know why? We love good stories. We love good animation. We love cartoons. We like great stories. We like good direction. We like action. We like drama. We like love stories. We would want better stories and games, period. It was obvious.

Now, there was a whole bunch of know-it-alls who said, "Oh, you don't understand games. Let me show you my metrics." You know, all that bullshit. And it was like, "Dude, you don't understand people." So, we started Oddworld on that very human note at the time.

Ramsay: Before you went to Sherry, was starting a company your only option? Did you consider other options?

Lanning: We did consider other options. There were a few people that had asked Sherry to run game companies that venture capitalists were about to finance for another $10 million or so. There were a few different efforts by a few different visual-effects companies. Richard Edlund was thinking about starting up a game department at Boss Film Studios. James Cameron had just started a new studio in Hollywood called Digital Domain. They claimed they wanted to do games. There was a lot of Sillywood hype about the "information highway." Silicon Valley and Hollywood were going to change the way we watch everything. Today, that has actually happened, but it didn't happen as fast as everyone claimed it would then. We wanted to get involved with games at Rhythm and Hues, too.

You have to understand, CG was very expensive. It was an $80,000 purchase just to put someone behind a desk. You had $40,000 in software, Wavefront, and another $40,000 in Silicon Graphics hardware. If you wanted decent-looking CG, that's what you had to spend. And that's not including salaries and other soft costs. If you had set up a network—a capable network that could push many gigabytes of data, which was a lot then—you didn't want to set that shit up from scratch, man. It was a lot of work, required a lot of brain power, and was very expensive. We were hoping to start doing games at Rhythm and Hues. Sherry was even asked to run the division, and I would work with her to get that going.

James Cameron had also personally asked me to work for him at Digital Domain. He was really interested and wanted to go for games. I just didn't believe any of those kinds of outfits would be successful. I listened to their plans, and I just said, "It's not going to work. If you don't take games ultra-seriously, you're going to fail because it's not as easy as you think." When film directors and studio heads look at games, they see toys. They go, "Ah, games must be easy." But they're not, right? Games are really hard. I've made movies, I've made television, and I've made photorealistic paintings. Games are the hardest. Games are really difficult because you're dealing with technology that the end user can break. That's not the case with any of these other mediums.

So, yes, we really did hope that we could start doing games somewhere else and not start our own company. At the end of the day, we said that if we don't start our own company, we don't think we'll be successful. That was a pretty depressing realization because I just didn't want to go through all the work of setting everything up, you know? Everyone dreams of having their own companies, but not many people are willing to do what it takes to actually pull it off. And I don't give a shit what anyone says—that's just the bottom line, and it's way harder than everyone usually thinks it is.

Ramsay: Did you have any experience with startups before?

Lanning: I had experience in the art world, so that was my experience, but I was still a young guy. I started Oddworld when I was 29 years old. And previous to that, I was at Rhythm and Hues. Previous to that, I was in aerospace working on the Star Wars, visualizing Reagan's Star Wars. Before that, I was in the art world in New York, and I was an illustrator who became partners with a painter named Jack Goldstein. I thought he was the best contemporary fine artist in the world. I felt fortunate enough to meet him, and then I felt fortunate enough to impress him, and then I felt fortunate enough to become partners with him.

As a kid from the street, I understood some basics, like you can't run a business and piss everyone off—pretty basic stuff, right? Big, successful artists never learn that basic principle, so Goldstein made all kinds of errors in his career and in his relationships. I saw that those problems could be fixed, and I was bold enough to present solutions. He was, I think, tired enough to take me up on my offer to help him implement them, and we got started. We turned his art into a good business. For example, when I met him in 1985, his paintings were $15,000 a piece. I looked at what other artists were getting, and I saw that he was clearly undervaluing his work. A year and a half later, we had his paintings up to $60,000 a piece. I was running a studio—well, let's just call it what it was, a factory that would manufacture ten of those paintings every eight weeks, and we were preselling them.

That was really my first startup. It was like an Andy Warhol factory operation. There wasn't a business plan. There wasn't an exit strategy. I didn't even know what an exit strategy was. I didn't know much about anything. I knew that people like these artists and their paintings, and they're willing to pay certain prices. I thought, "How do we build a business around that?" I also understood that unless you're Syd Mead or someone who has turned their art into a business, instead of just work-for-hire, you have to study the principles and science of business. In this land of capitalism, if you don't study business, you will get screwed. I knew I had a lot of learning to do, but I understood the basics. You need to keep people happy, you need work that stands out, and you need to separate yourself with excellence. These basics served me quite well, but I was pretty clueless.

Ramsay: When you started Oddworld, did you think your past experience would help you?

Lanning: Yes, because I really believe in evolving your skill sets. If you believe in evolutionary principles like that, you think, "Okay, what tools are in my cerebral arsenal now that I can apply and do the things I want to do and be successful?" Regardless of whether you got in a fight as a kid and got your ass kicked, you walked away with certain lessons. Regardless of whether you got a speeding ticket or whether your girlfriend broke up with you because you were an idiot, you learned lessons. And regardless of whether those lessons are professional or personal, they usually intertwine because they're really just lessons about life.

In the art world, I was lucky in a lot of ways. I was fortunate. I actually made more money than I thought was possible at that point in my life because I grew up as a poor kid. At the same time, I thought I knew more about business than I actually did. You hear people say, "If I could know everything I did when I was 18, I'd know everything." But the fact is that as we get older, we realize how much we didn't know. I think naïveté really allows people to take chances. If they knew what was really at stake or how hard starting a company was really going to be, they never would have gone forward in the first place. That's true for me, too.

Oddworld was so hard that if I knew how hard it was going to be, I probably wouldn't have done it. I probably would have been intimidated by the task and not believed that we could have actually succeeded. Just about everyone I know in the game business, including Peter Molyneux and Dave Taylor, says the same thing. If they knew how hard it was going to be, they probably wouldn't have done it. If someone doesn't admit that, I don't trust them. That's the truth. I hear people say things like, "We build games because we just love building games." I'm like, "Oh, shut up. You're just reading the script that you think people want to hear, but the fact is that you know you're getting screwed by publishers. You know you're getting a raw deal." The chatter in front of the camera is so different from the chatter in the backroom. When I hear these people, I'm thinking, "Are you kidding? Who do you think you're fooling? Building games is really fun? That's just bullshit."

I don't know anyone who builds great games who honestly believes that the process of building games is fun. I've had this conversation with many of the well-known names in the business, and I've yet to have one disagree. Whether they'll admit it to the world is another story. So, no, I probably wouldn't have done it, but I needed air, and naïveté really helped me to jump out there and take the bull by the horns.

Ramsay: When you were convincing Sherry to jump on this adventure with you, what was that conversation like?

Lanning: She thought I was stupid. Well, she didn't think exactly that. Sherry McKenna was the "it" producer for computer graphics. She has more Clio Awards than anyone. To this day, she has won more Clio Awards than any other single individual in television.

Her career started in the music business with The Doors, who were her kid buddies, and she was helping manage their business. When Michael Jackson or Mick Jagger wanted computer graphics, or when Steven Spielberg wanted to do the Back to the Future simulator attraction, they went to Sherry to produce all of that stuff. She was used to winning awards, being a hotshot, and being interviewed by HBO and all of these things.

She was making a fortune—literally hundreds and hundreds of thousands of dollars a year—and there I was trying to convince her, "But wouldn't you like to make more? Wouldn't you like to not be paid by the hour?" I pulled out every trick I could think of because I honestly didn't think I would be successful without her. I was an artist, so I was still an asshole. I'm not saying that I was early Steve Jobs, early Bill Gates, or Mark Zuckerberg in The Social Network. But you've got to be an asshole to just have your dream, be a dick and ignore everyone, and pursue it. Later, you might grow up and realize what an asshole you were. I wasn't an exception. So, Sherry loved movies, and there I was trying to show her Sonic the Hedgehog and why we should start a game company.

She was like, "Are you crazy? Why would I care about making stupid games?" That was probably a verbatim quote. I said, "Because let me tell you this story." I knew that she loved stories, so I told her the story of Abe. I told her this big, long story. I was working in her division at Rhythm and Hues, running the whole theme park division, which was called Special Projects. I was a strong advocate of that division and a strong advocate of having Rhythm and Hues recruit her from Universal. She had a relationship with these people anyway, but I was trying to move things along. I had worked on a project with her, and I was telling her that she should come to work at Rhythm and Hues. But it's not like this was unfamiliar territory. There was history. She had hired the people who founded Rhythm and Hues when they were working in coal mines in Pennsylvania.

So, she thought I was nuts, and then I told her the story of Abe. She fell in love with the story, and she was like, "My God, this is so awesome. Let's make a movie." I was like, "No, let's make five games." That was where the Oddworld Quintology got started, years before we launched the company. These stories were very close to me. These weren't something that a focus group sat around and cherry-picked. I had a pretty good idea of what I wanted to do, but I also wanted to bring in the influences of some creative partners, a team of designers and artists.

From that point, those original concepts were shaped into what I should say was more palatable and less extreme. I thought that the world was ready for quirky dysfunctional victims of the dark side of globalization—how appropriate that is today because look around us, man! I got Sherry to at least agree that if we could raise the money, we would start the company. I think she agreed just to humor me because I think she didn't really expect that we would actually get the money, but we did. She had given me her word, so it was too late to back out. That's how our adventure began.

Ramsay: You've mentioned several times that you grew up poor, that you were a kid from the streets. Can you tell me about where you grew up?

Lanning: I should say lower middle class, right? Not quite ghetto, but lower middle class. As a kid growing up in that environment, I was always afraid that we might not able to afford rent, and we might be out on the street. My dad was in the US Navy. My parents got divorced really young because he was always out to sea. He was in the submarines. My mother worked as a nurse as a single mom, raising two kids and just trying to get by. We were living in a low-rent neighborhood around the city of Meriden in Connecticut, and there was crime all around us. People were just feeding on other people. Not literally, of course. That's what I mean by lower middle class. It was a school of hard knocks.

Meriden was one of these rust-belt–type of cities, even though it was New England. It was an old silver-mining town that had since seen the heyday of its industry. There was a lot of racial tension and, in my opinion, a lot of bigotry, racism, and old ways of thinking in New England. The city where I lived had about an equal violent crime rate to New York City at the time. This wasn't new to Connecticut. New Britain, Bridgeport, New London, New Haven, and Hartford—these were hardcore cities. These cities aren't what you'd think of as Connecticut, but they're there. Ask anyone who went to Yale what the neighborhood was like.

I saw people who were just absolutely miserable to each other. They were resentful and criminal, and I thought a lot of that was related to the economic realities that they lived in. To me, it was always pretty clear that most people were always fighting over money. I didn't want to be like that. I didn't want to be living so hand-to-mouth that I had to be mean and miserable to other people and not use my brain. No disrespect to the lower class. In fact, I feel a great compassion toward people of lesser means because I think under capitalism, they've really gotten the shaft. And I'm even saying that as an entrepreneur.

If you and I were living in medieval Italy, we would be Catholic. We wouldn't have a choice. When you live in the United States, we don't have a choice but to play the capitalism game, but the capitalism game is failing us. That was very obvious to me 30 years ago. Its failure hasn't even fully materialized for most people to really understand just how badly it has failed and what's to come, which is, in my opinion, not going to be pretty. All of these influences aside, this is the game that we play. He who has the gold rules. This is the golden rule of capitalism.

As a result, we have to understand the economic realities of how money works and how the supposed free market works. If we don't understand that language, we're not going to get very far. Coming to understand how it worked did not mean that I was a devout follower of its faith. I always resented how it worked. I always felt like it was a game that didn't bring out the best in people or yield the best results. Learning about it in school, I just went, "I don't believe it. I just don't buy how one company becoming a monopoly and crushing others is good." I never could ignore when the richest people, like Rockefeller and Carnegie and J.P. Morgan, pressured others in the most wicked of ways. I never could buy into the notion that when you're in America, if you become one of them, you'll become enlightened and start building hospitals—that becoming a billionaire somehow makes you more human. That's our American myth. Having known a lot of billionaires, I don't think that's the case. I don't think you become more human by becoming more greedy.

Now, I'm not opposed to people making great amounts of wealth. I'm on a course for that myself, and I convince investors that is necessary every day. But how we go about it, and how we define ourselves in the process, I think, can use a lot of refinement. In our culture, we still worship the richest guy. But, come on, is that all? Is that really it? Is that how shallow we are? Is that all the fuck it's about? Take a look around you. Did I see his sailboat? Fuck his sailboat, and fuck him because the guy's a turd. When I look at the Rockefellers, the Carnegies, and the J.P. Morgans of the world, I see turds. When I see Oprah, not so bad. When I see Trump, who cares? I just see ego. That's all I can see. I don't see people trying to make the world better for anyone else. I see them trying to celebrate their greatness so that everyone agrees with them. I just don't buy that part of the picture, and I never did.

For me, I'm walking in a capitalist's shoes, but I'm not really a follower of the faith. This isn't the talk I give to investors, but this is the truth. I'm never going to lie about that. I just think humanity needs to wake the fuck up and stop being selfish little douche bags. I honestly believe that, and I believe that, as storytellers, we have the capability to try and effect that type of change. If I said my work was about anything, I think that's what it has been about: trying to effect that type of change. There's going to be war, so let's be good soldiers and at least try to shape it for the better, rather than just sitting on the sidelines, bitching and moaning like a lot of artists.

Ramsay: When you finally convinced Sherry to go along with you, she wanted you to get funding. Did you put together a business plan?

Lanning: Yeah. Before we continue, imagine this. I was driving forklifts in the South Bronx in one of the worst neighborhoods in the United States to pay for my education at the School of Visual Arts in downtown Manhattan. The School of Visual Arts wasn't cheap, but I paid my way because I wanted a good education. I didn't just get to go to college on someone else's dime. I worked really hard just to step through the door.

Although I was an artist in New York, I was also taking classes in business. The School of Visual Arts had a wide variety of offerings by really interesting people. I was taking classes with Wall Street brokers, venture capitalists, and finance people on how to raise money and how to put together business plans. I think being an individual of lesser means really drilled into me the difficulty of the road ahead. How hard is it to make something happen?

I asked myself, "Who do I love?" I loved Walt Disney. I loved the work of George Lucas. I loved the work of William Hanna and Joseph Barbera. I loved the work of Jim Henson. These guys had to figure out business, as well as master their crafts. I read as many biographies as I could about Hollywood moguls, early studio heads, and successful businesspeople, like the Carnegies and Rockefellers. I read whatever biographies I could get my hands on because I really wanted to understand how to succeed in the world. More importantly, I wanted to succeed with certain dreams, and I was under no illusion that my dreams would manifest themselves easily. Through all of these resources, I had learned the language and the structure for raising money.

When Sherry heard me say that I'll put together a business plan, I don't think that she really knew what she was in for. I pulled out the reference material for successful business plans. I copied those templates. I had been doing a lot of research. I've always believed in research, research, and more research. I had the data, but she had the experience to put everything together in a way that people would understand.

Ramsay: How much of a financial burden did you expect to undertake?

Lanning: Well, I learned something from the New York banking world, which was "never invest your own money." If you have good ideas, there are enough people with money who don't have those ideas. If you can't convince them, you're probably not going to make your idea successful anyway. I believed that you shouldn't invest your own money because it makes you less smart in the business because you're more scared. Fear doesn't manifest the best results.

Ramsay: You don't believe in having personal skin in the game?

Lanning: It depends on how many other parties are involved and how many parts can break. For example, we delivered games, and at times they couldn't find their way to the shelf. It had nothing to do with us. Had that been our money, we would have lost it all, and not because the game wasn't good. We would have lost it all because the distributor fucked up and couldn't get it on the shelf.

When people come to me and ask about whether they should invest their money in something, I advise people to understand what they'd be getting into, how many parts can fail, and how much control they have over those parts. There are a lot of ways that a great product can fail, and it can have nothing to do with the developers.

I think that it's better to not invest your own money and put your whole life on the line. I think if you do invest your own money, it's the nature of capitalism that you'll become a larger target. You're like a wounded gazelle. The predators will think that you can't walk. There's power in being able to walk away. The good news is that there's enough greed out there that you can always bank on greed. You can always know that if you have a story that stands a good chance to make people money, then you should be able to get someone who doesn't have any ideas to pay because that's what they do: they fund other people's ideas.

What we invested in Oddworld was time and sweat. I took a 50% cut to my salary to start the company, like I did when I went to work at Rhythm and Hues. I felt like I was investing a lot, even though it wasn't my life savings. It wasn't like I had much anyway. I think that people who do that are taking major risks with their own money. It doesn't always lead you to make the best decisions, so you really have to believe in what you're doing.

Ramsay: So raising money for Oddworld, you didn't have to sell your home or take on a second mortgage?

Lanning: No, I would never do that. I would never do that because in capitalism, that will be used against you. And I don't mean to be like the capitalist dog here, but the truth is what it is. I mean, read any good business book. Read Trump's books. I can't stand Trump, but I've read all his books, and I don't think he's a bad guy. The point is that what he'll always say that if you don't have the power to say no, you don't have any power.

So, if people know that you mortgaged your house, and you're going to be out on the street, they will take advantage of that. That is how this system works. I don't give a shit who says the opposite. I'd love to have that debate. It's like come on, man, it's pretty well damn understood. And if you have weaknesses—whether it's publishers or movie studios or venture capitalists—they're going to take advantage of them. That's their job. If you really understand how the system works, you get that that's their job. Now, you might have people within those organizations who have more credibility, who have different ethics, but at the core of this system, that's what it's about. That's what capitalism is about: taking advantage of little guys. And the more that someone has a vulnerability, the more people are rewarded for exploiting it, and that's just the way it is. I always saw that pretty clearly, so I was never going to put my life on the line, and then go out and ask other financial types to jump on the train with me because I knew where that would lead. I'd seen it at low levels and read about it at high levels. So, when I read about people making it, I think those are the fairytale stories. You know, there's one in a million that actually pulls it off.

Ramsay: What were your sources of funding for Oddworld?

Lanning: Well, at the time, it was sort of a pseudo-venture capital company that got created just for the purpose of creating a public company. They wanted to ride the same wave that Rocket Science was riding. If you remember that, it was riding that wave on the "information superhighway" that was the talk of the town in Hollywood, Silicon Valley, and Wall Street at the time. So, that was a group out of the Midwest that was basically run by the children of billionaires. The children were in their 40s and 50s, and they were more interested in making their own mark. They created this capital firm and started acquiring some companies. We rounded out their story quite well, so they chose to invest in us.

Their plan and our plan were not really the same, but that was what it took to get this company started. It started with that group. That was the only game venture that firm ever did. It was just a small group with a fair amount of money that had big ideas, and we kind of hit them at the right time, so we were able to get funded.

Ramsay: How much capital did you take?

Lanning: $3.5 million was what we raised.

Ramsay: What did you have to give up?

Lanning: At the time, 49% of the company, which people thought was unheard of. They thought you would absolutely give up more than 51%. We were in the negotiating room to sign the deal, and Sherry said she was willing to walk if she didn't have 51%. Their negotiator didn't believe it, so we started to walk. I was following her. He changed his mind and wanted us to stay! So, we had 51%, but it really came down to the fact that we had to walk. And if you're not willing to do that, you're going to be vulnerable.

Ramsay: You walked out of the meeting…

Lanning: Well, we tried! We tried to walk out, and we got stopped. Then it was like, "Okay, then. Let's be friends, and let's do this."

There were a lot of lessons learned after that, like about how various people can hold grudges, and you don't even necessarily know it. That caused a few rifts down the road. But again, it was also being financed by people who didn't really understand the game industry. They thought they understood Wall Street, and maybe they did. I don't know. But I know that they didn't understand the game industry. There were some unrealistic expectations.

Ramsay: Let's go back to 1994 and Rocket Science…

Lanning: Okay, so that was a big story in the game industry because it earned a lot of money in a really short time in the public market. But the whole story was "Hollywood meets Silicon Valley," and they had some guys from Apple and some well-known production designers like Ron Cobb and a few others. They were going to reinvent how games were made.

They did a Wall Street story and made a lot of money. And it kind of enflamed what I would say was a frenzy at the time—a bubble with people thinking they could start new game companies with 3D stories, take them public really quick, and make a lot of money. That was what our original investor was actually pretty clear about. I mean, that was just what the plan was. And for us, we didn't so much care about that plan as much as we wanted to build the company, and we wanted to build intellectual property. That was the misalignment. One was about how do you take it public, do a fast IPO on a good story, and just get out. And the other point of view, which was ours, was how do you build a great product, build a great company, try and have some fun, and make people money while you're doing it.

Ramsay: How much influence or control did they want?

Lanning: Control—full control. That's why we said we're walking out if we don't get 51%. That really is due to my partner. I mean, my partner's got balls of steel, she does. I probably would have been too wimpy on that front. What she said was, "Okay, if I don't have the ability to run the company, I don't want your money." It was really that simple. When it came to production, they really had to have faith that we could do product. So, that's how we got initial control of the company.

But I thought that by the time we delivered the product, these Wall Street types in these entities, which get created just to do public IPO plays, would be long gone. They didn't seem to have much interest in the process of making the product. I think that was kind of way beneath what their level of interest was. They were only interested in how quick can you create a timely story, how fast, and for how much can you turn it.

So, at the control level, they wanted full control of really nothing more than that. I mean, this was the basic model out there. It's not like a publisher that needs a game or a like a film studio that needs a film for a quarterly report.

When you're going for independent financing, it's all about the money. It's not so much about the company or the product. They need the controls to be able to make the types of deals that oftentimes people who are passionate about the product can easily stand in the way of and screw up.

What happens at contractual levels is that financial partners of that nature only have a singular interest in profit. They need the controls to make whatever financial decisions they want to make and move however they want to move. As a result of how the business financing world operates, they will always want those controls. Even if you're established, it's still the guy with the gold who's going to want those controls. It wasn't so much about product. It was more about destiny and the ability to have decisions made without the need for a common agreement.

Ramsay: As cofounders, how did you split your responsibilities?

Lanning: I demanded that she be the chief executive officer because I didn't want to do that, and I didn't think I'd be good at that. She was clearly far more skilled and versed in managing partners—whether they're financial partners or clientele partners—and that's half of the game right there.

If you want to build something—a company or a product—and you're passionate about it, you really need someone who knows how to deal with those partners. Those partners can easily and very quickly become overwhelming. They can divert a lot of time and attention away from the product you're trying to build. I mean, there's a whole slew of things where the partnerships need to be managed very skillfully to stay positive.

Everything in life is about trying to reduce friction, right? You want to try to make things happen easier. So, you need someone who manages the client very well—whether it's a financial investor or a publisher or a film studio or an advertising agency—they're all the same. Now, the difference is that pure cash investors don't have the vested interest in needing that film or needing that game for their distribution business. So, pure cash investors have their interests and it's very specific; whereas, if you're making a game and financing that way, you can be late and maybe not penalized because they're too afraid to piss you off because they really need that game.

But in the other space, in the financial space, it can be just more sterile and clinical and more upfront. The management of those relationships is critical, and I think the more people you talk to, the more that you'll hear that the people who succeed usually figure out a way to really manage those partners well. For me, my interest was creative, and Sherry was one of the few producers who I knew didn't think that she needed to get involved with that fun, creative process, too. Producers like that can be a real pain in the ass.

They're like, "Oh, let me tell you what color I think it should be." And I'm like, "I'm not really interested, dude." When there's that type of chemistry, it can be fractious and not result in a great product or a great company. There had to be a very clear delineation. It was my job to take out the compass and see which direction as a business we should go. I was really the vision of the business. Sherry was the implementer of that dream, and then I was more of the design director in the trenches.

Ramsay: How did you find that venture capital firm?

Lanning: They found us.

Ramsay: How did they find you?

Lanning: What happened was we were still in the film business, and we had put together the business plan for the game company. We sent that to our attorneys to bless some things, and word started getting around that we were looking to start a game company. We got contacted by a group. I remember they called me at my apartment on a weekend and said, "I heard that you guys want to start a game company. We have a million dollars to start a game company." I said, "Well, that doesn't work for us because we need $3.5 million." And he said, "Do you have the numbers to back that up?" I said, "Yeah." And he said, "Fax them to me." I did, and that was the beginning of that negotiation.

Ramsay: I wish more investors would call me out of the blue...

Lanning: It took a lot of prep. You know, my first thing in life is fishing, like fly fishing. Everything's really about tricking the fish into thinking it's exactly what it wants, right? The timing and the stars had kind of aligned, but we had invested a lot of time and energy so far in just putting together what in that investor's words was the best business plan he had seen in that space so far for startups. We didn't have the sophistication of a big publisher or anything like that yet. We were still kind of naïve on the business side, but we had some perspective and at least some clever ideas.

Ramsay: Since both you and Sherry were in the film industry, did you look for any outside advisors from the game industry?

Lanning: We did, actually. One reason we thought we had possible chemistry with our initial investor was they had bought another company that made games. That company made games the old way. They were a 16-bit company, and we were a 32-bit company. Things were going to start going 3D, and games were going to start having stories and all that.

I didn't have all the answers, but I knew quite well that games were going to be really hard. I knew they were already much more complicated than almost anyone in Hollywood would acknowledge. People were constantly underestimating the game industry. One thing that was clear about Rocket Science was they didn't have the secret ingredient that was really going to make great product and make audiences happy. At the same time, they underestimated what it was going to take. They raised a ton of money, but they really didn't recruit seasoned people who knew how to build games. But we were very concerned about what we didn't know about games.

A favorite saying of mine had been "I don't want to learn from my own mistakes. I want to learn from your mistakes." I hoped that I didn't even have to make the mistakes. Ultimately, that was kind of naïve, but it's true. I've had enough hard knocks that I recognize nothing comes easy, and everything is likely to be more difficult than you thought. So, I was actively engaging people who really understood the basic pipeline process of building games and the science of gameplay. To a large degree, I was often very disappointed with the creative solutions that class of people was coming back with. But we were seeking the help, and we sort of got it.

In terms of the package which came with that first investor, the chemistry between the two companies wasn't stellar. I think that adds more friction to the process, especially when you don't necessarily know what you're doing. We had a dream, and if you don't know exactly what you're doing, you tend to be a little more intense about it. You know, you tend to be a little more concerned, passionate, and like "no way I'm going to let this fail." You know, "I'm going to make this happen and really dig in." That can be exhausting. Without that, we probably would have a much harder time succeeding.

Ramsay: In that meeting with the investor, what would you have done without Sherry's experience?

Lanning: I would have believed them—everything they were saying. She was wise enough not to, you see. I would have been a sucker. I would have been a chump.

It's funny because the more you engage with financiers, the more you understand that they play by certain rules and behave accordingly. They'll tell you what you want to hear, and they're not going to tell you about all the bad things that could happen. They're not going to tell you about their interests, which they don't think you'd be interested in, which might throw your motivation off, or which make you question their commitment. You're going to be told what you want to hear.

So, if you said, "Look, I want to control the company," and they go, "You got it." But you're like, "Wait a minute. My attorney's saying that if you have this much stock, then you have control." And they say, "Yeah, but we don't want to exercise that right, so you have it." You have to be like, "Well, talk is cheap. On paper, I need it."

So, I was naïve enough at the time that I would have bought into basically that bullshit, and that bullshit is common. That's standard practice for almost everybody, and that's why people spend fortunes on attorney's fees doing deals. I would have fallen for it, and you never would have heard of me—at least not through the game channels, because we would have failed miserably.

Ramsay: You were 29 when you started Oddworld.

Lanning: Yeah.

Ramsay: Some entrepreneurs around that age had families when they started their companies. Did you?

Lanning: No. I've never had kids. I've never been married, but I live with Sherry. I'm straight. That's not my issue. But kids were never part of my plan. I wasn't wired that way. Some people hear that and ask, "You didn't have kids? How could you not have kids?" Well, once I sort of deprogrammed around 17, I started realizing that these ideas I have about the life I think I should lead, they're not actually my ideas. They were given to me by the system we live in. Once I started thinking for myself, I don't think that I ever wanted kids. I think raising kids is a really important job, and people should do it well, but I never had those families.

I knew people who started companies and families. If they could do it successfully, I really admired them. If their families suffered, I guess I judged them more harshly. If you're going to make the big step, the big commitment... I mean, anyone can go out and start companies, but the big commitment is birthing a human being, right? If you're going to make that commitment, you need to be really serious. And if you're out there trying to start a company and not paying attention to your family, and your kids are getting raised like shit, I think that's a sad testimony.

Ramsay: After you received your $3.5 million, what did you do? What was the first thing you did after getting capital?

Lanning: The first thing we did was go after the right talent.

Ramsay: Who were your first hires?

Lanning: I believe the first hire was Steve Olds. Steve was an incredible—and still is an incredible—production design talent. We were very much about design, having a creative culture, and really trying to be the best at design. I went after the guy who I thought was pretty much as good as anyone could get. I had worked with him at Rhythm and Hues. He's amazing.

Then we started rounding out the computer-graphics team, and we brought in some people. We also bought all Silicon Graphics workstations and really expensive seats—you know, $40,000 for software and $40,000 in hardware for each seat. The systems, networks, and all that back at that time were a lot more complicated and a lot more expensive than they are today, at least to set up and manage and get running, right?

We really started putting in our computer-graphics team first. It was hard to get game talent. It was hard to find people who shared our ideas about what games could be and who knew how to build games. Games, in general, seemed, for whatever reasons, kind of stuck in certain patterns. It's similar today, just on different levels, in the console market.

If you were around film directors, composers, screenwriters in that way, you'd know they were really thinking people. And, I mean, Hollywood's full of shit. There's a lot of bullshit down there, but there are also a lot of smart people—intellectual, smart, philosophical thinkers—and they're usually the talent. Hollywood's not full of them, but there's a lot of them.

Then you went over to the game industry, and you're trying to find like-minded game designers and programmers. Who we were finding had reference points which weren't Chomsky, Virilio, geopolitics, or international relations; instead, their interests were porn, sports, and video games. The industry had a reputation for being that way for a certain reason. People were just that way. It was pretty shallow and proud of being shallow. It was an interesting time. In hindsight, in a business like games, you have to balance your creative with your technical, but if you don't have the strong technical, you're dead. You don't have a chance no matter how great your creative.

Oddworld was driven from a top-down producer creative model that was hiring technical. We needed to make sure that we really had equal partnerships with great technical. But we didn't start doing that until our new company, which is more mature and wiser, hopefully.

Ramsay: You got right into building a development team, not management?

Lanning: That's right. We didn't focus on a management team at the time. We were focusing on—you're absolutely right—a development team because games were getting more complex.

Ramsay: You had the idea for Abe long before you started the company. What were the reactions of your first hires to the concept?

Lanning: They were excited because we were focusing more on the design, and the art team was taking advantage of Hollywood skill sets, so they were more driven by characters and story. Those things interested them more than gameplay, but they were excited by the possibility of what gameplay could be if we had more characters and stories. They were kind of bearing with gameplay, but they really cared about telling stories with computer graphics. At some levels, that's problematic, right? You need everyone really sharing the same dream. They thought it was risky, but it was kind of exciting. And the computer-graphics industry was getting tired because there was a lot of disappointment with being service companies to the advertising industry and to the film industry. If you know people and know sectors, they're always complaining about the client. And having been there, I'd say most of the time for good reason, but that's life.

Ramsay: How did you get those first few on the same page?

Lanning: You know, I don't know that we ever did. I just directed really strongly, and I don't mean that so much in the positive way. I mean that in the physical way. I just was relentless, and honestly, I was kind of terrified that it wouldn't work. I felt like I was learning every mistake the hard way. It was really scary at times. You're way behind. Things aren't coming together like you had hoped. You go through all these experiential anxieties, mini-failures, crises, and it's kind of a voodoo science building games and computer graphics.

We were trying to stick great production design, great computer graphics, and good gameplay together. Great production design is its own thing, but great computer graphics and good gameplay were like… Oh, it was a nightmare, man. It was really hard. What were we? Crazy?

Ramsay: Who published the Oddworld games?

Lanning: That was GT Interactive.

Ramsay: When did you start pitching the game to publishers?

Lanning: Well, here's what happened. We're in the Central Coast, and we thought that with our investors, we had a game company. We thought that we were building a game for the Sony PlayStation, and we were using their development systems and this and that. At that point, we were relying on the other parties to handle relations with Sony and give us good advice. So, one day, we received this letter from Sony, and it says we need to have our license verified, signed by the senior vice president at Sony, Bernie Stolar.

Bernie Stolar launched the PlayStation, he was the chief executive officer at Mattel for awhile, and he was president of Sega. So, Bernie, he's a big guy in the industry. And we have this letter, and Sherry goes, "Huh, I wonder if that's the Bernie Stolar I used to be really good friends with when we were kids?" So, she calls and leaves a message. She asked Sony, "Can I talk to

Bernie Stolar?" And, of course, they're like, "No, Bernie's a big guy, and you can't talk to him." So, she says, "Well, okay. Just tell him that Sherry McKenna called." And then a little while later, Bernie called. So, all of a sudden, the guy running the US PlayStation division was old pals of best-bud nature from back in the day. Bernie was like, "You're doing what? You're building games now?" And she's like, "Yeah, we're building for the PlayStation." And he's like, "No, you're not. You don't have a license." And she's like, "What's a license?" And he goes, "That's it. Get on a plane, and get up here." Sherry and I got on a plane, and we went up to Sony, and he said, "Well, what are you building?" We showed him, and he loved it. He completely fell in love right away.

We then started talking about how we could become a first-party title because we weren't with a publisher yet. We were still with our initial investor. And so we were going to be like a Crash Bandicoot or something like that. Bernie was starting to hook that up, and we thought we were going to be doing a first-party Sony game for the PlayStation. Then all of a sudden, Bernie calls up and says, "I'm leaving Sony, so, you know, sorry." And it was like, "Wow, are you serious?" And he goes, "Yeah, but this is the company you should go to." He turned us on to GT Interactive, and he said, "They have a lot of money. They need great games, and you have a great game, so that's the company you should be with." They flew out to San Luis Obispo from New York, saw what we were doing, and made a deal. They bought out our first investor right there, and our first investor right there doubled his money. He wanted a lot more, but things had become a little fractious between us. It was kind of like, "Look, we want to be with them as partners, and we don't want to continue the relationship as it is, so why don't you take the money and run?" That was an interesting episode.

Then we were partners with GT and started doing business with New York. They relaunched Abe's Oddysee, and they actually did it. It was really fun working with them.

GT was run by a guy named Ron Chaimowitz. He used to be the president of CBS Records in Miami, so he was a music guy, and he had helped build the careers of people like Gloria Estefan and Julio Iglesias. So, Ron Chaimowitz had been in the real entertainment business for a long time and was kind of a serious player. When we met with him, we really liked him, and they fell in love with Abe. They really gave him great support. Their people in marketing and all that really got behind it, and they were building that new company, so there was a whole energy of new and exciting possibilities.

So, we were riding that whole wave, and it was kind of fun at the beginning. We were starting up. They were going to take on the industry. They had a lot of money, and they had one of the few guys that seemed to really understand talent and how to work with talent. It seemed like the rest of the game industry didn't care about talent. It didn't understand the value of good creative. It was very technically-centric.

Ramsay: When you said that Bernie turned you on to GT Interactive, was he actually going to work for GT?

Lanning: No. I think he went to become president of Sega for Nakayama. Nakayama was the head of Sega out of Japan and kind of the guy that built it. He was sort of a cowboy Japanese, and I don't mean with the hat. I just mean he seemed more American than Japanese in the way he did business. Bernie basically started running Sega for Nakayama in the United States. Sega was coming out with either the Saturn or Dreamcast. I don't remember which came first. But he went over to Sega, and we were still on PlayStation. It wouldn't have made sense to go with Sega, although we certainly considered it. He was telling us where we should go—where he thought we would do the best—and he had a pretty good idea at the time. We took his advice and wound up in New York, while he wound up at Sega in San Francisco.

Ramsay: Do you know what Bernie said to GT to get them interested?

Lanning: I think what he said to GT was simply, "There's a product you should see." Bernie was the type of guy who'd say, "There's a product that you should see. It's what you need, and you should buy them. They need their investor bought out. You should do it. They're smart people. I've known them forever, and this is the deal you should do." And a lot of people would listen to him. So, if you can get those kinds of recommendations, you're in Fat City. It happened pretty easily with GT. I mean, it was complicated, but it was good stuff, and we're still friends with some of the best people that were there to this day.

Ramsay: Who contacted you from GT?

Lanning: I think it was Chris Garske. I don't know that Chris is in the industry anymore. Last I heard, he might be chilling in Hawaii, but he was a senior vice president and chartered us. He was out there finding titles, signing them, and doing acquisitions and stuff. There were a couple of guys in addition to Chris. There were Kurt Busch and Rick Raymo, and they worked for Chris. You know, they all were great. They all loved Abe. They were cool people, and we were thrilled to be with them.

Ramsay: What was your first major challenge after getting the publisher?

Lanning: Well, getting the game done. It was like impossible, man. There was a lot of friction at the studio. We had sort of different cultures. We had inherited some people from another company.

Company cultures really get shaped by different people with different interests. So, our company culture was one where we just wanted people who wanted to do great work. At the other company, there was a different culture, and great work was not the mandate. We never really sung well together. But because the investor owned the other company, when it came time to wrap that company up, we were in a position where we were depending on them, so we basically absorbed a lot of the staff.

There was a lot of risk there, and it was tough to get the game done. They weren't used to working with some maniacal director who wanted what he wanted. They were used to building games the old way, so there was a lot of friction. And the first couple of games kind of got done that way with that team.

There were shortcomings on both sides of the fence, but there were ultimately no bad people. Sherry had always said from day one that you have to hire the best people; you have to hire people who are smarter than you. Even though it's very logical that, yeah, that's what you should do, that's not what most people do. Most people are threatened by people who are smarter than them. So, you have some cultures where people don't want people who are smarter than them on any level, and it breeds different political situations within a company.

The bigger things get, the more difficult it becomes, and the more contention there can be between the staff. People start resenting other people and not feeling like they're pulling their weight. You've got people resenting people for feeling like they're too demanding, unrealistic, irrational, or whatever. We've all, I think, been accused of everything. Ultimately, you have to make some really hard decisions when you're building an organization because, at the same time you're putting your heart and soul into it, you're just trying to survive. It was really hard to do that at Oddworld. It wasn't a big company, but still, you're talking $400,000 to $500,000 a month, up to $700,000 a month, for 11 years as your burn rate. You have to make sure you're always paying people, so there's a lot of pressure to get product done.

Just getting that product done was a killer, partly due to the split in culture. Some people look at life and say, "I'm going to build the best game I can until I drop." And other people say, "I want to build the best game I can by 6 PM." So, you could imagine how people who were really intense and worked really hard felt when other members of their team didn't seem to be pulling their weight. They got resentful, and there was a fair amount of that.

Ramsay: Were there any particular conflicts that were impactful?

Lanning: Well, internally, I think it's typical company culture stuff. Externally, it was always really challenging. There are a lot of pieces to the machine that can fail that you have no control over. So, for instance, we built a game, right? At the distribution company we were in love with, some things started going south. I don't know the stories of what was happening inside the organization, but there were clearly tension and increasing dysfunction to the point where when our second game released, the distribution company was having its... challenges.

We knew through independent channels that they misplaced like a million games on forklifts in a warehouse somewhere. As commercials are running, as airtime was burning, there were no games on the shelves. There'd be like one in a store. We were dumbfounded. We were going, "This can't be happening." You kill yourself to do something, you run the ball all the way to the 99-yard line, and when you get there, bam, they just totally fumble. And you're just like, "You've got to be kidding me." Shit like that happens. What I've found is that's more common than not, and that's a lesson. I call it "idiot tax." We just hadn't paid our idiot tax yet. I was just like insane with confusion. Our ad dollars are being spent, and our games aren't on the shelf? I mean, it was just like suicide for the title.

Ultimately, it sold about a million and a half units, but it didn't do nearly what it could have, should have, and was supposed to do. What you find is that people don't go, "Yeah, you know we fucked up. We lost some games on the floor." You know, everyone's covering their ass, right? That's the corporate world. So, no one's admitting to it, and instead, they're saying, "Yeah, the game's just not selling too well. Sorry." And you're like, "What?" I mean, I was having people on the phone call every Wal-Mart, every K-Mart, and every "you name it." We just zeroed in on what the United States and Canada had at retail, and we put someone on the phone, and we documented every game that we could track in the United States. All total, we found like 1,500 games.

Now, we knew other companies out of Texas that were in the same position. We all were like, "What the hell's going on?" And we're all being told we're all losers because our games aren't selling well. We knew differently. That kind of shit is common, you know. Honesty is an endangered resource in the world. It's not an abundant resource. When things fail, it's very difficult to find out where, why, and how something is failing because it's very unlikely you're getting a straight story.

Ramsay: What were some of the things that you could have done differently that would have changed the outcome?

Lanning: Let's see. I'm 29, so the younger you are, the smarter you are in your own mind, right? The older you get, the more you realize how much you don't know. You know, there's a tipping point where you start going, "Wow, I really don't know that much." I thought I did. It's hard for me to assess what things I would have done differently. One of the absolute key things I know I'd do now is never make a hire out of fear again.

When you need someone in a noncritical role—say you need the lawn mowed—yeah, okay, just get somebody. But when you're talking about high-tech engineering or hardcore marketing or business or game design, you can't just get anybody. You need great people. I think, personally, a lot of my lessons were about making a number of hiring decisions out of fear because I just believed anything to do the job. Sometimes I would see the person I wanted as a talent-to-be, as opposed to what was right in front of me.

So, when we want something really bad, we have tended to see what we want to see, and that happens in the hiring process as well. You know, you want the person you're interviewing to be the solution you're looking for. If you don't have a great filter for checking and balancing your own desire against what you're really dealing with, you start compromising in a way that's going to be very painful. I've heard Jeff Braun, who was the cofounder of Maxis, talk, and he's full of lots of little bits of wisdom. He once said, "Hey, you can run a lot faster tied to ten guys than you can to five when one isn't running." I know I'm butchering that statement. You've probably heard it before. What he would say is you can move a lot faster if everyone is running together, but if one's slowing you down, they fuck everyone up. I think that's totally true. I'm not pointing the blame at any specific people—these are lessons learned.

When you're building a team, if you were playing a sport, you'd ask yourself, "What did I hire that guy as quarterback for? He can't throw." And you look like an idiot to everyone. But in a business, you go, "I can't do this or that. It's not as easy to tell." I think those are the biggest lessons in hiring. I actually forced my partner to compromise. She believed purely in only hiring the best. So, she would have taken it out more on a limb, and risked waiting for the right chemistry, whereas I was too afraid to burn too much money before I had the right people secured. There's all that normal angst that comes from wanting to start something, having a window, and having limited time and money, but fear will kill you.

Ramsay: Would you say that fear led you to make brash decisions—quick decisions with less consideration?

Lanning: I guess so. I'm not sure that's the word I would use, but I agree in principle, yes. I'm trying to articulate that in a better way. I have a friend of

mine who's a union psychologist. He says most people's issues come from
having unrealistic fantasies. And we might say less consideration, but I would
say "unrealistic fantasies."

Ramsay: Your expectations were higher than they should have been?

Lanning: Yeah, and misaligned, I guess. You know people do it in relationships all the time. One of my partners now, Daniel Goldman, has a dating
analogy for every possible thing you could think of that relates to business.
So, your friend comes back and says, "Wow, man. I met this girl, and I'm just
totally in love. I want to get married." He's saying all this stuff, and you're just
like, "Wow, she sounds really special." And then you meet her, and you realize she's a witch, or this guy's a jerk, or how can this girl be so in love with
him, or vice versa. That person has an unrealistic fantasy, right? Their friends
are looking at them going, "Dude, you just don't see it." I think that's kind of
like hiring. You want this date to work out, so you're kind of looking at it
blindly with hope. Hope is clouding your judgment.

Ramsay: What was the most serious case of this fear-driven decision-
making? Your game eventually came out, and it was extremely popular and
you were very successful. What actually went wrong?

Lanning: That's a good question. Let's take James Cameron as an example.
If you talk to anyone who's worked with him, they'll say they can't stand the
guy. They just can't stand him. They think he's a miserable, whip-cracking,
slave driver—an unrealistic, ultra-perfectionist who doesn't care about your
time or your energy. But the guy makes great movies, right? But he's afraid.
Anyone who can't stop making it perfect all the time is afraid. I don't care
how much money you have. It's a different type of OCD. That fight-or-flight
ability actually has its value. There's something to be said for just being completely relentless—for absolutely refusing to fail.

With what little I knew at that time, I can't say that I would have been more
mature in those areas. I wouldn't have failed for other reasons—the maniacal
drive and refusal of failure, which actually helped us through being terrified
to death of the saber-toothed tiger that gets you up the tree. If you have that
fear and you have the passion, then you tend to knock it out of the park. I
mean, all your best actors are totally insecure. All your best musicians are
totally insecure.

Being an artist is living with that never-ending dissatisfaction with knowing
everything is never done right. Most of the great talents that we've recognized through history weren't satisfied with their work, and that dissatisfaction compels them. They lose sleep just trying to make it better and better
and better. If you don't have that—if you don't have as much energy as it's

going to take—you're probably going to feel more comfortable. The guy who's hungry is going to prowl more. He's going to find more nuts than you're going to find. If you're getting lazy, cushy, and resting on your innate talents, that young whippersnapper who's paranoid and aggressive is probably going to eat your lunch. When you get into a comfort zone, you're dead.

Ramsay: Was Oddworld the only property you developed?

Lanning: Well, the whole concept of Oddworld was the planet Oddworld. So, Abe's Oddysee was just an episode that took place on that world. I always looked at it, and convinced Sherry to look at it, like it was Star Wars. We were building Episode I, Episode II, and so on. We would build our universe like a Middle Earth or the galactic universe of Star Wars. We'd have our own theme. Middle Earth had wizards, dragons, and good versus evil. Star Wars had samurai in space. We were going to have The Muppets meets The X-Files. We're going to have the dark side of globalization with a kick to the funny bone. I wanted to create this twisted brand that really represented the sort of unspoken truth of the world we're living in and try to make it humorous and ironic. Irony can be great humor, rather than just jokes for fun. It will tickle the funny bone with some counterculture. I wanted to do what great filmmakers did: tell stories in a new medium that lots of people spend lots of time with, and try to tell the stories I wanted to tell.

We did four titles in the Oddworld brand. We started on a few others, but we never delivered them. We never got them done and out the door. There's a lot of undeveloped material in that universe, lying in wait. To me, it's kind of like the Mexican bandito who has the two belts across his chest with all the bullets in them, right? Those bullets are like the characters, worlds, and stories of Oddworld, but I don't necessarily have the gun it takes to go out and shoot. I started a new venture to get that gun. One day, I'll go back to Oddworld and really do some damage.

Ramsay: Would you say what you're doing is similar to the Hollywood production model where every movie is an individual company?

Lanning: No. Every movie is a company in Hollywood to protect against legal liabilities. That's why every film has a new company created when it starts. But the way we were thinking of it was actually quite the opposite. We were thinking of it more like how Lucasfilm was looking at Star Wars, and how Jim Henson's company was The Muppets. We wanted to invest in one company that would make and keep developing a universe. The Hollywood model isn't about that. In Hollywood, you set up the company for the production, and you tear it down when the production's over.

Ramsay: Did you look at developing any properties outside of the Oddworld universe?

Lanning: Not really.

Ramsay: Were you ever worried that you'd get burned out on the Oddworld universe?

Lanning: Nope, I'm still not. I got burned out on releasing games, and not seeing them get the distribution or the exposure that I thought they were entitled to. I got burned out on being on a treadmill, and then finding out that my efforts weren't adding up. And those factors that are making them not add up are completely random at various times and beyond your control in various ways. You can't change them, so I got tired of that. I have a favorite saying: "I don't have to eat a gallon to know it's vanilla." A couple of spoonfuls, and I get what it is. If someone's a shitty partner, it only takes a couple spoonfuls. I don't need to hang around, tasting it with other people.

If you get burned two times, okay. If you get burned three times, you're kind of an idiot. What are you thinking? What were you expecting? We're very resilient when it comes to it. If we put our mind to something, we're going to do it, and we'll make it happen. But at the same time, we're not stupid. If you're fighting that battle, but not really winning anymore, then you go, "What's the world look like now?" You reassess everything.

With Oddworld, we never ventured outside the property because it was absolutely what we loved and still do. As I said, I've got a lot of undeveloped material, and I'm very passionate about it. I would like to get to it. I mean, it's my intent to get to it someday. The world was changing so quickly though that the idea of still building box product games with triple-A budgets that, well, that world became less and less and less sane. I shouldn't say "sane" as much it was just becoming less rewarding and more difficult with worse terms.

The world was changing, so I thought it was wise to just back up and wait a minute. I might be doing this thing, and we might have this company, but really, how is the world changing, and do we want to try to change this company to fit the world? Or do we love what we intended this company to be, and it's a different time now, so should we reprocess the new landscape? How has it changed? How do we take advantage of it now? How do we facilitate the thing that we love? It took us a few years to really start figuring that out, but we're, I think, very smart to have just said, "Instead of staying on a treadmill that's going nowhere, why don't we hop off the treadmill, cut our expenses, and realign? We're going to do a few different things." That was just before one of the worst financial periods in this country's history. Then those projects became more difficult to realize. Everything became more difficult around 2007.

We would never grow tired of the property, and that's why we didn't sell it. That's why we still have it. We want to return to it.

Ramsay: I asked because... Do you remember what Nolan said when we were in Napa? He has "five-year ADD" when it comes to companies.

Lanning: Yeah, he's also not a content guy. If you're just building businesses, I totally understand that. The company we just started? I have no desire to be here after five years—none whatsoever. Oddworld? I never want to sell it in my life. They're completely different motivations.

I know Nolan, and I respect Nolan, but he's not a storyteller. To him, it's just business. I mean, he's Nolan Bushnell. He's legendary. What I mean is that he's a creative visionary business guy, but he's not a content guy. There's a difference. Film directors, writers, novelists, animators—they really care about the work. Other people—businesspeople—what they tend to care about is the business. And a lot of what they do is interchangeable. For some guys, it doesn't matter that they're making toilets or golf bags. It's business. They get off on the business; that's what excites them. Maybe they get off on high-tech business, but when you get into content, you're really passionate, and you love that content like Henson and Dr. Seuss.

Ramsay: I get that. But how successful was the first title?

Lanning: I think Abe sold 3 million units or so. We didn't get sales like what you're seeing today, and not like what the Crash Bandicoot series sold. But it certainly put us on the map. And then just last year in 2010, Abe sold like another half-million units.

Ramsay: Was GT surprised or impressed?

Lanning: Well, we were favored. We certainly became golden kids in the stable, but they had Doom, Unreal, and Total Annihilation. We spent maybe about $3.5 million to $4 million on Abe. That was an enormous amount of money for a game. For it to be a success, they had to put like another $4 million into marketing it. That was fabulous exposure for us. If it wasn't a decent hit, they would have been really disappointed. At that level, they're investing in it to be right. They want them all to be hits, but they know their numbers. They know they're only going to get a percentage of winners.

Ramsay: How did they react to your success?

Lanning: The short answer is they weren't surprised, but they were happy that it worked out. Here's the problem with success. So, here's a perfect condition. They're thrilled—too thrilled—because what happens immediately is they go, "Okay, you know what? You did really well, but these other titles? They didn't."

A lot of their other titles didn't do well, and as a result, they, as a corporation, had a lot more financial pressure now to do better. More pressure and shorter deadlines got put on their successful properties. There was a lot of pressure to produce another game like Abe in a year, and deliver it in nine months. All of a sudden, we had to deliver a better game than the game that took us three and a half years to develop because we refused to deliver anything less than a better game. We had to deliver a better game in a third of the time. And that's a curse. So, the conditions are beyond you. The conditions of the people that are financing you can cause all different types of pressure to do things to help their business, and they are not necessarily the best things for your company.

Ramsay: What was the original deal with GT? How many titles did you create?

Lanning: They got half the company, so we were kind of half-owned by them. So, they could say, "We really need you to do this, and we love you." But on the other side of that, if we didn't, they we're going to hate us. You don't have a lot of choice, really. If you buck that system, you need to be in a stronger position. So, we did that game, and we did it on time. But that was when other elements started falling apart, like losing all those games in a warehouse somewhere.

Ramsay: Tell me about the warehouse incident.

Lanning: Well, it was kind of elusive. It was something that never got officially exposed. A lot of people knew what was going on. People inside the distribution company were aware, and they would let you know off the record that they knew, but it's not something that ever became news or anything like that. And it's not something that ever got cleared up, so it created a lot of tension. I was a really pissed-off guy. I killed myself for nine months. I was just really upset about it.

Ramsay: What got lost?

Lanning: Our games were part of like a million games that were lost in a warehouse. We don't know the details. All that we know is that they weren't on the shelf. So, apparently, it was like a warehouse in New Jersey. But it's just things that happen, and you suffer.

Ramsay: Were the cultural struggles still the status quo?

Lanning: Yeah. I've actually learned so many lessons since then. I mean, I don't think I was a mature manager. I was very, very demanding and emotional. There are many ways to screw things up, so I certainly had a lot to learn. In some ways, I think if you internalize your crises and reflect on them in what I would call a healthy way, you figure out where you're the problem. It's like, "Wow, she left me, but how was I really a boyfriend?" You have to really process where you think you might have been at fault.

I think I've matured. I hope I've matured a lot since the days when I was raising that money and being completely fried. Working 80 hours a week year after year, feeling like some spoke would break out there, and knowing that we've got to keep that pace... It just gets worse. It doesn't get better. That's what most of the development community, I think, would tell you. I think that even the most successful guys who have been in the game business for a long time know that it's been a really rough road.

Ramsay: During the production of the first title, how many hours were your employees working?

Lanning: How many hours? It was different. People who really were passionate? You couldn't get them to go home. Other people couldn't be counted on to stay past 6:00 PM. So, it was different depending on the individuals, and then there are labor laws that you have to abide by if you're paying them. I mean, we paid everyone exempt wages, so they didn't get paid overtime. We always paid well. Some people really killed themselves, but to others, it was a job. I told you how many hours I worked, but I absolutely refused to not deliver. You know, I refused to fail.

Ramsay: People really killed themselves? You're talking about work, right?

Lanning: They didn't literally. Yeah, I'm talking really hard. There were no suicides or anything like that, but I know companies where that has happened. They come in the morning, and there's a guy hanging there. Hollywood has seen that. Sherry worked at a company, Robert Able & Associates. They were legendary in the computer-graphics business. And they came in one morning, and a guy had just burned out. He was hanging. I know, amazing, sad... Work is bad enough where everyone's working that hard, and then one of you is dangling. It's like, "Oh, my God." But, you know, Bob Able was a maniac. I mean, he was like, "It's all about quality." He wanted everyone to work all the time. He was like Cameron, except maybe not nearly as well-known.

Ramsay: When you found out that the first title was selling so well, how did you feel about that success?

Lanning: Validated. Until that time, I just felt like there were a lot of ideas, but you didn't have proof, and any bozo could say, "Yeah, but you haven't done any better." And the fact was you hadn't, right? So, you know how that conversation goes. I mean, people have at it every day in every bar. When you've actually knocked it out of the park, you're validated in a certain way, and then you're looked at a little differently. You get a different reception. And I don't mean that in a star way. I just mean that in a credibility way. If you can walk in the door and your credibility precedes you, that's so much nicer a meeting than when you walk in the door and they're going, "Who's this guy?" Right? That makes a huge difference in business.

Ramsay: Were you cautious or overconfident about your success?

Lanning: I was always cautious. I mean, I always felt like failure is just around the corner. That was something that was very deeply ingrained in me. I mean, I never got therapy. I probably should have, but I ultimately started to realize that I took shit way too seriously.

Ramsay: You? Taking things seriously?

Lanning: Yeah, I know, right?

Ramsay: Isn't that similar to what you said about making fear-based decisions?

Lanning: Well, yeah, but we're talking about history. I'm claiming to be a little wiser now. I mean, I don't believe fear makes the best decisions. You know, as biological creatures, we have this fight-or-flight response mechanism. If we're living in fight mode all the time, it's just going to wear us down. It doesn't mean that you're not going to win the fight, if it's going to be a fight that might aid you a lot. But eventually, it's just going to wear you down; it's going to become really tiring. I think that fear-based decisions might keep you alive, but they're nothing to live on.

Ramsay: What expectations did you have? Obviously, it was to have a better game in nine months, but what were your expectations?

Lanning: I thought we would see sales that would give us more ability, and that ultimately means royalties. When you don't sell well, it puts a lot more strain back on the next day. Your next year is going to be that much more difficult. You're going to be insulted if people go, "Yeah, but you didn't sell as many units this time," and you're just like, "Fuck off, man." You know? You really start getting pissed. You get resentful because you believe you should have had a certain success that you didn't have, and rightly or wrongly, there's a tendency to point blame elsewhere. I felt justified many times. It's maddening.

If you feel like you did what you were supposed to do—you made good on your agreements—and someone else drops the ball, that affects your entire performance then and over the coming years. If you have a high burn rate, and you can get a triple, you can hit a home run, and it really affords you some flexibility. With a little breathing room, you're in a much better space. You're much more well-equipped to go climb those next mountains. Whereas if you don't have that success, it's kind of like starting over again. It's hard because now you just don't have the fruits of that success, and everything in this world costs money.

Ramsay: Did your cautiousness, in retrospect, ever lead you to miss some great opportunity or opportunities?

Lanning: Yeah. It's hard to quantify, but I know moments were lost. I know that I would be too passionate to seize an opportunity at a certain moment or too resentful—you know, basic failings of man. I can't remember. Oh, there's one. I really fucked that one up. I walked away from a film deal just because I, let's say, lost faith in wanting to be on a cycle that I didn't necessarily think could win—again, parameters beyond our control. Rather than get into something that you're going to resent, it might just be better to avoid it in the first place. But even now, I can't tell if that was a wise decision or a passionate decision. It's hard to tell.

I remember one of the smartest guys I ever met was a criminal psychologist at an extraordinary level of great success. I used to enjoy talking to this guy. He was an older cat, and I asked him, "How do you know when you're doing the right thing?" And he said, "Well, that's a great question. I don't know, but I think it's really easy to know when you're doing the wrong thing." I thought that was a great answer. If you tried to always do the right thing, you know it's a lot harder to know what might have been different.

Ramsay: There was a possible film deal for Oddworld?

Lanning: Not for Oddworld. For Citizen Siege, which was the company in the Oddworld universe. Oh, I'm sorry, you asked me before whether we entertained other properties. Actually, I designed and developed a new property for film, and they wanted it to be a game as well.

It actually got funded as a game first. Citizen Siege wasn't finished. The project was greenlit by EA in 2005, and then we walked away from that funding. We said, "Well, let's make the movie first, then let's come back and get funded as a game, and then let's use the database together." I was proposing this whole clever story that was maybe too clever for its own good at the time. It confused a lot of people, like attorneys who were trying to figure out how database rights would work between a game that was using the same data sets as the movie, and shit was just getting infinitely complicated purely on legal fronts. I had been working on it since 2004, and then we decided not to do it as a game. Instead, we then spent like another year doing preproduction, script writing—all that stuff to do a movie—and we had the full movie package. I'm still incredibly passionate about it.

In 2006, possibly 2007, we actually signed a film deal. We had the deal, but I guess you would say there was a creative difference. Without getting into specifics, I personally lost the faith that a good film could get made. In hindsight, I felt like I didn't want one to. This was another passion project for me. I mean, this was another property like Oddworld. And I didn't want to see it get mangled just due to the climate, or the conditions, or the business terms, or partnerships, or whatever. I felt too passionate about it to put it out there and risk it, so we backed off, decided to assess the landscape longer, and let the option expire.

Ramsay: Speaking of films, Hollywood used to think of games more as promotional tools, and you know, that might still be the case.

Lanning: Well, games would be used to ride the visibility being given to a movie. So, really, the games wouldn't really be used to promote it as much as the games were like parasites on movies. And "parasite" is a negative word. I don't mean it that way, but the game would be riding the back of the marketing campaign of the movie. Publishers would finance those games. They would pay a lot of money for the license because they believed exposure was everything. Then they'd make a crappy game, hoping that people just liked the license and would buy the game.

Ramsay: Who would approach whom about the license?

Lanning: It depends. You know, with something like Lord of the Rings, the publisher went after the movie. With something like The Matrix, I think it was Dave Perry who figured out how to get the Wachowski Brothers to give him the rights, which was amazing. In other cases, there are executives at studios, and their job is to go out and milk a property. If they're going to come out with a new film, their job is licensing, right? So, they want to go get as much money as they can to stick that brand on whatever they can.

Ramsay: So, the tables are turning. Instead of filmmakers looking toward games, game companies are looking toward movies. Now, there are game companies that want to extend their properties to the screen.

Lanning: Yeah. I mean, that was eventually going to happen. Historically, there have been a few attempts at that. One was Chris Roberts and Wing Commander. Two was Square and Final Fantasy: The Spirits Within. Square thought they could do it, too, but they did horrible jobs because they didn't understand the film audience. They understood the game audience, but because they made good-looking cinematics for games, they thought they understood the film audience. Well, they couldn't have been more wrong.

Ramsay: Did you explore any other media for the Oddworld universe?

Lanning: Yeah, television a little, but more for Citizen Siege. As a television series, well, as a live-action movie, Sam Raimi's company Renaissance Pictures wanted to do it. As a television series, J.J. Abrams' company Bad Robot was interested in doing it. Citizen Siege is a pretty rich, intense property. But Oddworld as a television show? I mean, we've always imagined that it could be a television show. We always thought and designed the characters, thinking that some day they could have television shows, but we never actually really developed for that medium.

We designed a whole Oddworld film, and we have hundreds of production paintings for that. Raymond Swan was doing some incredible work, the writing was developed, but we didn't do it. The financial climate was so bad, the terms were so bad, and the property was so intimate to us that we didn't try to take Abe out and shop it. We tested the waters a little bit, and it was pretty rough out there. Given the average licensing suspects, there's film, television, or video games, so there weren't many other places to take it. Dark Horse wanted to do something with comic books. But I think we were always just too distracted with trying to get things done as a struggling developer.

Almost all developers are always sort of in the mindset that they're struggling because building games is hard. With Oddworld, we left a lot of dinner on the table. You know, if we had more business acumen and more experience, we would have been able to enrich the business in different ways, and exploit licensing and merchandising in ways we didn't. We just didn't have the focus or the energy. So, we didn't develop in any other media.

Ramsay: Do you still own Oddworld Inhabitants?

Lanning: Sherry and I still have Oddworld Inhabitants today. Between the two of us, we own it 100%. We still own all of the titles, so if anything happens with Oddworld, it still comes back to us. That sounds like we're really clever in business, but the game industry grew up so fast around us. We found ourselves in a place where we didn't believe we could continue to be successful with the way the industry was changing.

We were looking at manifesting our other dreams as films and other media, and then the financial collapse happened in the West. When we shut down the studio, we saw the writing on the wall. How were we going to compete with Activision and EA against their frontline titles? How were we going to get a decent deal that isn't completely unfair? We just said we won't. We'll retool our business to move in other directions. We'll hold onto the property because we think the property is more valuable than anything we can get. We did something that a lot of people didn't understand. Why did you shut down your studio? Why didn't you sell it? Today, it's actually doing great, and we don't do anything! New generations are finding our games. Their parents are passing them onto their children. They sell on Steam, PlayStation Network, and in other stores every day. I didn't think that there would ever be nostalgia for video games.

I was a really early vocal proponent of digital distribution when a lot of other people were saying it would never happen, but even I didn't understand how digital distribution would bring us back. You know, Mark Rein and others were saying a lot of bullshit about what a joke digital distribution was, and I was saying that it was the key to the future. I didn't quite get that digital distribution would actually revitalize old titles—that it would create classics out of properties that seem to have come and gone. Digital distribution has been a wonderful thing, and shutting down Oddworld has worked out wonderfully.

We were naïve, even though we raised venture capital to start the company. Even though we bought the venture capitalist out before the first product was released. Even though Sherry was a brilliant manager, and handled the client and the bank. We were still, in my opinion, relatively naïve, even though the world saw us as successful.

Naïveté is a very powerful tool for starting businesses because if you knew how difficult it was, you might not have done it. You might not have believed in what you wanted to do if you understood all of the obstacles that you were going to encounter. You might not have believed in yourself if you understood how smart you would have to be, and how many ways you could fail. The number of ways you can fail is so enormous. But living through the process certainly gives you perspective. We learned a lot.

Ramsay: What are you doing now?

Lanning: We found another partner, Daniel Goldman. Daniel goes back with Will Wright to the original SimCity. He did the Windows versions for free because they couldn't afford to pay him. Daniel started his first venture when he said, "Okay, I'll do the Windows versions for free, and then I'll have some royalties." Daniel did very well. He built his first online network in 1983. He started Total Entertainment Network, sold it to EA, and it became

Pogo. We've got a guy who really knows his shit on the technical end and as a co-creative partner. So, together, we founded this new company, Oddmobb, which is more of a business than I've ever really been involved with before. It's exciting because there's a lot of learning again.

Ramsay: Did you invest your own money this time?

Lanning: Yeah, we put our own money in this time, but we have a different track record now. We have more financial freedom, and it wasn't like if we put it all in and failed, we would lose our house or face any of the really hard realities. There was enough buffer there so that we could self-fund, take a chance, and prove to people—in the most difficult financial climate most of us have ever seen in our lives—that it would be worth investing in. We needed people to get it. We believed in it enough, and we still believe that we would make good on it enough that we actually put in some substantive cash, sharing more than myself. Sometimes you've got to do it.

Ramsay: You said the new company is more of a business than you've ever been involved with before. What do you mean?

Lanning: This new company is more about business. It's less about my personal vision and telling my stories. This may sound a little silly, but I look at it like this: "Hey, man, if you're psychic, why don't you guess the lottery?" Do you ever hear people say shit like that? If you really think that you get what's going on, then why don't you really capture it? Why don't you really get on top of it? We were looking at changing the course of games. We were looking at changing the course of movies. We even got a movie deal, and the financial crisis happened. Some things didn't turn out to be as they appeared, and we left it on the table. Trying to raise money during a financial crisis was very enlightening because you see a lot of things that you otherwise wouldn't see. There's very little dumb money out there, so you need stronger stories. You need a better understanding of the marketplace and the big possibilities. Investors want a significant return on their money.

As things tighten up due to economic crises, as the banksters are ripping us off, and as you try to raise money in this climate, you're asked a million complicated questions. If you don't have the answers, you're not viable. It's a much more challenging climate to raise money in. It forced us to ask a series of questions and investigate answers that we never had before. Obtaining investment was a definitely more complicated game in 2008. We were financed in 2010. There still hasn't been an economic turnaround. In my opinion, we have to be headed for a collapse, but we'll see.

I've been expecting the West to be right where it is. I think the more that people look under the hood, the more that they expect it as well. We're not out of the woods yet. But it was a phenomenal experience, having to go around and sit with venture capitalists, billionaires all over Hollywood, and people who built mega successful businesses, and get their two cents, their feedback, and insights at a really clinical business level.

When you're in a hit-driven business like video games, if you can convince them that you've got a hit, you don't need all of the other business shit down. If you're Britney Spears, you don't have to convince them that you can run a record label. You just need to convince them that you can give the boys a boner that night on stage and make the girls love you, too. If you can do that, they'll take care of the business end. But when you're building real businesses and not hit-driven media businesses, investors are more careful about the firms they back. There has to be more substance to the business story. It requires a different level of discipline.

If you were a Stanford or Harvard MBA, you might have known a lot of this stuff before you got out of school. You wouldn't know what you know from learning the hard way. Some of the most naïve people I've met came from top-tier business schools. The point is that you have to be seriously well-versed in business as a clinical science to really grasp how to raise money in a dry climate. You have to really grasp how to raise money when you're not telling someone, "Look, we'll give you the hit you need next quarter because you need a hit next quarter." That's Hollywood, and that's the game business. Instead, you're going to investors saying, "Let me tell you about a business that you have no vision for. You don't need a hit next quarter or this Christmas. This is something you might not have even been thinking of, but let me tell you why you'll get a great return on your investment." That's a different argument, and that needs to be a lot sharper.

Chris Ulm

Cofounder, Appy Entertainment

 *In 1985, **Chris Ulm** cofounded Malibu Comics with Scott Rosenberg, Dave Olbrich, and Tom Mason. For more than a decade, Malibu was a fixture in the comics industry. Best known for the Ultraverse line of superhero comics, Malibu published several imprints, including the original launch of Image Comics and Eternity. When Malibu was sold to Marvel Comics, Ulm transitioned to video games, working with Lorne Lanning at Oddworld Inhabitants. He then served as chief design officer at Sammy Studios.*

After the merger of Sammy Corporation and Sega in 2004, Ulm, John Rowe, and Clinton Keith were among the executives at Sammy Studios who led the buyout that created High Moon Studios. Before the company was acquired by Vivendi Universal Games in 2006, High Moon Studios released its flagship cross-platform title Darkwatch to great acclaim.

In 2008, when ownership shifted to Activision Blizzard, Ulm and Emmanuel Valdez, Farzad Varahramyan, Rick Olafsson, and Paul O'Connor left to create Appy Entertainment, an independent developer of award-winning social mobile games. The studio's titles, such as SpellCraft: School of Magic, Trucks & Skulls, and FaceFighter, have been downloaded more than 11 million times by players around the world.

Ramsay: Tell me about how you started with High Moon Studios. How did you know your cofounders?

Ulm: High Moon Studios emerged from the management-led reorganization of Sammy Studios, the Carlsbad-based video-game arm of Sammy Japan. We started initially as the internal development group for Sammy, then morphed into an independent studio.

Emmanuel Valdez, Farzad Varahramyan, and Paul O'Connor were the key creative leads for art and design. As we went through the initial joys and pains of building that company and shipping our first game, I got a chance to work closely with chief operating officer Rick Olafsson, executive producer Steve Sargent, and senior programmer Marc-Antoine Argenton.

After High Moon was acquired by Vivendi, which is now Activision Blizzard, we decided to jump into startup mode again with Appy Entertainment.

Ramsay: At what point was a management buyout discussed? What were the reasons?

Ulm: The buyout for High Moon was discussed in 2005. After acquiring Sega, Sammy decided to discontinue game development in North America, thereby giving us, under studio president John Rowe, the opportunity to establish an independent studio with existing capabilities and resources. Darkwatch was ready to go to market, and we had built up a terrific team of amazingly talented developers, many who are still at High Moon today.

Ramsay: Transforming an internal development group into an independent studio sounds like no easy task.

Ulm: We had quite a few challenges in transforming our development group into an independent studio. The first was in completing our original game Darkwatch in a reasonable time frame, and then finding the right publisher to work with in bringing an original property to market. We eventually signed with Capcom in the United States and Ubisoft in Europe.

Building an original game is always hard, but we were also facing competitive pressure for talented developers, as well as teething hurdles with our own game engine on which Darkwatch was our first. We developed a very strong development organization to deal with these issues.

The most important thing we did was really focus on the quality of the new people that we hired. We had a pretty stringent filter: for every person we interviewed, we went through 100 resumes, and for every person we actually hired, we interviewed 12. And this was during a real shortage of key talent in the video-game space. In retrospect, I think this was exactly the right way to go and allowed High Moon to create quality products even when the going got tough.

Darkwatch made it to market for the PlayStation 2 and Xbox, receiving strong reviews and setting the stage for the Vivendi acquisition and the development of Robert Ludlum's The Bourne Conspiracy. Both Darkwatch and Bourne had real innovation within the games, but were challenged by transitions in publishing partners and marketing focus.

The teams that we built at High Moon were able to bring games to market through five publisher changes in six years, which is pretty extraordinary. I am incredibly proud of all the games that we were able to bring to market in my time at High Moon, and continue to be proud of the team that we hired and developed. They recently released Transformers: War for Cybertron to excellent reviews and strong initial sales.

Ramsay: Did you meet with other publishers? Were you turned down?

Ulm: We met with a few publishers, but it was really a matter of deciding which offer made the most sense for Darkwatch. Launching a new property is difficult and costly, and television advertising was very important to launching Darkwatch as a new game. The most important thing about the choice of publishers was their existing "consumer-facing" brand, such as what kinds of games are already associated with the publisher. We wanted a publisher whose portfolio of games was a good fit for Darkwatch.

Ramsay: Why was television advertising important?

Ulm: Television advertising is critical to launching a new console property because in-store support at key retailers—such as Target, Wal-Mart, and GameStop—depends on the strength of the publisher's other offerings and the perceived marketing spend that will drive gamers to buy the product. The best and most reliable way to reach gamers is through television, or at least this was very much the environment during the 2004 through 2005 period.

New properties that don't get a television spend generally don't get any traction or shelf space at retail, and therefore cannot be discovered. New properties are costly and difficult to birth and grow, so publishers tend to be very careful about investing in them. As development costs have skyrocketed, this has only become worse—much worse.

As publishers become more risk-averse and more reliant on their bread-and-butter franchises, they will more frequently invest in them, which means that a franchise eventually failing to excite the audience will have a much harsher outcome. No franchise is evergreen forever, and even the strongest and most popular need to be periodically put to pasture and renewed. It has been one of my biggest frustrations as a creative executive that new ideas are often treated as luxuries that companies cannot afford instead of as necessary components of the entertainment life cycle. Successful future publishers must figure out how to nurture new properties in a cost-effective manner if they want to survive in the long term.

Ramsay: Capcom and Ubisoft are strong choices. Why did you decide to publish with them?

Ulm: Both Capcom and Ubisoft already had strong skills in developing and marketing original properties in the action and shooter genres, so we felt they were already speaking to the audience that we wanted to reach.

John Rowe had many strong relationships in the industry, and Capcom was an easy choice, whereas Ubisoft was one of the strongest publishers for the European market. Splitting our focus across two publishers was done to build the best possible package for distribution, but it would have been stronger for us if we had a dedicated publisher from the start of production, rather than shopping for a publisher when the title was done.

Ultimately, Darkwatch came to market and was able to build an audience and a good reputation for High Moon Studios that helped us to make our next deals with both development talent and Vivendi.

Ramsay: What sort of competitive pressure for talent was there?

Ulm: At the time that we first started building Sammy Studios—and later High Moon—the industry was in a growth phase, and competition for programmers in particular was very intense. In fact, we ended up going to the United Kingdom and other European countries for qualified applicants.

We were also enormously picky about who we hired on every front, something I think contributed to High Moon's continuing ability to build triple-A games. We had a very motivated cross-disciplinary management team that focused a lot of our attention on hiring the best people. Our chief technology officer, Clinton Keith, was instrumental in bringing the agile methodology and Scrum process to High Moon, which allowed the studio to focus our efforts during the transition.

We depended on our past records at Oddworld Inhabitants, Midway Games, Electronic Arts, and Rockstar San Diego to interest talented developers. It also helped that we were developing a new property, which was a breath of fresh air to many of the talented artists, designers, producers, and programmers who signed on with us.

Ramsay: Looking back, were there any stressful moments? Any surprises?

Ulm: Any time a new studio is built from the ground up, there are a lot of stressful moments and constant surprises. I did not have enough appreciation for the technical, design, and art risks of building ambitiously featured games across multiple platforms with brand-new properties, an untested custom engine, and a team that had not worked together before. Any one of these issues could torpedo a project, but all of them together are a minefield of game production badness.

A late adoption of agile development helped us to better measure our progress and take appropriate steps to increase efficiency. But the one horrifying truth of game development is that throwing more people at a problem is only marginally successful, may increase your speed of production, but rarely, in my experience, increases the quality of the finished product.

When running a studio, all of your costs are tied up in the salaries of developers. The two things that matter are how focused they are on the right trade-offs with the product and how well they work as a team. Successful development teams work out the kinks on their first project, and then go on to do their best work on subsequent projects, if they are able to stay together and work on the same code base. It helps if they are working on a sequel to the first game as well, because after the first game is done, the team is painfully aware of all of the areas that they want to improve. Moreover, they know exactly how to execute these improvements.

We made quite a few rookie mistakes with the original Darkwatch. The design was very ambitious. Our internal measure of success was how well the game ran on the PlayStation 2 against a Halo benchmark, which resulted in feature creep and a finished game that did not live up to our expectations. A key feature—an open, streaming world that could be navigated by horseback—had to be scrapped at the eleventh hour.

Developers always have their hands in the cookie jar and never want to give up on aspects of their original design until they are forced to do so. This is important and commendable, but the artistic and creative elements of a game team have to be guided by at least one person who has a strong vision for the game and can make cross-disciplinary trade-offs on the fly. Our organization was too easily bottlenecked—something we tried to remedy for our next games through the institution of game directors and agile development geared around working demos every two weeks.

While I was at High Moon, we never built a second game on the same engine. So, as soon as we got the Darkwatch engine and pipeline working well for the PlayStation 2 and Xbox, we changed over to Unreal Engine 3 for the PlayStation 3 and Xbox 360, which was a less-than-smooth transition. High

Moon started working with the Unreal 3 technology very early, but at the time, Gears of War had not been released. Even on the Xbox 360, the technology and tools were still being formed, which took quite a bit longer than we had originally budgeted. We also had some internal resistance to working with a licensed technology and toolset after painstakingly building our engine using key pieces of middleware, so that was a small but persistent issue in our implementation of the Unreal technology.

Lastly, the project we had committed to build for Vivendi was a third-person action game with a heavy fighting component, as opposed to a Gears of War-style shooter. We had to make a lot of major changes to build The Bourne Conspiracy. These decisions significantly impacted our release schedule, as we had to deal with new technology, a new platform for the team, a new game genre, and a new publisher with ambitious expectations. This is a recipe for glitches and unexpected delays. As a leader, I learned to respect these variables and plan for much earlier trade-offs. Even at Appy, with much smaller projects, we are very cognizant of what we don't know and how much it can hurt us when we're planning projects.

Ramsay: You cofounded a company once before. Malibu Comics?

Ulm: Malibu Comics was formed at the tail end of the "Black & White Boom" that turned small, black-and-white comic books, such as Teenage Mutant Ninja Turtles, into giant publishing successes. The company was formed by president Scott Rosenberg, publisher Dave Olbrich, and creative director Tom Mason. I served as editor-in-chief.

The four of us operated the company for nearly 11 years and published an average of 25 books every month, with notable highlights, including the initial wave of Image comics, the Ultraverse line of superhero comics, and Men in Black, which was the original comic book that formed the basis of the movie that launched Will Smith to superstardom.

Marvel Comics acquired Malibu in 1994, and I remained as vice president of editorial for a little over a year before I left.

Ramsay: Can you point to any specific experiences at Malibu Comics that helped you with your later endeavors?

Ulm: The experience of building a company from four individuals into a leading publisher was formative for me. We were very young. The members of the staff were, on average, in their mid-20s. We worked hard and tried a lot of ideas.

It was a great experience in every way. The fact that we had the ability to "greenlight" our publishing portfolio was incredibly satisfying and allowed us to experiment with different characters; licensed properties, such as Star Trek, Robotech, Terminator, and Planet of the Apes; as well as business models.

We had to wear many different hats, from editor, creator, writer, and producer to advertiser, attorney, salesman, and public relations guy. I found that enormously satisfying. That flexibility is a big part of the reason that I continued to build companies over the years.

The Apple iOS environment reminds me of the early days of Malibu. At Appy, we have to think beyond the role of developer and wear all those startup hats all over again. Like Malibu, we have the ability to greenlight our portfolio and live and die by our own judgment. It feels great when you connect with the audience, but not so great when you don't!

Also, like the 1980s and 1990s comic-book industry, the app business is full of idealistic developers that own and control their own projects and are fundamentally changing the nature of the video-games business.

Ramsay: You are now on your third company?

Ulm: Appy Entertainment was founded on Halloween 2008 with the premise of creating "games for the rest of us"—small blasts of fun that players can share with their friends and play anywhere. The company's founders all came out of High Moon and cover the disciplines of engineering, design, art, brand management, and finance. It's a great team, and I am very lucky to be able to work with them.

Our three game apps are all very different and are only possible on touch-based mobile devices. Our bestselling title FaceFighter has been downloaded over eight million times and allows users to "reach out and punch someone." Users can incorporate any face from any photograph—such as bosses, dogs, best friends, political figures, and athletes—and have a full-fledged fighting experience, then send the bruised-and-battered face through e-mail, Facebook, and Twitter. Zombie Pizza is our darkly comedic take on the puzzle genre, where players have to create disgusting pizzas made up of human organs and get them to the zombies before they storm your pizzeria. Tune Runner is our music game that lets you use any song in your iPod and compete with the entire world.

Ramsay: Social games seem to be the big thing these days. Why did you decide to go mobile and enter the app space?

Ulm: Social games are very interesting, and all of our apps have social aspects, and ties to Facebook and Twitter. But we decided to focus on the app space because of its rapid growth and much smaller capital requirements to build out our own proprietary technology.

Ultimately, we wanted to create a company based on our own properties and unique brand. Most importantly, we felt that the console industry had become so risk-adverse, because of the high cost of development, that it was more and more difficult to do something that was not a sequel or movie tie-in.

In the app space, we have the ability to greenlight ideas that we feel are interesting and try them. It's also the chance to communicate with a completely different audience than the folks who are buying console games and see if we can connect with an enormous group of underserved mobile gamers with a revolutionary device.

Ramsay: Some people have said that the app space is not only Apple's house, but also a house of cards. Is there really a promising future for game developers who specialize in this market?

Ulm: The app space is a very tough and competitive arena with enormous price pressure. It is not easy to grow a professional company solely on the basis of revenues from games, although there have been some standouts within the space. However, the platform is growing rapidly, and business models and consumer expectations are settling in. The total number of iOS devices has passed 250 million and should continue to grow. I believe that the space will consolidate, and the successful iOS-centric companies who are able to connect to consumers will form stronger entities that really understand the mainstream digital environment.

In terms of Apple as a partner, I feel that they do an excellent job in curating the iOS platform and have set the standard for user experience in hardware, software, and digital retail. Development approval times are not even close to those required on game consoles. We average about seven days for approval time, which is reasonable in my view. The censorship is not a problem for us because we are trying to connect to mainstream consumers. Flash support is a nonissue for us as well because we have always written directly to the platform.

Apple puts the consumer experience first, which means that they have more stringent rules about third-party technologies that affect battery life and stability, which is understandable.

Ramsay: Focusing on Apple platforms sounds just as risky as focusing on Sony platforms or other embedded systems, since developers must rely on manufacturers for support as well their commitment to increasing market share. Should game developers in the app space be hedging their bets by developing for Android and Symbian, too? What is your strategy at Appy?

Ulm: The larger picture here is that networked smartphones that can run third-party applications will rapidly replace cell phones to become the dominant computing platforms on the planet. Penetration of these devices in 2010 is relatively small compared to the base of total cell phones, but this is changing rapidly as every manufacturer seeks to beat the iPhone.

Apple will certainly set the bar and the terms of engagement, but others like Android, Windows 7 Phone, Nokia, HP Palm, and RIM will all be competing hard on features and, most importantly, price. The iPhone can be had for $99, and many others are lower than that.

The key difference between platforms today is the quantity of apps. It's a powerful statement for Apple to say there is an "app for that." However, future competition between platforms will be dominated by app quality, and that's why it is so critical for the platform curators to find ways to monetize app development so that developers like Appy can continue to take risks and spend more time, money, and creative personnel on our projects.

We are constantly evaluating other platforms, but they must be competitive to the standard that Apple has set in order for us to justify a development budget. Right now, it is hard to make games that sell at a reasonable retail price on any platform, but it is exceptionally hard on platforms that don't have a robust retail experience that makes it easy for people to discover and purchase games.

Ramsay: What is Apple doing to facilitate the shopping experience? What would you like to see done?

Ulm: Apple has, by far, the best consumer retail experience of any app curator, with one-click payment, iTunes gift cards, and a well-laid-out store stocked with a lot of variety. That being said, I would like to see more efforts at improving speed and responsiveness, at separating the various parts of the store into more comprehensive layouts, and in improving the consumer rating and reviewing process.

It would be great to attach the Genius function to the mobile version of the App Store so that users would get a customized list of apps they might find interesting. Ultimately, our problems as developers are all about discovery and browsing, which are hard problems.

Ramsay: Most entrepreneurs would be lucky to pull off one successful venture, but you have managed three. Have starting and leading new companies become any easier for you?

Ulm: Companies succeed or fail because of the team, not because of one individual. At Malibu and High Moon, I was only part of the executive teams that built those companies. I've had the privilege of working with some great mentors, including John Rowe, Lorne Lanning, and Scott Rosenberg. I've been very lucky in my career to work within cultures of trust and achievement that made the challenges of the startup possible to overcome. At Appy, the founding partners and I have carried these same values with us.

In some ways, having experience with other startups makes it easier to operate a company in that the obvious mistakes are more easily identified. However, each company has had totally different products, business models, and development-time horizons, and therefore has required a different approach. At Appy, the Wild West aspects of the digital retail business model and the inherent product unknowns in building successful game apps are challenges that often require the mind of a student. Sometimes experience can send you down the wrong path if you're not careful.

Ramsay: What advice do you have for the entrepreneurs out there?

Ulm: Do what you love. Be patient with yourself and your team. Don't make the same mistake twice. Most importantly, share whatever success you are able to achieve with the people that made it possible.

Tobi Saulnier

Founder, 1st Playable Productions

*When Activision acquired Vicarious Visions, where **Tobi Saulnier** was vice president of product development, she left the company. Having spent 12 years in research at General Electric, she was familiar with the culture and operations of a large enterprise. Saulnier, however, longed for the small-business environment. As a mother of two, passionate about children's education, Saulnier was inspired to set out on her own, and she founded 1st Playable Productions in 2005.*

Unlike other studios, 1st Playable is a client-centric game developer that specifically works with licensors and publishers, such as Disney, THQ, and D3Publisher, to extend major children's brands to video games. Since the beginning, 1st Playable has created a number of games for key properties, including Club Penguin, Kung Zhu, and Yogi Bear. Saulnier continues to serve as chief executive officer.

Ramsay: What were you doing before you started 1st Playable?

Saulnier: When I started 1st Playable, I had been in the game industry for five years. I was vice president of product development at Vicarious Visions. In that role, I had learned about the game industry and shipped 60 different SKUs, ranging from Blue's Clues for Game Boy Color to DOOM 3 for Xbox. Previously, I worked at GE Research and Development for 12 years as a program manager and researcher in the computer networks field.

Ramsay: What prompted you to move from a large enterprise to a small business?

Saulnier: Even before I joined Vicarious, I was interested in small-company culture. While I was at GE, I was volunteering at a local Montessori school. I was a board member and board president for several years. That was my first experience with the responsibilities within a very small business. Yeah, it was a school, but it was also a business. We had 12 staff members. Nothing was computerized, and the financials were a mess. I was in this very active, almost second full-time job for a few years during my time at GE.

It became really apparent to me how much of an impact that an individual can have in a small company. In a big company, you're just one of thousands of people. If you want to get anything approved, you have to deal with huge infrastructures, and you have to go through layers of management. The upside is that you don't have to worry about how anything is done. The downside is that everything comes about very slowly.

When the opportunity at Vicarious presented itself, I was intrigued. I was thinking that might be a place where I can have an impact. It was a relatively small company at around 40 people. I could help them quite a bit with my training. I thought I should do something more useful like that, as opposed to just fighting bureaucracy. I also wasn't happy about being forced to implement certain destructive policies in my group. My thinking was that I could fight that big battle, which was really worthwhile but could take years, or I could join a small company and quickly have a significant impact.

Ramsay: Were people in that company still wearing many hats?

Saulnier: It was very informal. When I first joined Vicarious, the company was fairly young, at least in terms of process and project management. As vice president of product development, I brought in more process to help the company start to understand how money was spent, how projects were earning money, how to keep to schedules, and things like that. The processes and the training I received at GE were very helpful in assisting and setting up a structure that made the company very healthy, able to deliver great games, stay within budgets, and become a profitable organization that the publisher Activision eventually sought to purchase.

Ramsay: After achieving success in your role at Vicarious, why did you want to break out on your own and start up 1st Playable?

Saulnier: I started 1st Playable when Vicarious joined Activision. I had fallen in love with the spirit of the independent game studio, and since there was now one less independent studio, I thought I should start another. In addition, I was very passionate about education for children, and there weren't many developers focusing on that area. There aren't a lot of options for people who want to make educational games for kids, so I thought this would be a great niche to focus on.

Ramsay: How did your past experience prepare you for 1st Playable?

Saulnier: Well, I didn't know too much. I knew business though. My GE training was fantastic from that perspective. I wasn't an MBA, but I learned marketing, strategy, business, and finance. I was able to refine my knowledge and skills through my work at the Montessori school.

Honestly, I don't think I would have started 1st Playable if had not received so many words of encouragement. There were a few different things that I might have decided to do at that time, but many people were so supportive and pushed me to at least give this a shot. I hadn't always dreamed of starting my own studio or anything, but I felt at that point, it was something that just needed to be done.

Ramsay: Did you put together a business plan?

Saulnier: By April 1, 2005, I hadn't yet thought about how exactly I was going to make this venture happen. In retrospect, I've learned that I don't need to know every step that I'm going to take along the way, but being able to articulate, and proceed in, a general direction is a huge advantage. In a startup, you don't have many details or a lot of control over the future, so you need to be really confident in where you want to take the company.

But I actually didn't have a clear plan at first, and the plan that I had partially formed wasn't viable. By the middle of April, I changed my approach completely. I had this idea that the company would be comprised of me and some contractors. We'd effectively have a virtual production office. I asked a few people who I knew in the industry for their feedback and listened to their reactions. I realized that if I was a publisher, even I wouldn't hire myself under that model. If I wouldn't hire me, who would? I needed a more compelling approach. I needed about a dozen people on the team, co-located, and we'd need to work together to make something over the summer. That approach became far more successful than the original plan could have been.

Ramsay: How much of a financial burden did you expect to undertake? Did you look for any investors to alleviate that burden?

Saulnier: When I left GE, I cashed in my stock options. I was lucky because I left at a time when the economy hadn't yet crashed. I had that amount in my mind for startup capital. Then I came up with a budget, and I realized that I was going to burn through it in six months. I decided that if I did not take the risk on this strategy, I might save money, but I wouldn't be able to get started.

In a strange way, I was fortunate to have been over 40 when I started 1st Playable. I was frugal, didn't spend much money, my spouse didn't spend much money, and we've always tried to live on one salary, so we had financial security. We did without a lot of extras, even though we were sort of envious of our friends' huge houses and cool cars. Just living like that long enough paid off. I didn't have to get funding from anyone else. I could do things the way I wanted to do them. Well, at least as long as I could get clients and find people for the team that shared the same ideas.

I also paid everybody from day one, which is what I spent my savings on. We had benefits, too. Payroll began in mid-May, and health plans began at the start of June. I started the company the way I wanted the company to be—a sustainable local employer that wasn't going to have a liquidity event that would pay out stock options.

Ramsay: You mentioned a spouse. Did you have a family then? How did the startup life affect them?

Saulnier: Yes, my husband and I have two kids, eight years apart. The youngest is my son, who was an important part of my startup experience. He was three years old when I got into games, and eight years old when I started 1st Playable.

Eight years old is a very impressionable age. The interesting thing about that age is that we still think our parents are superheroes. We think our parents are invincible and they can do everything. Two years later, our parents are ignorant and annoying, but at the grammar-school age, parents get a ton of admiration and confidence from their kids.

My daughter was a teenager, so she was involved in the company, but her world revolved around her friends, and not so much around her mom at that age. However, my son had incredible confidence in me. When he heard his mom was going to start a company, he was sure that we would be successful. He would tell everybody that we were starting a company, that we were going to have 12 people by June, and he'd go on and on. I'd be thinking, "Oh, my! Now I have to actually make this work." Disappointing myself is one thing, but this little kid has so much faith in our success that I had better deliver. It was amazing how much his belief influenced me to overcome my own doubts.

And you know what? Sure enough, it worked. So, he became someone who would take on these grand projects without a doubt as to whether they could be done. I remember an administrator at the school called me up and said, "I just want to check before I send this home. Eric gave me a flyer, inviting everyone to your house for dinner because he has this idea that you're going to start a restaurant." He had gotten together with his friends, and they had decided to start a restaurant. They decided that the dads were going to cook because, of course, the moms were busy. They made up menus that they were going to send to the entire school because to them that's perfectly normal for starting a restaurant. It was hilarious.

I think the kids definitely have to be affected when they're exposed to or involved with entrepreneurial activities. My son is a teenager now and brings all of the fun of being a teenager into our lives. In the long term, I think it will be interesting to see how this experience affects him.

Ramsay: Other than your son, who else did you convince to take on this challenge with you? How did you put together your initial team?

Saulnier: You don't have enough things to do when you're starting a company because you're waiting for people to get back to you or make decisions. That was my experience anyway. Despite being a programmer, I wasn't programming games initially, so I was bored. I discovered a little wireless phone game company in the incubator center, and I began helping out with its production, prioritizing bugs, testing, and that sort of thing.

One of the employees ultimately joined 1st Playable, and then there were a few other people that left Vicarious at that time. I had signed a noncompete agreement, so I couldn't just go out and convince the people who I wanted to join me. But the people who were leaving around the same time became natural allies. We had worked together previously in different roles, but we had made games the same way. I also sought out students at Rensselaer Polytechnic Institute (RPI), talked to professors, and attended IGDA meetings. I looked for people who were pursuing their first jobs, who were inspired by our social entrepreneurship mission. It's through those approaches that we pulled our first team together.

Ramsay: Did you focus on recruiting management, or did you get right into building a development team?

Saulnier: 1st Playable is still an extremely flat company. We don't have a lot of people who are strictly managers; in fact, nobody is only a manager here. We have groups and group leaders who attend to the people-type things, but the company was designed to stay under 50 people from the start. I purposely avoided the type of larger structure that I created for Vicarious.

We have little structure, management, or administration. I'm almost entirely responsible for the business side. We have an office manager. I recently started a finance person on a once-weekly schedule. We have a human resources person on the same schedule, too. We have somebody focusing on recruiting when needed. We have this very, very, very slim administrative staff because we want to be sustainable.

One of my goals was to not sell the company to a publisher, but instead try to create a sustainable business that didn't need a liquidity plan. What does it take to be sustainable? An important lesson that I learned at the Montessori school and at GE is to ensure that you keep your overhead down. If you let your overhead get bigger and bigger, you have to work harder and harder to pay for the overhead, and you may actually spend less on your product every year. That scenario has a finite lifespan.

I realized early on that keeping overhead low meant I would have to accept imperfections in the many things we would do, and we were going to have to accept a degree of disorganization. It is in my nature to prefer more polished processes and be more systems-focused, which is perfectly appropriate for a 120-person group. If you want to keep your group under 50 people though, you can't have very many administrative people unless you have an impressive profit margin, which is definitely not the case for game development.

Ramsay: Why did you want to keep the company under 50 people?

Saulnier: One reason for staying under 50 people is that I wanted to create a company that has an informal creative atmosphere, where relationships are critical, and where everyone is mission-focused. Over 50 people, there are systems, processes, and infrastructure that you have to put in place. Staying small isn't an easy goal to achieve, but it was an intriguing challenge.

Ramsay: Was recruitment simply a matter of dollars for work, or did you have to be more persuasive?

Saulnier: What I primarily did first was ensure that we were clear about what we were doing and what we were all about in our public communications, to attract people who resonated with the mission-focused company I was trying to start.

Initially, I didn't think that too many people were going to respond positively to our message, but I learned that the message sold itself. I found that there are a lot of fresh graduates and experienced developers who are very motivated to do meaningful work in this area. We've changed our messaging slightly, but it's still very much the same mission we articulated our first year.

Ramsay: Did you have any external advisors—people you could count on for insight into issues that cropped up?

Saulnier: An uncountable number. I'm very proactive in seeking advice and interpretations of different experiences. That first year especially, I would visit other studios—such as Backbone Entertainment, High Voltage Software, and Cyberlore—and learn about how other people meet challenges and discover role models. There were many people who were generous with their time in terms of just tolerating me dropping in, so I could have somebody to talk to about how it was going and find out what they were doing.

I never actually ended up creating a formal board, partly because I'm concerned that board members can expect you to take their advice or direction. But I had learned I have a very strong sense of direction. People can give me advice, but if I don't agree, I don't follow it. That can look like I'm ignoring them, and I'm not very good at smoothing over ruffled feathers. That was one of the main reasons I didn't set up a board.

Fortunately, there were many people—RPI alumni—at the incubator center who are entrepreneurs and made themselves available for feedback, too. I took advantage of every speaking opportunity that came up at the center. I'd present to whatever venture capital group or whoever wanted to have us present to them, which is ironic because we weren't looking for money. But they were opportunities to evangelize the potential of using games for education, to talk to more people about the company and our mission, and to get their reactions.

Ramsay: Sometimes business models arise out of a need to land deals with publishers or to obtain venture capital. Since you didn't require outside money, what was your business model?

Saulnier: We did need to earn revenue, even if we had some initial capital. I had a theory: focus on the entertainment space provides the skills to make games fun, with the appropriate production values, on a tight schedule. You could then take those skills and apply them to the educational domain. In the long term, I thought we should do about half of each. The retail space would keep us sharp and on top of our game, and then we could apply those skills to make great, engaging games for the educational space. But although we wanted to make educational games, it was clear that that market was very soft and not likely to be a great place to generate revenue in the near future.

In the kids entertainment market, I knew that there was a strong demand for developers who genuinely wanted to work on kids games. I knew that many clients who needed our expertise were not going to have Vicarious Visions to do these games anymore because they would now be exclusively Activision. So, our immediate strategy centered on proving we could deliver high-quality game experiences that met this demand.

And then, in parallel, we focused on finding ways to cultivate a larger future market for educational games. So, all of the presentations I did were about educational games, despite the fact that our initial revenue was from games that are more in the entertainment space.

Ramsay: Your first title was Cabbage Patch Kids, right?

Saulnier: The first title that we developed was Cabbage Patch Kids for the Game Boy Advanced. D3Publisher had just opened a US office, so they didn't have existing developer partners. 1st Playable was also a startup. So, the relationship was perfectly suited to us because we could provide what they needed.

Ramsay: Cabbage Patch Kids is a licensed property. Do you work with many properties that were created by third parties?

Saulnier: That's what it's called in the retail space. It's a preexisting brand.

I know people use "license" to refer to an existing brand in a derogatory way. There are some people who think that if you didn't invent it, it's not worth working on. I can understand that point of view. I used to think that my solution was better, so I didn't want to work with other people's ideas, but now I find that there's far more challenge in helping others succeed.

It has been really interesting to work with creators and brands at different stages, figuring out the best ways that brands can be made into fun video games that elicit the right responses from consumers. And even if you create your own brand, you are going to need to be able to establish a clear vision, which an entire team can work to. This is really not that different than working with creative owners outside the company.

Ramsay: How do you determine which brands to bring into video games?

Saulnier: We want to work with our clients' most important kids properties, such as Cabbage Patch Kids, Disney Princesses, and Ben 10. For these high-profile titles, I know that the project success is important to them because their business depends on it generating revenue. If the project is less important to them, the company can take a bigger risk, and hire with one of many, many low-cost studios around the world instead of us. If we're in a higher cost labor market, like upstate New York, we need to be very proactive in the pursuit of working with our clients' most important brands and delivering successful games.

Furthermore, a significant amount of customer service is required to guide brand owners through the process of adapting successful brands to games, which are themselves very complicated products. As part of that service, we work with clients to determine which games would best support their brand-building efforts. That means aligning games with the core brand values, and identifying gameplay, characters, art style, and content that are appropriate for the target age group.

There's another dimension to going after the most important brands. When there's an economic downturn, we don't want to be the first ones on the cutting block. Our employees depend on the studio maintaining a below-average cancellation rate.

Ramsay: How did the Cabbage Patch Kids game come about? How did you get the project?

Saulnier: I was going around, showing a first-playable demo to everybody who I knew had an interest in quality kids games. I'd show them our work in progress because I was building a case that we could do an awesome job, and I wanted the feedback.

For startups, I thought that the best match would be another small organization that really needed our expertise. A startup publisher really needs a high-quality game to win over new licensors. That's where D3 was at the time; they had just obtained the license to publish a Cabbage Patch Kids game.

I had worked with Brian Christian, who was vice president of product development at D3. Brian knew about 1st Playable and that we were actively looking for a game to develop, so he sent out a team to perform their due diligence and ascertain whether we really existed. They found that we were doing high-quality work, so Brian called and offered us the contract. That was a critical step because after we produced a high-quality game that won some parenting awards, D3 showed that title to Cartoon Network, secured the license for Ben 10, and had us launch that handheld video-game series.

Ramsay: Can you tell me about the demo you showed around? Was the demo based on Cabbage Patch Kids?

Saulnier: No, our first-playable demo was a practice run at making a game that was representative of the type of games that we wanted to do. We chose to create a game based on a Disney property called Rolie Polie Olie. The show features round robot characters and bright, poppy colors. If you ever watch that show and you're an adult, you'll want to turn the volume down because it's definitely aimed at young kids!

We treated the game as though we had the contract. We went through the steps, we stumbled, we had to train people, we figured out our processes and the design, and we built the necessary technologies. We wanted the demo to look and feel like a slice of the final game because when a publisher or a brand owner plays a first-playable version of a game, they expect to see a final-looking slice, have fun, and imagine the game on store shelves.

Ramsay: You built a technical demo to exhibit your core competencies?

Saulnier: Well, yes and no. It was more than a technical demo. A technical demo might have just the character on the screen that can be moved around in a game environment. The first-playable milestone is the end of preproduction and the beginning of production. At the first-playable milestone, you have all of the game mechanics and a complete, polished level.

You can make the rest of the game from that foundation because a lot of the ambiguities have been clarified. You can bring in playtesters and evaluate whether the game is any fun. Today, some call this a "vertical slice." The benefit of doing this is that we had started with a brand-new team that hadn't worked as a team before, so we were able to work out the kinks before we had a publisher counting on us to hit deadlines. I used to call it "spring training."

Ramsay: In terms of product development, are you focusing on extending third-party brands or developing original intellectual property?

Saulnier: We're doing both. Our studio focuses on understanding and developing games for underserved, mostly young audiences. For example, we might develop a game for boys, ages three to six; a game for both boys and girls, from six to twelve; or a game for teachers to aid struggling middle-school students in a science class. But we're also a resource for really high-risk, important projects that are also small-scale games. We don't want to do anything that's a Grand Theft Auto with equally grand budgets, partly due to the issues of scale. We're specialists in smaller games because that's part of being sustainable and not being able to absorb immense financial risks of huge projects.

Many retailers are attracted to games that are based on either established brands or other media which have "household name" recognition. Games that are sold at retail need household name recognition because mass-market consumers are going to need to find them on crowded shelves, and these games rarely have large marketing budgets themselves. As a counterpoint, we've been working on games for the Nintendo 3DS. The household name recognition of an established brand isn't so critical for a new platform, since there is less product. We can do more original titles and take a chance on cool emerging genres like augmented reality. I don't expect that window of opportunity to stay open for long, but we try to take advantage of these openings because we know that consumers will take a chance on unknowns when there isn't much competition from known brands.

Ramsay: You mentioned games for education. Are serious games part of your offering?

Saulnier: Serious games are a really fast-growing area for us. We've found that we can be a really valuable member of a research team that's applying games to education, health, or some domain new to the application of games.

These groups have subject-matter expertise, and there's demand for a game developer who can borrow that expertise, be very inventive and creative, and find game solutions for their focus areas. I think there's a lot of demand here, probably because nobody is going to get rich doing these games. Studios that are incentivized by big paydays aren't going after these opportunities, but they're potential high-value targets because we can take what we learn in the retail space and bring them into this area. Our mission to have social impact, instead of to merely make a lot of money, makes us a compatible partner for nonprofit groups.

Ramsay: Are you interested in other markets?

Saulnier: Downloadable content is interesting. I'm curious about how the Apple App Store, Amazon App Store, and other app stores will evolve in relation to business models. We're monitoring how downloadable content might become more of a professional market versus a strike-it-rich market because a small company with salary commitments can't really do a lot there unless we dedicate the scale to take a variety of risks.

Ramsay: Do your projects typically come out of talks with publishers, or do you go directly to content and brand holders?

Saulnier: We did a direct license once so far. Based on what I learned during that project, I don't pursue those as much now because of the stakeholder issues when it comes to retail distribution. A publisher who also has a distribution channel is more interested in promoting their own products than something they have a smaller share of because we licensed it.

I've come to realize that everybody needs to have skin in the game. Everyone involved in getting a game onto the shelves has to feel like it's their game and they have some control over the outcome. I'm more appreciative of partners who can handle their part of the process. The publishers we work with are fantastic because they offload all of the care and feeding of the brand-ownership team. That can be very time-consuming, quite risky, and it's very hard to do that and focus on making a great game.

So, currently, we're very involved with the creative teams at brand owners, but I haven't looked into obtaining direct licenses with their organizations because I like our publisher partners. We like working with them. We have established roles, and we work together really well. If they're not in the equation, then we have a whole set of problems that we have to troubleshoot.

And to keep the company small, we need to develop great partnership skills instead of trying to do it all ourselves.

Ramsay: When a brand owner comes to you, do you pass on the opportunity? Or do you match them with a publisher?

Saulnier: In the serious games space, people come to us who want to make a game, and we may try to match them up with a publisher depending on their go-to-market needs. If they need to get to the retail shelves, we might have them visit our offices and educate them, so that when they talk to the publisher, they have a stronger understanding of the process. We just try to be a good citizen and a resource for market and development information. In some cases, the same brand owner will come back to us after they've teamed up with a publisher, so everybody wins.

Occasionally, brand owners will approach us because they want to have a developer when they go to a publisher. We haven't pursued many of those opportunities because they're typically not prepared to invest financially in making the game, and realistically, any publisher would and should want to choose the developer if they are risking their capital.

Ramsay: How many titles do you have in development at any one time?

Saulnier: We are set up to have four to five projects in development at one time with 40 to 50 people, roughly averaging 10 people per team. At certain times of the year, we have many projects finishing and some starting up, so I feel like we have twice that number, but that's the math.

We don't have many projects that are the same size as each other. We'll have big projects, and then we'll have smaller projects because they're for a really young age group or an educational game. We run the gamut. The upside of a diverse portfolio is that it helps us manage risk in a volatile market.

Ramsay: When you have multiple titles in development, how many of those are usually licensed properties?

Saulnier: We think about licenses so much differently than a lot of people in the industry. The majority of the revenue that we earn is from brand owners who can justify big budgets because they're already household names, perhaps through different media, and they already have a market revenue stream. That translates to a higher profit potential, so they're more likely to hit the "important" or "vital" criteria for a publisher. So, we do tons of very popular entertainment properties. It's great to see kids playing games we've made for characters and worlds they love.

We compete for that niche—that segment of the market—because that's the segment that can pay for an American developer. We've done games for

Rio and Yogi Bear. Movie games really need that type of developer who can be really adaptable and flexible, and integrate content details at a very late stage when the movie-production process finalizes.

We've done several toy brands, like Kung Zhu, which we thought was a great experiment with how to create a version of the very cool Zhu Zhu Pets robotic hamster toys to appeal to boys. And Pillow Pets is another toy brand which has seen a lot of response from parents. Toy brands require more story and creative development, from art style to backstory, since their main focus will have been simply the fun factor. And we've done a game for Pinkalicious, which is a very popular children's book title. It's even a musical on Off Broadway. We worked with another book based on a real-life story, Winter's Tail.

Working with authors is also rewarding. Here, we have people who have very strong narrative and sense of values that they are conveying, perhaps some art style, and very little preconception of game mechanics that can support those. Those are just some of the brands that I think people would call "licensed." Our team really enjoys learning about and immersing ourselves in a new creative world. I think of it as virtual-world "tourism," in the best possible sense of traveling outside one's comfort zone and enjoying other cultures.

We're a service business. We provide a service to clients who've worked really hard on a brand they love and suddenly it's exploding. Their advisors are telling them that they have something that people care about, so they should expand into other media. We can help ensure this is done in a way that preserves their vision and unique positioning.

Ramsay: Did you set out to be a service business? Why?

Saulnier: I learned at GE that services were where you wanted to be. If you were just selling product, there was very little potential to maintain pricing in a global market. It is too easy to become a commodity. You really wanted to be in a differentiated service-oriented market. A high-end professional services business requires a lot of communication ability, cultural awareness, and technical knowledge. And if you have expertise, you can compete on a global scale.

Ramsay: What are the unique challenges of working with multiple licenses?

Saulnier: I think the key is to make sure all of your clients' information is confidential and you're not allowing information to leak across projects. We use code names and strictly protect information. Everyone here is well trained and knows that we're working on things that are secret to our different clients, and that are key to their survival and ability to thrive in an unforgiving industry.

Every client has to be confident we care about their project as much as any of our other projects and that we're going to put their needs first, before ours. That doesn't mean we put everyone to work on one project. It just means that we have to make sure that nobody feels like they're being given the second shift. Happily, we have always found that putting our clients' needs first always ultimately benefits us, too. It's the cliché of win-win. Having a team that can think through solutions from our partners' perspective is invaluable to both the project success and repeat business.

So, "customer service" is critical. One aspect is how we communicate with the customer and the information that we provide. If I hired a company like 1st Playable, I'd want the head of the company to care about my project. I wouldn't want to be handed off to someone else. I'd want the head of the company to care. When my daughter's school was being built and I was heading the building committee, the CEO at the construction company attended all of the meetings to show us that he was personally committed to the outcome. He personally showed a commitment and willingness to do what it took to make it the best possible result for us. Even at GE, it's the head of a business that will talk to the head of a utility about a sale because it's that degree of personal commitment that they are buying in addition to the work.

Of course, there aren't just challenges to working with multiple licenses; there are advantages, too. Our artists get to work with an incredibly diverse set of art styles, our programmers get to work with a variety of genres, and we get experience with many different audiences.

Ramsay: Do you sometimes have clients who are in direct competition with each other?

Saulnier: They're all competing with each other, but we try to avoid doing two products that are competing with each other for the same audience and the same shelf time. In reality, Club Penguin competes with Ben 10, right? So we only work with clients for whom that's okay.

We can't do a noncompete agreement. We wouldn't be able to survive as a company if we had to do a noncompete. But the market is so big, it shouldn't matter if there's more than one 1st Playable game out there. That should be the least of their problems because there are so many different games out there. By itself, that's not enough of a competitive hindrance.

It's more important to them that they can work with a team who knows how to work with licenses, knows how to adapt to asset availability, knows how to listen to other points of view, is able to recognize whether our great idea isn't actually a great idea, and knows how to manage creative and software risk to deliver the game on time! I think the business relationship is often more important than the products of that relationship. The product has to be great, sure, but working with us has to be a greater experience.

Ramsay: When you started 1st Playable, where did you want the company to be by now?

Saulnier: That's a good question. I'm not the sort of person that looks five years ahead in any level of detail. I just don't do planning that way. If I had been forced to think five years ahead, I think that what we've been able to achieve is where I wanted us to be—maybe more. We've earned a great reputation with our clients, we have many repeat clients, and we were able to get on the leading edge of a platform transition.

The company was formed right after the Nintendo DS was introduced, so we were in catch-up mode. We started out with the Game Boy Advance. We didn't do a DS game until the third or fourth generation. With the 3DS though, we were able to be at the forefront. That was a great accomplishment and quite necessary to our sustainability.

Ramsay: Did you think all of that was possible?

Saulnier: I must have. But I don't have very fixed detailed goals. I have more of a sense of exploration. Let's find out what happens, you know? For instance, I started the company with the goal to develop 50% entertainment games and 50% educational games. I thought it would take maybe ten years before we could achieve that balance. When we started doing educational games much sooner, I was surprised. But I try to not have definitive goals, and instead try to find an exciting direction and broad destination, and go that way. My ancestors were Norwegian sailing captains. I suspect I inherited this from them. They needed to cross the ocean, but every trip required a different approach.

Ramsay: Would you say that your willingness to take risks hasn't changed?

Saulnier: Right, exactly. If it did change, I'd go find a different job because it's a very bad job for anybody who's not tolerant of risk.

Ramsay: How has your role changed since you've started?

Saulnier: When the company first started, it was very boring for me. When you're starting out, you really don't have very many people to work with. For a few weeks, I had nobody to work with yet, and I'm very much a team-oriented person, so I really disliked that aspect of the experience. I went from having 14 milestones on a given day to a job where I felt like I was just waiting for other people. That downtime gave me a chance to play World of Warcraft quite a bit though! My role at the start was very different in that there was a lot more waiting, a lot less specifics to handle, a lot more tasks related to getting people up and running, establishing processes, and establishing how we're going to do things.

I also didn't return to programming initially. It was a couple of years in before I realized I could contribute in this way. I wouldn't consider myself a great programmer, but I am great at filling in the gaps to support a busy team. Being a programmer, I am not sure why I had never delved into that aspect of games previously while at Vicarious Visions. I suspect I was just too busy learning about the art and design disciplines.

By the time we had our first team at 1st Playable, we had a few very experienced people, but there were quite a number who had never made a retail game or a professional game. I was a lot more hands-on during that time, although initially focused on process and quality. As the company has grown, we have a core group of people who have a lot of expertise and take on a lot of responsibilities. Nowadays, I might be really involved in only a few projects at any given time.

Now there are more wheels in motion. Because we have to maintain a low overhead, our flat organization with an informal structure keeps me plenty busy. I'm still wearing many hats. I still do accounting, finance, and sales. I get involved with high-risk projects when it comes to sorting out technology issues or what features can we scope into a particular game. I could hire full-time staff to address those needs, but generally speaking, I would rather create another job for a designer or artist than an administrator. It's not that I don't like administrators. I simply see the company purpose being partly to create jobs for creative talent, to keep them in our community.

Ramsay: What's your long-term vision for 1st Playable? How do you want to manage succession?

Saulnier: I think the direction we need to go is toward a professional partnership, like that of an architecture or legal services firm. Basically, what that means is you have a partnership structure that partners can buy into, and you have means for adding and removing partners to allow for people moving. The company's success would become more of a group leadership effort. If you look farther out than the game industry, you'd see sustainable business models for groups of experts, which is what we're becoming. We need to evolve our organization into something more appropriate for such a group.

Ramsay: Do you currently have a program for cultivating new leaders?

Saulnier: Yeah, I would say we have an informal mentorship program. Every week, the production team that manages projects meets. I try to encourage cross-mentoring and sharing of techniques and approaches.

Ramsay: How has the culture changed over the years?

Saulnier: When we started, we had a very informal self-starter culture. That really hasn't changed. I've never had time to manage every little detail, nor have I seen that as healthy for the group to be too dependent on me specifically. So, when people come aboard, they adjust and learn that the workplace is very much an environment where you have to take ownership of activities and tasks that need to get done.

On some occasions, the organization has become too bureaucratic. When that happens, we try to pull back and regain the informal atmosphere that we've had since the start. At the same time, we've had to formalize some systems and processes, like how time off is determined, in order to maintain a positive culture where everyone is contributing.

For example, we effectively used the honor system for time off. The assumption was that everyone would be responsible and confirm with their team members. But it's really hard to ensure that everybody does just that. We've had a few cases where too many people were out during specific deadlines and a few people were being left to carry the workload. That wasn't working so well because it wasn't fair to those left. Now we require that employees get explicit permission for time off to ensure there is a balance.

Ramsay: What values characterize the culture?

Saulnier: We value collaboration; your own point of view isn't always the most important one. Listening to other people's needs and perspectives is really important for games, regardless of whether you're listening to your teammates, your clients, or the brand owner.

We value craftsmanship, or attention to detail. Everyone on the team should be jointly responsible for the quality of the entire product and should be able to affect and improve the quality.

We value capability, which means that we like things that are hard to do from a technical or creative perspective. We're not looking for easy solutions because, due simply to salary costs in our location, we're going to be more expensive than some other solutions across the globe. We have to take on the harder jobs to justify our higher price.

Finally, we value community. Many of our decisions are driven by our community orientation.

Ramsay: You've been involved with the IGDA for awhile. That association places a premium on quality of life. What have you done at 1st Playable to improve the overall quality of life?

Saulnier: I think there are different perspectives as to what defines quality of life. In the game industry, "quality of life" is usually related to the abuse of mandated hours over sustained periods for staff for whom it's inappropriate to be requiring overtime. Our staff normally works a 40-hour week most of the time. Our challenge is, in some ways, the opposite: to make sure that people know that they're working in a really competitive industry and that the number of hours we work does factor into salary amounts, especially when handling peak development periods. Our smaller projects help manage those time periods to be more on the order of weeks than months.

From an IGDA standpoint, quality of life in the game industry is a tricky thing because it's often referring to situations where people had to work seven days a week, ten hours a day. At the same time, I have family members in factory jobs, which have regular 12-hour shifts expected, and in one recent situation, 27 straight days of 12-hour days. So I don't think the occasional 9- or 10- or even 12-hour day will kill us.

Most professional jobs require some amount of crunch, working more than eight hours in a given day near a project's end or in a particular season—for example, retailers and holidays, accounting and tax season, and obstetricians and birth peaks. That's just the way it is. That's the way it has always been for me as an engineer outside the game industry, although I don't recall being told to work late. I was just following the lead of older engineers, and if a project was late, we worked more to get it done on time. It was considered a professional responsibility to meet deadlines.

We're not like a movie studio or a construction firm, where you might have people working around the clock across three shifts to finish a project. What we do is provide infrastructure and processes so that we can avoid having a lot of work pile up at the end. By keeping hours down and thus salaries lower, we can also avoid some longer hours by hiring additional people when we need them during peaks.

I think the game industry's challenge for recent graduates is communicating that crunch is not a nine-hour day. That might be your job, depending on the deadline. Or you might have multiple 10- to 12-hour days. The problem comes when specific hours are enforced throughout a huge project, with a workforce which has been defined as "exempt." Measuring results in terms of hours in a creative field is not reliable and can lead to dysfunctional teams.

Ramsay: How much time would you say that you personally put into 1st Playable and your role on a daily basis?

Saulnier: I would be the exception to the typical hours of a 1st Playable employee. I work probably 12 to 14 hours a day on most days. I work less on weekends though, because we don't have projects that are so ambitious that we have to spend many weekends to accomplish our goals. The weekends require fewer hours for my 1st Playable work—maybe four or five hours a day. But keep in mind I have unending lists of things to do and things I want to try to accomplish beyond that. I can always think of more that I should or could be doing. This is just my nature and isn't unique to my current job. I've just never had jobs which could be "done" at a given point.

My alarm goes off at 5:00 AM, and I'm ready to work by 6:00 AM. I can hop on my computer and get a couple hours of focus before I need to wake up my son and get him ready for school. I come into work around 9:00 AM before most people arrive, leave at around 7:00 PM after most people have departed, have dinner, and then return to my computer and work until I'm too sleepy.

My balance comes from adding yet more things to my plate. I have always been an active volunteer in community organizations. I love the outdoors and have a homestead with a lot of outdoor work available. So, on some evenings, I have to attend a community event. If I'm a member of a board, I might have to go to a board meeting for three hours. I have farm animals, and that gives me other things to do, morning and night. I just fit a lot into my time. There are these other uses of my time, but I don't watch TV or anything like that.

Ramsay: Do you ever reflect on your schedule and think that you should be doing less? Do you ever feel like you overextend yourself?

Saulnier: We only have so much time to positively impact our world. Why would I want to do less? I've had a chronic illness. I know what it's like to be in the hospital, thinking that I might never leave and reflecting on how I used my freedom. When my illness was more active, I did all the sitting and watching television that I'd want to do in a lifetime, and I just have no interest in passive activities as long as I am healthy enough to walk and work and interact with the world. I learned that life throws you curveballs. One day, you can do anything you want; the next, you are bedridden and fighting to just survive.

As an entrepreneur and possible role model, people want your time, and there are plenty of worthy causes. That can be a problem because the demand is always more than it's possible to meet. You have to budget your time and take on things that you can do because you don't want to be stressed when you find that you can't do everything. I'm still learning how to keep myself from being overloaded. Sometimes just a small amount of work can weigh a ton. But then again, a lot of things turn out to be not that important, so I reevaluate priorities a lot and try to let go of things that aren't really needed.

Ramsay: When you look back on how far you've come, what are your thoughts? Are you surprised?

Saulnier: I asked myself this question the other day. We recently moved our office, and we had news media and local politicians over here. We're in the middle of something that's so important to people. I didn't plan for us to be where we are. We just followed our instincts and seized opportunities as they came about. There's no way I could have predicted what I'm doing now, how I spend my time, or even the roles that I'm playing.

Ramsay: Entrepreneurs ultimately leave their companies. When you leave 1st Playable, what legacy do you want to have left behind?

Saulnier: I think that all of our employees will work here for only a finite amount of time. They will eventually move on to accomplish other feats, and perhaps even start their own companies. So, I try to cultivate a workplace experience that will inspire them to be better leaders.

I had experiences like that in my first jobs. There were a lot of people who had a huge influence on me. I learned what was possible because I had seen how they approached business and the world. Those experiences gave me the confidence to try things that were unconventional or that other people said were not possible.

We try to build for our employees' futures. We take on the additional expenses of having our service providers come in and explain details to people. We have people involved in selecting health-care plans so that they will gain that experience and understand the factors that will affect them in the future. We're really trying to run the company to have the biggest future impact.

I've definitely enjoyed working with this group of people. They are some of the most optimistic, positive, and idealistic people I've ever worked with. I am confident they will carry that spirit forward and beyond my involvement. What could be a greater accomplishment?

Christopher Weaver

Founder, Bethesda Softworks

 An MIT-trained scientist who inspired Jeff Goldblum's character in the box-office hit Independence Day, **Christopher Weaver** founded Bethesda Softworks as an experiment in 1986. Today, the studio has proven his experiment, becoming one of the most prosperous developers in the video-game industry.

For nearly 20 years, Bethesda Softworks has produced the best-selling series of fantasy role-playing games The Elder Scrolls, which was created by Weaver and Julian Lefay. Skyrim, the fifth game in the series, was released in 2011 to universal acclaim. Before then, the company was one of the most innovative startups of the time.

Bethesda Softworks launched with the most physically realistic football game ever made, Gridiron, which provided the technical foundation for the Madden NFL series, later unveiled by Electronic Arts. In 1990, the studio released The Terminator, which was the first game based on James Cameron's famous science-fiction franchise.

In 1999, Weaver and Robert Altman, who became chief executive officer, reorganized the company as a division of ZeniMax Media, which they cofounded as part of a plan to attract investors. From that point onward, Weaver gradually reduced his responsibilities, leading to his ultimate exit from the two companies in 2002. Weaver refocused on his work at MIT, where he continues to teach today.

Ramsay: What were you doing before you started Bethesda Softworks?

Weaver: Before creating Bethesda, I was a technology forecaster and tele-communications engineer for the television and cable industry. I had the good fortune to work at the American Broadcasting Company in a transition era as a young researcher, fresh out of grad school. After writing numerous memos about the importance of alternative distribution systems and how satellites and broadband networks would impact network television, I was made manager of technology forecasting. I reported to Herb Granath, the executive in charge of new ventures, as well as Leonard Goldenson, the chief executive officer at the network.

I wrote a few articles about the exciting prospects for cabled distribution systems, and I was quoted in a number of national magazines. This attracted the attention of the National Cable Television Association, which offered me the opportunity to create an Office of Science and Technology for them. In that role, I was to help the cable industry appreciate that television was only one aspect of what cabled distribution systems were capable of doing.

It was an amazing sandbox to play in. I helped numerous member companies design some of the earliest experiments in high-speed data communications and other nontraditional uses for their cable systems. I also worked with many government organizations, and eventually was asked to be chief engineer to the House Subcommittee on Communications. Among other things, I helped write documents which influenced legislation to break up the telephone monopoly, dealt with international data and satellite issues, and allowed the cable industry to compete more fairly with television broadcasters.

After a few years, I left the subcommittee. I created Media Technology, which did engineering and media consulting for various Fortune 500, network, and government organizations. One of the engineers, Ed Fletcher, suggested that we expand into new areas, such as video games. I supported the idea because I believed that personal computers would become far more widespread. Ed's passion was football, so we went to work on a football game. I knew very little about football, but I did know a good deal about physics and display interaction, which were offshoots of the work I had done as a grad student.

Ed initially started down a path of using classic lookup tables, similar to other games of the day. But the lack of dynamic interaction wasn't interesting to me. By combining our perspectives, the result was Gridiron, which was released in 1986 to wide acclaim as the most realistic physics-based football simulation ever created for PCs.

Ramsay: What was your rationale for pursuing a completely different line of business, especially video games?

Weaver: It wasn't a completely different line of business for a number of reasons.

First, much of my undergraduate and graduate career focused on computers, networks, user interaction, simulation, spatial data management, and synthetic environments. In fact, a friend from the Architecture Machine Group and I decided after graduation to commercialize some of the lab's work which had been funded by DARPA grants.

We put together a business plan, which was almost 400 pages long! The Industrial Liaison Office at MIT helped connect us to venture capital. We went with a wealthy family in the electronics industry whose daughter had also attended MIT, in the School of Engineering and the Sloan School of Business.

Together, we formed VideoMagic Laboratories. We went on to produce the first commercial videodisc-based environment simulator. The background video was shot on the Universal Studio lot by some of the best technical gurus in Hollywood. Along the way, we created some core technologies which allowed users to interact with the display screen using gesture recognition—long before it was popularized by Apple—as well as the tools to edit interactive video. While we didn't know it at the time, the combination of techniques, technology, and tools we developed predated the market by many years.

While VideoMagic's technology was radical and cutting-edge, our market timing was premature. Videodisc location-based entertainment systems were untested. The market was impressed from a technical perspective, but it was slow to respond from a commercial one. The family who funded us was also experiencing financial troubles in their business. They decided to pull out of the venture prematurely, and tried to sell off some of the company's innovations, rather than stay the course.

We weren't willing to abandon the vision, so one of the senior lab engineers and I decided to go off on our own, and we began consulting in communications, computers, and interface. After a few years, I had saved enough money to start Bethesda Softworks, and our experience in military and commercial development from the VideoMagic days helped us create our first simulation product.

Ramsay: The business plan for VideoMagic was 400 pages long. Did you apply the same rigor to planning Bethesda Softworks?

Weaver: Bethesda was self-funded, as it was an internally generated idea, so the rigor was there from a self-critical standpoint. There were discussions with other colleagues to test the idea, but there wasn't a formal business plan.

Ramsay: Even without a formal plan, I assume you knew what you wanted to accomplish. What were your goals?

Weaver: In order for me to answer this question, you need to remember the context. This was a fledgling industry. Even companies such as Electronic Arts were in their infancy then. Unlike with VideoMagic, I didn't write a formal business plan because Bethesda was more of an experiment to prove out my belief that personal computers would be used for entertainment as much as business. And because the investment was all mine, I was the only one who had to be "convinced."

In my opinion, too often people get caught up in the process and don't pay enough attention to the core issues. Bethesda was formed as a test to see if my analysis would hold and whether we could compete in the marketplace.

Ramsay: How much capital was necessary to get Bethesda going?

Weaver: I started Bethesda with roughly $100,000 and a lot of sweat equity, doing virtually everything. There were only three or four of us at the start. It's difficult to give a definitive figure of the total invested because I reinvested most of our income back into the company on a continuing basis.

Ramsay: $100,000 is a considerable out-of-pocket sum. Did you have a family at the time? What impact did the startup life have?

Weaver: At the time I started Bethesda, I was not married. That allowed me to invest more time in the enterprise than I would have had available if I had a family. I regularly worked long into the night and on weekends. In looking back, I'm not sure I'd have been able to maintain family obligations and work as hard as I did to establish the company. There were few of us, and a lot of things needed to be accomplished.

As for the way we spent money, we were very careful to make every dollar count, and to not allow ourselves to get on the wrong side of the curve. Any good manager is supposed to pay attention to the spend, but when every dime is your own, you tend to pay even more attention to the bottom line. It's always a high-wire act—without the net.

Ramsay: Some people say that having personal "skin in the game" can lead to bad decisions. When your own money is on the line, you can become more concerned with how business decisions will affect you personally.

Weaver: Skin in the game is the quickest way to establish a real sense of connection to whatever enterprise you're undertaking as an entrepreneur. While I've heard this argued, in my experience, if you possess the intelligence, skill, drive, and self-assurance to take the steps necessary to achieve your vision, then skin in the game amplifies upon the process. If, however, you're forever second-guessing yourself and refusing to make hard decisions, then no amount of personal investment will help, and may even interfere. But, ultimately, real entrepreneurs thrive on the passion of building to achieve a vision. If skin in the game scares you, then maybe you're not ready to leave the farm leagues.

Ramsay: Do you remember your spending goals? What initial problem were you intent on solving as part of the startup process?

Weaver: I don't remember having any particular spending goals, other than generally trying to ensure our spending did not exceed our income for too long! Unlike so many of our competitors, we were extremely frugal. And once we had some early success with Gridiron, we refused to allow ourselves to become complacent about that success. All of us were painfully aware that many large competitors had suffered or fallen because they had not prepared for possible disasters. We did.

That bunker mentality saved us time and time again when economic downturns torched our competitors, who were simply not prepared for steep dips in the sine wave. While much smaller than Software Toolworks, Mediagenic, Epyx, Commodore, and other companies, we were able to survive the storms.

Ramsay: Who were the others working with you?

Weaver: Ed Fletcher was the principal programmer in the beginning. We had worked well together at VideoMagic, and I respected Ed's work ethic and creativity. VideoMagic was very influential to my willingness to create Bethesda, as over the previous two years, we had developed tools and technology to do real-time, photorealistic, arcade-based video games using customized laser-disc technology. We had also created some of the earliest commercial electronic catalogs for major retailers. Ed was the main programmer on Gridiron.

Benni Jensen, who's from Denmark and who programmed under the name Julian Lefay, was the second key coder. Julian came to Bethesda from another studio with a reputation as one of Europe's best underground programmers. If I'm credited with giving birth to The Elder Scrolls, then Julian deserves credit as the one who fathered it. Julian is one of the most creative and brilliant programmers I've had the pleasure to work with in all my years in the industry.

There were a few other early employees who were mostly administrative, but I consider Ed and Julian linchpins in those early days. They had very different personalities, but each possessed a unique ability to see the larger picture, even as they were immersed in developing the code to create the realization of it.

Ramsay: The answer seems obvious, but I have to ask. Was your first office in Bethesda, Maryland?

Weaver: Yeah, Bethesda Softworks was started on the proverbial kitchen table in Bethesda, Maryland. We moved into our first commercial space a year or two later after Gridiron came out, and then progressively moved to larger spaces as time and success allowed.

Ramsay: Was Bethesda Softworks always "Bethesda Softworks"?

Weaver: I had originally called the company "Softwerke" because it seemed like an interesting turn of word—close to the German, and yet descriptive of what we did. We had a legal problem with a Virginia-based software company that went by the same name. While the lawyers, in typical fashion, wanted to fight about it, the president of that company and I mutually agreed to coexist if I changed our name to something else; hence the name Bethesda Softworks. By the time I thought seriously of changing the name to something more unique, I decided against it. We had developed a very loyal following who knew us by that name, and so the die was cast.

Ramsay: What other names did you consider?

Weaver: I dabbled with the idea of using a name that incorporated the word "magic" out of respect for Arthur C. Clarke, who said, "Any sufficiently advanced technology is indistinguishable from magic." But, in the end, Bethesda Softworks stuck.

Ramsay: Location is important to some businesses. How did you choose the commercial space? Where was it?

Weaver: A commercial location became important because the original place where I started the company was my house, which was not zoned for a commercial enterprise. I lived in Bethesda at the time, and chose a space in Rockville that was convenient to the closest major highway, but in a direction opposite to normal morning commuter traffic.

Ramsay: Why did that matter?

Weaver: That was simply a logical assumption on my part to try to lessen morning commuter fatigue. Many of us lived in Washington or the suburbs. Commuting "out" was a lot faster and less hassle-prone than commuting in with everyone else. The D.C. area is legendary for its traffic jams. I thought that the Rockville location would be more palatable for employees coming into work. It turned out I was right.

Ramsay: During that period between setting up in Bethesda and relocating to Rockville, how many titles did you have in development?

Weaver: Well, as I said, we initially worked out of my home in Bethesda for over a year, creating our initial game, Gridiron. As Gridiron was our first game, it was necessary to build not just the game, but the tools to develop it, as well as the physics engine.

In those days, computers were extremely underpowered, and games were limited in terms of their ability to simulate reality. Gridiron addressed many problems of the day, especially with presenting the intricacies of football play using the most realistic physics-based engine at that time, despite the fact that graphics in those days were minimal. EA had their Gamestar football game, and Mattel and Atari had their consoles, but their games could not match Gridiron for realism. Our initial sales demonstrated that players chose Gridiron as the next-generation sports game.

We were invited to join EA as an affiliate and develop their new John Madden Football game, which we did. While we did not end up completing the game for legal reasons, the work we did under contract with EA, using Gridiron's underlying engine and game-system technology, heavily influenced the early Madden series and paved the way for what it is today.

Hockey simulation seemed a natural progression for our physics engine and game technology. We initially reached out to Bobby Orr in Boston and our local Washington Capitals hockey team, who became instrumental in helping us understand the nuances of their sport. To this day, I cannot say enough good things about the hockey community. Hockey players were very approachable. Many of them had played video games and knew of Gridiron. Many well-known players, such as Larry Murphy, and coaches, such as Terry Murray, gave us a huge amount of their time and counsel. They provided us the opportunity to make our hockey simulation accurate. While we'd have loved to call our game "Bobby Orr Hockey," Wayne Gretzky was the number-one player at the time. With the help of our hockey friends, we were able to show our simulation to Gretzky's manager, Mike Barnett, who himself had been a longtime hockey player. We ended up with the license and went on to put out Wayne Gretzky Hockey to universal acclaim.

The Terminator, which we released at the end of the 1980s, had been a favorite movie since it was released in 1984. We thought it was such a brilliant film on so many levels that it would make an amazing game. As the industry was comparatively new, I approached the licensor for the game rights and was fortunate enough to gain his trust. We started out on a small scale, but with the repeat of hit games, I was able to parlay that relationship into a longtime partnership and friendship that continues to this day.

Ramsay: Until then, you were focused on sports games?

Weaver: We weren't really focused on sports per se. Our software development was a logical extension of the real-time physics engine and tools we had created, so we tried to apply its unique capabilities in as many areas as possible. The Terminator was our way to break into another popular category and create a more realistic first-person shooter in the process. We thought we could apply our imagination and software skills to create something novel, and push the genre forward, just as we had in sports.

Judging from trade buzz and sales numbers, we achieved our goal, and simultaneously influenced the future development of that genre. Many others, including the boys from id Software, came down and looked at what we had done at a games show in Chicago. People loved our "down-the-barrel" perspective, and id Software certainly made good use of it in the games they eventually brought out with great success.

Ramsay: Where did you get the idea to implement the "down-the-barrel" perspective?

Weaver: That first-person perspective seemed a far more realistic and interesting way to accentuate the feeling of "being there." As with so many other supposed breakthroughs, the reality is that it just seemed like a logical visual enhancement at the time—nothing more.

Ramsay: What effort did you invest in balancing licensed and original properties? Are either or both essential to driving early revenue?

Weaver: This was so early in intellectual property licensing that there were no set guidelines. It was more a matter of balancing the cost of a license against the desire to break out of the noise floor and into the signal domain. The product had to be able to amplify upon the license to some exponential degree. Otherwise, there would be little interest on my part because the cost-benefit ratio wouldn't justify the cost and restrictions of a license.

Category was important as well. For example, sports are a natural for licensing, while role-playing games are generally not. In addition, I knew from the earliest days that creating original intellectual property would ultimately yield the greatest long-term benefit for the company. We just had to reach a certain critical mass, in the mind of the public, to be in a position to capitalize upon our developing reputation. And we had to create a library of intellectual property that would be able to develop and maintain its own traction.

Ramsay: Like other developers, did you start the company intending to go through publishers for distribution?

Weaver: Well, no, we were always a publisher, except for a few brief periods where it was advantageous to develop for others. For example, we did contract work for THQ on Where's Waldo and Home Alone, and we distributed Gridiron through EA during the period when we worked on John Madden Football. But overall, we always developed and published our own products.

In fact, to the best of my knowledge, we were the only ones who owned our own duplication and packaging plant. That ended up being one of the best economic decisions we ever made. It allowed us to manufacture for less cost, and to create our own just-in-time inventory-control system for distributors.

Ramsay: What were your cost savings?

Weaver: I don't know my exact savings, as we didn't have that level of information with respect to most of our competitors. What I can tell you is that we were able to keep a large percentage of net that others were spending on third-party fulfillment. And, just as important, we were able to respond to orders from distributors more rapidly than virtually anyone else. This allowed us to maximize sales while not being forced to overstock.

We could manufacture and ship 50,000 units a day. Turnaround was virtually instant because we could run up to three parallel lines, and then have the pallets taken directly to the shipping docks, which were downstairs from our offices. We literally had a soup-to-nuts facility, where every aspect of the process was controlled in-house.

Ramsay: What events really tested either the company or you as a leader prior to 1999? How did you meet these challenges?

Weaver: Managing resources, getting product out on time, and staying above water were always challenges. The Wayne Gretzky Hockey franchise really helped us. That game quickly became the best-selling hockey game on the Atari ST, Commodore 64, and Commodore 128, just as Gridiron had been the best-selling football game before Madden.

All too often, we were committed for a big marketing push, only to find that beta testing had pointed out some bugs, which would push us out a few extra weeks or a month. And then would come the inevitable scramble to shift marketing dates and not lose money to cancellation penalties, etc. In order to prevent such headaches, we implemented more and more procedural development techniques before making marketing commitments. Two of my "bibles" became Rapid Development and Code Complete by Steve

McConnell. As budgets and development complexity rose to meet demand, our early days of Wild West code development were over.

Ramsay: Were there any other issues with which you had to contend to scale and run the business?

Weaver: The most pressing issue in the beginning was that we didn't have enough hands to spread the load. We did everything in-house, including conceive, design, program, manuals, box art, distribution, and sales. It was a tall order because sales started growing quickly, and I wanted to stay lean until I really understood if Gridiron was a fluke or Bethesda was a long-term business.

Ramsay: In 1994, the first game in the series that defined the company was released: The Elder Scrolls. Can you tell me about its inception?

Weaver: There were many important hands in the development of The Elder Scrolls series. One of the key influences was that many of our senior development people were addicted to the classic pen-and-paper Dungeons & Dragons-style games, and they thought we should attempt to achieve that kind of depth in a computer game.

To do proper justice to the team, the credits that accompanied the first chapter of The Elder Scrolls: Arena show how many people were responsible for bringing the game to fruition. If you look at the credits for the latest Elder Scrolls chapter, Skyrim, you will find many of the same names that appeared in the credits of Arena in 1994.

The Elder Scrolls has made everyone who has ever been associated with it proud. Along with naming the series, I was executive producer for the earlier chapters. But in the grand scheme of things, it has been the passionate dedication of the coders, artists, producers, and designers that has made the series the success it has become.

Ramsay: Did you plan The Elder Scrolls as a series?

Weaver: We always envisioned it as a series. We just hoped that we'd be given the opportunity to follow through on the vision. While it was a rocky start, the first chapter, Arena, convinced us that we were on to something, even as we kept tweaking the world and what you could do within it. The second chapter, Daggerfall, provided the test bed to learn from our previous mistakes, and push the boundaries to create a pen-and-paper game for the computer. User feedback was critical to helping us stay focused and improve each release.

Ramsay: When would you say Bethesda peaked during your time there? How much had the company grown?

Weaver: For a strictly internally funded company from our inception in 1985, we had grown steadily over the years. But the best was yet to come after 1999, when the company transitioned to ZeniMax, and we began to implement the plan for broader growth.

Ramsay: What was that plan? Was succession part of that plan?

Weaver: We were so busy trying to grow the business and manage the day-to-day that I did not put a real succession plan together until later in the company's life. In 1999, I started looking for management talent to help grow the business and broaden our administrative structure.

The company was reaching a point where people more versed in business skills were needed to be brought in to better manage what was basically a technical organization that sold things. I'm a technologist by training. I saw an explosion of opportunities in media distribution, such as customer interaction and direct purchase through increased website presence, as well as customer service and bulletin boards. I was also convinced that there would be a market for object-oriented, cross-platform tools, and we started a few projects to attract those types of customers. But I knew that to really grow, we had to break out of the feast-or-famine cycle that affects every small, seasonal company. To do that, we needed to diversify our product base and attract different types of users.

Ramsay: How did you achieve these goals?

Weaver: The way that you become a real force is to have enough quality teams that you can asynchronously develop and release triple-A products, and capitalize on their quality at the same time your previous product is converting from its main sell cycle to a secondary one. If you can get the multiple timelines to overlap properly, you can keep the sine wave at positive values.

Bethesda has always been the core. We were known as a boutique house that pushed boundaries. While the company has grown around the initial studio, I believe that Bethesda's core philosophy hasn't really changed.

Ramsay: Who did you find to help you pursue those opportunities?

Weaver: I brought in someone who I believed had better business and administrative skills than me. Robert Altman is the current chief executive officer, and has been there since I brought him into the company.

Ramsay: How did you proceed from there?

Weaver: During the first two quarters of 1999, in order to bring in outside funding, which I had never done previously, it was recommended that I change the legal structure of the company to attract investors. This was done by transferring the intellectual property of the existing entity into the new one, and the new company taking over the employment agreements and other key obligations of the former company. The new company was Zeni-Max Media.

Ramsay: Why did you need outside funding?

Weaver: Outside funding provided a necessary cushion to allow development without as much regard for the calendar as before. Quality improves when you have the luxury of being able to concentrate on the job at hand, with a degree of insulation from the financial demands to release a product to feed the monster.

Ramsay: How did your role change?

Weaver: I started the company in 1984 as its founder, chief cook, and bottle washer. I remained in that position until 1999, when I stepped into the role of chief technology officer.

Ramsay: Why did you step down?

Weaver: Robert and I agreed that he would step into the chief executive officer role and I would take the lead technical role. He was more grounded in finance and business, and my interests were in pushing technical boundaries on the research-and-development side. At the time, the division of responsibilities seemed to be a logical way to grow the company.

Ramsay: Was there ever a point where you thought, "This is too much"?

Weaver: I don't know about "too much," but I often felt overwhelmed with all the things that needed to be done, and how few people and little time there were to do those things. Luckily, I've always had the capacity to push through challenging times. Nevertheless, it was a lot easier to handle it all when things were going well than when they were not, and I have the scars to prove it.

Ramsay: How did you feel about the company's success?

Weaver: One of my favorite lines is the fighter-pilot parlance to always "check your six." In other words, keep an eye on your tail, so you don't get shot out of the sky. Maybe it's my personality, but I was always wary about our success. In the game business, you are only as good as your last hit.

Ramsay: So, you were careful. Were you too careful?

Weaver: Well, in terms of the big one that got away, one event immediately comes to mind. When we were hired to make John Madden Football by

Electronic Arts, they offered us a lower build price, but they were willing to give us royalties. I rejected their offer and negotiated a larger development price. In hindsight, after Madden became the bestselling sports game of all time, I realized that making sure we got the larger initial payment was one of my biggest mistakes and a life lesson.

Ramsay: How much effort did you put into the intellectual capital of the business, into perhaps creating "name" developers?

Weaver: There were key people within our organization who managed development teams and created products, who were always respected for their contributions internally and publicly. In the early days, people were far less interested in developer names than the product itself. Having started as a developer myself, when we received awards, I made sure the people who did the work received the recognition they were due, and that they got to accept awards on the company's behalf. My position was that executive management does not create the underlying value in an intellectual property-based company.

Ramsay: As you said earlier, in the 1980s, the game industry was really just getting started. Did you encounter any problems with attracting and recruiting development talent?

Weaver: Not from the standpoint of competition, but definitely from the standpoint of having to separate wheat from chaff. Uniquely talented people are always difficult to find. In those days, no colleges had programs oriented toward game studies. We were always looking for the best of class and rebels who wanted to do cool things on small computers within special-interest groups and similar communities. In those days, I was very active in the Game Developers Conference, when it was an organization to serve the needs of the actual development community, not the moneymaking behemoth it has become today. There was a purity of old that has become diluted as more and more money has flowed into the industry.

Ramsay: Did your recruiting challenges become easier in the 1990s?

Weaver: Recruiting was never really a problem. People interested in games tend to gravitate toward companies that make them. Finding "good" people was occasionally a problem. Finding "great" people was always a problem.

Ramsay: Tell me about the early culture of Bethesda Softworks. How did it emerge? Was any effort directed at its care and development?

Weaver: I would like to think that we had an inclusive family culture in the early days. The structure was extremely horizontal. Anyone could and did come into my office about anything at virtually any time. We usually made decisions as a group by holding company-wide meetings and going over major issues of the day. There were no cabals or secrets. We had a very open structure. Everyone mattered. Quite frankly, we were too small to play politics, and I never liked office politics anyway.

Things that posed personal challenges were aided, absorbed, or shared. I bought cars for people who did not have transportation, helped others get houses by helping with down payments or countersigning their loans, and even helped broker a few marriages! I tried to be as much friend and counselor as possible. We also had the best health plan we could afford. I made sure the company put aside 15% of each person's salary into a personal employee bonus account, which was the maximum amount allowed by law, and contributed 100% of that amount without requiring the employee to put in anything.

If the company did well, we all did well. That was a big commitment. Everyone valued the company for going that extra mile. The result was very little turnover. We had a lot of personal commitment going in both directions. That held us together as an "us against the world" unit.

Ramsay: How did the culture evolve between the establishment of the company and your departure?

Weaver: As we got larger, it became more difficult to do certain things I had done before because we had to follow more stringent policies. For example, to make sure we complied with legal requirements to treat everyone equally, I couldn't give cars away to any one person, lest I be required to do it for everyone. I understood the legal reasons, but it often grated against me. I would often just do something out-of-pocket because that did not, technically, commit the company legally.

Ramsay: How important was quality of life at Bethesda?

Weaver: Quality of life was of paramount importance because I believed that companies which create intellectual property live or die on the quality of their creative employees. In addition to the medical and bonus plans, knowing that programmers often forget to eat, or eat junk, I built a complete restaurant in-house and hired a local chef from a good Italian restaurant in Bethesda to run it. We initially just gave everyone lunch, but the IRS was going to impute the value of the lunches, so we charged everyone $3 to $4 for meals that were worth up to five times that amount. The restaurant was such a big success that it was expanded from just serving lunch to serving all-day meals. We also put in an ice cream freezer, drinks, and snacks that were available 24/7. Whoever says that companies do not run on food has never run a software company.

There's an old Chinese expression: "Ruling a large kingdom is like cooking a small fish." The expression is derived from Tao Te Ching. The translation of which by Arthur Waley is my favorite. You can interpret the writing in many ways, but I think its philosophy sums up brilliantly what running a software company is really all about: do as little to harm as possible, and allow each to bring forth their best to contribute to the betterment of the whole.

Ramsay: What were the events that led to your departure?

Weaver: The founder of a company isn't always the best person to take that company to the next level. I left the day-to-day operations in the summer of 2002. While it was a painful separation, I came to realize that creative companies, like people, go through growth cycles. I was invested in the technology and building cool new things, which I continue to do at MIT. Altman, as a former banker, was more interested in the finance and profit side of the business. Friction between founders and chief executives is legion. But at the end of the day, only one person gets to fly the plane, or run a company.

Ramsay: What did you do after you left ZeniMax?

Weaver: I wrote and relaxed that summer, and then consulted with some game and media companies. While I had taught at MIT throughout my career, I was able to increase responsibilities there, including being elected to the board of directors at a major university and industry consortium in the Microphotonics Center that was helping to shape the future of optical communications.

Ramsay: Do you have any immediate plans in the game industry?

Weaver: Well, I teach games studies in the Comparative Media Studies department in addition to my class in Materials Science and Engineering so in terms of the games industry, I really just moved from being in front of the camera to behind it. And I now have dozens of students in all phases of the games industry.

But the social gaming landscape is also exciting because it reminds me of the time a small team could bring out a fully developed product at a reasonable cost. As the genre moves to 2.0, the new kids on the block are just beginning to appreciate the value of tapping into the old guard. After all, building yurts is very different than building skyscrapers. So every time I think I may be through with games, it is clear that games are not through with me. Whether or not I decide to get back into making games is something only time will tell, But for the moment I am proud of my legacy at Bethesda and happy for the continued success of the company I started.

Jason Rubin

Cofounder, Naughty Dog

Jason Rubin and Andy Gavin cofounded Naughty Dog in 1986, becoming two of the youngest contractors to develop for Electronic Arts. During its rise from a scrappy startup to an industry powerhouse with three of the top-ten games for Sony PlayStation, Naughty Dog established a reputation as one of the most innovative developers of video games on the planet.

In 1994, the company created its first major franchise, Crash Bandicoot, of which the titular character became the de facto mascot of the Sony PlayStation. Now spanning at least 16 titles, the Crash Bandicoot series has since sold more than 50 million units worldwide, and the third title in the series was the top-selling foreign-made video game in Japan. After parting ways with its publisher, Universal Interactive, Naughty Dog followed Crash Bandicoot with another bestselling series, Jax and Daxter, but not before being acquired by Sony Computer Entertainment in 2001. Rubin and Gavin left the studio in 2004.

After Rubin and Gavin had left the company, Naughty Dog released Uncharted: Drake's Fortune for the PlayStation 3 in 2007, and then the sequel, Uncharted 2: Among Thieves, in 2009. The sequel received critical acclaim and won more than 100 awards, including the coveted Game of the Year awards at both the Interactive Achievement Awards and the Game Developers Choice Awards.

Ramsay: When did you get started with Naughty Dog? How did you know your cofounder, Andy Gavin?

Rubin: Andy and I met in school at around age 13. We both owned Apple II computers, and the work we were doing with them at the time—from simple programming to pirating—was much more interesting than what the teachers were teaching. So, we would sit in the back of class and talk about computers and programming. We were very young, and there weren't books, websites, or other teaching materials for computers yet, so we learned by experimentation and communication.

I vividly remember thinking that if I kept compressing a file, it would shrink until it was one byte. Andy replied that you certainly couldn't do that, as the unlocking key would expand until it was the entire file you started with. It was thousands of simple realizations like that, and sharing ideas and tips, that led the two of us to figuring out how to make "full games" on our own. It is worth remembering that a full game in those days could be written in a long weekend. There were many false starts, such as a mostly finished golf game that I had created, which Andy destroyed by copying something onto the disk it resided on—this was before hard drives. We also had a mostly realized Punch Out clone that we eventually couldn't finish due to technical issues. And there were many other games that fell in the category now called "not safe for work."

At around 15, after returning from a ski trip, I did the art and code for a game called Ski Stud. The game looked good, but the game slowed down as the skier got further down the slope. I had reached the limit of my coding ability, so I took it to Andy. He rewrote the core of the game, and it screamed! We decided this would be our first published game, so we applied for a commercial license to use the tool we had been using for sprite drawing. We were going to "publish" the game by putting it in Ziploc bags and selling them around Washington, D.C., the area where we lived. Don't laugh. That was competitive packaging at the time! The company that created the sprite tool saw the game and asked if they could publish it for us nationally. We agreed and received a check for $250. We had become game developers!

Ramsay: When you entered the business world, do you remember ever feeling that you were treated differently as a result of your age?

Rubin: I think we were probably too young to notice how young we were. I do remember going to an EA developers' symposium, a big convention of internal developers that EA held every year. Andy and I were both 17 at the time—the youngest contractors to work for EA and well below legal drinking age. The hotel bar didn't seem to mind. I vaguely remember meeting all of my heroes: Bill Budge, Will Harvey, and Brent Iverson. They were early game developers who were all significantly older than me. And I definitely remember having a lot of drinks!

I think you have to have a certain amount of blind, naïve faith in yourself to be an entrepreneur. I truly believed that it was inevitable that I would be successful. If I hadn't had such an unfounded certainty in myself, I would have taken a safer route through life. As a result, success, at any age, never seemed like success so much as part of the logical progression toward something bigger. That sounds arrogant, but I wasn't elitist. I never thought I was special, and I would have supported anyone else who told me that they, too, were destined for greatness.

The serial entrepreneur Jeff Stibel wrote in a column for Harvard Business Review that entrepreneurship is a disease. I have the disease, and part of the disease is not seeing the world for what it is. Perhaps I was treated differently because I was young, but I never noticed.

Ramsay: After Ski Stud was published, what did you do next? Did you incorporate as Naughty Dog and put together a business plan?

Rubin: Business plan? We were 16. Our business plan was to do whatever we thought was cool. Income? Whatever we could make. Expenses? Ask our parents; they paid for the power and rent.

We agreed to do another game for Baudville, now the long-defunct publisher that put out Ski Stud, which had been renamed Ski Crazed for political correctness. The next game was called Dream Zone, and it was a graphic adventure for the Apple II, Amiga, and Atari ST. After selling 10,000 copies of Dream Zone, we decided, as two 16-year-olds, that we were ready for the big time.

So, we cold called the help line at Electronic Arts, which was at that time the largest game publisher in the world, and managed to get a producer on the other end of the phone. A few months later, we were working for EA on Keef the Thief, another graphic adventure for the same systems. Frankly, I still don't know how we pulled that off. It would be the equivalent today of a kid who has a half-million views on YouTube cold calling Warner Brothers and getting a movie deal.

Keef sold well, compared to its development budget, so EA signed us for a second title. That game, Rings of Power for the Sega Genesis, was our first console title. Rings of Power took three years to make because it was a massive title, and because Andy and I were working from colleges in two different states. Rings was critically acclaimed and sold out of its first pressing.

Unfortunately, so did a new game called John Madden Football. When Sega told EA that they could only reorder a fixed number of cartridges, EA chose to go with 100% Maddens. As a large role-playing game, Rings had more ROM than Madden and an EEPROM for saving your game, and had been developed externally. Each Rings cartridge was far more expensive to print, had a royalty attached, and was thus less profitable than a Madden cartridge. Obviously, it was a smart business move for EA. But as the developers getting the short end of the stick, it sucked! EA just decided to shut off the money flow.

Frustrated, Andy and I took some time away from game development, but it didn't last long. Eight months later, Trip Hawkins called us and told us about his new project—the 3DO. He is a persuasive man, but possibly his strongest argument for the system was that on a disc-based console with plenty of memory and discs that were readily produceable, we wouldn't get screwed by cartridge-printing decisions again! It didn't take long to discuss the opportunity. Trip gave us free development kits, and Andy and I began work. We had no publisher attached, it was a full-time endeavor, and we financed the game out of our own pockets. Way of the Warrior for the 3DO marked our exit from game making as a hobby and our entrance into game development as a profession. But we still didn't have a business plan.

Ramsay: Was that the first time you had talked to Trip?

Rubin: I don't remember when Andy and I first met Trip Hawkins. It must have been before we began Rings of Power. EA was a small, developer-centric company at that time. I'm sure he was curious to meet the 17-year-old hackers he had under contract! We certainly already knew him by the time we began Rings of Power in 1988.

Andy and I were walking through EA's offices that year after finishing Keef the Thief, and Andy spied a silver box with a cord attached to a computer. He immediately identified it as a reverse-engineered Sega Genesis platform. EA had hacked Sega's system and was developing games for the Genesis without Sega's permission. They planned, and eventually did, use that ability to negotiate a better platform rate from Sega. But at that point, the hardware was top secret. Andy pointed at the reverse-engineered system and said, "You reverse engineered a Sega Genesis?" The next thing we knew, Trip and EA's lawyers were in front of us with nondisclosure agreements. Andy and I signed the documents, and then Andy said to Trip, "Rings of Power would make a cool Sega game." We were already under a nondisclosure agreement, and Trip wanted us invested in the top-secret program's success, so he immediately agreed. That's how we became console developers.

Ramsay: In 1996, Naughty Dog released Crash Bandicoot, which became your first major franchise. How did this project come about?

Rubin: When we were almost done with Way of the Warrior, we rented a three-by-three-foot space at the Consumer Electronics Show—an early E3—for $10,000. It was the last money we had to our names. Our "booth" really consisted of a one-TV-wide nook in the greater 3DO booth. It turned out that we had called the market just right with our game. The publishers had put their developers on titles they were grandly calling "multimedia." Basically, multimedia titles consisted of lots of badly shot, interactive video, and weird semi-gaming crap. They all realized too late that this stuff wouldn't sell and that they needed to be publishing real games. Unfortunately for them, there was only one real game that was nearing completion: our game Way of the Warrior, which was a half-decent knockoff of Mortal Kombat. So, a bidding war ensued for Way of the Warrior, and for a variety of reasons, Universal Interactive Studios won.

One of the reasons that we chose Universal was their enthusiasm for funding our next title and letting us choose what that title would be. We set out by car from Boston to our new home at Universal Studios in Hollywood, determined to decide what to develop along the way. We had "successfully" knocked off a fighting game, we reasoned, so why not try for a character action game? This time, with a real budget and a real team, why not go beyond "borrowing" ideas from past games and try to do something that had never been done before? Fighting games and racing games had gone 3D, but character action games had not been done in 3D. But how would a 3D character action game look and play? We titled the concept "Sonic's Ass" because we realized that in 3D, you would be looking at the back of the character most of the time. What did Sonic's ass look like? Who knew, but in our new game, the character's ass would have to look amazing because you'd be staring at it for hours!

At the same time, somewhere in Japan, Miyamoto-san and Naka-san were thinking the same thoughts. Both were responsible for creating the most popular and emblematic characters for their systems: Mario for Nintendo and Sonic for Sega. The new systems their companies were bringing out—Nintendo 64 and Saturn—would enable them to bring these characters into 3D for the first time. Miyamoto-san went for it with a fully open playground for Mario 64, creating a form of gameplay that is copied to this day. Naka-san balked and created a game with 3D characters and art, but with gameplay fixed firmly in a 2D space. Because of this, or perhaps because he thought the risk of 3D was too much to risk on a Sonic game, Naka-san also chose to launch a new character called Nights.

Unaware of any of the incredibly important decisions that two of the greatest minds in video games were making, Andy and I solved the same question in another way. Most levels would be into z space, or into the screen. We let the character move in full 3D, but significantly restricted one dimension of freedom: the x axis, or left and right movement. This created "paths" that were only a few characters wide. It was truly 3D gameplay, but also allowed us to keep the challenges firmly in the classic 2D sweet spot of platforming, timing, and simple interactions. It also made it impossible to run around enemies, get lost, or get attacked from off screen or behind the camera—these were weaknesses of Miyamoto's 3D efforts. We also solved the "ass" problem by keeping some paths mostly in what is called "x and y space." In these levels, you got to see the character from the side. For good measure, we even had levels that came "out of" the screen's z axis. Gamers will remember these as the boulder levels. Controlling a character that ran at the camera allowed a full frontal view—with shorts on, of course.

Most importantly, Andy and I made the audacious decision that because Nintendo and Sega already had mascots, we would make our game for the Sony PlayStation. Sony was new to video games, and therefore, they had no legacy characters. We were in Utah after two days of solid discussion when we made the decision. Two 24-year-olds, who had never made a successful game, with all of their worldly possessions in the back of their car, were going to drive to Los Angeles, hire their first employees, figure out what made a great action game, work on their first 3D title ever, and create a compelling character and franchise. Then all that would remain to do would be to put in a call to Sony and tell them we had created the PlayStation mascot. It was simple, really.

Ramsay: Were you aware at the time that all of this would be quite difficult? Or were you two still just winging it?

Rubin: We were both aware of the difficulty, and yet completely sure that we would manage to overcome the barriers and create the Sony mascot. This, despite the fact that we had no way of knowing whether Sony itself was working on a mascot internally, which would have guaranteed failure. Remember, at the time we were working with Universal, not Sony. Sony had no way of knowing about what we were doing, and we had no way of knowing how they would react. Of course, who were we to attempt a game of this complexity and against such great competition? Again, to succeed as an entrepreneur takes a certain amount of blind faith, bordering on raw audacity and possibly entering the realm of stupidity. Andy and I had that kind of faith.

By this time, we were certainly doing business planning. We had a budget, we had employees, and we had deadlines. Naughty Dog had become a business.

Although we were both computer hackers, Andy and I were comfortable with business and management. I was treasurer of my senior class and an economics major. I had run multiple small businesses of my own on the side over the years, including a t-shirt printing business while I was at college that sold 50,000 t-shirts in a year. I knew how to use Quicken and budget time on spreadsheets. We never had problems running a business.

Ramsay: When you arrived in Los Angeles, where did you set up shop?

Rubin: As part of our deal with Universal, they paid to put us in a space on the back lot of Universal Studios. We received free phone lines, fax machines, secretarial staff, etc. Originally, we didn't even owe them a product for all of this free help. They just wanted "talented people" working on their lot, and hoped that would lead to good things for Universal. It sounds strange, but this strategy had worked for Universal. We had roughly the same deal that Steven Spielberg had at the time, although our entire space was the size of his office!

This methodology is totally different from what the game publishers would have offered. EA had given us a budget and expected to get a game in return. If we needed power or desks or a roof over our heads, then we had to figure out how to get that for ourselves. You are either internal or external to publishers. Internal teams get everything done for them, but don't own or control anything. External teams have to fend for themselves.

We had something in between at Universal. We liked the Hollywood "housekeeping deal" arrangement, and in the end, we signed a three-project deal with Universal that eventually produced hundreds of millions of dollars in revenue for them. So, it worked out for everyone.

Ramsay: Were there other internal teams on the Universal lot?

Rubin: Naughty Dog was the first team that Universal brought on the lot under a "housekeeping deal." Mark Cerny, vice president of Universal Interactive, felt confident enough about only one other team to bring them on the lot—Insomniac Games. All other teams were off-lot and operated under the standard terms of a development deal.

It is fair to call Naughty Dog and Insomniac's relationship competitive, but only in the best of terms. We critiqued each other's work, we shared code occasionally, and we even had each other's characters do cameos in our games. We also spent time with each other outside the office, and I'm still quite close with the Insomniacs today. During the day, we were all business, but at the end of the day, there was nobody else that understood what you were going through more than someone who did what you did. So, we were also friends.

The competition continues today. In my opinion, Naughty Dog had the edge in sales and quality in the Crash days versus Insomniac's Spyro. But I think it is only fair, in retrospect, to say that Ratchet & Clank was a more successful franchise—sometimes in sales, but also in impact—than Jak and Daxter. I'll leave it to the fans to judge Resistance versus Uncharted. The games are less comparable than past titles because they don't share a genre, but I know that in their hearts, the guys at Naughty Dog and Insomniac still measure themselves against their brother development house.

Ramsay: By 1998, Crash Bandicoot was an iconic trilogy that defined the PlayStation, but the three-project deal had ended. I assume that Naughty Dog had to vacate the premises soon after?

Rubin: Naughty Dog made the decision to not renew its deal with Universal Interactive. By the time that Crash 3 rolled around, Universal's role had shrunk to nothing. Sony was financing and publishing the games, and additionally providing valuable worldwide production advice. Mark Cerny, who started at Universal and was a large contributor to Crash's success, had become an independent contractor and continued to work with us. And, of course, Naughty Dog was doing the heavy lifting of developing the titles. Universal was simply being paid for the intellectual property rights.

Andy and I decided that we were not willing to split the developers' share of revenue with an entity which was contributing nothing to the mix, which was extremely difficult to work with, and which was actively trying to take credit for Crash's success. So, we announced that we were not renewing our contract and we were leaving the lot after Crash 3. At that point, Universal Interactive's management lost their minds.

We were forced to develop Crash 3 in the hallways of their offices. Although they still had a contract to give us office space, they decided to make our lives as miserable as possible. We were under extreme deadlines for a Christmas release, so we couldn't move the team in the middle of the project. We had to stay in those hallways until the game was done. Naughty Dog was working 16- to 20-hour days that year with no weekends. To make matters worse, Universal refused to pay for the air conditioning in their offices, and thus their hallways, after hours. Los Angeles summers, especially in the San Fernando Valley, are extremely hot. At night, and especially during the weekend, the heat on the thirty-fourth floor passed 100 degrees. This is not an exaggeration. We had to buy thermometers and measure the temperature constantly because the heat was affecting more than our comfort. Our servers were going down because the internal temperatures of the hard drives were going over 130 degrees. And the building wouldn't let us bring in portable air-conditioning units, so we were forced to cool the servers by blowing air over a bucket of ice with a fan. That solved the problem until we managed to disguise an air-conditioning unit as a mini-refrigerator and sneak it in.

I could tell endless tales of Universal Interactive's spite and contractual misbehavior that year, but that's all history. They tried to break us. They couldn't. Although we all worked shirtless at desks in hallways that year, we got Crash 3 done. To put all of this in perspective, Crash 3 was guaranteed to make Universal hundreds of millions of dollars in profit. Yet, as a company, they didn't have the decency to accept our decision as independents to chart our own destiny. And they were vindictive enough to risk their financial windfall had their nonsense caused us to fail. If Universal had been more humane and reasonable, it is possible that Naughty Dog would still be making Crash products today.

The day Crash 3 was finished, Naughty Dog moved off the Universal lot and started work on a kart game. We didn't have characters attached then. The first versions had nondescript block-headed kart riders. Our relationship with Sony was always incredibly close. We offered to make the game based on Crash characters, if they dealt with Universal and obtained the rights. At that point, Naughty Dog couldn't even speak to Universal's management they were so… apoplectic. Sony managed to do so, and thus our first title after leaving Universal was a final Crash product: Crash Team Racing.

At the same time, Naughty Dog decided to start fresh. While most of Naughty Dog worked on Crash Team Racing, Andy, Stephen White, and Mark Cerny started working on a next-generation engine for what eventually became the PlayStation 2. Andy and I risked $4 million of Naughty Dog's cash into starting development of Jak and Daxter. This was well before thoughts of selling Naughty Dog entered our minds.

Ramsay: That's quite a significant investment in a new, untested property. Why did you leave Crash for Jak and Daxter?

Rubin: Naughty Dog would have liked continuing with Crash beyond Crash Team Racing, but the relationship with Universal was untenable. Originally, we had signed a three-project deal; however, when Sony became enamored with the game and eventually negotiated to publish Crash, Universal cut a deal for a sizable yet much smaller cut of the game than they would have received as the publisher. Our contract with Universal never contemplated this occurrence. We were effectively crammed down into a cut of their cut. This made no sense. Our costs and recoup were the same. Our effort was the same, but we were getting a much smaller amount per copy sold.

On the other hand, the arrangement meant that Universal had no more marketing costs, very little internal management costs, and eventually they even managed to push the financing costs back to Sony. It is perfectly fair to say that they did next to nothing on the project and yet reaped a larger amount on the early games' profit than we did. The only reason I cannot say that Universal contributed nothing is that Mark Cerny, a Universal employee, was our producer. He was a massive force in the success of our games. His salary and work could be called Universal's contribution to the first few Crash titles. But Mark eventually left Universal, and we started contracting him directly. Sony effectively paid for his work. While Mark continued to be incredibly important to our titles, his contribution could no longer be attributable to Universal. From that point forward, they did literally nothing but collect royalties that should have been, at least in large part, ours.

Obviously, this situation couldn't last forever. We had to strike out on our own and start fresh. Jak and Daxter was the result. It is sad that Naughty Dog had to leave Crash and that Crash went on to be in so many average titles—I'm being kind—after Naughty Dog stopped developing the games. He is still a very endearing character with a huge fan base. In 2010, I looked at Crash's Q Scores—rankings done by a third party for every major intellectual property. Crash does incredibly well for a character that has had such a long hiatus from the spotlight. This is especially true with adults 18 to 49. Those that remember playing Crash remember him fondly.

When Activision merged with Vivendi Universal—itself a merger of Vivendi and Universal Interactive—the Crash rights passed to Activision's hands. I have high hopes that they will someday dust off Crash and bring him back to his original glory.

Ramsay: Were you looking to repeat the success of Crash?

Rubin: Jak and Daxter was not an attempt to repeat the success of Crash so much as move forward on the Naughty Dog "dream." That game, or at least the outline of that game, existed when we started Crash, but would not be realized for over a decade and a half. It involved weaving plot and adventure together seamlessly and continuously with tight gameplay—basically, a fully playable movie.

Originally, Crash was supposed to be laced with plot points and action sequences. But both our code and the PlayStation utterly failed on that promise. Instead, we fell back on almost 100% platform gameplay. As the Crash games progressed, more and more plot came in—basic plot, but plot nonetheless, driving the game forward. Jak was an attempt to take that to the next level with even more showpieces—large physical destruction and change—and story.

Ramsay: After leaving what was effectively an abusive relationship, did you think that Naughty Dog could survive as an independent, external studio?

Rubin: Andy and I had no fear that Naughty Dog could go it alone. We were generating significant income from Crash Bandicoot royalties, and the band was still together. Everyone was excited to move forward and try something new. Mark Cerny, who had been the only major contributor to the success of Crash from Universal, was now freelance and continued to add his abundant talent to our endeavors. Sony Computer Entertainment was still giving us advice from over 70 countries around the world. It was just such local knowledge that had made Crash so popular in Japan and elsewhere. It was the fact that we were all so comfortable working together that led Andy and I to make the investment in Jak and Daxter.

We knew that we'd eventually work out terms with our friends at Sony. Our relationship could not have been better. Why bother negotiating a contract upfront when there was a game to be made? We had also learned, from self-financing Way of the Warrior, that there is no such thing as a great game that can't find a place on store shelves. If you build it, there will be a way to get it to market. And the longer the developer takes the risk, the greater proportion of the reward they reap. We were ready for that risk.

The PlayStation 2 was just hardware. As much as everyone worries and complains, new hardware is just new hardware. At the end of the day, hardware never holds up a good team. In fact, new hardware makes good teams shine. Not only were we ready, but we also had everything we needed to succeed.

Ramsay: Where did you eventually set up shop? Did you want to stay near Los Angeles, or did you look at other locations?

Rubin: We moved to Santa Monica. It seemed like the most comfortable place for the team. Hollywood was of small importance to Naughty Dog by the time we left Universal. Initially, we had thought it was important to be established where the entertainment action was. That was one of the reasons we moved to Los Angeles instead of signing with a San Francisco-based publisher. At that time, in 1994, it seemed that games were going more "multimedia" and that Hollywood would provide better talent. But it didn't pan out that way. While it was certainly nice to be in the Los Angeles area—where great voice actors, cartoon designers, writers, and other Hollywood talent reside—other teams have been able to harness that talent from other cities with little trouble. Los Angeles is certainly a great place to live and work, but other major cities have their advantages as well.

Location is not that important for developers, but there are tradeoffs to make. If you are in a big, game-centric city like San Francisco, Los Angeles-

Orange County, Seattle, Vancouver, Montreal, or Austin, then there is a lot of talent. But there's also a lot of competition for your staff. On the other hand, if you are the only player, or one of the only players, in town—like say, Epic Games in Cary, North Carolina—then it is harder to attract talent but easier to keep it. I think anywhere works, so long as it works!

Ramsay: When Naughty Dog relocated to Santa Monica, were you aware that Sony was establishing a studio of its own there?

Rubin: We had been aware of the other Sony studio all along. Alan Becker, who ran the studio, was involved in the Crash, and Jak and Daxter, projects. But even after the acquisition, Sony left Naughty Dog to do its thing. Before Andy and I left, Naughty Dog was a wholly owned subsidiary of Sony Computer Entertainment America, a company that was completely owned by its parent but had its own board and management. Our relationship with the other Sony studios, including Santa Monica, was very close. And we remained close with Insomniac, who was not under the Sony corporate umbrella.

Ramsay: Did that proximity inspire Naughty Dog's sale to Sony?

Rubin: There is a good story about how the sale of Naughty Dog came about, but it had nothing to do with the Sony studio. Andy and I were in Tokyo at the Lexington Queen, a Roppongi nightclub that had been a debaucherous hangout for the touring heavy metal bands of the 1980s before it became our favorite 4:00 AM spot in the late 1990s. We were with Kelly Flock, who was then head of Sony's game division in the United States, and Andy McNamara and Andy Reiner of Game Informer magazine. Suffice it to say, we were not in any shape to drive home, were we to have had cars.

We were arguing about what Naughty Dog should do after Crash, and even Kelly wasn't privy to what we were already doing at that point. Naughty Dog had started Jak and Daxter, but Shu Yoshida and Connie Booth, our long-term producers, were probably the only non-Naughty Dogs who had seen it at that point. Kelly threw out the idea that Naughty Dog was at the top of the business. We had the number 2, 4, and 7 best-selling games on the PlayStation, and Crash Team Racing was fast catching up, so there was nowhere for us to go as developers but down. That piece of sick logic hit Andy Gavin and me like a brick. The Andys from Game Informer fought back, literally. They both jumped across the table to wrestle Kelly and defend Naughty Dog's honor. But Andy and I looked at each other, and we both realized that he just might be right. That is when we first contemplated selling the company.

Ramsay: How was Jak and Daxter different from your success with Crash? Was Uncharted an evolution of your earlier vision?

Rubin: By Jak 2, the Naughty Dog vision started to show through. Through the Jak games, we still had to separate gameplay from story with pretty harsh cuts. We tried to do both at the same time here and there, but there was only mild success in this endeavor. Jak was more serious, more adult, and more interesting in its weaving of plot and game, but it was far from our dream title. Uncharted finally realized the dream. I'm elated and proud that Naughty Dog finally saw the dream to fruition, and sad that I wasn't there for the final steps. When Uncharted 2 came out, I finally saw the pieces come together and click. Uncharted 2 was the game Naughty Dog set out to make when we started Crash. It took well more than a decade to get there.

From a business standpoint, Jak would release us from our shackles at Universal. Finally, the pie was to be split between only the parties who were making and publishing the game: Naughty Dog, and Sony. But Sony also wanted to be freed from its shackles. They didn't want to create another de facto mascot just to see the character go multiplatform like Crash. Naughty Dog asked for the same deal that had been struck with Universal, but Sony wanted more.

Ramsay: What did Sony want?

Rubin: Sony wanted insurance that Naughty Dog wouldn't do with Jak what Universal was doing with Crash: publishing it on competitive hardware. In the end, it only made sense for Sony to own the intellectual property outright. However, Naughty Dog wasn't willing to spend another six years working on a property that it didn't own. The only solution was an acquisition of Naughty Dog by Sony. So, Sony solved the problem by making Andy and me an offer that we couldn't refuse.

It was a smart financial move on Sony's part. That was true by the time Andy and I left, but when you add the Uncharted series, it becomes obvious. It was also a good move for the Naughty Dog team. From that day forward, we had a comfortable place to focus on making the best games we could with all the support that only a company like Sony could provide. That focus and support continues to this day. But was it a smart move for Andy and me personally? In retrospect, I think so. But who knows what would have happened were Andy and I still leading an independent Naughty Dog!

Ramsay: When did you and Andy leave Naughty Dog?

Rubin: Andy and I left Naughty Dog in October 2004 at the end of our contracts. There were many reasons. The two major factors were our lack of vacation and the needs of those directly below us in the company hierarchy. I guess it's fair to say that we desired the first and were enabled to pursue it because of the second.

Triple-A video-game development has progressed from one man and a computer in a weekend to teams of hundreds working in multiple specialties for years. But that progression was not smooth and organized. Andy and I had started making games in 1985 at the end of the "one man and a computer" period. By that time, teams were specializing, with an artist or two, a programmer or two, and sometimes a specialist for sound. There was very little hierarchy on the teams. The developers worked together, but there usually wasn't much in the way of leadership.

By the time Crash rolled around a decade later, teams had become eight to twelve people on average, and one or two of the members needed to be decision makers. The structure at the time of Crash was flat. In other words, as director, I spoke to everyone on the team directly and I knew what everyone was doing. That meant that Andy and I were usually the first ones in and the last ones out of the offices. Budgets were rising quickly, although they were still what seems today to be a pathetic $2 million. That meant limitations on hiring.

Bottom line: in 1997, I was in the office for 364 days and averaged 16 hours a day on the computer, according to the computer's logs. The single day that I was out was during the worst part of a bad cold. Lunch that year came out of a vending machine more days than it didn't. I don't think Andy missed a single day that year. After finishing a game, we were already late for the sequel. It took 21 months to make Crash with 8 Naughty Dogs, 13 months to make Crash 2 with 13 Dogs, and 11 months to make Crash 3 with 16 Dogs. And the bulk of Crash Team Racing—aside from the new engine—was done in 8 months and 6 days with 21 Dogs, which must be some kind of record. We hit four Christmas releases in a row—30 million units. Big money, but we had no breaks, and it showed on us physically.

Unfortunately, the PlayStation 2 brought even bigger challenges. The team size ballooned, and we didn't have the time, experience, or foresight to radically change the team structure. This was not unique to Naughty Dog. And as the age of the average Naughty Dog, and developers industry-wide, was increasing, families and children came into the picture. This created time issues. Some Naughty Dogs were happy working from 6 AM to 6 PM, while others were working from 4 PM to 4 AM. This is not an exaggeration. This couldn't work. A single game character was no longer the task of a single person. There were modelers, riggers, texture artists, and animators all working together. If one was an early bird, and the other was a night owl, they might not be in the office for more than an hour or two together.

So, I created the then-novel idea of "core hours." Everyone had to be in the office from 10:30 AM to 12:30 PM and 2:00 PM to 5:30 PM. Those weren't complete hours. Those were just the hours that an individual Naughty Dog absolutely had to be in the office, so they could work together. I vividly remember the meeting that Naughty Dog had about this new rule. Employees were yelling in ways that had never been seen before. I lost two employees—one that day and one a few weeks later—over the core-hour rule. Naughty Dog was one of the first, if not the first, developer with core hours. Three years later, almost everyone in the industry had them.

And the team sizes just kept expanding! Budgets doubled from $2 million to $4 million on the PlayStation 1 and from $10 million to $20 million on the PlayStation 2. Although we tried to create hierarchy and middle-level management, the team lead was still on top of everything. We had over 60 employees, and I still needed to know what almost every one of them was doing. Assuming a ten-hour day, that was only ten minutes per person, if I wanted to check in with everyone.

The work was stressful, so we started giving the entire team a month of vacation after every project. The cost of this, from a budget standpoint, was over a million dollars per project. To minimize this cost, the team had to be ready on the day they got back. Andy and I had to work during the month off, preparing everything with Evan Wells, Stephen White, and a few other key people.

In addition, bigger games with bigger profits led to bigger marketing campaigns. This created press tours around the world to speak with local media about the titles. The longest one was 20 days in 14 countries. I truly loved the press tours, but it wouldn't be fair to call them vacations. So, we lost the only month we might have taken time off.

When I decided to leave Naughty Dog, I was looking at two seemingly intractable issues. The first was that I couldn't see myself continuing at the pace I was going. The second was that, in creating hierarchy and promoting Evan and Stephen, we had created two incredibly talented individuals who had then gained the experience and talent to run teams on their own.

Teams were bigger and budgets were higher, but the console business was still in its heyday. There were publishers itching to expand and create new teams. I feared that Evan and Stephen would leave to jump on that opportunity, and I didn't want Naughty Dog to go through that division. This was not our imagination. I had managed to pull Stephen back from the brink just before he left Naughty Dog for another opportunity.

We might have split into two teams, with Evan and Stephen running the new team, but I felt at that time that Naughty Dog was at the top of its game and shouldn't take risks like that. Two mediocre, or even two very good products, wouldn't be as lucrative as one great one. Historically, this has been true in hit-driven industries. If you look at the sales curves of titles, you will see that this is certainly the case in video games.

So, in 2002, Andy and I decided to leave Naughty Dog. We told Sony of our decision, and promised that we would spend the next two years making sure that Evan and Stephen were ready to lead the team when we left. We did exactly that. By the end of Jak 3, I was not in the biggest office; Evan was. I did less and less direct management, and more looking over his shoulder. By the time Jak 3 finished, Evan was ready. Andy did the same with Stephen. Stephen eventually decided that he didn't like running a team, probably for many of the reasons that I've mentioned. Christophe Balestra was right there, ready to go. That created the seamless transition that allowed the team to continue to perform at such a high level of success and which led to Uncharted 2, a game of the year.

A few years later, hierarchy had come to the business, and that meant teams self-healed and were more efficient to run at scale. Hierarchy also brought more sanity to development schedules. This is not to say that development has become easy, or that developers don't put in extremely long hours, but the industry is now more sustainable and less brutal to team leads. There was a certain aspect of the Wild West that disappeared from triple-A development. It was fun at times, but I think we were all happy to see the industry mature and grow out of it.

Other things have changed as well. Smaller teams have returned with social, mobile, and casual games. Deadlines outside of the console space are looser. Christmas is not much of a factor for them. Games are patchable and continue to have add-ons, so development is not so focused on a single-disc release. In the console business, the opportunity to strike out on your own and create a new team is now basically nonexistent. Triple-A teams are being cut in huge numbers. Certainly, a second-in-command can leave to start a smaller developer making smaller games, but the fear of losing your number two to a similar triple-A project isn't hanging over anybody's head. Since triple-A managers only want to make triple-A titles, you don't worry about losing your talent like you did.

Had Andy and I continued through the early PlayStation 3 development transition with our sanity, I think we probably wouldn't have left thereafter. Had we split into two teams and managed to keep up the quality, maybe we'd be even more successful. It is hard to say for sure, but at the time I made the decision to leave Naughty Dog, I felt like I had no other choice. Some people live for a single purpose—to do the one thing that they love doing. I loved working at Naughty Dog. I loved the team, the process, and the success, but

I also love diversity of life experience. I have done things that I never would have been able to do had I stayed at Naughty Dog.

The road had two paths, and I chose what seemed like the more interesting one at the time. You can never see too far past the branch, and you always wonder what you might have given up had you followed the other. I would not give up what I've done since October 2004 to be able to go back and change my decision. I'm incredibly proud of Evan, Christophe, and the entire Naughty Dog team for what they achieved after we left.

Ted Price

Founder, Insomniac Games

In 1993, Princeton University graduate **Ted Price** left his uncle's concierge medicine business, driven by a need to be "artistically creative." He established Insomniac Games that year, aiming to build the company's first title, a first-person shooter called Disruptor. Soon, Price was joined by Al Hastings, a programmer who was also a Princeton graduate. They were introduced by their mothers.

Price and Hastings worked together to build a demo, and pitched the title to publishers up and down the West Coast. Unsuccessful, the duo was about to call the venture off, but took a last stab at Universal Interactive Studios. They landed a three-game deal. Hastings' brother Brian then joined the company, and the three formed the core executive team, which today includes chief operating officer John Fiorito. A few months later, they relocated from San Diego to Hollywood, and were welcomed onto the Universal lot. While on the lot, Insomniac formed a lasting relationship with their lot neighbor, Naughty Dog.

In business for nearly two decades, Insomniac Games is recognized as a model employer, with countless workplace awards. The studio has developed three of the Sony PlayStation's signature franchises: Spyro the Dragon, Ratchet & Clank, and Resistance. Altogether, Insomniac has sold more than 35 million units, and produced several of the highest-rated PlayStation games of all time. Price continues to serve as the company's founding chief executive officer.

Ramsay: What were you doing before Insomniac Games?

Price: I was very fortunate to attend Princeton University where nothing I studied had anything to do with games. However, I did play a lot of games in college thanks to the Nintendo Entertainment System in my shared dorm room. In fact, I think my grade point average was at least half a point lower than it should have been because of Metroid and Zelda.

When I graduated from college in 1990, I moved to San Diego to work for my uncle, Dr. Gresham Bayne. Dr. Bayne had started a one-of-a-kind house call service named Call Doctor where doctors and technicians would take high-tech vans to patients' homes and provide the same level of care one can find in an emergency room. It was, and is, and incredibly valuable service for the many, many people who aren't ambulatory or are deathly afraid of hospitals. Even better, because the service is partially covered by Medicare, it saves taxpayers a ton of money; the alternative for most of these patients is to visit an emergency room for even the smallest ailments. And that can be very, very expensive.

My uncle wanted to see if he could train a college graduate to perform the kind of diagnostics needed to support the doctors' efforts in patients' homes. So, as the resident guinea pig, I learned how to take and develop X-rays, perform all sorts of blood tests, and even assist the doctors in minor procedures. We saw fascinating cases—a woman whose lung we drained by sticking a needle through her back, a 600-pound bedridden man who had bedsores the size of hollowed-out grapefruits, and folks with serious dementia—you name it we saw it. In every case, the doctor's presence at the patient's own bedside provided incredible emotional, psychological, and medical benefits that just could not be obtained in a sterile office or a chaotic emergency room.

One of my responsibilities was to drive the medical vans from house to house. However, I have a very poor sense of direction. And even after a year and a half on the vans, I was still getting lost on the way to patients' homes. The doctors finally asked for someone who could read a map.

After being kicked off the vans, I began working in the Call Doctor offices. I started by creating databases to collect and report on the market research we received during every house call. This information was important for us because we were trying to get better Medicare reimbursement for the doctors. We needed to prove that we were providing an incredibly important service for patients, many of whom would simply die alone in their homes without Call Doctor's ministrations. The data we collected at each call helped to demonstrate this.

I truly enjoyed the database programming. But, after a few months, our financial controller left the company to get married. The same week my uncle walked into my office, dropped a college accounting textbook on my desk and said, "You've got a week to learn this. You're our new controller." It was probably the best thing that could have happened to me because I knew nothing about finances at the time. But with the pressure of a real deadline, and real consequences if I failed, I dove in.

Pretty soon, I got the hang of debits and credits. And soon after that my uncle set me loose on our business plans where I began creating revised financial projections as we prepared for expansion. I got to work with the venture capitalists who were helping fund the company and learned quite a bit from them as well. I loved it.

Despite how much fun it was to help shape the business and run the financial side, after another year I realized that I wasn't passionate about the medical field. I liked the idea of helping people, and I really liked the technical aspects of the database programming that I was continuing to do alongside my financial responsibilities. However, I missed the opportunity to be artistically creative. And I missed games.

In late 1993, I left Call Doctor to start Insomniac Games. I continued to work with my uncle, providing support for the market research databases I had created. But he had hired a new chief financial officer and other staff. I was able to turn my full attention to building Insomniac and our first game, Disruptor. Our articles of incorporation were officially accepted by the State of California in February 1994. Four months later, my first partner Al Hastings joined me in our small San Diego offices where we began putting together the demo for our debut game.

Ramsay: How did you know Al? Why did he get involved?

Price: Al was also a Princetonian. However, he was in the class of 1994, and I was in the class of 1990. We had never run into each other at school. I met him because my mother was explaining to a friend of hers that I had started a video game company. Her friend had a son at Princeton whose roommate was Al. My mother's friend had heard her son refer to Al as the most brilliant programmer he had ever encountered. So, my mother connected the dots, and told me about Al.

I called him during the spring of 1994 as he was getting ready to graduate. Al flew out to San Diego and we immediately hit it off. He agreed to join me as soon as he graduated. In June, he moved out to San Diego and we spent a month putting together the demo for our first game Disruptor.

Al programmed an amazing engine in a few weeks while I slapped together some art, animations, and sound effects to flesh things out. We drove up and down the West Coast in my Saturn, presenting the demo to any publisher who would let us in the door. We got rejected by every one.

At the time, Al was sleeping on my couch when he was sleeping at all, and I didn't have the money to pay the next month's rent. We were on the threshold of failure. We took one more shot, and visited the newly formed Universal Interactive Studios. Within 24 hours, we had a verbal agreement for a three-game deal. It was an incredible moment for both of us.

Ramsay: Aside from having no other options, what made their offer attractive? Was working on the lot part of the original deal?

Price: The offer was attractive because we were out of money; we had been turned down everywhere else, and Al and I really liked Mark Cerny, who was the executive producer, after spending only a few hours with him. Mark was thoughtful, attentive, and clearly knew games inside and out. We were looking forward to working with him.

Insomniac is an independent company, so we get to choose what to do in terms of where to work and how to make our games. In fact, we started developing Disruptor in San Diego. We eventually moved onto the "lot" at Universal for a number of reasons. The first reason was that, other than Al's brother Brian Hastings, we couldn't find team members in San Diego.

We wanted to hire artists, but it seemed like all of the artists lived in Los Angeles and San Francisco. The second reason was that we really didn't know what we were doing at first. Well, I didn't know what I was doing. Al and Brian were doing awesome work on the engine, artificial intelligence, and tools. When we missed our first milestone, it became apparent that we needed production guidance. Moving to Los Angeles would put us much closer to Mark. The idea was that he could coach us, or me specifically, on how to approach game construction less haphazardly.

So, we uprooted, packed up our development kits, and took the trip north. We ended up in a low-slung building, previously occupied by Amblin Entertainment. The best part was that we were right next door to the Naughty Dogs. We got to be great friends as a result.

The worst part was that the building's air conditioning broke down often, especially during that first brutal summer in Los Angeles. I kept wondering about which we would lose first to overheating: our devkits or our team. Fortunately, no one died from heat exhaustion, and we found a better spot on the lot within a few months.

Ramsay: Some developers start up, thinking that they will only create games in specific genres. Your first game, Disruptor, was a first-person shooter. Is that what you initially wanted to focus on?

Price: I was a big fan of Doom and initially wanted to make a first-person shooter. But instead of doing a first-person shooter for PCs, I thought it would make more sense to do it for consoles given that 3DO seemed to be the future. Al Hastings and Brian Hastings shared those sentiments. We believed that console games would continue to become more popular. And, frankly, we didn't want to deal with the headaches of supporting different PC configurations. When 3DO took a nosedive, there was a moment when it looked as if we had guessed wrong. Fortunately, Sony stepped up with the PlayStation and the console market took off like a rocket.

Ramsay: So, you were betting on a platform more than any particular genre. Was your bet about profitability? Or did you think that the console would displace the PC as the platform of choice for video games?

Price: The idea of working on fixed hardware was far more attractive than trying to keep up with ever-changing PC technology. We also guessed that with a small team, we'd be better off focusing on one console and "going deep." That way, we would have a better chance of staying on the cutting edge for that particular console. In our case, that was the PlayStation.

In the mid-1990s, industry insiders foretold the death of PC games. With the advent of the PlayStation and its penetration into the mass market, it was easy to buy into that particular philosophy. So, we never seriously considered moving into the PC game market. Of course, the reality is that the PC game market faltered a bit, but has now grown and evolved in some really interesting ways. Yet, if we had to do it again, knowing what we know now, we'd still stick with consoles.

Ramsay: They seem like polar opposites. One is a serious sci-fi first-person shooter. The other is a flighty fantasy third-person adventure with a cute, purple dragon. How did you get from Disruptor to Spyro?

Price: After we had finished Disruptor, we needed a breath of fresh air. We were a small team at the time and had spent the previous two years immersed in a dark and humorless universe. Actually, the cheesy full-motion videos in the game were pretty funny but not by intention. Anyway, we needed a breath of fresh air, something a bit more lighthearted.

At around the same time, Mark Cerny, our executive producer at Universal Interactive Studios, pointed out that there was a vacuum on the PlayStation. No one was trying to take on Nintendo who completely owned the family market. He suggested that we think about something other than a shooter, something that had broader appeal. We began to brainstorm and one of our team members, Craig Stitt, said "I've always wanted to do a game about dragons." At that point, Spyro was born.

While Al Hastings began prototyping a brand new engine that was designed to promote open areas and long views versus the confined environments of a first-person shooter; we moved quickly into character design. Charles Zembillas, a very talented artist and animator who we contracted to help us out, created Spyro's initial look. What I remember was Spyro being fairly angry and intense-looking at first. He had heavy, bunched eyebrows and a mischievous smirk. Almost a snarl. After several iterations, we began softening him, increasing his head-to-body ratio which gave him a more wide-eyed, innocent expression. But despite the doe-eyed look, he was still a cocky little bastard. At least until the sequel.

Ramsay: How did Spyro change for the sequel?

Price: We introduced new abilities for Spyro, including power-ups and the abilities to hover after a glide, swim underwater, and climb ladders. We also introduced new non-player characters, new enemies, and a new boss, Ripto. The story was a continuation of the first game's story, though a year had passed in Spyro's universe, and the worlds which players got to visit were entirely new. The reasons for the changes were simply that we felt the need to create a sequel that offered more than the original. We weren't reacting to the market necessarily. We just knew that we had to up the ante with any sequel we did.

Ramsay: Why did you feel that you had to push the envelope with each successive title?

Price: I don't think you can succeed with game sequels unless you push for fresh experiences. Gamers expect better content with each iteration of a franchise. Very few people want more of the same; it gets old fast. However, it's a tough balancing act. We learned the hard way later with Ratchet Deadlocked that if you deviate too much from the franchise's roots, you can alienate your fans. So what one provides has to feel fresh and familiar at the same time.

Ramsay: At the same time, your friends at Naughty Dog were working in the hallways at Universal. Did Insomniac receive equal mistreatment? Did you have to find another publisher, too?

Price: Actually, all of the Spyros were published by Sony. Universal sublicensed the publishing rights for Spyro and Crash to Sony. It was a great opportunity to get more exposure for both titles. Ultimately, it paid off for Universal, for us, and for Naughty Dog since Spyro and especially Crash became de facto mascots for the PlayStation.

Ramsay: So, you stayed on the lot and didn't have to relocate the studio?

Price: Actually, we did relocate to an office space a couple of miles away from Universal. We moved off the Universal lot simply because we lost our space to an internal department at Universal. Since we weren't officially a part of Universal, our sweet "your rent is free" deal didn't compete well when internal Universal groups needed to expand. We did get plenty of warning from Universal, so we had time to look around for other offices that were the right size. So, the physical separation was just fine with us.

Ramsay: What was your criteria for office space? Why'd you move there?

Price: We chose the space because it was fairly close to where many of us lived at the time in Hollywood. Since 1994, we had moved spaces at least four times, so moving offices wasn't too traumatic. The only problem with the new space was that it wasn't conveniently located close to any restaurants. It made us nostalgic for the not-so-great Universal cafeteria…

Ramsay: How successful was the Spyro trilogy for the company?

Price: It certainly put us on the map, and brought us closer to Sony with whom we did deals for over a decade. Total sales for the three Spyro games we created were north of 12 million units, which we didn't think was too bad given that the games only appeared on the PlayStation.

Ramsay: How did the trilogy put you on the map? What sort of interest did you attract? Did anyone ever approach you about selling the company?

Price: I think what was most important is that gamers took notice of what we had done. Gamers began to recognize the Insomniac brand thanks to Spyro. Today, we still hear from many of our fans whose first game experience was with Spyro the Dragon. Aside from making some of us feel old, it's extremely gratifying to know that we were affecting people's lives positively with that little purple dragon. And, yeah, we've been approached many times by all sorts of entities that were interested in buying Insomniac. It started after we shipped Spyro. In this business, I think that's the norm once you prove that you can ship a quality title.

Ramsay: At that point, you had been running Insomniac for six years. You were out of money when you signed with Universal. After 12 million units of Spyro sold, were you ready to really grow the company?

Price: Well, I still had $1,000 in my bank account when we signed with Universal. So, we weren't exactly out of money. But after Spyro, growing wasn't really our goal. Our goal was to move onto the PlayStation 2, and make even better games. Because gamer expectations and our own expectations were much higher, it was necessary to have a bigger team to do more with our games. We grew out of necessity.

Things were toughest when we hit 50 people on Ratchet & Clank: Going Commando. At that time, we were still operating like a garage developer. Personally, I was going insane, trying to manage way too much. I was doing a very poor job with trying to lead projects and run the company. So, we established departments, and set up a more logical hierarchy within the company. Things settled down, and my wife began talking to me again.

Ramsay: What was next for the studio?

Price: Ratchet & Clank arose out of our failure with a game we were calling "Girl with a Stick". Girl with a Stick was our attempt at a more mature action-adventure game on the PlayStation 2. It featured a female human magic caster in a Mayan-influenced fantasy world. She would perform martial arts katas to unlock and cast spells. Plus, there was a lot of melee combat... using a big stick. I thought it was pretty cool.

We had a deal with Sony, and both their and our own team were lukewarm about the game. We were having a hard time transitioning from the whimsical world of Spyro to something mature. But I kept pushing it. Six months into preproduction, I realized I had made a mistake. We killed the game and decided to go back to what we did best at the time: platforming.

Brian Hastings, our chief creative officer came up with the initial idea for Ratchet two weeks after we had deep-sixed Girl with a Stick. He suggested we do a game featuring an alien character who rockets from planet to planet using cool weapons and gadgets. Everyone loved it and began contributing. Within a couple of months, we had the first test of Metropolis up and running. At that point, we knew we had something special.

Ramsay: When did your friendly rivalry with Naughty Dog and their Jak and Daxter franchise begin? What did that entail?

Price: When Naughty Dog and Insomniac were on the lot at Universal, we were right next door to each other. We used to share equipment and testing space. We'd go to each other's parties, have Quake LAN matches... At the same time, I think there was definitely a friendly competition between the groups because we were both working with Universal and Sony, and we were both in the platformer space. Of course, this continued through Ratchet & Clank and Jak and Daxter.

And, by the way, the resemblance between those franchise names is entirely coincidental. When we came up with Ratchet & Clank, we had no idea what Naughty Dog was doing and vice versa. I remember the day we found out about Jak and Daxter. There was a lot of "what?" and "are you kidding me?" going around. I'm sure that the same thing happened in their office. I guess we were both playing to our strengths.

However, Naughty Dog really helped us out at the beginning of Ratchet & Clank. We were building our PlayStation 2 engine, and Jason offered to share some of their rendering techniques. It was a huge kick start for us. In return, we offered code of our own. Thus began our back-and-forth sharing, which continued throughout the PlayStation 2 era. But we'll always be extremely grateful for that first extremely generous gesture.

Ramsay: Several employees left during the development of the second Ratchet game and started a new studio called High Impact Games. Their first title was a Ratchet game later down the road, so I have to ask: was that an outcome of anything that was happening at Insomniac?

Price: I think we were going through a growth spurt, and several people yearned for the small developer environment again. To their credit, they took a big chance, and were successful in delivering several great games.

Ramsay: You had the platform games Spyro and Ratchet & Clank, which were light-hearted fare. And then there was Resistance: Fall of Man, your second first-person shooter. Why did you return to that genre?

Price: There were a lot of reasons we went with Resistance. First, we needed to branch out creatively to stay sane. Platformers are great, but there were many of us who were ready for something different. Second, despite Disruptor, we were becoming known as a company that only made platformers, and it was important for a lot of us to not get pigeonholed.

We wanted to prove to gamers, and to ourselves, that we were capable of doing more. We had also decided to develop a launch title for the PlayStation 3, and we knew that we had to create something with more of an edge to attract early adopters. A first-person shooter seemed to be a logical choice. Finally, many of us were and still are first-person shooter fans. I certainly am. Personally, I was really excited to get back to what we had started out doing in the first place.

Ramsay: Where is the Resistance franchise today? How much of a boon has this series been for the studio?

Price: In terms of sales, Resistance has been an extremely successful franchise. Resistance 3 has just been released, and we're waiting to see how the holiday sales fare. Conservatively, it looks like our average unit sales per Resistance game will end up being over 2.5 million worldwide, or more than 8 million total units sold across three games, and that's on just one platform.

Aside from the financial benefits, we've learned a lot of good lessons from Resistance—lessons about what it takes to do a launch title, scope control, better storytelling, etc. It was also very useful in helping us make a transition from the super-stylized worlds of Spyro and Ratchet into something a bit more believable. At the same time, I think the series has helped us figure out where we want to go in the future. I can tell you now that, despite my own love for the series, our future does not involve Resistance.

Ramsay: Your next title is being published by Electronic Arts. Why aren't you publishing with Sony again?

Price: Overstrike is a multiplatform game. Thus, it wouldn't make sense for Sony to publish it. Imagine a Sony-published game on the Xbox 360. That would be a first! We also own the intellectual property for Overstrike, and that's not something which works for most publishers. Or, at least it didn't a couple of years ago. Fortunately, Electronic Arts Partners publishes titles from independent developers who own and control their intellectual property. Electronic Arts has been a fantastic partner on the title.

Ramsay: Many developers have a number of bets between hits and franchises, but Disruptor was your only one-off. Is your catalog indicative of strategic genius? Or would you say you were just lucky?

Price: Frankly, I think you make your own luck. We've had our share of ups and downs just like everyone else in this industry. And we've certainly made plenty of mistakes; it's fortunate that none have been fatal. But I think what's gotten us to where we are is our internal need to keep pushing for better and better content. If we ever settle for doing the same thing over and over again, I believe it's a recipe for disaster both financially and emotionally.

Ramsay: Insomniac has consistently won "best place to work" awards. What are you doing that other companies are not?

Price: That's a big, broad question, and I could probably go on for hours with answers. I think, at the core, we never stop trying to encourage collaboration and communication. We want people here to take ownership of the games, and have a meaningful impact on the final outcome, which necessitates involvement from all. That's really, really hard to do consistently because with big teams, communication and collaboration are the first things that tend to break, especially when deadlines are looming.

When things aren't working, which is often, we fess up and attack the problem. Personally, I want to work at a place where people feel like they can speak out about problems and offer solutions that work. To me, nothing is worse than feeling like you can't do anything about issues going on around you. If and when either our chief operating officer John Fiorito or I see that happening, we jump on it and force change.

Again, we're not perfect by any means, and I'll admit that we do make a lot of the same mistakes from game to game—something that many of us are trying extremely hard to change. But we recognize that, and I think we get better each year. The challenge we always face is that what we do isn't static. The processes, the technology, the genres we're in, and gamers' expectations are changing all the time. We have to work twice as hard to avoid the same pitfalls, which are often disguised as new problems.

For example, even though we've gone from first person to third person to first person back to third person, we don't always remember that the same core mechanics apply. Whether it's auto targeting, character and camera responsiveness, enemy reactions to projectile hits, we often take a new approach based on our excitement about the fresh new game concept until we realize that the fundamentals haven't changed. In other words, good character control is good character control. Satisfying weapon play shares the same basic ingredients across platforms and across genres. Anyway, after almost two decades, I think it's finally starting to sink in.

Ramsay: Specifically, what have you done to cultivate business and creative leaders within the studio?

Price: We've often made the mistake of putting people in leadership positions before they're ready. Hell, that was me, too. I certainly didn't know much about leadership when I started Insomniac.

Another mistake I've made is asking people to take leadership positions when they really don't want it. A lot of people like the thought of having a management or lead position. But when they realize that it actually means stepping away from what they truly love doing, like coding or art creation, and instead dealing with people problems, life becomes painful.

Fortunately, we've found plenty of folks at Insomniac who enjoy the people management challenges as much as the production challenges. And they're very good at both. These are the people we want as department heads and leads. There are others who develop guru-level skills, but who aren't interested in managing people. We've created the "principal" path where folks who uniquely contribute to Insomniac's success can become principal artists, principal programmers, etc.

Another important philosophy we have is "promote from within." We occasionally bring in folks from the outside to become department heads or leads. But those are exceptions rather than the rule. We find that those who understand the "Insomniac way" through their experience at the company function well as leaders because they really get the idiosyncrasies that make us who we are as a creative team.

In terms of leadership development, we do a lot more than we did 10 years ago. For those who we think are ready to take on more responsibility and who want to take on more, we put them on a specific leadership path, which involves mentoring, outside leadership training, and the gradual assumption of more and more responsibilities.

And we do encourage Insomniacs at all levels to get out there and talk about what we do, unless it conflicts with delivering a game on time...

Ramsay: You've been in business for 18 years. That's a long time. Compare the early days to today. What's different at Insomniac?

Price: I don't think our basic philosophy has changed at all. I've mentioned how collaboration and communication is key—that's something we've held dear since day one. We have also always tried hard to raise the bar with everything we do, and we've done whatever it takes to deliver on time every time. But, outside of our basic tenets, a lot has changed.

We now have around 215 people in two offices, we have a much more structured approach to making games, we're developing for multiple platforms, and we've sold over 35 million games. Basically, we've gone from being a garage developer to a mostly professional company. I say "mostly" because we do try hard to keep bureaucracy to a minimum. I think a lot of us are still wary of tipping over into a more corporate existence. As a game company, I believe it's crucial to focus as much as possible on what will makes the games great. Politics and bureaucracy are wasteful distractions.

Ramsay: Insomniac has only ever done PlayStation games. With the end of this console generation on the horizon, and with, as you said, the PC game market having "grown and evolved in some really interesting ways," do you see Insomniac developing for other platforms in the near term?

Price: We made the decision to move to multiplatform development several years ago. It was a necessary business move. At the same time, reaching a new gamer audience is exciting for us. Currently, we have games slated for release on the Xbox 360, PlayStation 3, and the PC through our Insomniac Click group.

Ramsay: Is your role different now?

Price: Aside from doing the more corporate run-the-company kind of stuff, I used to be the creative director at Insomniac. Then I became one of the creative directors. Now, I've abdicated that responsibility altogether. By Resistance 2, I had definitely become a bottleneck. I wasn't doing a good job in either of my roles.

Today, each of our projects has a different creative director or a pair of co-creative directors, and that setup works much better, in my opinion. Part of my job is to "oversee" the creative directors, but I also believe in providing as much autonomy as possible. Our creative directors, and, in fact, everyone on our teams, should feel ownership in their projects. They shouldn't be worried about my second-guessing their decisions. So, I try to stay in the background. With that said, John and I do provide a lot of creative feedback on all of the projects. Part of our jobs is to look ahead and identify problems with the games' directions, so that we can attack them early. Fortunately, there are plenty of people on each production team who do that as well because they really care about shipping something that rocks.

Outside of development, I spend a lot of time negotiating contracts, working with our publishers, working out long-term strategies, helping John with suggestions for the production process, soliciting feedback from the team, and things like that. I really like everything I do because it's kind of a potpourri. It's certainly never boring.

Ramsay: You said that you've had your share of ups and downs, and you've made plenty of mistakes. Can you tell me about any particular down times? Any particular mistakes that you try to not repeat?

Price: Well, I already mentioned the Girl with a Stick episode. I wasn't listening to the team. That was an important lesson for me, one which I try hard to not repeat. If we don't function as a team, we don't function at all.

Another trying time was when we were trying to ship Resistance: Fall of Man. We had trouble running the game consistently on the PlayStation 3 until about three weeks before gold—and the game was a launch title! Yikes. One mistake we made was developing systems for the PlayStation 3 on PCs, and neglecting to optimize them until it was almost too late. We now make sure that every game can run in memory and on disc at the alpha stage. I'm sure it sounds logical, but it has been a huge challenge for us over the years.

Ramsay: When you reflect on your 18 years at Insomniac Games, knowing that most studios will never last as long, what are your thoughts?

Price: I'm still learning lessons every day, and that's what makes both game development and running a company so exhilarating. However, I suppose I could offer a few suggestions to new entrepreneurs.

First, remember that employees at your company aren't working for you. You're really working for them. It's your job to make sure that everyone is happy, creatively challenged, well-informed, and being given honest feedback about how he or she is doing. It's also your job to represent your team's best interests through the decisions you make because your team is your company. And you can't do that without always being available to listen to what each person has to say.

Second, you can't abdicate setting the vision for your company. If you're the leader, you're the one who has the responsibility of communicating and constantly reminding everyone of that vision. The vision itself doesn't have to be your idea, but people will look to you for it. It's also your job to make sure that the vision is shared and embraced by the entire team. Otherwise, it's probably never going to pan out.

Finally, accept and embrace change. Nothing ever goes as planned in a creative endeavor. When you or anyone else holds too tightly to some preconceived notion of how things should be, it stifles innovation and halts progress. In my opinion, those companies who remain flexible, who embrace change, and who always push for innovation are the ones that change the world. I'm still trying to improve in all of the above.

I

Index

CPSIA information can be obtained at www.ICGtesting.com
Printed in the USA
LVOW06s1923181114

414348LV00001B/126/P